My First Recession

V2_/NAi Publishers

My First Recession

Geert Lovink

Critical Internet Culture in Transition

Introduction

Currents in Critical Internet Culture

"Are you living in today's world?" Marshall McLuhan

After 9/11

By 2003, Internet euphoria had all but disappeared. After the fall of the dotcoms, the mainstream media started to report on the "death of the Internet." In the aftermath of 9/11, both civil-rights activists and Internet pioneers voiced their concern over the rise in surveillance, tighter laws and the subsequent "closure" of the once-open Internet. There were stories about a plot by IBM and Microsoft to take over the Net.[1] Even the neo-liberal weekly *The Economist* complained, "The Internet Sells Its Soul" (referring to the introduction of subscription fees on many sites after the failure of free services during the dotcom age). Hard-nosed commercialism had left its traces. Users were increasingly asked to pay for information and services, while advertising became more intrusive.[2] Over a period of roughly seven years, enormous changes had occurred.

The Internet proved unable to "route around" steadily rising state and corporate control. The post-9/11 "War on Terrorism" demanded a dramatic swing of regulatory concerns towards surveillance and control. Libertarian anti-state values could easily be pushed aside as "unpatriotic." The undermining of civil liberties by government anti-terrorist legislation is presented in a rhetoric that claims to preserve the so-called "fundamental values of liberal societies." But what "Total Information Awareness" is in effect imposing is an intellectual property-rights regime instigated by the entertainment industry. Student dorms are raided and their Internet connections shut off, their users suspected of "trading in copyrighted music and movies." Orrin Hatch, chairman of the US Senate Judiciary Committee, even suggested that people who download copyrighted materials from the Internet should have their computers automatically destroyed.

Jeff Chester, director of the Center for Digital Democracy, has sounded another warning of the "death of the Internet as we know it."[3] So far, most users (in the USA) still pay a flat fee for Internet access. However, with the gradual rise of broadband, telecommunications companies have suggested introducing bandwidth caps after which users pay for each Mb they download. The fundamental characteristic of the Internet today is that it lacks precisely these kinds of tolls, barriers and gatekeepers (with the exception of some places, like Australia, where most users pay for every Mb they download).

Writing for the UK Web publication *The Register*, Andrew Orlowski also portrayals the Internet as a dying organism. "E-mail is all but unusable because of spam. Even if our Bayesian filters win the arms race against the spammers, in terms of quantity as well as quality of communications, e-mail has been a disaster."[4] An architect friend told Orlowski e-mail had become the biggest productivity drain in his organization: not just the quantity of attachments, but the mindless round-robin communications, requests for comments that get ignored. Even the Google search engine has its own spam problems, as Andrew Orlowski points out. There is "a tiny number of webloggers and list-makers whose mindless hyperlinks degrade the value of its search results, and create the Web equivalent of TV static." But what's dying here isn't the Internet – it remains as open as ever to new software and new ideas. Orlowski says, "What's dying is the idea that the Internet would be a tool of universal liberation, and the argument that 'freedom' in itself is a justification for this information pollution."

Stories of the decline of the Internet are not just myths, though. The growth of users in the USA has indeed leveled off. This is a trend reflected in the growing scarcity of "cool" sites. Glenn Davis, founder of the once-popular online destination Cool Site of the Day, has not only kicked his Web habit but also almost completely given up the medium. The Cool Site of the Day still exists, but Davis, who no longer has the enthusiasm to surf the Net, no longer runs it. "We lost our sense of wonder," he told *The New York Times*. "The Web is old hat."[5] The "creative class" (Richard Florida) had become bored with the medium – even worse, it had become bored with boredom itself. "What else have you got?" Glenn David asks.[6]

Some question the blurry ownership of the Internet and demand global governance. Michael Geist, writing for *The Toronto Star*, remarks, "In recent years, the world has begun to grapple with Internet policies that are established in one jurisdiction (typically, though not solely, the US), but applied worldwide. That policy imbalance has left many countries resentful of foreign dominance of the Internet."[7] Increasingly, conflicts over domain names, copyright, privacy law, and free speech run into contradictory, unilateral (US) policies in which global rules only apply to "the rest of the world." At the same time, courts claim jurisdiction over foreign countries. Geist mentions the case of a US court that ordered the cancellation of a domain name owned by a Korean registrant – despite the existence of a Korean court order prohibiting the cancellation. The US court simply ruled that its decision trumped that of the Korean court, suggesting that US law may enjoy greater control over domain name disputes in other countries than does local law. Why should the Pentagon have the power to shut off entire countries from the Internet? The cynical answer – because it rules the world – may not satisfy everyone. On the other hand, "courts in France and Australia have asserted jurisdiction over US publishers such as Yahoo! and Dow Jones, which both claimed that the speech in question would have been protected under US law." Michael Geist also reports that "ISPs in Canada and Australia regularly receive notice and takedown notifications from US companies despite the fact that US law does not apply in those countries." Would you comply?

Alarming reports of increased levels of surveillance and control can easily portray users as victims. The Internet infrastructure makes certain kinds of human action possible that did not exist before, as Howard Rheingold claims in his 2002 study *Smart Mobs*. He writes: "The 'killer apps' of tomorrow won't be hardware devices or software programs but social practices. The most far-reaching changes will come, as they often do, from the kinds of relationships, enterprises, communities, and markets that the infrastructure makes possible."[8] Smart mobs are able to act in concert even if they do not know each other. *My First Recession* brings together the common experiences of such groups. Social networks, as described here, are actors which shape technology, not consumers of a finished product. Online communities are not effects or byproducts that simply obey the technological *a priori*. As Linux inventor Linus Torvalds says, "It is society that changes technology, not the other way round. Technology just sets the boundaries for what we can do, and how cheaply we can do it."[9]

A social network is not an aftereffect or a spinoff but originates in a "techno event." What the French philosopher Alain Badiou says about events could be applied to social networks and their role in the making of technology: "Something must happen, in order for them to be something new. There must be an encounter, there must be something which cannot be calculated, predicted or managed."[10] Networks are rooted in unknown events that need to be described and cannot be reduced to casual opinions or instituted knowledge. For Badiou, we are actors, "but in such a way that we are targeted by, carried away by, and struck by the event." Without a doubt this also goes for the Internet, where standards and applications cannot be separated from the "events" that constitute them. It is the task of "Net critics" to identify and describe such events and unearth the social and cultural layers beneath technology. Badiou also reminds us that not every novelty is an event. It is time for critical Internet discourse to oppose opinion as "representation without truth" and analyze the "anarchic debris of circulating knowledge." If there is something to be learned from the dotcom era, it is the old phrase "don't believe the hype." It is necessary to radically dissociate technology from the world of finance and its consultancy vaporware and unveil its effect on social events.

The Whereabouts of Theory

Karl Marx's saying that "the tradition of all the dead generations weighs like a nightmare on the brain of the living"[11] also counts for Internet studies. The new, struggling to push aside old traditions and structures, cannot afford to be haunted by shadows of a past it claims not to have. On the other hand, to many the Internet stands for a liberating move away from the past, a "crusade of hope against history" (Edna O'Brien). In its own popular mythology, technology blindly marches on, indifferent to recession or crisis, unaware of its past, solely focused on the future. 1980s avant-garde cyberpunk claimed to live in the future. We may have arrived there (for cyberpunks, "the future is now"). It is now time to liberate the Internet from its engineering history. Once information technology is installed and society is networked, the rhetoric of the cool revolting against the establishment no longer works and the mood changes. This study looks in particular at the moment of transition, as the "economy of the cool" is fading away, its cultural residues are being absorbed into the everyday, and "all-too-human" characteristics are hitting the interface surface.

By now, Internet culture has created its own history. In 2003, ten years after the introduction of the World Wide Web, talk about the Internet as the final frontier and a cornucopia for all has faded away. Streams of messages about corporate collapses and cyberterrorism have replaced popular cyberculture. There is a rising awareness of backlash. A part of this new consciousness could be translated as Internet culture's need to write its own history. It has to leave its heroic, mythological stage behind.

With L.P. Hartley, one could say the Internet past is a strange land. The Net criticism project, of which this study aims to be a part, contributes to the writing of such histories-in-the-making. There are uses and disadvantages of technology history for life. Critical Internet research is faced with a dilemma: it does not seek to glorify high tech or (post-) dotcom business models, nor does it buy into the cynical reasoning that in the end everything will remain the same. The critical history-of-the-present approach proposed here operates in an elective affiliation with "media archaeology."[12] Media archaeology is first and foremost a methodology, a hermeneutic reading of the "new" against the grain of the past, rather than a telling of the history of technologies from past to present. No comprehensive overview of the media archaeology approach is yet available, but we could mention a few scholars, such as Friedrich Kittler, Siegfried Zielinski, Werner Nekes, Jonathan Crary, Katherine Hayles, Werner Künzel, Avital Ronell, Christoph Asendorf, Erkki Huhtamo, Paul Virilio and others. Although I do not trace Internet culture back to the 19th, 18th or even 17th century, I see a *Wahlverwandschaft* (elective affinity) between my research and the media archaeology approach. The dynamics of social networks on the Internet need not be reduced to models from existing disciplines such as psychology, anthropology and ethnography. They are as much a part of the history of the medium itself as the heroic tales of its inventors.

❦ –

"Whatever thing I name exists" (Toni Negri). New concepts open up dialogues and imaginative spaces, be they in the past, present or future. But all too often history is used as a strategic weapon against concrete work by new-media practitioners. It may be a truism that the uptake of media takes a cyclical form, from avant-garde to sellout and back to the spotlight of obscurity. Nothing is as easy as turning history against the Internet. Artists, academics and other intellectuals who have felt threatened by the power of the rising medium have tried to prove that there is nothing new under the sun. They want to make their audiences believe that the Internet's fate will be the same as those of radio and television: to be tamed by national regulators and the market. There is an iron law that after an invention has turned into a mass product, early adopters drop the fad in search of the next one. It may seem like a historically inevitable process, but that does not make the passions and interests of the players involved any less real. In the case of the Internet, "Net criticism" is one such player – and a passionate one – though its existence may not yet be well known outside certain circles. The call for Net criticism should not be read as yet another obsession to carve out a terrain.[13] There are enough churches and cults. Instead of stressing popular cycles, attention should focus on the marginal status of critical Internet culture, a more urgent danger. After a decade of great excitement, the outside world remains by and large unaware of new-media culture and, because of its relatively small size, can ignore it, treating it as the activity of a "mafia" that talks only to itself and curates its own artworks. Self-referentiality, a precondition necessary for any culture to flourish, is becoming a major obstacle for growth and transformation toward a next stage.

Because of the speed of events, there is a real danger that an online phenomenon will already have disappeared before a critical discourse reflecting on it has had the time to mature and establish itself as institutionally recognized knowledge. Internet research, Net criticism, techno-cultural studies and media philosophy are still in their infancy.[14] Often the object of study has already disappeared before the study of it is finished. But that doesn't make the issues irrelevant. Critical Internet research must distance itself from vaporware and accept its humble role of analyzing the very recent past. Internet researcher David Silver has distinguished three stages. During the first stage, which he calls "popular cyberculture," Internet research is marked by its journalistic origins. The second stage, "cyberculture studies," focuses largely on virtual communities and online identities. In the third stage, "critical cyberculture studies," research expands to "online interactions, digital discourses, access and denial to the Internet, and interface design of cyberspace."[15] This study would fit into the third stage. In particular, it re-examines the notion of virtual communities as actual social networks and the way in which they both reflect society and anticipate (and embody) new forms of social interaction.

As I made clear in Dark Fiber,[16] Net criticism as I see it is not primarily targeted against the libertarian values of pre-dotcom Internet pioneers – those of decentralization, open standards, cryptography, the right to own your own words, the sharing of online resources, code and content, and anonymity remain essential and worth defending. If anything, it is aimed against the cynical, populist IT journalists and PR consultants who used to sell the Internet as a commodified spectacle and are now doing the same with "scandalous" dotcom stories. It is this class of mediators who have systematically refused to do their homework and analyze the power structures within this emerging global medium. This bad practice, or perhaps sloppiness, continues today, well after the dotcom crash. Hardly any investigative journalist anticipated the dotcom crash or the rise of weblogs and wireless networks. The news media fail to catch up with the facts and are often complicit in maintaining the hype machine until the last minute, when yet another tech or telecom company collapses.

Net criticism is a call for critical intellectual engagement. It is not a critique of information or technology in general. The critic-as-organizer must navigate between the economic hype of "the creative industries" and the really existing futility of arts and culture compared to the science and technology giants. New media, in my view, deserve society's best cultural resources, ones that can think and operate beyond the fluctuations of pop and fashion. The recognition of the user as an "imperfect machine" is pending. In *The Future of Ideas* Lawrence Lessig launched a dramatic call to defend the original Internet values in order to save capitalism from its own monopolies (see Chapter One). However, there is a growing disbelief that "the market" is the appropriate partner in defending, and defining, Internet freedom. Lessig's US-specific common-sense position leaves us with the question of how the economics of an independent "digital commons" might look. One thing is sure: the Internet is not a parallel world somewhere out there, it is an integral part of society. The social networks described here are not isolated but should be defined as osmotic interfaces between inside and outside.

The word "critical" does not, for me, automatically refer to the so-called Frankfurt School critical theory of Adorno, Horkheimer, Marcuse and others, no matter how tempting it may be to frame Net criticism within that particular theoretical tradition. The crisis of continental critical theory as an obscure academic niche has taken its toll. There is no neo-Marxist network theory that critically engages with new-media culture, and we might wait in vain for the aging 1968 generation to grasp the Internet and take it serious as an object of theory. "Critical," in this context, refers to the urgent need for reflection and thinking,[17] combined with action, felt by many in the 1990s to be necessary to counter hyped-up, buzzword-obsessed media coverage. What was needed was an informed discourse that could transcend the slogans of the day and combine the shared drive towards public domain, free software and open standards with a (self-) critical view of business and the role of culture in the formation of the "network society." Net criticism, in my view, is not a call to establish an academic discipline, nor an appeal to existing sciences to please take notice of the Internet.

The marketing discourse that was dominant in information technology was not criticized (enough) by the technologists who were pushing the medium. Thinkers such as Jean Baudrillard do not have hands-on knowledge about Internet issues and keep talking in general terms about "cyborgs" and "virtual sex,"[18] ignoring the dominant techno-libertarian ideology and its neo-liberal fetishization of the "market." The call for critical reflection on the emergence of a global communications medium of such magnitude does not necessarily equal "anti-capitalism" (or "radical pragmatism" for that matter). It is most of all an endeavor to "beautify" this astonishing "junk" medium (à la McLuhan), to create a gift of excess, joy and pleasure within the Internet itself. Life does not function by rules alone. Net criticism has no obligations. It is an aesthetic undertaking as much as a field of social-political contestation. Both engaged and informed, utopian and negative, empirical and general, it should be a sophisticated and intellectual enterprise of the highest order. This is the challenge, in my view, that the Net criticism project is embarking upon.

The call for Net criticism is not a Luddite escape route, a search for an essentialist or "alien" outsider position. It is a call for engagement and responsibility born out of a deep concern that the Internet, bit by bit, is being closed down, sealed off by spam filters, copyright lawyers, bureaucratic firewall builders and a patchwork of security measures. There is a joint operation under way by corporations and governments claiming they are creating a "secure" and "safe" information environment free of dissent and irritants to capital flows. With the technical and law enforcement measures in place, any bit can be labeled "dissent." Radical pragmatists like myself believe that the picture is not gloomy, that there's still enough space for intervention and freedom for off-the-radar initiatives. This confidence is built on the presumption of an active minority of Net users who are willing to act, skilled enough to lobby, and equipped with enough experience to build social alliances in order to uphold or indefinitely circumvent closed systems based on profit through control and scarcity, while reinforcing open, innovative standards situated in the public domain that anyone can access and modify. One might think of Eric Raymond's metaphorical battle between the cathedral (Microsoft) and the bazaar (open source), or Manuel DeLanda's distinction between open markets and anti-markets (which he took from Ferdinand Braudel). Radical media pragmatism is not satisfied with some ideal notion of how capitalism, or socialism for that matter, might work in theory, assisted by well-meaning engineers who've found the perfect technology to run a "GPL society"[19] based on "free" goods, barter or "open money." Rather, the daily complexities of online cooperation must be enjoyed. The pragmatism I employ requires vigilant efforts to articulate the Net with materiality, for herein lies the possibility of a politics that recognizes how "embedded" technology is in social practices. Technological models can inspire, mirror and assist, but not replace, social struggle.

The ideas and experiences gathered here do not openly draw from contemporary debates on the philosophy of technology. Net criticism does not need the support and protection of general theories or grand thinkers. If it is to be viable, its techno-discursive practices will have to stand up by themselves and engage in the battle against new closures and alternative architectures. Net critics are not the eunuchs of cyberspace, let alone anthropologists studying exotic tribes. Theory, as presented here, is a living entity, a set of proposals, preliminary propositions and applied knowledge collected in a time of intense social-technological acceleration. The discourse is not primarily assembled from books, but takes shape out of a mist of private e-mails and encounters, mailing-list posts, weblog entries and database retrievals. It is not yet time for a general network theory. First of all, we must go back in time, be it to yesterday, last year or 50 years back. There is a lot to be learned and borrowed from older fields of study, such as cybernetics, systems theory and mass psychology. In this period of "permanent transition," scholars are stuck between print and online forms of knowledge hierarchies. Online publications are still looked down on. Despite the hype, huge investment and commercial success, there is no systematic networked knowledge to speak of in the "Western" world around the turn of the millennium, assuming such a grand theory would even be possible in the wake of postmodernity. Institutional power remains wary of network potentials, particularly the danger of losing intellectual property and offline privileges. The network society-in-the-making is reluctant to theorize itself.

One question keeps returning: Why use the concept of "criticism" in the first place? Isn't it a dead horse? Since the 1980s, *Kritik* has been severely out of fashion, and for good reason. My generation has perceived the critic as a bored, aged, cynical outsider who is openly disinterested in what is going on. The critic as authority fueled the war between the generations and staged "culture wars" about politically correct topics (but never technology), promoting a curious mix of neo-liberal populism and highbrow institutional culture. Criticism became indistinguishable from the "culture of complaint." Employed by magazines and daily newspapers, the critic aimed to talk down, and if possible destroy, technological, artistic and intellectual experiments – at least, that's how we experienced criticism. Contemporary cultural theorists only made matters worse, as they limited themselves to the Gutenberg galaxy of printed matter, thereby further widening the decades-old gap between the humanities and the world of the engineers and scientists who were building the architecture of global computer networks. It was hard enough to "think television," let alone theorize algorithms of Internet search engines. The jump to the "visual culture" discourse had yet to be made; meanwhile, there was already a new technology and its attendant discourses. All this constituted an avalanche of the new and is symptomatic of the futility of criticism as fashion.

Within this context I am not referring to classic contemporary critics, such as Edward Said, who remain strictly within the realm of print (daily newspapers, magazines and books). The few public intellectuals around do not deal with new-media issues. Said's integrity to some extent stops him from facing the cynical nature of the media intelligentsia. I was therefore tempted to go back to one of the classic postwar texts on the role of the critic. In *The Anatomy of Criticism* (1957), Toronto professor of literature Northrop Frye opposes the mainstream view of the critic as a parasite or artist manqué. We could replace art with information technology here and make a similar observation: we could say that Net critics are intellectuals who have a taste for IT but lack both the power to produce it and the money to patronize it, and thus make up a class of cultural middlemen who distribute IT culture to society at a profit to themselves.[20] This is a social formation which media critic McKenzie Wark has termed the "vectoral class."[21] Although the mediating function still exists, today's intellectuals can no longer claim to represent the creative online other. It is not the task of the "virtual intellectual"[22] to verbalize the ideas of programmers, designers and artists. For Northrop Frye, criticism had to exist because "criticism can talk, and all the arts are dumb."[23] In this age of interviews and specialized websites and magazines, workers in the "creative industries" are adept at expressing themselves. They do not need critics to do it for them. Furthermore, one could question the paternalistic assumption behind mega-terms such as "creative industries" or "the knowledge nation." After all, new-media workers, by definition, have established the competencies needed to function within networked societies. Some would even say that the "vectoral class" has no choice, since it must write applications and academic papers to make a living. The rise of general writing skills, computer literacy and the Internet are closely connected.

In his book *The Function of Criticism* Terry Eagleton argues that modern criticism was born of a struggle against the absolute state. Eagleton describes how, after a golden age in the late 18th and 19th centuries, criticism gradually declined. "It has ended up, in effect, as a handful of individuals reviewing each other's books. Criticism itself has become incorporated into the culture industry as a 'type of unpaid public relations, part of the requirements in any large corporate undertaking.'"[24] Writing in 1984, Eagleton sees the role of the contemporary critic as a traditional one: "Criticism today lacks all substantial social function" (p. 7). At the same time, he expresses the hope that criticism will retain its timeless potential "to disrupt the consensualism of the public sphere" (p. 21).

Eagleton admits that today the battleground is no longer English literature. Much like Frye (but unlike Raymond Williams, Marshall McLuhan, Friedrich Kittler and other literary scholars-turned-media theorists), Eagleton hesitates to make the "technological turn." He remains safely on the Gutenberg side of the fence, and confines his analytic rigor to past centuries. But if we can forgive his pessimism, *The Function of Criticism* should be considered a key text for Net critics. There is a lot to be learned from the ups and downs of literary criticism as described by Eagleton. The same could be said of film criticism, which was at its height in the 1970s. We see a growing tension between various media and their respective scholars. In a climate of fierce competition, there is an immanent danger that new-media studies will take away resources from film, theatre and literary studies. Nonetheless, film theory could be a rich source of inspiration for new-media critics. One need not start with the latest school of thought and go through the lengthy process of deconstructing deconstructionism, as Eagleton does. Like their historical predecessors, Net critics "must reflect as well as consolidate public opinion, working in close touch with the broad habits and prejudices of the public" (p. 47). If the Net criticism project is to succeed, Eagleton's sober judgment of today's intellectual poverty must be taken into account. The anti-intellectual attitude that "clever isn't cool" is criticism's biggest enemy, whatever media it operates in.

In recent decades, the role of the critic has only further diminished. Let's face it: public intellectuals are not the gatekeepers of cyberspace. Most of them look disdainfully down on the "new." That attitude should not concern us. What critics and theorists can do is to contextualize work and give the multidisciplinary reality of media works a discursive turn. Frye declared literary criticism an art form; this is not my intention here for Net criticism. It can make only modest claims, given the overall decline of the intellectual's position in society. According to Frye, the notion that the poet necessarily is or could be the interpreter of him- or herself or of the theory of literature "belongs to the conception of the critic as a parasite or jackal" (p. 6). There is indeed a tendency within new-media culture to look down upon intellectuals who stick to the old rules of the Gutenberg galaxy, in which a select group of editors inside publishing houses and newspapers decided what was and wasn't theory.

The humanities have been mostly preoccupied with the impact of technology from a quasi-outsider's perspective, assuming that technology and society can still be separated. This also counts for key media theory texts which are frequently either not available in English translation or not online because of copyright issues. The transfer of critical knowledge and activities into the networks has yet to take place, and the process might take decades, if not generations, pushed by a growing number of "netizens" who risk ignoring publisher's contracts, old-media reputation systems and academic publication requirements. But do not despair: the "napsterization" of text is at hand.

Defining and exchanging key reference texts has been an important element in the Net criticism project. Free-content clearinghouses, based on peer-to-peer file exchange principles to ensure that essential reading does not get locked up behind firewalls, are under construction.[25] But we are not there yet. I will go into detail about this topic in the first chapter, in which I discuss the work of Lawrence Lessig. As he explains, the general tendency is in the opposite direction. Closed image databases, filled with a cultural heritage that once belonged to the general public, will hold up if not stifle the wide use of the Net. A growing awareness of the potentialities of the "technologies of freedom" (Ithiel De Sola Pool) goes hand in hand with a control that is growing ever faster, fueled by users' uncertainty and fear. An important task of the Net criticism project is therefore to be inside the network, in the form of e-mail, uploaded texts, links and databases. It is precisely this being inside that is necessary for reflexivity, as opposed to the society/technology split of traditional criticism.

This study describes beginnings, or formative processes, of networks. The Internet is still an unfinished project. After the peer-to-peer networks of the late 1990s, wireless networks and weblogs emerged. The emergence of all three can be read as a response to dotcom culture and proof that the medium is by no means dead. I will not focus again on the early mythologies and promises, but I would like to map some of the first accounts of actual cultural life on the Net. Unlike George Steiner, I believe "beginnings" are still possible.[26] The call for Net criticism is first and foremost a quest for quality research into actual online relationships. *Netz-kultur is das was der Fall ist.*[27] Net criticism is neither descriptive nor prescriptive but reflexive. It is only a decade ago that the only texts about the Internet available were popular how-to manuals. The bulk of Internet reporting is cheap and quick journalism, undistinguishable from public relations. A medium used by hundred of millions deserves to have the most sophisticated and imaginative criticism possible, one that positions itself at the heart of technical, legal and commercial developments. Internet criticism should place itself explicitly at the center of operations. This requires a proactive research approach. It is not enough to study the implications of technology, as so many social-science studies do.

Like books, films and theater, the Net is in need of a lively public debate about its content and direction. This discussion has not yet hit the mainstream; there was no room for it in the late 1990s. One could even ask if Net criticism has not already passed its sell-by date. Small website-review sections have already started to disappear from daily newspapers. The confusion remains: is the Internet part of the media section, along with radio, film and TV? Does it belong on the business pages? Or should it rather be classified under "faits divers," covering hackers' attacks, spam, child pornography and other controversial topics? Or should Internet issues return to the technology supplement, if there is one? Staying with the newspaper table-of-contents metaphor, I would suggest that the best place for writing about the Internet is in the opinion pages, combined with background analyses in the arts and book review sections. Instead of labeling the Net as "pop" culture, it would be a better strategy to position it as part of traditional "high" culture and world politics. I in no way wish to return to the futility of the high/low culture wars; rather, I wish to emphasize that a Net criticism can only be "pop" for 15 minutes. This, after all, is the economy of contemporary media culture. Net criticism is a call for thorough, long-term scholarship – inside or outside academia. Its "pop" phase is only a brief interlude in what Braudel calls the *longue durée* of socio-technical life.

The prisms envisioned here are not meant to smooth the cultural anxieties of the elites. In the early days of the Internet, science-fiction writers, followed by academic researchers and business gurus, took on the critic's role. We are now witnessing the dawn of the cultural Net critic. It is no longer enough to produce images of a bright cyber-future (there are plenty of those anyway). Instead, Internet theory should map the limits and possibilities of materiality. The current state of the Internet is one of conflict. Infowars are multi-spatial, fought out in electronic, material (physical/sex/gender/race, institutional, geographical) and imaginary ways. The Internet is not a parallel world, and it is increasingly becoming less dominated by its technicalities because of user-friendly software. Computer networks are penetrating society deeply. They are spreading so fast and so far that it is becoming next to impossible to define Net specificity separately from society at large.

To get a critical understanding of the Net, with all its functionalities and standards, is already a monumental task. In my view, Net criticism would not just aim at the technical level, even though software critiques, discussions of operating systems, open-source principles and the larger network architecture could all benefit from encounters with a broader (non-technical) audience outside programmers' and system administrators' circles. The criticism I have in mind is as polymorphous and perverse as its topic, having the difficult task of bringing together aesthetic and ethical concerns and issues of navigation and usability, while keeping in mind the cultural and economic agendas of those running the networks at the hardware, software, content, design and delivery levels. That's a lot. Still, the scope may be large but the task is small and precise. The Internet is not the universe – it's just one galaxy among many. This is proved by the phenomenal rise of "cellspace," which by 2003 had twice as many users (1 billion) as the Internet.[28]

In the new millennium, information warfare is on the rise, and this is more than just a construct of the Rand Corporation financed by the Pentagon. DARPA's Total Information Awareness program is but one example of this development. The Internet is slowly but inevitably shifting from a model of consensus to one of control and conflict. But the strategy of tension and control in the context of "infowar" is not just a state policy (along the lines of "counterterrorism") but rather points to a global civil war in the making, with a multitude of players. Even to those who have not (yet) personally faced fatal data loss or been involved in flamewars, it must be obvious how the general mood on the open Internet has changed into one of suspicion, untraceable tension and despair. Electronic civil disobedience[29] is only one of the "positive" strategies available. There are also plenty of negative ones, which further fuel a climate of tension and uncertainty. Counterattacks can come from any side, inside or out. Much of this is still unconscious, and little of it has been theorized.

Information warfare is a general state of affairs, not just a military technique. In this context, it is remarkable that Manuel Castells, in the same "Computer Networks and Civil Society" chapter of *The Internet Galaxy,* describes the downfall of the Amsterdam Digital City and then immediately moves on to security and cyberwar issues. Castells: "Informational politics naturally leads to the possibility of information warfare." Online projects, in one way or another, can easily deepen the "crisis of political legitimacy."[30] Still, "us and them" divisions are not very useful in this context. Hackers' knowledge is generally available. Attacks can come from any direction, not just from one specific subculture. Cyber-attacks are coming from Beirut as well as Pittsburgh, and Kuala Lumpur, Melbourne and Tel Aviv. Online "hacktivism," mostly playful and innocent and testing possibilities, can easily change its character and bring down not just the World Bank's Web server, but yours too. In my conclusion, I will return to this dual aspect of both fostering and managing conflicts on the Net.

By 2001, the spirit of the widely propagated Information Age had turned nasty. A cloud of (self-)censorship hangs over the Net. The climate is one of electronic tensions, e-mail overload and disengagement. The general excitement, curiosity and openness that marked the 1990s were overturned by security concerns. Online energies and desires are now flowing towards wider debates on globalization, global warming, missile defense systems and the "war on terrorism," and away from the topic of the Internet as such. A new generation of students takes the Web for granted and no longer projects any expectations onto the medium. People have woken up from the libertarian-consensus dream of the neutral, positive hacker ethic. Unlike Pekka Himanen in *The Hacker Ethic*, I believe that the distinction between good hackers and bad crackers, endlessly reproduced by the mainstream media, is one of the past.[31] There is more to hackers than the "post-Protestant work ethic" Himanen cites. A polarization is becoming visible between those who stick to worn-out New Economy tales of "good capitalism" (against the bad state) and others who question the disastrous dictatorship of the free market. The critique of globalization is not a backlash, as conservatives like Thomas E. Friedman like to suggest. The movements active under the "Seattle" umbrella have a clear blueprint of global justice and economic democracy on offer. The countercommunication is as global as ever. Opposite the branch model (logo) are active translocal exchanges between the "multitudes" of (nologo) nodes. The days of offline activists – condemned to perform street actions while fighting with the print media to get recognition and a hearing for their arguments – are numbered.

An exciting renaissance of media activism is undoubtedly taking place at both a global and a local level. Protests during numerous summits of politicians and business leaders have boosted local activities that in turn strengthen the highly publicized global confrontations. Techno-geek and eco-feral cultures, separated in the past, are now mingling. "Hacktivism," with its collective denial-of-service attacks on government and corporate websites, though controversial, is on the rise. But there are also signs of a global civil war among hackers (Chinese against US Americans, Serbs against Albanian sites, Israeli and Palestinian hackers fighting each other, Pakistanis vs. Indians). Activist methods aimed at enemies backfire, leading to an arms race of ever more sophisticated info "weapons" and a further rise in restrictive network security, corporate countercampaigns and repressive state measures, sold under the goodwill slogan of "usability." The exercises in Net criticism presented here do not explicitly deal with the strategies of tactical media and online activism; I have written about these issues elsewhere.[32] However, the rising tensions on the Net described here should be read in the same light.

The steady rise in conflicts on the Net, combined with the battles over Internet standards – ownership, if you will – is not a development that I particularly oppose. Instead of arguing for a (nostalgic) return to a time where a handful of engineers sought consensus through "requests for comments," I argue for the need to analyze different positions and expectations. In her book *The Democratic Paradox*, political philosopher Chantal Mouffe develops a critique of the dominant liberal-democratic consensus approach. She calls for the need to acknowledge "differences," pointing out the impossibility of complete reabsorption of alterity. It is her argument that rivalry and violence, far from being the exterior of exchange, are its ever-present possibility. She concludes that "modern reason needs to acknowledge its limits."[33] All this applies to the Internet and its quasi-neutral and "rational" engineering culture. Applying Mouffe's ideas to the Internet, I would argue for an "agonistic" approach to network architectures. As Mouffe explains, conflicts must be situated not between enemies but between "adversaries." The prime task of "agonistic pluralism," she tells us, is "not to eliminate passions from the sphere of the public, in order to render a rational consensus possible, but to mobilize those passions towards democratic design."[34] It is in this spirit that I have conducted my case studies. I will try to deconstruct, both in code and culture, Internet consensus as a "temporary result of provisional hegemony, as a stabilization of power that always entails some form of exclusion."[35]

The IT consensus culture, with its hippie-entrepreneurial New Age positivism, has dominated Internet circles long enough. This is, in part, a question of scalability. Up to the early 1990s, the worldwide Internet community was small and relatively homogeneous. With half a billion users in 2003, that picture has changed dramatically.

The "democratic project," as Mouffe calls it, that I take up in this study is different from the scalar dimension of the liberal nation-state and its models of representative democracy. A call for the "democratization" of (critical) Internet culture need not end up in a debate about regulatory issues. Mouffe privileges the term "the political" over "politics," since the former, as a field of social relations underpinned by the potential for antagonism, constitutes the possibility of politics. "The political" in this context is embedded in software. For Net criticism, software is a field of social relations that constitutes the possibility of online discourse. For many political scientists, democracy is still a legal form of power, executed within the boundaries of the nation-state. Internet culture, however, is a global medium in which social networks are shaped by a mix of implicit rules, informal networks, collective knowledge, conventions and rituals. It would be foolish to reduce the Internet to a set of legal-technical standards and presume, for instance, that "regulative ideas" would stop information warfare or spam from spreading further. Instead, I will point to possibilities for advancing the social "settings" within software and network architectures in order to experiment with a pluriform and agonistic "post-geek" form of hegemony.

In "Against the Digital Heresy," the opening chapter of *On Belief,* Slavoj Zizek formulates what could be the philosophical underpinnings of the Net criticism project. For Zizek, the overcoming of "myth" is not simply a departure from the mythical but a constant struggle with(in) it. "Myth is the Real of logos: the foreign intruder, impossible to get rid of, impossible to remain fully within it." Following Adorno and Horkheimer's analysis in *The Dialectic of Enlightenment,* Zizek's enlightenment itself is mythical. "The dynamic, rootless postindustrial society directly generates its own myth," and the Internet is a particularly strong and appealing one. Zizek does not analyze the Internet directly but makes reference to the mythological nature of computer engineering culture. "The technological reductionism of the cognitivist partisans of Artificial Intelligence and the pagan mythic imaginary of sorcery, of mysterious magic powers etc., are strictly the two sides of the same phenomenon: the defeat of modernity in its very triumph."[36] Translating this to the case of Net criticism, we could say that the idea of a pure global communication assisted by software algorithms and decentralized network architectures is itself a mythological construct, loaded with ideology. This study looks at only one tiny element, mailing list software, and investigates its social imprint. But beyond that, I am interested in the dynamics of critical Internet culture itself. I am eager to find out what pitfalls there are, for the obvious purpose of being able to circumvent them in future projects.

It is now common sense that the window of opportunity for the unfinished Internet is rapidly closing, even before the medium has reached a mature stage. Would the conclusion point to a "spineless" Internet, similar to the "spineless" parliamentary democracy of the 1930s? There is plenty of evidence for dismissing Internet officials as soft-minded appeasers of the corporate regime. As we speak, the Net is not yet a monolithic broadcast medium. I remain wildly optimistic about its potential. The recent ascent of peer-to-peer networks, weblogs and free software could be a sign of a coming Internet renaissance. Before the "Battle of Cyberspace" reaches its critical stage (or fades away), research into list cultures may be crucial. Lists (and weblogs) form the communication backbones of so many of today's movements and cultural/intellectual undercurrents. It is not my intention to make public claims about the essential "truths" of the Internet based on the experiences gathered here. Still, I feel that it is of strategic importance for the future of "computer-mediated communication" that the inner dynamics of list communities become better known. It is time for precise questions, free of nostalgia or bitterness. What can be learned from the mid-1990s Web excitement? What models became predominant in the cultural non-profit Internet scene? How did artists' communities on the Net distribute power?

Methodology

My aim is to write a contemporary form of media archaeology in which I map the social and cultural usages of the Internet. Here I continue a series of histories of a selected group of techno-cultural networks.[37] The methodology used in these case studies consists of content analysis of publicly available Web archives of lists and sites. I went through thousands of individual posts, looking for general patterns and significant quotes. From the list archives I selected a number of significant threads and then did close readings of particular debates. Selection was motivated by instances in which the discursive limits of online debate manifested in terms of an articulation of social, political, economic and cultural dimensions within the time and space of the mailing list itself. Filtering e-mail and critically selecting Web links are essential if one is to avoid being overwhelmed by the vast amount of online information. This problematic is addressed throughout this study. During the filtering process, I searched for general discursive patterns and shifts in the exchanges and then selected a limited number of posts. I combined a detailed analysis of Web archives with my personal knowledge as a participant in each of these networks.

No matter how urgent or attractive, it is not my intention to perform a discourse analysis of the dominant techno-libertarian Internet agenda, with its anti-statism and preoccupation with biological metaphors. My aim is a limited one. I am mapping out the diverse spaces that constitute critical Internet culture. What is presented here is a "communicology" (Vilém Flusser) or grammar (Marshall McLuhan) of the Internet. I am looking into the internal dynamics of those who did not follow the commercial mainstream and tried to develop a critical Internet culture. In the

case studies presented here, I describe how these networks were founded, and how they grew, defined their topics and discovered their boundaries. One of my key questions is: What are the forces that produce
change in Internet mailing-list cultures? How are ownership and internal
democracy arranged beyond the good intentions of anti-censorship and
open publishing? I will investigate how social relationships are embedded
in software. Beginnings are arbitrary in such cases. For some of the actors
in this didactic play it would have been 1993; for others, 1995.

Research into Internet Mailing Lists

A good part of this book is dedicated to Internet mailing lists.[38] Josephine
Berry describes lists as one of the most important significant materials
and theaters of operation. "These often long-running lists, generating
dozens of mails each day, produce an informative, critical and sociable
'virtual community' against which and through which artworks are made,
circulated and discussed."[39] According to Berry, list cultures result in
"group authorship, hyperlinked structures and a high level of mutual quo-
tation and/or plagiarism." The origin of list culture goes back to early
engineering circles' use of lists to exchange ideas and reach consensus on
how to develop an application or standard. An oft-cited 1992 quote by
David Clark (MIT) about the work of the Internet Engineering Taskforce
(IETF) says it all: "We reject kings, presidents and voting. We believe in
rough consensus and running code."[40] This is complemented by another
famous Internet saying that describes list culture: "Inside every working
anarchy, there's an old boys' network."

The number of academic studies that investigate lists is still relatively
low.[41] Most of the research I found deals with other aspects, such as
online virtual communities in general (mostly MUDs, MOOs and other
types of games), chatrooms and Usenet newsgroups. Sydney-based Jon
Marshall has written a detailed ethnographic analysis of a turbulent early
list called Cybermind.[42] Cybermind was founded in 1994 by Michael
Current and Alan Sondheim; its aim was to "discuss the philosophical and
psychological implications of subjectivity in cyberspace." The list covered
a wide spectrum of 1990s topics, from French theory and film studies to
MUDs, MOOs, Net sex and a wide range of personal off-topic stories.
According to Jon Marshall, "Cybermind people engaged in mutual support, attempted to cooperate in furthering their careers, sought pair
bonds of a less temporary nature. At the least, they simply found people

with compatible interests, experience and politics with whom they can engage in non-routine 'play', when the embedding society is perceived as hostile to such aspirations." Subjects in the beginning included spelling and style; the nature of community, and whether virtual communities were similar to other forms of community; the nature of identity, and the congruence between virtual and "real" identities; and virtual reality.

By mid-1995, flamewars had started to dominate Cybermind, and the list soon went out of control, dominated by the conflict between those in favor of unconditional free speech and those who preferred moderation in order to create space for less noisy contributions. Cybermind continued to function through unspoken compromise, with occasional further disruptions. Jon Marshall concludes that communication on the list "was bound up in a degree of conflict or paradox, between demands for openness or authenticity, and the kinds of hiddenness which actually resulted. Ways of indicating authenticity (strong language, aggression, etc.) tended to be ambiguous and undermine the appearance of list harmony."[43] The Iraq invasion by US-led forces in March 2003 proved a stressful episode for Cybermind, with issues of national identity rising to the fore. Many Americans, even those opposed to the war, seemed to find the criticism of US policy expressed by non-American list members easy to classify as "anti-American," and left or refused to participate. Membership declined, as did the number of on-topic posts. This event, according to Marshall, changed the nature of the list far more than any previous crisis.

I am reluctant to present Internet mailing lists as "virtual communities." Coming from a Euro-continental background, I tend to associate the community *(Gemeinschaft)* concept with romantic notions of pastoral unity, comfort and dictatorial consensus rituals. This may or may not be the Anglo-Saxon tradition, in which the term community has a more neutral meaning.[44] Nonetheless, for me the word community is first of all an implicit reference to the domain of order, refuge and withdrawal. Howard Rheingold, the author of *Virtual Community,* has answered such criticisms in a new afterword he wrote for the second edition.[45] I would rather not do the obvious and again debunk Rheingold's 1993 position, as David Bell does in his *Introduction to Cybercultures.*[46] Ten years after the publication of Rheingold's groundbreaking book, it is common knowledge that the "healing" Internet is not delivering spiritual communion. This is why I don't want to be dogmatic and have decided to use the term occasionally. That said, a considerable number of virtual-community studies contain consensual New Age talk. Take, for instance, Anna Du Val Smith, writing in one of the countless mass-produced cyber-anthologies, *Communities in Cyberspace*. She writes: "If in their attempt to control behavior, communities drive out ideas by suppression or exclusion, or escalate into chaos as a consequence of power struggles, their life and purpose will be threatened. To avoid this they must not silence the voices of their members, but give them expression. As Scott Peck puts it, communities must not give up fighting, but learn to 'fight gracefully.'" Against such idealism, I am arguing that the *realpolitik* of information warfare is necessary in order to guarantee the very survival of today's online forums. For me, nothing is as terrifying as being totalizing, so I will use the (virtual) community concept occasionally, since it cannot be reduced to narrow New Age visions or Third Way phantasms.

What Is Critical Internet Culture?

Culture is the aspect of information technology where knowledge transfer happens. Access and training are not enough. It is only when a culture emerges that social interaction on a larger scale starts to happen. The object of this study is neither the Internet in general nor new-media theory as such. Instead, I will look into "social software" that supports group interaction. The number and variety of mailing lists, e-groups, Usenet forums, weblogs and virtual game worlds is vast. I will not even attempt to give an overview of the thousands of topics they deal with. Rather, I would like to exemplify the choices I have made and what I understand to be the constitutive elements of "critical Internet culture." I refer here to a specific emerging "milieu" of non-profit initiatives, cultural organizations and individuals primarily based in Europe, the USA, Canada and Australia and a steadily rising number of other countries. Cosmopolitan in nature, critical Internet culture can be positioned at the crossroads of visual art, social movements, pop culture, journalism and academic research. Its interdisciplinary intention is to both intervene and contribute to the development of new media.[47]

Critical Internet culture manifests itself both in the virtual world, as websites, mailing lists and chatrooms, and at festivals, screenings and public debates. It stresses the need to go beyond oppositional gestures and create a lasting independent infrastructure. Besides such countercultural characteristics, what is specific here is the desire to intervene in the early stages of technological development. Technoculture is not just a lifestyle. The subject of critical Internet culture is the user as producer. The aim is not consumer choice. Although access-related issues are important, the demands go beyond equal dissemination of technology throughout society. It is the architecture of the networks and the underlying code which society should question, and change. This is why a critical understanding of standards and ownership plays such a key role in this context. The intent of critical Internet culture is to shape and anticipate, as much as to reflect on, existing IT products and their inherent social relationships.

Technology is not a neutral tool, and this is of course true of the Internet. Its structure is a result of particular historical settings. But most of all, culture at large plays a key role in the making of new media, even though most technologists deny the fact. Critical Internet culture is therefore not just about artists working with technology. There is no longer any avant-garde dream of the artist as a first user who will bring society into an aesthetic future. Instead, there is an ongoing debate about the parameters of technological culture. What are the properties of "the new" and who are its agents? The critical aspect is related to the urge to reflect upon the dominant discourses while at the same time positioning one's own contribution. Critical Internet culture is driven by the desire to address issues that ultimately affect hundreds of millions of users, and it is perfectly aware of the limited and marginal position of such non-profit cultures.

My First Recession is a chronicle of a handful of social networks. It tells the story of critical Internet cultures in their first years of existence. Neither the theory nor the practices presented here heralds a triumph of technology. These case studies reveal real boundaries, internal contradictions and conflicts that arose once the projects had surpassed the initial stage of euphoria. What happens when the party is over, when you run up against the borders of commonly used software standards and group dynamics, when the cyber-spectacle fades away and the everyday, with its dirty politics, takes command?

Chapter Overview and Biographical Elements

In the following section, I will give a brief summary of each chapter along with an account of my personal involvement in each of the stories. Many of the archives I deal with here have an online component. This means they are accessible to any scholar and, if they are preserved carefully, as I hope, to any future historian.

Chapter One opens with three positions I selected from the fast-growing body of work being done in the field of Internet research. What unites the studies by Hubert L. Dreyfus, Manuel Castells and Lawrence Lessig, all published in 2001, is their post-introductory mode. The choice is personal and may or may not be representative. None of the three is asking any longer what the Internet is all about. This may sound futile but is in fact a big plus. Writing at the end of the dotcom era, these three authors all deal with the complex relationship between the Internet and society. Whereas Hubert L. Dreyfus takes a more conservative-moralistic stance, Manuel Castells tries to give a "neutral" overview of a wide range of academic literature. In his view, the growing use of the Net, for instance in education, could lead to a loss of reality. Law professor Lawrence Lessig, on the other hand, plays the role of the concerned liberal citizen, warning of the danger of a state-sponsored corporate takeover of the Internet, which could cripple its innovative role.

In Chapter Two I provide the reader with an overview of the "dotcom mania" literature that looks back on the e-commerce hype of the late 1990s. In order to situate the challenges of non-profit critical Internet culture, I analyze the dotcom boom and bust as its "mirror." After describing the general characteristics of dotcoms, I examine a collection of dotcom biographies published after the fall of the Internet stocks in 2000. I have been a dotcom watcher from early on. I did not work in a dotcom myself, but I have been reasonably close to the phenomenon because of friends' and colleagues' involvement in this area. All the initiatives I have started have been non-profit businesses. I had a few personal experiences with the first wave of Internet commercialization (1994–97), and witnessed the quickly fading catalyst role of artists, designers and content producers like myself, followed by the dotcom business hype (1998–2001).[48] The reluctance of independent Internet initiatives to critically engage with business is a topic in itself. The historical fact is that, apart from a few moments in the early-to-mid-1990s, the traditional separation between theory, academia, arts and culture on the one hand and business on the other was reproduced during the late-1990s dotcom boom, despite the popular rhetoric of fluid boundaries. At most, the others were watching the tech boom from a near distance.

Cultural studies, with its emphasis on identity politics in "old" print and broadcast media and broad analyses of globalization, has strangely over-looked the Internet boom and its techno-libertarianism. Maybe that's because, in short, it all went too fast. Both traditional NGOs and new global movements have so far shown little interest in the financial machinations of the managerial class. Instead, activists' investigative research focused on the environment, racism, migration and gender issues. Some investigations into the media and telco markets and institutions such as the IMF, World Bank and WTO did touch on some of the dotcom topics. Studies such as Dan Schiller's *Digital Capitalism* reduced the New Economy to the old-style monopolist strategies of well-known big corporations, overlooking the specific dotcom dynamics of overnight multi-billion-dollar start-ups of companies that folded the next day.[49] Such studies all too easily deny the involvement of progressive activists and artists in the making of the Internet, including its dotcom stage. The Net cannot be reduced to a corporate environment.

Over the past few years I have often been asked about my apparent obsession with dotcoms. Why bother in the first place with this financial bubble and this greedy yuppie culture that had no clue about the Internet's economy and technology? A considerable part of "generation @" was actively involved in one the thousands of dot-companies. For me, writing about dotcom mania had little to do with a return to economic determinism. The "dotcom question" is one of what sustainable economic models exist for a critical Internet culture outside (disappeared) venture capital, grants and sporadic state subsidies. The gap between the frantic production of innovative interfaces, software and content and the lack of "economic competence" with respect to how these prototypes could be utilized by wider audiences indicated a looming crisis for a sector that many brilliant people had invested much of their passion and energy in. Dealing with dotcoms as an intrinsic part of the Internet story was one way for me to question the dominant "gift economy" and rampant self-exploitation. In my view, voluntary labor and giving away your code and content should be a free option, not a default one.

Chapter Three describes the rise and fall of the Syndicate mailing list. Founded in 1996, the Syndicate network slowly built up a critical mass of subscribers. The aim of this post-1989 project was to open dialogue between new-media arts practitioners in Eastern and Western Europe. After a number of meetings, workshops and publications in early 1999,

Syndicate found itself caught up in the controversies of the Kosovo war. The list became a lively platform for debates about ethnic cleansing and the NATO bombing of Yugoslavia. But it did not survive these harsh debates. In 2000, while still an open and unmoderated list, Syndicate became the target of "trolls" and other "infowar" strategies of Net artists. In mid-2001, it fell apart, unable to resolve the issue of moderation.

Chapter Four concerns Xchange, an early network of non-profit streaming-media initiatives. The Xchange list was established in late 1997 and has always been a pragmatic, hands-on network. In this case study I describe and analyze the collaborative projects between the audio artists and Net radio initiatives that make up the Xchange network. Owing to the stagnation of broadband rollout and the rising uncertainties about intellectual property rights, the streaming-media sector found it difficult to reach its full potential. This also had an impact on the independent non-profit networks. Instead of expanding in dotcom style, Xchange was forced to remain small and "sovereign."

Although I know a reasonable number of the Xchange network members, I would not consider myself part of it. Besides sporadic posts on the list, I have made Net radio programs in collaboration with e-lab, DFM, Zina Kaye, Ralf Homann and others, doing streaming sessions wherever possible. This research builds on my 1992 essay "The Theory of Mixing" and a few related pieces from the same time, in which I described the techniques of Amsterdam free-radio producers.[50] It uses an Adilkno concept from the same period to explain Xchange's strategy of "sovereign media": the liberation from any possible audience, or media without audiences. This strategy aims to go beyond the idea of "alternative media" or "subculture." I have been interested in the economics and politics of bandwidth from early on. Independent streaming-media networks such as Xchange depend heavily on the availability of cheap Internet connectivity. In this chapter, I explain how the self-image of such networks is related to the (relative) stagnation in bandwidth that the Internet has faced since the late 1990s.

I deal with critical issues in new-media arts education in Chapter Five. Because models in education affect future generations of the new-media intelligentsia, and because so many theorists and artists are employed in this field, I have decided to devote a chapter to this emerging topic. What is the status of software courses and vocational training in general? It is tempting to presuppose technical skills and immediately jump to the more interesting critical and conceptual issues, but that is often unrealistic. How great is the "market pressure" upon academic institutions to deliver masses of creative young "code slaves"? What is the place of theory? Thousands of educators worldwide are struggling with these issues and many more. The ideas I present here have grown over the years and are based on a decade of experience. I have taught new media in a variety of schools, in Zürich, Bucharest, Stuttgart, Osaka and Sydney and on the US West Coast. As not much written material is available, I have chosen to conduct e-mail interviews with experienced new-media educators, all of them colleagues that I find inspiring.

Chapter Six looks at free software and open source from a cultural perspective. This is obviously a vast field, but it is of such strategic importance in my opinion that I felt the need to engage with it even though I am not a geek or programmer myself. I have chosen to tell my version of the story through debates on the German mailing list Oekonux, which explores the possibilities and parameters of a GPL society. The General Public License, introduced to protect free software against misuse and keep source code open, is discussed as both a model and metaphor for an alternative socio-economic metastructure. Because of the extent and the depth of the Oekonux discussion, which kicked off in mid-1999, it has proven impossible for me to summarize the 7,000 or so posts, but I have tried to anyway. The ability to "transport" concepts from one context into another displayed here is fascinating, and it is yet another proof that there are no strict boundaries between technology and culture.

In the Conclusion, I bring together the experiences of different lists and communities and focus on the issue of moderation and how internal democracy within Internet-based networks could be shaped. The rise of "weblogs" is one way of dealing with issues of information overload and moderation. I will describe how I see "open publishing" Web tools as a possible answer to the limitations of existing Internet community models (and e-mail-based mailing lists in particular). The possibilities – and limitations – of weblogs are a direct response to the "benign dictatorship" of lists and the linear "collaborative text filtering" model. Towards the end of the chapter, I address the wider issues of (internal) democracy and ownership of Internet projects and discuss how software mediates between social experiences and technical possibilities.

The post-1989 period is drawing to a close. The fall of the dotcoms, and the following recession, combined with 9/11 and the wars in Afghanistan and Iraq, form the necessary setting of this study – but they are not its topic. Instead of providing the reader with a preliminary big picture of the post-millennial George W. Bush era, it is my intention to investigate in detail how virtual communities function, a decade after the Internet was opened to the general public. This undertaking needs a somewhat longer timeframe. It is important to stay on-topic and not leave the scene. In my view, post-dotcom and 9/11 new-media discourses should no longer advocate an unusual, unheard-of future. The age of global civil infowar, peer-to-peer networks and weblogs confronts the reader-as-user with problems and perplexities that need further investigation. There have been enough speculative philosophies. What this maturing medium needs is less religion and more scrutiny; not cynical statements or sales talk but serious engagement. It's still a monumental task to leave the 20th century behind, despite the fact that its deconstruction is in full swing. The global network society is no longer a promise but a fluid and dirty reality. Instead of proclaiming the next future, it might be more interesting to presume that we have already arrived there, and start to explore its workings.

Post-Speculative Internet Theory

Three Positions: Dreyfus, Castells, Lessig

"I'm feeling so real. Take me away." Moby

From Vision to Research

Since the mid-1990s, we have witnessed the emergence of academic research into the Internet from a social-science and humanities angle. Parallel to the scientific approaches are art-related, activist and critical discourses growing out of cultural and political contexts. In the mid-1990s, personal websurfing diaries and dotcom-business titles were hot, but these have gradually disappeared from the shelves. The biggest market area for Internet books remains that of program manuals and DIY books (a genre I won't discuss). Instead of deconstructing all the intellectual currents and their ideologies and respective roots, I'd like to jump to theories that reflect, at the edge of recession, on the Internet after it was opened up to the general public. I will analyze the research of three US Internet theorists: Hubert L. Dreyfus, Manuel Castells and Lawrence Lessig. I have not chosen them as representatives of different "schools." It is not relevant whether or not they are part of the emerging academic Internet research canon. What matters is that they take positions. I have refrained from properly summarizing their books. What is missing in Internet culture, in my view, is strategic debates and polemic discussions. There are plenty of reviews available online. Instead, I have given priority to "criticism."[1]

The three works discussed here were all published in late 2001 – a fact that, in theory, should not be important, but is because the Internet is such a rapidly changing environment. They were written after the speculative dotcom phase of Internet development had come to a close (but before the big corporate scandals and 9/11). The fact that all three are male US university professors based in California indicates that, conceptually speaking, the USA, and the West Coast in particular, is still the epicenter of the Internet, despite efforts to geographically diversify the discourse.[3]

Retrospectively, we can now start to map 1990s popular cyberculture. There are Esther Dyson, George Gilder, Kevin Kelly, Raymond Kurzweil, John Perry Barlow and Nicolas Negroponte, who have been carefully styled into cyber-libertarian idols. Then there are researchers who look at the identity aspects of cyberspace, such as Howard Rheingold, Sherry Turkle and Sandy Stone. William Michell contributed to the "virtual architecture" hype with his book *City of Bits*. Work of a more philosophical-speculative nature came from Sadie Plant, Manuel DeLanda, Pierre Levy and Derrick de Kerckhove. Slightly more "underground" would be writers such as Hakim Bey, Erik Davis and Mark Dery. One could also go back in time and mention the technical founding fathers, such as Internet Society boss and (former) WorldCom executive Vint Cerf, the late Jon Postel (administrator of the top-level domain-name system), *Whole Earth Catalogue* publisher Stewart Brand, free-software guru Richard Stallman and Web inventor Tim Berners-Lee. Recently, Katherine Hayles, Peter Lunenfeld and Lev Manovich have become influential thinkers in cultural new-media circles; their intellectual production, like that of other media theorists, mostly deals with the underlying structures of information technology and does not address specific Internet issues. Rather than deconstructing the founding myths and utopian promises or entering cultural studies territory, I am more interested in the recent work of authors who reflect directly on the Internet as a medium in rapid transition.

Hubert L. Dreyfus's Reality Romanticism

Berkeley philosophy professor Hubert L. Dreyfus, known for his book *What Computers Can't Do* (1979), was commissioned by Routledge to write a four-chapter essay on the Internet for the "Thinking in Action" series. Dreyfus develops his version of "Net criticism" in four different fields: the limitations of hyperlinks and the loss of the ability to recognize relevance; the dream of distance learning (no skills without presence); the absence of telepresence; and "anonymity and nihilism," which concerns the way the Internet presumably promotes a life without meaning. In principle, such topics could be relevant, yet they do not address real concerns. There is no mention of pressing issues such as the free versus proprietary software issue, domain-name politics, the dangers of corporate takeovers, techno-libertarianism, cryptography and censorship, the "digital divide," intellectual-property regimes, and so on. What counts for Dreyfus is the ontological deprivation caused by today's social networks: the Internet deprives users of "essential embodied capacities."

Dreyfus centers *On the Internet* around an unfortunate misunderstanding.[4] He confuses the very particular Extropian cyber-dream of "disembodiment," popular in the mid-1990s, with the Internet as such. Unfortunately, Dreyfus is by no means alone in this. The mix-up between virtual 3-D immersive environments and the rather primitive 2-D Internet goes back to the early 1990s, when futurist techno magazines such as *Mondo 2000, Boing Boing* and *Wired* treated all new technologies as part of one and the same "revolution of the mind." But no Internet agency ever promised "that each of us will soon be able to transcend the limits imposed on us by our body."[5] There is in fact a whole range of competing ideologies – such as pragmatism, communitarianism, statism and libertarianism – fighting for hegemony of Internet discourse. Global-governance models are competing with the policy interests of nation-states and the commercial agendas of transnational corporations. There are engineers, corporate gurus, telecom suits and geeks, all with different agendas and cultural backgrounds. "Civil society" is increasingly trying to get a grip on the decision-making process and figure out who is setting the agenda for the "information society."

Posthumanism is only one of many factions. A decade after the rise of posthumanism, the claim that cyberspace will bring about the super- and infra-human is hardly discussed anymore. Instead, people argue over things like globalization, the "war on terrorism," and Internet governance models. A consensus has emerged, growing from the observation that "we are all cyborgs," which says that we are increasingly becoming dependent on, and even physically inseparable from, technology. Dreyfus carefully routes around economic and political aspects of the Internet debate, thereby contributing to an influential undercurrent of cyberculture: the media ecologist's call for a return to "reality." According to this backlash philosophy, "the Net is making our lives worse rather than better."[6] Instead of dealing with complex issues of filtering, linking, moderation and ranking, media ecologists call for a general crackdown on information production in order to stem the glut that, in their view, cannot be processed.

According to Dreyfus, "life in and through the Web may not be so attractive after all."[7] After an initial period of curiosity and excitement, Dreyfus's reassessment of the Internet coincides with the post-dotcom hangover. In such a post-bubble climate, a conservative backlash can easily gain popularity. Like household appliances, the Internet has become an invisible part of everyday life. It may be a liberating relief for some that there is more to life then the Internet, but such a truism can hardly be the foundation for a philosophical investigation.

It seems tempting to confuse popular-culture virtual reality motifs with the rather dull *realpolitik* of network architecture. So why can philosophers no longer distinguish between substance and appearance? Paul Virilio and Slavoj Zizek, for instance, and with them countless others, have had the greatest difficulty distinguishing between literary fantasies, demo design, marketing video clips and Hollywood dreams, on the one hand, and really existing technologies, with all their imperfections and incomplete versions, on the other. The press release and advertisement do not equal the actual product, no matter how often public relations people repeat New Age mantras of becoming "virtual." But for certain philosophers they have become one and the same. That may be fine for luxury cars and perfumes, but it doesn't work for software. Body politics may have been significant at some point, but they cannot begin to cover the variety of all-too-real issues that the Internet as a global medium faces. The Internet is not in need of "re-embodiment," as Dreyfus suggests. Instead, it cries out for a strong coalition able to come up with a design for a digital commons, and to defend and redefine core values such as openness and access.

Philosophers are in great need of help in defining ideas such as "freedom," "liberty" and "property" that underpin open-source and free software. Many won't listen anymore to free-software guru Richard Stallman talking about "free as in free beer." There is no free lunch. Or was it no free speech? Is geek culture really as dazed and confused as it seems, or is there more significance to the Richard Stallman-Eric Raymond controversy?[8] This would be an ideal case for a techno-philosophy aimed at doing "the proper study of mankind" (Isaiah Berlin) online by updating notions about what "positive" and "negative" freedom will look like in the digital age. What, for instance, is the difference between "free" and "freedom" in this particular context? Do terms such as "liberty" and "autonomy" provide a way out?

This leaves us with Dreyfus's phenomenological preoccupation with the body. Numerous Internet critics looked into the mythological disembodiment dreams of 1990s cyberculture. Around 1990, science-fiction futurism was used to popularize and electrify the still-unknown "cyberspace." There was a lot of speculation about "virtual bodies." But by 2001, the year Dreyfus's pamphlet appeared, excitement and curiosity about disembodiment had faded away. From early on, there had been thorough (feminist) critiques of male dreams of leaving the "messy" body behind, none of which Dreyfus mentions. Meanwhile, a range of artistic practices had been created that left the Extropian tendency far behind, developing a critical "body politics" within the virtual arena. Scholars such as Cameron Bailey and Arthur McGee have done work on race in virtual communities, arguing that online communication is never "disembodied" but always carries racial and cultural markers. One might, therefore, expect criticism of this commonsensical approach rather than a return to the same old adolescent cyberpunk culture.

"All this chatter about sociality and community is partly inherited hypocrisy and partly studied perfidy" (Kierkegaard). Not surprisingly, Hubert Dreyfus outs himself as a cultural pessimist. To be more precise, he is a media ecologist comparable to Neil Postman, George Steiner, Hans-Jürgen Syberberg, Peter Handke and, most recently, Rüdiger Safranski.[9] The deluge of meaningless information disgusts these media ecologists. Nonsense should not be just filtered but banned. It is the high task of civilized intellectuals to decide what should and should not enter the media archive. Driven by good intentions, the media ecologists secretly dream of an authoritarian regime of enlightenment in which chatting and rambling are serious offenses. Along these lines, they denounce the World Wide Web as a "nihilist medium." "Thanks to hyperlinks, meaningful differences have been leveled. Relevance and significance have disappeared. Nothing is too trivial to be included. Nothing is so important that it demands a special case," Dreyfus complains.[10] It is one thing to call for "self-limitation," as Safranski does, but who will design the "immunity armors" he calls for? If the questions get too difficult, as in the case of bio-ethics or network architecture, one is to turn away from the world – and sell this gesture as a philosophically superior sign of wisdom.

In *On the Internet* Dreyfus confuses elements of popular cyberculture with the agenda of the creators of the Internet. He seems unaware of the Californian Ideology debate, the *Wired* clan's agenda of digital Darwinism, and the critiques of techno-libertarianism in publications such as *Cyberselfish* by Paulina Borsook and Thomas Frank's *One Market Under God*. For Dreyfus, the Internet equals Hans Moravec plus Max More times John Perry Barlow plus Ray Kurzweil. Dreyfus focuses on the wrong assumption that the Extropians embody the "truth" of the Internet, instead of analyzing them as a subcultural undercurrent and post-religious sect. He then sets out to deconstruct this presumably dominant Platonic wish to leave the body behind, without analyzing in detail the specific political, economic and cultural agenda of this tendency and its relationship to different new-media discourses.

Dreyfus then turns Nietzsche against the Extropians to illustrate that human beings, rather than continuing to deny death and finitude, "would finally have the strength to affirm their bodies and their mortality."[11] When we enter cyberspace, Dreyfus answers the disembodiment advocates, we might "necessarily lose some of our crucial capacities: our ability to make sense of things so as to distinguish the relevant from the irrelevant, our sense of the seriousness of success and failure that is necessary for learning." To sum up: "If our body goes, so does relevance, skill, reality, and meaning." That could be the case. As an analysis of the Extropian movement, *On the Internet* is a classic case of belated *Ideologiekritik*. This leaves us with the general question of how knowledge stored in books can operate in a fast-changing environment like the Internet. Often, the object of criticism has long disappeared by the time the theoretical objections have been well thought through. The answer can only be a theory on the run. Internet-related critical knowledge is not only forced to operate in the present, it also expresses itself in a range of ways, as code, interface design, social networks and hyperlinked aphorisms, hidden in mailing-list messages, weblogs and chatrooms and sent as SMS messages.

Dreyfus makes no mention of users and groups creating their own meaning and context on the Net. He has apparently never heard of mail filters and thresholds. Like a small child wandering around a library, touching the shelves, Dreyfus is overwhelmed by the sheer quantity of accessible information that doesn't make sense to him. "One can view a coffee pot in Cambridge, or the latest supernova, study the Kyoto Protocol, or direct a robot to plant and water a seed in Austria."[12] The data ecology of the Web is not all that different from the information universe on offer in a Borders bookstore, where "the highly significant and the absolutely trivial are laid out together." Perhaps bookstores should also be cleansed. How about shortwave radio, or the rising mud floods on the peer-to-peer networks? With John Stuart Mill and Alexis de Tocqueville, Dreyfus fears the coming of the digital commons, where every citizen will have to do his or her own information filtering.

On the Internet traces the origins of media ecology back to Kierkegaard's 1846 book *The Present Age*. Kierkegaard blames the "leveling" of society ("Everything is equal in that nothing matters enough to die for it") on the Public. What Kierkegaard, and with him Dreyfus, really finds scary and disgusting is democratic nothingness. The public and the press – these days renamed "the internet" and "the media" – should not be allowed to celebrate radical uselessness. Instead, the elites should restrict the public sphere and direct the masses towards progress, war, socialism, globalization, or whatever is on the agenda. The fear of the black hole of the commons is widespread and ranges from left to right. "In newsgroups, anyone, anywhere, anytime, can have an opinion on anything. All are only too eager to respond to the equally deracinated opinions of other anonymous amateurs who post their views from nowhere."[13]

What Dreyfus finds particularly disturbing about the Internet is its anonymity, which he reads not as a feature to ensure one's freedom but as a sign of indifference. Nowhere does he actually demonstrate how widespread anonymous communication on the Net is, nor does he note what measures security officials have already taken to crack down on effective anonymity and free, unmonitored browsing (if that ever existed). As everyone should know by now, online privacy is an illusion, as is anonymity. The saying "On the Internet, no one knows you're a dog" should be deconstructed as yet another Internet myth. These days, security experts are able to identify even the most intelligent hackers. Apart from that, only in rare cases, such as reporting from war zones, is anonymity really useful. Usually, the anonymity cult is a sign of boredom, exhibited as a hobby in the late hours. Not everyone is into anonymous role-playing. Anonymity is one of the many menu options, used in specific cases, not the essence of the Net. It is not the default option, as Dreyfus presumes it is. With all the security and surveillance techniques available today, absolute anonymity is arguably getting harder and harder to maintain these days. Anonymity may soon go underground, as everyone will be obliged to show his or her Microsoft Passport before logging onto the Internet. Both chip and operating system will reveal a user's identity in a split second to any authorities who ask for it.

For Dreyfus, surfing is the essence of the Net, and with it comes solitude and boredom. The undirected surfing and chatting he so despises may have happened in the early days of excitement. But by now, users know what they are looking for and no longer get lost. Dreyfus does not distinguish between phases: the academic Internet of the 1980s; the mythological-libertarian techno-imagination of *Mondo 2000* and *Wired;* the massification of the medium, accompanied by the dotcom craze; the consolidation during the 2000–02 depression. Because of this inability to distinguish, old-fashioned essentialism gets projected onto a rapidly changing environment.

In one aspect Dreyfus is right: online learning won't solve the problems of mass education. But that's an easy statement. The fact is that knowledge is increasingly stored digitally and distributed via computer networks. This is not done out of a disdain for the body, to purposely prevent real-life gatherings of students with their teachers, as Dreyfus implies. The Will to Virtuality has a political agenda, aimed at the privatization and commodification of public education. As David Noble shows in his *Digital Diploma Mills*,[14] the aim of the .edu managerial class is to run the universities as if they were corporations – with or without bodies. Public education demands quality and accessibility, regardless of its real or virtual character.

The question Dreyfus poses is an old one: who decides what is sense and nonsense? The debate over filtering the Internet (and mailing lists in particular) is a central topic in his book. Though few list participants would support Dreyfus's position, there is certainly a silent majority that favors (manual) filtering by editors in order to prevent information overload. Managing information flows is a main concern for users – but one they do not like to trade for a loss of freedom. Internet enthusiasts point to the crucial difference between old media, based on scarcity of channels, resources and editorial space, and the Net with its infinite room for parallel conversations. For the first time in media history, the decision over the sense-nonsense distinction has (potentially) moved from the medium and its editors to the individual user. Dreyfus doesn't mention the opportunities and problems that come with this important techno-cultural shift. According to him, curiosity as such is dangerous. Groups "committed to various causes" could potentially bring down the ethical sphere. In the end, this debate is about the freedom of speech. Dreyfus doesn't want to openly raise the sensitive question of who is going to judge content. Censorship should probably come from within the self, as voluntary self-restraint with respect to daily information intake and production.

Ever since the rise of virtual communities in the 1980s, there have been ferocious debates about how to distinguish – and balance – noise and meaning. A wide range of (self-)moderation models and filtering techniques has been developed. How this well-informed and Internet-savvy

Berkeley professor can ignore all this is a mystery. *On the Internet* is therefore a setback in terms of Internet theory. At the same time, the book also embodies the common desire to walk away from work (on the computer) and take a well-deserved break. The ethical-aesthetical position Dreyfus calls for could be developed without much effort. For him, however, the "morally mature" must avoid the virtual sphere in a search for extramedial "unconditional commitments."[15] Kierkegaard would reject the Internet, according to Dreyfus, because in the end "it would undermine unconditional commitment. Like a simulator, the Net manages to capture everything but the risk."[16] Bankrupt dotcom entrepreneurs would say otherwise. Looking at the tension and confusion caused by viruses and trolls, one wouldn't say the Internet is such a safe place.

The Net is not "a prison of endless reflection," as Dreyfus suggests. I would analyze it rather as a challenge in the direction of a lively agonistic democracy (Chantal Mouffe), filled with controversies and irreconcilable positions.[17] Neither a separate realm nor a numbed consensus factory, the Internet could foster structural dissent (to be distinguished from protest as a gesture, lifestyle or even opinion). The more the Internet matures, the more it will become a both fierce and fertile battleground for "adversary" social groups. The digital divide will not be bridged but will create new forms of conflict. Today's communication bridges are built to facilitate the redistribution of wealth, be it software or knowledge. In this understanding of a lively electronic democracy, the naïve discourse of "consensus without consequences" Dreyfus so despises will be undermined anyway by those reconnecting and redistributing "virtuality" within society. As Manuel Castells points out in *The Internet Galaxy,* there is no return possible to an era before the network society: The Network is the Message. Reality romantics, similar to their historical predecessors in the late 18th century, can point to the blind spots of the Network Society, but will not succeed in outlawing or overturning the technological nature of, for instance, knowledge production and distribution.

The "reification" of the Internet's "nature" is classic techno-determinism. In this sense, Dreyfus falls into the same trap as those he criticizes. For Kierkegaard and Dreyfus, salvation from techno-determinism can only come from the religious sphere of existence, experienced in the "real" world. As if a pure and unmediated world ever existed. "Real" and "virtual" are becoming empty categories. A call for a return to the "real" can only be nostalgic and makes itself irrelevant as it runs away from the present conflicts over the future of global network architecture. Dreyfus's sentiments are outdated but still popular because they appeal to nostalgic feelings of a lost world that existed before the rise of new media. What is needed is a radical democratization of the media sphere. The material and the virtual have become one, and separating them is conceptually misleading and practically impossible. The same can be said of the made-up dichotomy between old and new media, often used within institutional contexts facing rapid changes. Castells' formulation of "real virtuality" could be more useful in this context. "Real" education free of ugly computers might sound attractive to some, but as a critique of technology it runs the risk of further deepening the crisis between the rising online masses and the elites who are rich enough to retreat into Fortress Reality, safely sealed off from cheap, dirty cyberspace.

Manuel Castells' Network Pragmatism

After his influential trilogy *The Rise of the Network Society*, Berkeley professor and urban sociologist Manuel Castells published a survey solely dedicated to the Internet. *The Internet Galaxy* reads like a hastily assembled, broad overview of recent academic literature. After detailing the history and culture of the Net, Castells discusses a wide range of contemporary topics, from business models and virtual communities to privacy, the digital divide and the geography of the Internet. Manuel Castells has the brilliant intellectual capacity, connections, and frequent flyer miles to produce a global overview of Internet research. However, the cultural "Net criticism" ideas and networks presented here make up a world largely unknown to Castells. Being a structuralist, he sketches wide landscapes of academic research, avoiding close reading. His aim is "strictly analytical" but not particularly critical. What Castells is concerned with is the shifting morphology of society from hierarchies to networks. He persistently talks about a "new economy," by which he means something other than dotcoms. According to Castells, the architecture of the economy is becoming more flexible due to the ability of IT networks to combine flexibility with control, aiming to beat hierarchies at their own game: the focused marshaling of resources. Yet, with this long-term shift in mind, Castells avoids deconstructing emerging hegemonic discourses. Remarkably, he fails even to mention techno-libertarianism as the dominant Internet ideology of the 1990s. Unlike the technology gurus, he is wary of future predictions and moral admonitions. One possible reason for his blindness to techno-libertarianism is the lack of academic research into this ideology. Only phenomena that have reached academic credibility in the United States make it into the Castells galaxy. References from websites, lists and e-mails are virtually absent in his study. With the Internet in a state of "informed bewilderment," Castells admits that the "speed of transformation has made it difficult for scholarly research to follow the pace of change on the whys and wherefores of the Internet-based economy and society."[18] This may also count for his own study – and that of anyone else trying to capture the fluid Internet *Zeitgeist* in a comprehensive study.

The Internet Galaxy opens with lessons from the history of the Net. Castells briefly sums up how ARPANET engineers mixed with a utopian counterculture, resulting in a spirit of freedom hardwired into code. He then moves on to describe the e-business and New Economy that dominated the Internet in the second half of the 1990s. For Castells, e-business does not equal dotcoms. He sees the network economy and the changes it unleashes as real, not a bubble. In the next chapter, I will go into further detail about Castells' dotcom arguments. His next topic is the social implications of virtual communities. On these he gives a brief overview of work done by scholars who belong to the Association of Internet Research (AoIR).[19] This is followed by a chapter on networked social movements and citizens' networks, in particular the Amsterdam Digital City project, whose demise I described in detail in *Dark Fiber.*

Castells is a pragmatist, not a prophet or a pessimist – and this is what he and I perhaps have in common. Written in the midst of the dotcom crash, his *Internet Galaxy* reads like an upbeat reminder that the networks, in the end, will be victorious. Castells really wants his "network society" to work. We should all stick around and convince ourselves that the Internet will survive the current volatility. Like many of his academic colleagues in this field, Castells is wary of conflict. He likes to formulate carefully balanced observations. This puts him, unwillingly, in the position of an innocent outsider, a diplomat at best. There may be a need for journalistic-scientific works written by generalists such as Castells who take up the position of the general – surveying the battlefield from a hilltop. But analysts, in my view, have to get their hands dirty in order to deconstruct the agendas of the different, increasingly clashing cultures and factions inside the Internet at large. If the Internet is a battlefield, what we need is war reporting. His aim to "better our society and to stabilize our economy" would be better served by posing uncomfortable questions to technologists, CEOs and community networks.

The Internet Galaxy takes up the well-known US position that privacy no longer exists. It charts the dilemma of many Internet advocates: is it useful to look for government assistance in the protection of liberties – from the same government that is stepping up restrictive legislation? *The Internet Galaxy* closes with Castells' remarks on the geography of networks, a field he is widely acclaimed for. His conclusion is that geography does exist: the Internet has not erased locality. Global nodes spring up; yet this "glocality" is not confined to industrialized nations. In the same way, the digital divide also exists. "The rapid diffusion of the Internet is proceeding unevenly throughout the planet."[20] The Internet did not correct the growing gap in knowledge, technology and living standards between the developed and developing worlds. Castells advises a new model of development that requires leap-frogging over the planetary digital divide. It calls for an Internet-based economy, powered by learning and knowledge-generation capacity, able to operate within the global networks of value, and supported by legitimate, efficient political institutions.[21] If this does not appear, the digital divide "may ultimately engulf the world in a series of multi-dimensional crises," he predicts.

The dotcom visionaries took their ideas from conservative US business circles and energized different discourse fragments into a strong, appealing image of the Wired Future. As a frantically productive belief system, the dotcoms drew on an accelerating feedback loop with the *Zeitgeist,* riding on much bigger currents such as privatization, deregulation and globalization, embedded in a structurally unstable situation. The 1990s economic boom also profited from the post-(cold)war dividend. Castells knows the limits of the bureaucratic categorizations he uses and counters his own quasi-neutral instrumental rationalism with ambivalent conclusions. As a former Marxist, he is afraid of being labeled "anti-corporate" or even "anti-capitalist." This fear eventually hampers his capacity to analyze the 1990s fusion between technology, business and culture with all its ups and downs.

No matter how much realism prevailed, the dotcom crash and downfall of telecom giants such as WorldCom and Global Crossing did happen, and this history needs to be analyzed. These "scandals" are not exceptions but an integral part of the Internet story (particularly if you look at the role of Internet founding father Vint Cerf in the WorldCom saga). One can therefore expect Castells to modify his mild judgment of e-business in the near future, stressing the need for "corporate accountability." Having said that, Castells makes valuable observations. He points out that most innovation coming out of Silicon Valley in the past decade has been focused on the business side rather than the technology side. "After all, most technology these days is open source or 'off the shelf': the real issue is what to do with it, and for this the essential item is talent."[22]

In *The Internet Galaxy,* Manuel Castells rightly defines Internet culture as the "culture of the creators of the Internet."[23] It is not the users but the pioneers that set the parameters. Internet culture is characterized by a four-layer structure: the techno-meritocratic culture, the hacker culture, the virtual communitarian culture and the entrepreneurial culture. According to Castells, these together contribute to an ideology of freedom that is widespread in the Internet world. The four cultures are interrelated and have loosely distributed forms of communication. However, they are not equal. First of all, there is a hierarchy in time. The techno-meritocratic culture was there first, and this is how it claims its authority. "Without the techno-meritocratic culture, hackers would simply be a specific counter-cultural community of geeks and nerds. Without the hackers' culture, communitarian networks would be no different from many other alternative communes."

He continues: "Similarly, without the hacker culture, and communitarian values, the entrepreneurial culture cannot be characterized as specific to the Internet."[24] Castells summarizes in an almost holistic overall view: "The culture of the Internet is a culture made up of a technocratic belief in the progress of humans through technology, enacted by communities of hackers thriving on free and open technological creativity, embedded in virtual networks aimed at reinventing society, and materialized by money-driven entrepreneurs into the workings of the new economy."[25] The critical Internet culture mapped out in this study would probably fall under the "communitarian networks" category. The Internet may be a "cultural creation,"[26] but if we look at Castells' categorization, it doesn't really have a cultural arm. There is no mention of any cultural theory in *The Internet Galaxy.* In Castells' galaxy there are no designers, artists, theorists or critics. Even mainstream issues of human-computer interaction and "usability" remain unmentioned. There is some truth in this, as critical Internet culture remains marginal and has had a hard time proving its very existence and conceptual urgency, lacking both media visibility (in terms of celebrities) and academic credibility.

Lawrence Lessig's Legal Activism

Warnings about the rise of state-corporate control over the Internet have been around for a few years. At the height of dotcom mania in 1999, two studies dealing with the legal and political threats to "cyber-freedom" appeared: Alan Shapiro's *The Control Revolution* and Lawrence Lessig's *Code and Other Laws of Cyberspace.* Lessig warned that Internet developers were closing their eyes. "It is the age of the ostrich. We are excited by what we cannot know. We are proud to leave things to the invisible hand. We make the hand invisible by looking the other way."[27] *Code and Other Laws of Cyberspace* is a friendly yet persistent dialogue with the dominant libertarian forces that rule the Internet. Two years later, Lessig shifted his attention to large corporations, in particular the media/entertainment industry.

In The Future of Ideas, the Stanford law professor becomes outraged over the assault on the Internet. As Lessig says, his "message is neither subtle nor optimistic."[28] Corporate control is crippling "the creativity and innovation that marked the early Internet. This is the freedom that fueled the greatest technological revolution that our culture has seen since the Industrial revolution."[29] Lessig is a classic anti-trust liberal and by no means anti-capitalist. For Lessig, the fight is not between progressive and conservative but between old and new. His tone is almost apocalyptic. After having lost the Eldred vs. Ashcroft case in the US Supreme Court, Lessig said at a conference in Oxford, "When I wrote *Code,* people told me it was wildly too pessimistic. It turned out not to be pessimistic enough. Things changed in a negative way more quickly than I predicted – so I guess however pessimistic I've been, I've not been pessimistic enough."[30] We are moving from an architecture of innovation to one of control. The content owners are taking revenge over the hackers. Noticed by hardly anyone, freedom and innovation have been lost. "Those threatened by this technology of freedom have learned how to turn the technology off. We are doing nothing about it."[31] In the chapter on streaming media and the Xchange network, I go into detail about one such threat: Internet-radio initiatives being forced to close down because of intellectual-property issues and high traffic fees.

In the first part of *The Future of Ideas*, Lessig describes the conditions of openness. The crucial element in the design of such an "innovation commons" was the "end-to-end" principle. In the "e2e" model the network itself is kept relatively simple. The "intelligence" is not located in the heart of the network but allocated in the terminals, the individual machines that are connected to the network. As a result, the Internet itself is kept "simple, in the sense that it handled all packets equally, without regard to content or ownership."[32] But this structural design is changing, both legally and technically.

Lessig calls the open space the Internet once created a commons. "A commons is a place, a real physical space or an more ephemeral information space, that is not privately owned. Natural commons include the oceans and the atmosphere. Garrett Hardin's famous article 'The Tragedy of the Commons'[33] argued that such commons would inevitably be degraded and used up – like a village commons where everyone would feed their livestock until there was no grass remaining. Information commons hold the shared history of our cultures, such as myths and folksongs. Information commons are unique, because as ideas are taken from them to provide inspiration, they are not used up. Those ideas remain for the use of future generations of creators."[34] Against Hardin, it is often argued that the exhaustion of the commons is no longer a danger when you can make infinite perfect copies without implications for the "original."

It was the Harvard law professor Charlie Nesson who mentioned the idea of a commons in cyberspace to Lessig. "He spoke of the need to support a space in cyberspace free from control – open and free, and there for the taking." Why would anyone need to build a commons? Lessig wondered. "Cyberspace was not a limited space, there would always be more to build. It is not like the American continent was; we're not going to run into the Pacific Ocean someday. If there's something you don't have in this space, something you'd like to build, then add it, I thought."[35]

Digital commons are usually situated in between the state and the marketplace and easily squashed by either – or both. "The civic sector represents our collective selves, in other words, particularly in all of those affairs (such as community action and cultural expression, education and social welfare) that are neither driven by the profit motive nor derived from the authority of the state."[36] The digital commons, in one possible reading, is nothing more then the lost dream of a fading middle class, a harmonious picture of a consensual society free of conflict. In this view,

NGOs and artists are essentially intermediate buffers who create the illusion of "civil society." Advocates of the digital commons are therefore easily portrayed as "useful idiots" who are there to soften up the harsh side of global capitalism.

The idea of a digital commons could be compared to the public sphere as described by Jürgen Habermas.[37] According to Terry Eagleton, Habermas' concept of the public sphere "hovers indecisively between ideal model and historical description and suffers from severe problems of historical periodization. The 'public sphere' is a notion difficult to rid of nostalgic, idealizing connotations; like the 'organic society', it sometimes seems to have been disintegrating since its inception."[38] The same could also be said of the digital commons. Similar to the tragedy of the commons, the tragedy of the digital commons may already have happened. Yesterday's utopia may no longer be in reach today. At the same time, the legal documents produced for today's commons can be read as ideal models, utopian in nature.

A long time ago, back in mythological times, before 1993, the entire Internet was "public domain." All code, applications and content were publicly owned and accessible to all – so pioneers from the early days report. In this rational and egalitarian environment, built and maintained by well-paid engineers, tenured academics freely exchanged ideas and resources. Money was no issue, because all the actors had either tenured jobs or were employed by companies. In this climate, it is understandable that the issue of proprietary versus free software became the main controversy. This economic paradise created a paradox which early Internet developers have not openly dealt with: before "the public" everything was public. As soon as the masses invaded the new-media arena, the precious public domain was overrun by "dirty" market forces and even more "evil" government regulators. Ordinary users requested easy-to-use interfaces, tailored entertainment and, above all, safe and reliable systems. Business took over, and as a result, the digital public domain vanished. Lawrence Lessig does not talk about this strange circular movement of the digital commons concept – even though he must be aware of the eternal return of the tragedy. After every legal defeat, Lessig takes up an even bigger task. His is a clear case of "pessimism of the mind, optimism of the will."

According to Lessig, free software published under the GPL license is part of the digital commons. So are the public streets, most parks and beach-es, Einstein's theory of relativity and the 1890 edition of Shakespeare. These are the carefully chosen examples given in *The Future of Ideas*. But Lessig knows very well how little content and software is actually public domain. In the USA, the period of copyright has been extended 11 times over the past 40 years. So instead of thinking of the digital commons as an identifiable "sphere" with actual info bits in it, we should instead read it as a proposal for a legal framework. After the publication of *The Future of Ideas*, Lessig and others launched the Creative Commons initiative, a practical toolkit of adjustable licenses. Creative Commons is a direct result of Lessig's and others' intellectual work, offering the public a set of copyright licenses free of charge. "For example, if you don't mind people copying and distributing your online image so long as they give you credit, we'll have a license that helps you say so. If you want people to copy your band's MP3 but don't want them to profit off it without your permission, use one of our licenses to express that preference."[39]

By now, there are many versions of the Fall of the Net. In most, the public domain does not really exist, and what could labeled as such is all but a shadow, an echo of glorious days gone by. Paradoxically, it is society that spoiled the purity of the early cybersettlers' paradise. The "tragedy of the digital commons" was provoked by individuals and corporations that drew on the value produced by the commons, which they then consumed privately. In *The Future of Ideas*, Lawrence Lessig's lost freedom is the creativity and innovation that marked the early Internet and fueled the greatest technological revolution of our time. The globalization theorist Benjamin Barber paints a similar grim picture: "Citizens are homeless: suspended between big bureaucratic governments which they no longer trust ... and private markets they cannot depend on for moral and civic values ... They are without a place to express their commonality. The 'commons' vanishes, and where the public square once stood, there are only shopping malls and theme parks and not a single place that welcomes the 'us' that we might hope to gather from all the private yous and mes."[40]

I am aware that I am making a similar move concerning the ups and downs of critical Internet culture. The fall of independent initiatives can cause the rise of cynical or apocalyptic sentiments. Like Atlantis, the mythological empire that sank into the ocean, destroyed by an unknown catastrophe, the digital public domain lives on as a ghost of the past, always ready to return. In the common view, the digital commons has to be "reclaimed" so it may then be "stewarded." In this line, we should see the Founders' Copyright initiative, under which "publishers and copyright holders can choose to dedicate their works to the public domain after a 14-year period with an option of renewing for another 14 years – just as America's first copyright law, in 1790, would have had it."[41] The slogan of the campaign is "Create like it's 1790." One wonders how many 21st-century digital artists share Lessig's belief that US law determines social reality. In etymological readings, the commons is described as land communally held, fields where all citizens might pasture their sheep, for example, or woodlots where all might gather firewood. Against such a harmonic, communitarian viewpoint, one could suggest other, less innocent definitions, in which social spaces like the commons are defined in the antagonistic act of becoming media, rather than by their legal or spatial frameworks.

Instead of lamenting the disappearance of public space, in the tradition of Richard Sennett[42], today's artists, activists and coders are actively shaping and radicalizing the "dot.commons." The "dot.communists" may have to accept that the digital commons are temporary, unstable and fluid in nature. Software and websites easily outdate and are wiped away by the next technological wave. Digital information may be easy to copy, but it disappears from the Net just as easily. Looking at Lessig's Creative Commons project (www.creativecommons.org), which allows users to download and modify their own licenses, we might find out that the digital commons is a really existing yet negative utopia. It should be seen as a program or ideology for the worried few. One could think of it as a temporary event, a fluid environment, not a fixed entity. Electronic civil disobedience is a major force in the creation of a digital commons. Breaking the law is often a starting point for the creation of better legislation that opens up the media sphere. The Creative Commons website offers an important set of online legal documents that users can customize according to their needs ("some rights reserved"). But the digital commons as such should, in my view, not be limited to legal issues (implicitly always those of US law). Creativity may end in legal battles, but that's not its source. It is good to have lawyers defending your case in court, but should they appear in every aspect of life? Even those who reject copyright altogether will in the near future be forced to "metatag" their work with a legal document. Like wearing seatbelts, licensing may become compulsory, irrespective of your opinion on "intellectual property rights." Before the licensing rage kicks off, perhaps it is time to point at the specific US elements in the Creative Commons project and design variations of the CC licenses that are beyond "localization," tailored for specific countries, languages, regions and cultures. In the meantime, we should be realistic and demand the impossible: "A license-free world is possible."

The advantage of an imaginary or even utopian definition of the commons over the legal definition is that it comes closer to what techno-citizens are actually experiencing. Lessig's digital commons has an ambiguous time frame: it existed in the future or is about to happen in the past. Arguably, the music file platform Napster, at the height of its use around mid-2000, was the biggest digital commons of our time. Then Napster was closed down and the company went bankrupt. It is time to tell peer-to-peer stories and draw inspiration from them.[43] No doubt wi-fi wireless networks will be the next to be regulated, along with existing peer-to-peer networks such as Gnutella and KaZaa. The public sphere on the Net only exists in retrospect. This is a methodological challenge – not a reason to become cynical or nostalgic. After the coming tragedy, no doubt a new cycle will start.

Anatomy of Dotcom Mania

Overview of Recent Literature

"Two guys go camping, and they're barefoot, and they run into a bear. And one guy stops and puts on his sneakers. And the other guy looks at him and goes: What are you doing? And the first person says: I don't have to outrun the bear, I just have to outrun you."[1]

Intro: Non-Profits vs. Dotcoms?

The dominant Internet rhetoric of the late 1990s was embodied in the "dotcoms."[2] Dotcoms were more than just "e-commerce" startups experimenting with how to make money out of new media. They came to embody the era of greedy market populism. With the Cold War over, stock markets souring, and a limitless hunger for new technologies, there was nothing that could stop corporate globalization and its Internet vanguard from taking command. The dotcoms set out to rule the telecom and media sphere, business and society at large. Not a single aspect of life seemed untouched by the commercial Internet paradigm. Dotcoms embodied a distinctive next phase in the development of the Internet now that it had left the safe walls of academia. The Internet fitted perfectly into the libertarian anti-state pro-market agenda, at its height during the mid-1990s, summarized by the "Contract with America" of the conservative US Republican "Gingrich revolution" that gave unprecedented powers to corporations and financial institutions.

In this chapter I will browse through a number of dotcom histories, as told by the believers who were in the eye of the storm. The accounts and analyses presented here were written in the immediate aftermath of the tech wreck, and do not include recent books about corporate collapses such as Enron and WorldCom.[3] If 2000 was the year of the NASDAQ crash, inevitably in 2001 pitiful dotcom biographies followed. As a theoretical entrée I will evaluate concepts from Manuel Castells' *The Internet Galaxy* and his take on the New Economy. I will then go through David Kuo's *Dot.Bomb* (about the e-tailer Value America) and *Boo Hoo*, the story of boo.com's founder Ernst Malmsten. From there, I will look into broader analyses: Michael Lewis' *The Future Just Happened* and Brenda Laurel's *Utopian Entrepreneur*, reflecting upon her vanished girls' games venture Purple Moon. But first I will make a few general remarks.

Critical Internet culture developed relatively remotely from the dotcom spectacle. Here and there, dotcoms and the cultural non-profit sector had common interests and met through personal interconnections, but by and large one could describe the two as parallel universes.[4] The proximity of a blossoming arts sector to "creative industries" is no more than vaporware for Third Way politicians. Having creative minds around may be a nice setting for business culture, but the new-media arts sector itself hasn't benefited much from the dotcom craze. For a short period (1998–99), pressure built up on (state-funded) non-profit initiatives to transform their activities into dotcom ventures, but only a few made the actual step. One of the reasons for this could be the speed of events. Dotcom mania was over before it could have a lasting impact. This is perhaps also why there was hardly any fundamental critique of dotcom business culture before the year 2000, when, parallel to the fall of the NASDAQ, the first critical studies started to appear.[5]

Independent intellectual circles such as the Nettime mailing list mainly focused on the underlying techno-libertarian, neo-Darwinist discourse of the early dotcom phase, the so-called "Californian Ideology," named after a 1995 essay by Richard Barbrook and Andy Cameron. Early critics included Mark Dery and Critical Art Ensemble. Their critique was mainly focused on certain pseudo-religious transhuman (Extropian) tendencies, which stated that the "telos" of technology was to leave the body behind and establish a posthuman regime. This type of cultural criticism did not explicitly focus on dotcom business models as such. The dotcom scheme – from business plan, startup and attracting investors to stock-market launch and sellout – did not appear on the radar screens of critical arts and theory. Whereas *Wired* and *Mondo 2000* were widely read – and criticized – IT-business magazines such as *Red Herring, Business 2.0* and *Fast Company* remained largely unknown within critical Internet circles.[6] Dotcom culture had come up in a period when most activists and digital commons advocates had already given up the fight against commercialism.

If any, the feeling of the critical new-media intelligentsia towards dotcoms was ambivalent. Jealous of the ease with which the "baby suits" could get millions of dollars as seed funding for their shaky business plans, cultural community pioneers were on the other hand unable to translate this discontent into a cohesive counter-program for safeguarding and (re-)defining the Internet as a public domain. Dotcoms, and in particular the new telcos, took initiatives where the (federal) state had failed. National telcos had been reluctant to get into the Internet business. But from 1995 onwards the commercial tidal wave seemed unstoppable. Many agreed that more infrastructure and access were badly needed, and this is where dotcoms and the non-profit critical Internet culture teamed up against the vested interests of the (former) state-owned telcos such as Telstra, Deutsche Telecom, Telefonica, KPN and BT. Yet privatization of the telecom markets worldwide had not led to fair competition and open markets, and instead had further strengthened the quasi-monopoly position of privatized state firms.

The failed deregulation of the telco, satellite and cable markets eventually led to a stagnation of broadband rollout, capacity badly needed by both the dotcom e-commerce vendors and non-profit content producers. No one wanted to come up with the huge investment sums necessary to bring fiber optics into every home. However, this (potentially) common interest did not articulate itself in any political way. Cyber-lobby groups have mainly focused on electronic civil rights issues and network technologies' effects on democracy, wary of putting the hard economic issues on the agenda. The ambivalent attitude towards the telecom giants remained, as they were one of the main forces that had sabotaged the takeoff of the new-media industry. With a completed fiber-optic network reaching households, businesses and small institutions, the dotcom story would have taken a different turn. With little broadband infrastructure in place, though, the financial "bubble" aspect of the dotcoms only became more pronounced.

Get There First

What is striking in all the different narratives is the desire to capture the excitement, the drive to "get there first," and the strong belief in slavish (yet playful) hard work. In the "Himanen ethic" the foundations of the Protestant work ethic remained untouched. The eight-hour work day was merely extended to "24/7." Belief in "friction-free" network technologies and trust in commercial applications were overwhelming. Every idea presumed a multi-million customer base. Remarkably, in all these works the ideological origins of the dotcom model remained uncontested, no matter how different the backgrounds of the authors were. Just a few years after the bubble, the dotcom stories are about to fade away for good. Let's, therefore, look back at some of the elements of the dotcom golden days and how they were reassessed during the Internet's first recession of 2001–02.[7]

The late-1990s bull market convinced analysts, investors, accountants and even regulators that, as long as stock prices stayed high, there was no need to question company practices. That changed drastically in 2000. While publicity after March 2000 focused on the ever-rising list of dot-com bankruptcies, 2001 overshadowed these cases with a much bigger overall recession, 9/11, and serious collapses such as those of energy giant Enron and telco Global Crossing. Enron's demise has been called the first morality play of the post-boom era, and the enormous media attention it generated indicates a symbolic turn. After 9/11, confidence and optimism waned. "And then, as if to confirm that an era had ended, the nation's seventh-largest company, one that had reinvented itself using the tools of the moment – technology, faith in markets, canny lobbying and an ability to exploit deregulation to create new businesses – went poof."[8]

According to *The New York Times*' Bill Keller, Enron "embodied the get-obscenely-rich-quick cult that grew up around the intersection of digital technology, deregulation and globalization. It rode the *Zeitgeist* of speed, hype, novelty and swagger." Keller describes Enron as a "thinking-out-side-the-box, paradigm-shifting, market-making company. In fact, it ranked as the most innovative company in America four years in a row, as judged by envious corporate peers in the annual *Fortune* magazine poll."[9] The core – and most profitable – part of Enron was its Web-based ener-gy trading platform. The Internet turned out to be the ideal vehicle for it. Blind faith in the New Economy had become paradigmatic for the late-1990s anything-goes attitude. Some blamed it on the 1960s, liberalism, born-again materialists, Clinton, or even the environmental movement.[10]

Keller wrote: "Petroleum was hopelessly uncool; derivatives were hot. Companies were advised to unload the baggage of hard assets, like fac-tories or oilfields, which hold you back in the digital long jump, and con-centrate on buzz and brand." Accountants who tried to impose the tradi-tional discipline of the balance sheet were dismissed as "bean-counters" stuck in the old metrics. Wall Street looked to new metrics, new ways of measuring the intangible genius of innovation, and the most important metrics were the daily flickers of your stock price. When the stock plum-meted, Enron immediately died. Liquid modernity, it turned out, was not crisis-proof. Keller sums up new mood, so different from that of a few years earlier: "The louder someone yells 'free markets!' the closer you want to look at his files (assuming they have not been shredded)." Or-dinary customers (formerly known as citizens) had enough of the milking, lagging and parasiting of the bottom-line accounting practices of share-value-obsessed corporations. The slogan "People Before Profits" began to make sense. Eventually, the purpose of business itself was in question: was it making money? Or creating value, providing a service for customers?[11] There was suddenly a big contrast between "the blue-collar firemen that did their duty without quibbling over widows' pensions before they went into the burning building and senior Enron managers selling their stock as the price sagged, without warning humbler employees who subsequently lost everything on their 401(k) investments in the company."[12]

By mid-2002 a chronology of events was beginning to emerge in which the 2000 fall of dotcom firms, followed by telecom high flyers, had triggered a selloff on the global stock markets, setting off an economic recession. Then a widely announced recovery in 2001 was further and further delayed by 9/11 and the collapse of Enron, the biggest dotcom ever. Both the NASDAQ and the Dow Jones index fell back to 1998 levels. With higher oil and gold prices and a devaluation of the American dollar, the greedy dotcom schemes were moving quickly into the land of fairy tales. Although general discontent had not reached the point of questioning global capitalism, some fundamental questions were put on the table. Whereas the dotcom stories could still be dismissed as "excess," Edward Chancellor went further and put the managers' pursuit of shareholder value at the heart of the problem. Alan Kohler called share-based remuneration "the root of all corporate evil." For a good 15 years, only stock value counted, not profits or revenues. The presumption was that stock value reflected the general health of a corporation and its future. This ideology can remain uncontested as long as the market goes up but endangers entire sectors, jobs and savings once the market goes down.

One way to talk oneself out of responsibility for the larger financial crisis following the dotcom crash is to dissociate the "pure," innocent, spiritual, alternative (California) IT industry from the "dirty," money laundering, gambling East Coast Wall Street mafia. A psychoanalytic reading could uncover a traumatic paradox, going back and forth between the multicultural, eco-queer "light" side and the dark Anglo-Jewish oligopolies that lured the innocent entrepreneur with dirty money. Or, to put it in different terms, new, risky venture capital versus safe institutional investment. Kevin Kelly, *Wired* editor and author of the 1998 bible *New Rules for the New Economy,* retrospectively covered over his personal responsibility into the whole affair: "Three trillion dollars lost on NASDAQ, 500 failed dotcoms, and half a million high-tech jobs gone. Even consumers in the street are underwhelmed by look-alike gizmos and bandwidth that never came." This revised view of the Internet, as sensible as it is, Kelly wrote in *The Wall Street Journal*, "is as misguided as the previous view that the Internet could only go up. The Internet is less a creation dictated by economics than it is a miracle and a gift."[13] Kelly was hastily running away from the CEOs he had hung out with during the roaring 1990s. In order to cover up his own involvement he then praised the army of amateur website builders: "While the most popular 50 websites are crassly commercial, most of the 3 billion Web pages in the world are not. Companies build only thirty percent of Web pages and corporations like pets.com. The rest is built on love, such as care4pets.com or responsiblepetcare.org. The answer to the mystery of why people would make 3 billion Web pages in 2,000 days is simple: sharing."[14] It was a comfort, for both those who had missed out and those who had lost their savings, to hear such quaint words. Voluntarism was to be the penance for all the bullish sins.

John Perry Barlow, co-founder of the Electronic Frontier Foundation, took a more down-to-earth approach. Speaking in early 2002, Barlow admitted that being an Internet guru wasn't what it had used to be. "I lost probably 95 percent of my net worth. But it's been good for the Internet, and in the long term it's going to be very good for the dot-communists. Never has there been a time when there are so many young people who have been poor and then rich and then poor again. I think it's an educational experience that teaches you what's valuable in life. To have a whole bunch of money at a really young age and see how completely useless it is – it trains a lot of folks in the real value of things."[15] Like Kelly, he interpreted dotcom mania as a hostile takeover attempt led by forces from the past. Barlow refrained from naming names, such as those of venture capitalists, investment banks or other established industries. Instead, he used the familiar biological metaphors. "The whole dot-com thing was an effort to use 19th- and 20th-century concepts of economy in an environment where they didn't exist, and the Internet essentially shrugged them off. This was an assault by an alien force that was repelled by the natural forces of the Internet." However, unlike Kelly, Barlow admitted his own errors in all this, "trying to evaluate where to go because we've so massively screwed up."[16]

In his first mea culpa interview with Gary Rivlin for *Wired*, technology guru George Gilder confessed: "When you're up there surfing, the beach looks beautiful. You never think about what the sand in your face might feel like until after you've crashed." While Gilder had avoided investing in the companies he'd written about in his newsletter because of the potential for charges of conflict of interest, the Global Crossing telco was a notable exception. According to *Wired*, it was Gilder as much as anyone who had helped trigger the investment of hundreds of billions of dollars to create competing fiber networks. Then everything imploded, and company after company went under. The telecom sector saw an even greater financial debacle than the dotcoms. *Wired*: "'Global Crossing going bankrupt?' Gilder asks, a look of disbelief on his face. 'I would've been willing to bet my house against it.' In effect he did. Just a few years ago, he was the toast of Wall Street and commanded as much as $100,000 per speech. Now, he confesses, he's broke and has a lien against his home."[17] The article failed to mention that for all these years *Wired* had been an all-too-willing megaphone for Gilder, putting out one uncritical interview after another, all conducted by senior editor Kevin Kelly.

Underneath the dedicated excitement of the late 1990s, we can find a deep sense of inevitability. I hesitate to say fatality, because that might sound pompous. Unfortunately, dotcoms lacked suspense. Like other aspects of the "transparent society," they were driven by essential human blandness. Generation @ were nothing but ordinary people, and there is, perhaps, no secret to reveal. There are no signs of despair or hope. At best, there was white-collar crime. Theft and robbery were presented as perfectly legitimate ways of doing business. The dotcoms, filled with excitement over all the vaporware business opportunities, in fact lacked sufficient conspiratorial energy. It is questionable whether the schemes can be reduced to individual cases of white-collar crime. There is a sense of cold cynicism about a gamble lost. No depth, only light. There was no such thing as wrongdoing.

In 2001, the former dotcommers were still baffled. Claiming that everything in their New Economy would be different, they had been unaware of the historical reality that every revolution eats its young. The unjust crisis without cause overwhelmed the heralds of virtual enterprise, who had hardly anyone to blame. Lawyers might have advised the dot.bomb authors not to dig too deep: class actions might be taken. This could explain the stunning lack of (self-)analysis. More likely, though, it is the

superficial and packaged experience, sensed as something uniquely exciting, that the dotcom generation went through worldwide. Dotcom antagonists had history on their side. Opportunities could only multiply. So
what went wrong?

To say that the US economy goes through periods of boom, bust and
cyclical downturn may sound like a harmless, obvious statement, but it
was heretical knowledge during the late 1990s. The overall presumption
was that victorious technology had brought real growth, and the expansion was reflected in rising stock values. To question skyrocketing equity
prices was like attacking the computer itself: irritating but irrelevant.

Castells' New Economy

Until late 2001 there had been a widespread belief that the IT sector
could not be affected by economic downturn. It was presumed that there
would always be strong demand for technology products and services;
after many decades of growth the tech industry simply could not imagine that it could be hit by a recession. "Moore's law" of the doubling of
chip capacity every 18 months was presumed to be applicable to the tech
business. Overproduction could not occur. The industry was only familiar
with overdemand for the latest models. Technology was in the driver's
seat, not Wall Street. Even Manuel Castells, in *The Internet Galaxy*, was
not free of this dogma. He wrote: "For all the hype surrounding the
dot.com firms, they only represent a small, entrepreneurial vanguard of
the new economic world. And, as with all the daring enterprises, the business landscape is littered with the wreckage of unwarranted fantasies."[18]

Castells could see only bright futures ahead, and uncritically copy-past-
ed Maoist-type forecasts of e-commerce growth predictions into his text,
fabricated by Gartner, a bullish consultancy firm that was itself highly
dependent on the continuous (share-value) growth of the IT market and
never predicted the coming of the 2001–02 IT recession.

Castells denied that economic growth in the 1990s was "speculative or
exuberant," or that the high valuation of tech stocks was "a financial
bubble, in spite of the obvious over-valuation of many firms" (p. 111). At
odds with his proclaimed "strict analytical purpose," Castells refrained
from analyzing the ideological aspects of the New Economy paradigm
and its agents such as the "business-porn" magazines with their confer-

ences, management celebrities and godlike IT consultants. Instead, he neutralized the term "New Economy" by lifting it onto a general level of all economic sectors that use network technologies. The "network enterprise," for Castells, was neither a network of enterprises nor an intra-firm networked organization: "Rather it is a lean agency of economic activity, built around specific business projects, which are enacted by networks of various composition and origin: the network is the enterprise."[19]

Unlike New Economy prophets such as George Gilder, Tom Peters and Kevin Kelly, Manuel Castells did not have to sell a business model. He abstained from electrifying his readership with upbeat concepts. He "correctly" pointed to the two sides of the coin in an ongoing attempt to reconcile industry and community. One thing he did not want was to upset technologists and business people. He switched back and forth, praising the "real" changes of IT while playing down the long-term effects of the speculative bubble. As a techno realist and "natural capitalism" sympathizer, Castells favored regulation and sustainable growth models. Facing the legitimacy crisis of governments Castells still saw the necessity of political representation and effective public policy. "Until we rebuild, from the bottom up and from the top down, our institutions of governance and democracy, we will not be able to challenge what we are facing" (p. 105). These are huge tasks, and he projected a huge responsibility onto the Internet to solve pretty much all of today's problems. Castells did not travel to the edges of the galaxy to explore the possible limits of his own discourse. For him, society equaled network. We were being drawn deeper and deeper into cyberspace. There was no room to question possible limitations of the network as a metaphor, or question its agenda. There were no parallel poetic universes. Like many techno-determinists, Castells declared history a one-way street, leaving no option to quit the network society.

Within Internet theory, Manuel Castells represents a third generation of pragmatic social scientists who have come after the computer scientists and cyber-visionaries. For Castells the impact of network technology on business, culture and society was anything but empty: "betting on the technological revolution was not a foolish idea" (p. 105). On the other hand, the current economic laws were still in place. Ever since the mid-1990s financial markets had been dictating to the technology sector, not the other way round – and Castells was well aware of this fact. Technology in itself was no longer the driving force. "The new economy is not the fantasy land of unlimited high economic growth, able to supersede business cycles and be immune to crises" (p. 111). Two pages on, Castells again switched position: "To consider that the Internet or genetic engineering are the driving forces of the technological engines of the 21st-century economy, and to invest in firms that are producers or early users of these major technological innovations, regardless of their short-term profitability, do not seem irrational."[20]

In the society of risk, theory could no longer produce a fixed ethics from a meta perspective. But neither did Castells want to become a degraded PR tout for the "Internet age," characterized by systematically volatile, information-driven financial markets. The ability to live dangerously had become a part of the business way of life, he said. But how dangerous is Castells' thinking? His combination of both speculative thought and ironic negativism puts him in a somewhat difficult position. Castells wanted to be part of an accelerated *Zeitgeist* while safely covered by an insurance policy. As a result, his careful positioning refrains from risk-taking, avoiding both speculative futurism and critical analysis. A worthy position, but not very innovative. It provides the reader with an impressive overview of new research, but the accomplishment of *The Internet Galaxy* cannot be other than modest. However, these tempered thoughts do not really help us to understand the wild fluctuations in the state of the Internet.

Throughout the "dot.bomb" period, when he was researching *The Internet Galaxy* (March 2000–March 2001), Castells made a few critical remarks about the (dominant?) discourse of "exuberance." One could label this viewpoint, as if there had only been a "speculative financial bubble," as old-economy liberalism. Castells: "I think the 'bubble' metaphor is misleading because it refers to an implicit notion of the natural market equilibrium, which seems to be superseded in the world of interdependent global financial markets operating at high speed, and processing complex information turbulences in real time."[21]

Both the overvaluation of tech stocks in 1996–2000 and the following devaluation happened "regardless of the performance of companies." Castells searched for a valuation of the network economy outside the financial markets – and failed to find it. He described the 2001 downturn as "a new form of business cycle." What he attempted here was the heroic task of conceptually unraveling the technology sector and the stock market. He was right in saying that the volatility is systemic. Post-Marxists would perhaps describe it as a "permanent crisis." It is significant that Castells does not blame fraudulent schemes but the "naysayers of the old economy of the industrial era."

Here I disagree. Capitalist logic is fundamental to the IT sector – perhaps only a massive delisting of IT companies on the stock exchange and a closure of the NASDAQ, both very unlikely moves, could disentangle capital from the computer industry. There was no "alien" assault from "tired" old-school capital on "new" and innocent West Coast hippie engineers coding for the common good. Silicon Valley should not be portrayed as a victim of Wall Street. Still, Castells' intention of thinking together business and society is the right strategy. There is no longer any "pure" Internet that can be situated outside the market. Capital rules computer technology (and this may always have been the case). Despite the utopian work of coders, artists and activists, the Internet cannot easily be disassociated from the capitalist logic. Castells' message – we live inside the Internet Galaxy (as if we could pretend otherwise!) – is a pragmatic one. It remarkably resembles Michael Hardt and Toni Negri's thesis in their millennial *Empire:* we live inside Empire (and pretend there is an outside). Castells' closing remark reads as follows: "If you do not care about the networks, the networks will care about you. For as long as you want to live in this society, and at this time and in this place, you will have to deal with the network society."[22]

Even after the dotcom crash, technological innovation will be economically driven – more so than it ever was. The fight has just started over the terms and conditions under which a techno-renaissance might unfold: free software, open source, copyleft, barter, peer-to-peer, "love," etc. The role of cyclical financial market movements and profit-oriented corporations in this process of "freedom enhancement" is highly disputed – and yet unclear. If the trajectory from bubble to burst is not to be repeated, the Internet community at large will need to quickly dream up alternative economic models; otherwise capital will, again, knock at the door.

Dot.Bomb and Boo Hoo

It is an ironic detail that the dotcom ur-parable, Michael Wolff's *Burn Rate*, appeared in 1998, well before the phenomenon was given its "dotcom" label. Wolff, a "leader of an industry without income," describes the

1994–97 period in which his New York new-media publishing company turned out to be an "Internet venture" that attracted venture capital. He was the creator of the best-selling *NetGuide,* one of the first books to introduce the Internet to the general public. As one of the first movers, he quickly turned his company into a "leading" content provider. With a "burn rate" of half a million dollars a month, Wolff New Media LLC subsequently got dumped by its venture capitalists. He explained the hype logic by which he operated: "The Internet, because it is a new industry making itself up as it goes along, is particularly susceptible to the art of the spin. Those of us in the industry want the world to think the best of us: Optimism is our bank account; fantasy is our product; press releases are our good name."[23]

The company operated under "Rosetto's law" – named after *Wired* founder Louis Rosetto – which says that content, not technology, is king. Early Internet entrepreneurs with a media and publishing background such as Rosetto and Wolf held the utopian belief that technology would become a transparent and low-priced commodity. Revenue streams would come from marketing partnerships, advertising, direct sales and, most of all, content replication – not from technology-related businesses. Views diverged as to whether or not consumers would be willing to pay for content. So far, Internet users were only paying for hardware, access and, to a certain extent, software. "On the West Coast, the *Wired* disciples believed information wanted to be free; here in New York they blissfully believed information wanted to be paid for."[24] Neither model worked. Users were mistaken for customers. Around the same time Michael Wolff left the scene, the nearly bankrupt *Wired,* after two failed IPOs (initial public offerings), was sold to the "old media" publishing giant Condé Nast in May 1998. Wolff: "My early belief that the Internet was a new kind of manufacturing and distribution economics, was replaced" (p. 328).

The dotcoms became victims of their own speed religion. They wanted the crops without planting. The dromo-Darwinist belief in the "survival of the fastest" (you are either one or zero, with nothing in between) dominated all other considerations. Overvalued stocks and an unquestionable belief in techno-superiority turned geeks into moral supermen: "My strength is as the strength of ten because my heart is pure." The "amazing over-the-horizon radar" capacity (John Doerr) broke down almost immediately after the first signs of a recession set in. The hyper-growth dogma and the drive towards the dominance of a not-yet-existing e-commerce sector overshadowed economic common sense, fueled by the presumption of something very big out there, an opportunity as untouched and beautiful as a virgin, waiting to be snatched.

The dotcoms have to be defined by their business model, not their technology focus. There was hardly any emphasis on research ("too slow"). The domination of high-risk finance capital over the dotcom business model remains an uncontested truth. These companies were depending on capital markets, not on customer bases or revenue streams. Michael Wolff sums up what would become a dotcom mantra: "The hierarchy, the aristocracy, depends on being first. Land, as in most aristocracies, is the measure. Not trade. Who has the resources to claim the most valuable property – occupy space through the promotion of brands, the building of name recognition, the creation of an identity – is the name of the game. Conquer first, reap later."[25] Or to use the terminology of Jane Jacobs, the dotcom class of '99 consisted of religious warriors, not traders. But once they had besieged the Y2K monster, the fight was over and financial reality kicked in.

David Kuo's *Dot.Bomb* is perhaps the most accessible story in the genre thus far. Unlike Michael Wolff with his investigative new-journalism style, Kuo lacked critical ambition and just wrote down what he had experienced. The book tells the story, from an employee's perspective, of the rise and rise and sudden fall of the retail portal Value America.[26] Craig Winn, a right-wing Christian with political ambitions who had already gone through an earlier bankruptcy case with Dynasty Lighting, founded the retail portal in 1996. Like mail order, Value America rested on the basic idea of eliminating the middleman and shipping products directly from manufacturers to consumers. Winn got powerful financial backing, but the portal didn't quite work, and it attracted only a few customers and offered poor service. In the face of rising expenditure, the board of directors forced Winn to resign not long before the company was liquidated in August 2000.[27]

Value America was a perfect example of a dotcom scheme that rested on the coward's mentality of messing up knowing that someone else would deal with the carnage. As David Kuo wrote of the underlying logic: "We were supposed to do the Internet shuffle – get in, change the world, get rich, and get out."[28] The New Economy could only function under the presumption that in the end the "old economy," in one way or another, was going to pay the bill; either in another round of venture capital financing, or investments by pension funds, institutional investors, banks, employees or day traders. Somebody was going to bleed. In dotcom newspeak, akin to that of pyramid schemes, everyone was going to "prosper." Not from the profitability of e-commerce, but from the large sums of money that would change hands quickly, in a perfectly legal way, covered up by official auditing reports, way before the world found out about the true nature of the New Economy.

Towards the end of his account, David Kuo wondered why events hadn't turned out the way they'd been meant to: "We discovered that the prevailing wisdom was flawed. The Internet is a tremendous force for change, but the industry chews up more folks than it blesses" (p. 305). A true Darwinist of his age, Kuo admitted the chances of getting rich so quickly and easily weren't really that high. Remembering being in Las Vegas, watching an IMAX movie about the Alaska gold rush of the 1890s, he mused: "More than a hundred thousand people ventured near the Arctic Circle in search of their chunk of gold. Of those only a handful ever found anything of any worth. A few thousand covered the cost of their trip. Most came back cold and penniless. Thousand froze to death."[29] And then came the revelation: "The truth hit me over the head like a gold miner's shovel. Despite the hype, headlines, and hysteria, this was just a gold rush we were in, not a gold mine we found. We might look like hip, chic, cutting-edge, new economy workers, but in fact, a lot of us were kin to those poor, freezing fools, who had staked everything on turning up a glittering of gold."[30]

The comparison with the 1890s gold rush might be an attractive explanation for those involved. The gold-rush narrative reinterprets business as lottery. There are no concepts or decisions, just chance statistics. The historical parallels would perhaps be tulipomania (Amsterdam, 1636), the South Sea bubble (UK, 1720), railway stocks in 19th-century Britain, and the Roaring Twenties boom that ended in the 1929 stock market crash. Compared to the Alaskan gold rush, there was no hardship during dotcom mania. Long hours were voluntary and compensated with parties and stock options. Other than some social pressure to comply, there was no physical endurance to speak of. All participants still seem to be in an ecstatic mood and willing to go for it again if they could. None of them froze to death. They enjoyed themselves. As a boo.com analyst said in a now-famous quote: "For the first nine months of its existence, the company was run on the economic rule of the three C's – champagne, caviar and the Concorde. It's not often you get to spend $130 million. It was the best fun."[31]

Boo, a fashion, sports and lifestyle venture, is another case of the pursuit of arrogance. Sold as entrepreneurial and courageous, it found itself in the fortunate position of fooling around with investors' money while flouting all existing economic laws. Boo.com was supposed to be become a global e-tail empire. Way before a single item was sold, it was valued at $390 million. Founded by two Swedes, Ernst Malmsten and Kajsa Leander, in early 1998, when the New Economy craze was picking up in Europe, it was supposed to become the first global online retailer of sports and designer clothes, "using only the most cutting-edge technology." Boo Hoo is Ernst Malmsten's stunning hubris-laden account which tells of the excitement of how easy it was to collect millions for an over-hyped business plan, assisted by offline 3-D demo design and the right buzzwords. London-based Boo got backing from the Bennetton family, a small British investment firm called Eden Capital, the luxury-goods magnate Bernard Arnault and a number of Middle Eastern investors. Despite, or thanks to, all the money, boo.com turned out to be a management nightmare. A Swedish report analyzed the company thus: "Ericsson was no good at systems integration. Hill and Knowlton did not know how to sell the story to the media. JP Morgan was not bringing in investors fast enough. The chief technology officer was not up to his job. Even Patrik Hedelin, a fellow founder, was too much of an individual to be a good chief financial officer."[32]

The Boo dream imploded only six months after its launch. After having burned $130 million, boo.com folded less than a month after the NAS-DAQ crash in April 2000. Retrospectively, Ernst Malmsten admitted that the core of the problem had been speed, the belief that Rome could be built in a day. "Instead of focusing single-mindedly on just getting the website up and running, I had tried to implement an immensely complex and ambitious vision in its entirety. Our online magazine, the rollout of overseas offices, and the development of new product lines to sell on our site – these were all things that could have waited until the site was in operation. But I had wanted to build utopia instantly. It had taken eleven Apollo missions to land on the moon; I had wanted to do it all in one."[33]

Those who taught Kuo, Malmsten & Co. these New-Economy truisms remained unnamed. George Gilder, Kevin Kelly and Tom Peters did not show up in these chronicles. As if in a psychedelic rush, the dotcom actors had gotten caught up in events, and moments later been dropped into the garbage bin of history, left behind with nothing but question marks. Ernst Malmsten: "In my head I see images of all boo's employees, who worked day and night with such enthusiasm; and the investors who were so confident of our future that they had put $130 million into the company. Two years' work, five overseas offices, 350 staff. All these people trusted me and now I have failed. What have I done? How could things have gone so wrong?"[34]

As instructed by "leadership" gurus, Ernst and Kajsa wasted a lot of time and resources creating a brand for their not-yet-existing business. The company image got turned into a *Gesamtkunstwerk* (total art work). The founders showed total devotion. "We determined that every aspect of our business, from the look of our website to the design of our business cards, should send a clear message who we were and what we stood for."[35] The launch of the (empty) boo brand throughout 1999, fueled by press releases, demo designs and parties, created the risk of media overexposure at a time when the Web portal itself was nowhere near finished. On the technology front, Ericsson, responsible for the e-commerce platform, was doing a lousy job. As Malmsten explained it, "The breaking point had come when its 30-page feasibility study landed on my desk ... The first thing that struck me how flimsy it seemed. Then I got the bill. At $500,000, it was roughly five times more than I'd expected. As we had been having considerable doubts about working with Ericsson, I saw no reason why I should accept it."[36]

This left Boo without a master plan, thereby creating a delay of many months: "There was one thing guaranteed to bring us back down to earth again. Technology. As we began to pull together the different parts of the platform, more and more bugs seemed to pop up. So many in fact that no one had any clear notion when the launch date would actually be."[37]

Still, "technology felt more like a pip in the tooth than something we really had to worry about. It barely dented that summer's mood of bullish self-confidence" (pp. 215–216). In early August 1999, only weeks before launching the boo.com site, Malmsten discovered that pretty much nothing worked. "Systems architecture, the user interface, product data, the application development process – there were problems in pretty much all these areas. Our overall project management was a disaster too. We were now working with 18 different technology companies who were scattered around the world. What they needed was a central architect."[38] Boo didn't have any version control. A central system of management should have been in place to track versions and create a central code base.

In the cases of Boo and Value America, it is significant that there was no executive technologist on board in an early stage of each venture. The lesson Malmsten learned from all these disasters is a surprising one. Instead of scaling down at a crucial moment, thereby giving technology more time to develop and technologists a greater say in the overall project planning, Malmsten retrospectively suggests outsourcing. "We should never have tried to manage the development of the technology platform ourselves" (p. 308). However, in e-commerce there were – and still are – no out-of-the-box solutions. Unaware of the imperfect nature of technology, the dotcom founders displayed a regressive understanding of the Internet. Instead of entering deeper into the complexities and the ever-changing standards, they simply instrumentalized technology as a tool, which was supposed to do the job, just like the ads said.

Surprisingly, both Kuo and Malmsten admitted they hadn't used the Internet before they got involved in their dotcom ventures and did not even particularly like the medium. In both stories technology was portrayed as an "obstacle," not the core and pride of the business. As technological outsiders, Kuo and Malmsten were visibly irritated with the imperfect nature of technology. The permanent state of instability is a source of eternal enjoyment for geeks – and should be a permanent worry for those who are in it for the business. The anxiety may be understandable coming from suburban moms and dads, but executive level managers of major Internet startups? The Internet in the late 1990s was anything but perfect, especially in cases where a complex variety of operating systems, networks, databases, applications and interfaces had to talk to each other. Dotcom management lacked the passion to fiddle around. There was simply no time for bugs in the now-or-never schedules.

The fact that these *Über*-yuppies were unaware of the non-functionality of new technologies illustrates the guest-appearance role of the dotcom workforce in the larger Internet saga. David Kuo was a political adviser and CIA operative. Boo founders Ernst Malmsten and Kajsa Leander ran literary events and a publishing house. Lawyers, former humanities and arts students and corporate employees went back to their previous professions, disappointed about the millions they failed to make. The class of '99 did not have the marketing expertise to lift its dreams beyond the level of good ideas, nor the technological experience to understand the very real limitations of the Web. They were blinded by financial deals, and their religious optimism forced them to believe that technology and markets did not have to be developed and therefore their companies could become mega-successful instantaneously. There was no time scheduled for mistakes. Didn't Darwinist doctrine teach that those who hesitated would be slaughtered? The dotcom class did not hesitate – and was slaughtered nonetheless.

Boo.com investors may have been lured, not to say fooled, by fancy offline demonstration models. "Boo.com suffered from delays, technical hitches and a website that made broadband access a prerequisite for purchasing sneakers," wrote www.tornado.com, a venture capital network that itself died in early 2002. The home computers of most potential boo customers, with their slow 28-56K dialup connections, were unable to access the high-bandwidth 3-D images of the products on sale. Yet Malmsten doesn't touch on this problematic aspect of the boo concept. Potential customers lacking bandwidth did not cross his mind. Like so many dotgone leaders, Malmsten presumed the latest technologies to be flawless and omnipresent. The future had already arrived. Those without ADSL or cable modem were losers and dinosaurs. Everyone was presumed to have seamless bandwidth at his or her fingertips. Fire up your browser, surf and buy. What's the problem? The six months boo.com was online were too short to look at bandwidth and usability issues. None of the investors pushed for a low-bandwidth version of the website. They all blindly bought into the glamorous beta versions – until reality kicked in.

In his dotcom study *No-Collar,* Andrew Ross tells a similar story about the startup 360hiphop.com. The 360 team overloaded their site with video, audio and animations that took an eternity to download. "Java, Flash and DHTML were crucial ingredients behind the navigation," Ross reports. "Access to the site's full range of content required applications like Shockwave, QuickTime, RealPlayer and IPIX. The result was technical overkill." During the launch of the site, fans got nothing but "404 Not Found" messages. The next day, when the site was finally ready, users found a homepage that took up to ten minutes to load or crashed as a result of limited bandwidth.

Boo's scheduled IPO was postponed. Investors produced a list of demands. A signed supplier agreement had to be secured with either Nike or Adidas, there had to be clear evidence of further revenue momentum, and so on. Staff had to be cut by half. The first department closed was boo's "lifestyle" Web magazine, boom. It had been Kajsa Leander's brainchild. "The notion that art and commerce could be mutually supporting – that we could be mutually supporting – that we could create a loyal customer base through a magazine that had its own independent validity – appealed enormously to her" (p. 322). It had failed to work out; like most online magazines, it was run by a staff of editors, designers and programmers and a pool of freelance writers who all needed to be paid, and brought in little or no revenue. In April–May 2000, there was a sudden mood swing in the press. Boo.com felt victimized. Investor confidence dropped below zero, and on May 18, 2000, boo.com became one of Europe's first dotcoms to close its doors. "In the space of one day our glorious schemes for expansion had vanished in a puff of smoke" (p. 318). In a matter of weeks, boo.com followed the downfall pattern described by Kuo: "Company after company followed the same death script: 'restructurings' that would help 'focus on profitability' led to explorations of 'strategic alternatives', which led to 'further layoffs' and finally to bankruptcy" (p. 311).

The dotcom generation provides, in part, an example of the dominant credit paradigm. Borrow first, let others pay back later. This pattern had already been visible in earlier practices of the boo.com founders. Their earlier publishing house, Leander Malmsten, survived on "delaying what payments we could," leaving their printers with unpaid bills. Their next project, a Swedish Amazon clone, www.bokus.com, which sold books online, didn't even have to make decent revenues: the venture was immediately sold to an old-economy retail giant, which then had to figure out a business plan. The Value America story was even weirder in this respect. It was only towards the end of his engagement that David Kuo discovered the true magnitude of a huge bankruptcy scandal caused earlier by Value America founder Craig Winn. Despite Winn's bad reputation among some Wall Street analysts, he was still able to borrow $200 million, until creditors again pulled the plug.

Michael Lewis' Future Sagas

The Future Just Happened by Michael Lewis followed the model of his last bestseller, *The New New Thing,* the story of Jim Clark and the Netscape IPO. Lewis wisely kept quiet about the whereabouts of his New Thing heroes and the tragic marginalization of the Web browser company Netscape after its takeover by AOL. For Lewis, dotcom mania moved from being a process shaped by technologists to a scheme run by financial professionals. Lewis wrote: "In pursuit of banking fees the idea that there was such a thing as the truth had been lost" (p. 47). The active role that his own immensely popular book might have played in talking up stocks remained undiscussed. Instead, Lewis set out to map the social impact of the Internet. *The Future Just Happened* accompanied a television series of the same title Lewis wrote for the BBC. In both, Lewis developed a wildly uncritical crackpot sociology. Well-known usages of the Net were suddenly sold as an "invisible revolution." In order to avoid dealing with the flaws of dotcom business models, the Microsoft monopoly, intellectual property rights, surveillance and other urgent issues, Lewis cast himself as an "amateur social theorist" who had discovered a new set of pioneers uncorrupted by Wall Street money and corporate greed.

Like many of his contemporaries, Lewis noticed that "capitalism encourages even more rapid change" (p. 6), without mentioning what kind of change. Lewis shared with Manuel Castells an attraction to the diffuse term "change," away from the old towards anything that seems to tend towards the new. For Lewis technology seemed to have no agenda, only heroes driving a wild and unspecified process. "The only thing capitalism cannot survive is stability. Stability – true stability – is an absence of progress, and a dearth of new wealth" (p. 125). Lewis equated change with economic growth. Instead of looking into marketing techniques, the production of new consumer groups and the role of early adopters, Lewis reversed the process. He mistakenly presumed that the first users of a technology actually drive the process. Sadly enough for the early adopters, this is not the case. If any identifiable agency drives technology, it is arguably the military, followed by university research centers, in conjunction with large corporations and the occasional startup.

In the television series and book *The Future Just Happened,* Lewis' heroes were not dotcom CEOs but ordinary people, and in particular adolescents. Finland provided his key example. The Finns had been successful because they had been especially good at guessing what others wanted from mobile phones. Lewis followed the corporate rhetoric of Nokia, which presumably spent a lot of time studying children. However, the assumption he makes is a wrong one: Finnish schoolchildren did not invent instant messaging. What they did was use existing features in a perhaps unexpected way. An interesting detail is that SMS is a relative low-tech feature. Nokia anthropologists picked up on this informal mobile phone use in their marketing strategy.[39] In short, Finnish youth neither invented nor further developed the SMS standard. It found new social uses in close feedback with the corporate (research) sector. The loops between marketers and "cool" rebels were stunningly subtle and banal at the same time. Such dynamics were perhaps too complex for Lewis, and so he set out to merely celebrate them, in the same way as he had done earlier with Netscape/Healtheon entrepreneur Jim Clark.

The Future Just Happened also tells the story of 15-year-old Jonathan Lebed, "the first child to manipulate the stock market" (p. 15). In September 2000 the US Securities and Exchange Commission (SEC) settled its stock-market-fraud case against this computer whiz who had used the Internet to promote stocks from his bedroom in Cedar Grove, New Jersey. "Armed only with accounts at AOL and E-trade, the kid had bought stock, then, using "multiple fictitious names," posted hundreds of messages on Yahoo! finance message boards recommending that stock to others" (p. 16). Lebed agreed to hand over his gains of $285,000. Lewis' inability to frame events becomes clear here. He completely fails to mention that only a few months after the Lebed case these same fellow day traders lost billions and billions of dollars. But Lewis is not interested in the losers, especially losers who can't be fitted into his success story about the "democratization of capital." Instead, the impression of the reader is supposed to be: clever kids can make a lot of money on the Net and the establishment doesn't let them; how unfair.

Lewis' attack on the established Wall Street experts may seem attractive, but it's a safe form of rebellion, backed by long-term developments within the financial system itself. First the trading floors of the global stock markets were wired, and then trading moved to offices outside Lower Manhattan. It was only a matter of time until Wall Street was no longer a physical center but a hub of computer networks, located – especially after 9/11 – anywhere but Manhattan. Day trading is part of this overall process but certainly doesn't drive it; its numbers are way too small compared to the vast sums institutional financiers move around. The professionals are based in New Jersey offices, Atlanta, Tokyo, anywhere. They operate from walled communities in the suburbs, equipped with laptops, broadband, PDAs and cell phones, busily tracking stocks and global news.

Within this process, which began in the mid-1980s, Lewis rightly classifies the SEC as a conservative force. "Right from the start the SEC had helped to reinforce the sense that 'high finance' was not something for ordinary people. It was conducted by elites." Hobbyist day traders such as Lebed weren't going to change that fundamental fact. Over the past decades, the rich had become richer and the middle class had come under increased pressure in terms of maintaining its lifestyle. The New Economy did not turn out to be the big leveler promised. At best, it convinced a whole generation that life was a gamble. The ticket to prosperity was the right lottery number, not a sustainable, balanced business plan. Dumb luck.[40]

Lewis argued that it was unfair to punish Lebed for pushing shares by confiscating his profits. That could be so. Regulation works to protect those in power. Lewis' sense of injustice expressed itself in oppositions: young versus old, mass versus elite, outsiders versus insiders. Because reason tells us so, the Internet would prevail over the "old rules" and would eventually claim victory. This iron-fisted historical determinism seems to attract many. The stubborn naïveté of the argument overwhelms me each time I read it. To support the cause of the Internet, I would argue, a deeper understanding of current power structures is essential. Reason will not triumph, nor will newbies, no matter how brilliant. There is no friction-free Internet world without setbacks or responses by the establishment. For instance, Michael Lewis discusses Gnutella, peer-to-peer (P2P) software launched in March 2000 by twenty-year-old AOL employee Justin Frankel. The Gnutella case was a real challenge for the capitalist Lewis' belief system. He interpreted the post-Napster free exchange movement in an interesting way. For Lewis P2P stood for post-1989 "capitalism without alternatives," which "allowed" peer-to-peer networks to experiment. "Now that the system is no longer opposed [by communism] it could afford to take risks. Actually these risks were no luxury. Just as people needed other people to tell them who they were, ideas needed other ideas to tell them what they meant."[41]

In other words, now that capitalism has vanquished all alternatives, corporate technology needs its own internal antagonists such as Linux, PGP and Gnutella. All the virus does is test the system: "That's perhaps one reason that people so explicitly hostile to capitalism were given a longer leash than usual: they posed no fundamental risk" (p. 145). Herbert Marcuse couldn't have expressed it better. In Lewis' one-way street model, the rebel had no option but to integrate. Duped by a fatal cocktail of historical necessity and greedy human nature, the Internet rebel would ultimately change sides. Sooner or later, wrote Lewis, playing ventriloquist for the voiceless hackers, "some big company swoops in and buys them, or they give birth to the big company themselves. Inside every alienated hacker there is a tycoon struggling to get out. It's not the system he hates. His gripe is with the price the system initially offers him to collaborate."[42]

In order to explain the very real struggles between inside and outside, Lewis trotted out a good-evil distinction. Capitalism from before the Fall of Man is pure and good in its very nature and cares for the Internet. As with Kevin Kelly and Manuel Castells, it is the lawyers, CEOs and financiers who are the evil elements. These imperfect, greedy human beings try to frustrate "change" as practiced by the young. Yet Lewis does not ask himself the obvious question of why the Internet has not been able to dissociate itself from these elements. Lewis' own book *The New New Thing* described in detail how finance capital took over the Internet in 1994–95.

A pure and innocent capitalism, without evil monopolistic corporations, ruled by the market, is an old idea that can be traced back to Adam Smith. Lewis set out to reinterpret youngsters' "socialist" intentions as "rebel ideas of outsiders" whose only wish, and legitimate right, it seems, is to be incorporated. Here, Lewis really shows his cynical nature, overruling the legitimate concerns of hackers in favor of his own conservative political agenda. Lewis advises us not to take notice of anti-capitalist sentiments. "Socialistic impulses will always linger in the air, because they grow directly out of the human experience of capitalism" (p. 124), Lewis reassures us. However, "the market had found a way not only to permit the people who are most threatening to it their rebellious notions but to capitalize on them" (p. 125). Daniel, a 14-year-old English Gnutella developer, "didn't see things this way, of course. He was still in the larval state of outsider rebellion."

In reference to the debate sparked by SUN's senior technologist, Bill Joy, on the ethical borders of technological knowledge,[43] Lewis states that such questioning is dangerous because it could stop "change." In his purist techno-libertarian worldview, progress is a blind process, without direction or values, which cannot and should not be directed. What remains is friction between the generations. Lewis calls for the Old to make way for the New. "The middle-aged technologist knows that some-where out there some kid in his bedroom is dreaming up something that will make him obsolete. And when the dream comes true he'll be dead wood. One of those people who need to be told to get out of the way. Part of the process."[44] But power doesn't exactly follow the logic of knowledge production as Lewis describes it. Those in power worldwide perhaps do not produce "change." But they are perfectly aware of how to own "change" once it has reached the point of profitability. Giving up power is not "part of the process." Change is a disruptive affair, often caused by revolutions (some cultural), wars (civil and otherwise) and recessions. It is a violent act. The baby-boom elites are in no danger of being overruled because the young lack a basic understanding of how power operates (and Lewis would be the last one to tell them). It's pathetic to suggest the elderly will voluntarily make way for the next generations just because they know more about how technology works.

In his review of *The Future Just Happened,* Steve Poole writes: "By the end of his series of meetings with horribly focused children, there is a whiff in Lewis's prose of real, old-fashioned nostalgia – nostalgia for the past, when kids were just kids, and authors could more easily get a handle on the changing world around them."[45] Lewis is not ready for the looming conflicts over intellectual property rights, censorship and ownership of the means of distribution. The possibility of an enemy from outside the technological realm – for instance, Islamic extremists or other funda-mentalists – doesn't cross his mind. The *a priori* here is technocratic hege-mony, determining all other aspects of life. This is perhaps the most out-dated idea in Lewis' work: that technologists are the only ones who shape the future.

Brenda Laurel's Purple Moon

The last dotcom testimony I will analyze here has firm roots in cultural IT research. *Utopian Entrepreneur* is a long essay by Brenda Laurel, author of *Computer as Theatre* and female computer games pioneer. It is an hon-est and accessible account of what went wrong with her Purple Moon startup, a website and CD-ROM games company targeted at teenage girls.[46] Sadly, Laurel's economic analysis does not cut very deep. After having gone through the collapses of computer and games company Atari, the prestigious Silicon Valley Interval research lab, and most recently Purple Moon, Brenda Laurel, along with many similar good hearted "cultural workers" seems to be gearing up again for the next round of faulty business. Nervous how-to PowerPoint-ism prevails over firm analysis. As long as there is the promise of politically correct ("humanist") popular computer culture, for Laurel any business practice, it seems, is allowable.

Laurel is an expert in human computer interface design, usability and gender issues around computer games. She is a great advocate of research; "Utopian Researcher" could perhaps have been a more accurate title for the book. Laurel is insightful on the decline of corporate IT research, on how the religion of speed, pushed by venture capitalists and IPO-obsessed CEOs, all but destroyed long-term fundamental research: "Market research, as it is usually practiced, is problematic for a couple of reasons. Asking people to choose their favorites among all the things that already exist doesn't necessarily support innovation; it maps the territory but may not help you plot a new trajectory."[47]

Laurel's method, like that of many of her colleagues interested in computer usability, is to sit down and talk to users: "learning about people with your eyes and mind and heart wide open. Such research does not necessarily require massive resources but it does require a good deal of work and a concerted effort to keep one's assumptions in check."[48]

Laurel declares herself as a "cultural worker," a designer and new-media producer experienced in communicating to large and diverse audiences. However, this does not necessarily make her a utopian entrepreneur. Like other authors discussed here she doesn't want to articulate her opinion about the world of finance. She hides her anger at those who destroyed her promising venture. It has to be said here that Purple Moon's business model predated the dotcom schemes. Revenues did exist, mainly from CD-ROM sales. Despite solid figures, high click rates on the website and a large online community of hundreds of thousands of girls, investors nonetheless pulled the plug. The recurring problem of *Utopian Entrepreneur* is Laurel's ambivalent attitude towards the dominant business culture. Laurel, like countless others, keeps running into the very real borders of really existing capitalism. The difficulty of developing a (self-) critical analysis is becoming apparent throughout the "cultural" arm of the new-media industry. The references Laurel makes to America as a culture obsessed with making more money and spending it are not very useful: "In today's business climate, the story is not about producing value but about producing money" (p. 66). Yet the book does pose the question: What role does culture play in the dynamics of business and technology?

While *Utopian Entrepreneur* is able to describe the chauvinism of "new economy" gurus, the analysis proceeds no further than moral indignation. Sadly, the economic knowledge Laurel calls for is not evident in her own writing. One of the fundamental problems may be that she equates critical analysis with "negativism." Her passion for doing "positive work" backfires at the level of analysis because it does not allow her to investigate the deeper power structures at work behind companies when they keep crashing. Theory can be a passionate conceptual toolkit and is not necessarily "friendly fire." Criticism, in my view, is the highest form of culture, not "collateral damage." Organized optimism, so widespread in the New Age-dominated business and technology circles, effectively blocks thinking. Critique is not a poison but a vital tool for reflecting on the course technology is taking.

Laurel seems to suffer from the curious fear of being criticized by radicals, which results in an unnecessarily defensive form of writing. She writes: "A utopian entrepreneur will likely encounter unexpected criticism – even denunciations – from those whom she might have assumed to be on her side." Laurel doesn't distinguish between a tough assessment from an insider's perspective and public relations newspeak. Purple Moon was tremendously successful amongst young girls, and got killed for no (financial) reason. Contrary to the Darwinist dotcom philosophy, I think such "failures" should not happen again. There should be other, less volatile, more hype-resistant business models, to provide projects such as Purple Moon with enough resources to grow at their own pace. There is no reason to comply with unreasonable expectations and buy into speculative and unsustainable "speed economics."

Brenda Laurel is on a mission to change the nature of the computer games industry, move it away from its exclusive focus on the shoot-'em-up male adolescent market. She outs herself as a Barbie hater and says her aim is to get rid of the "great machine of consumerism." Although she sums up the problematic aspects of short-term profit-driven technology research, she does not propose alternative forms of research, collaboration and ownership, out of a fear it might "activate the immune system." Laurel's fear of being excluded from the higher ranks of the virtual class is a real one, not easily dismissed. She carefully avoids mentioning dotcom business gurus such as George Gilder, bionomics priests and others who Europeans, for better or worse, tend to think of as representatives of the "Californian ideology." Laurel may never have been a true believer in the mold of Kou or Malmsten, but she remains as silent as they about the once so dominant techno-libertarian belief system.

Compared to other dotcom crash titles, Laurel's book's agenda remains a secretive one. In *Dot.Bomb* David Kuo is remarkably honest about his own excitement – and blindness – for the roller coaster ride; Laurel's report remains distanced, general and at times moralistic ("live healthy, work healthy" (p. 92)). It is as if the reader is only allowed a glimpse inside. Laurel is on the defensive, reluctant to name her protagonists. Perhaps there is too much at stake for a woman to be a perpetual outsider. Unlike with Kuo, who goes on about all the ups and downs inside Value America, we never quite understand Laurel's underlying business strategies. Her motivations are crystal-clear. Her attitude towards the powerful (male) IT moguls and venture-capital *Übermenschen* is implicit and has to be decrypted like a Soviet novel. There is no reason to describe those who destroyed a corporation as (anonymous) "aliens," as she does. The "suits" have names and bring with them a particular business culture. In this sense, *Utopian Entrepreneur* brings to the fore the question of "inside" and "outside." Laurel is desperate to position herself as an insider. "It took me many years to discover that I couldn't effectively influence the construction of pop culture until I stopped describing myself as a. an artist, and b. a political activist. Both of these self-definitions resulted in what I now see as my own self-marginalization. I couldn't label myself as a subversive or a member of the elite. I had to mentally place my values and myself at the center, not at the margin. I had to understand that what I was about was not critiquing but manifesting."[49]

Laurel is afraid of theory, which she associates with critical academism, cultural studies, art and activism, thereby replicating the high-low divide. For her, theory is elitist and out of touch with the reality of the everyday life of ordinary people. That might be the case. But what can be done to end the isolationist campus-ghetto life of theory? Instead of calling for massive education programs (in line with her humanist enlightenment approach) to lift general participation in contemporary critical discourse,

Laurel blames the theorists. This attitude, widespread inside the IT industry, puts those with a background in humanities and social sciences in a
difficult, defensive position. It also puts critical analysis of the dotcom
chapter of the Internet history in an "outsider" position. As soon as you
start to reflect on the inner dynamics of Silicon Valley, you seem to be
"out." Instead of calling for the development of a rich set of conceptual
tools for those working "inside" Laurel reproduces the classic dichotomy:
either you're in (and play the capitalist game), or you're out (become an
academic/artist/activist and complain and criticize as much as you can).
Despite the strong tendency towards the corporatization of universities,
the mutual resentment between those involved in technology and business on the one hand and the ivory-tower humanities on the other seems
more intense then ever.

On the other hand, postmodern theory and cultural criticism haven't been
very helpful for Laurel, Castells or the study of the Internet in general. As
long as "celebrity" thinkers such as Slavoj Zizek continue to confuse the
Internet with some offline cybersex art installation, there is not much
reason to consult them. Contemporary thought urgently needs to be
upgraded and fully incorporate technology in all debates. This also goes
for Michael Hardt and Toni Negri's *Empire,* the presumed bible of the
"anti-globalization" movement. Despite the worthy and abstract category of "immaterial labor," critical knowledge of both the Internet and the
New Economy is virtually absent in this fashionable millennial work. The
dotcom saga has virtually no connections to identity politics and body
representations, two favorite research angles within the humanities.
Today's leading theorists add little to Laurel's conceptual challenges in
the field of user interface design or the criticism of male adolescent geek
culture. Cultural studies armies will occupy the new-media field only
when IT products have truly become part of popular culture. This means
a delay in strategic reflection of at least a decade. Meanwhile, there is
hardly any critical theory equipped to intervene in the debates over the
architecture of the Network Society and its economic foundations – of
which the dotcom bubble was only a brief chapter.

The baby-boom generation, now in charge of publishing houses and
mainstream media and in leading university positions, shares a secret
dream that all these new media may disappear as fast as they arrived.
Lacking substance, neither real nor commodity, new media are failing to
produce their own Michelangelos, Rembrandts, Shakespeares and Hitch-

cocks. The economic recession which followed the NASDAQ tech wreck only further widened the gap between the forced "freshness" of the techno workers and the dark skepticism of the intellectual gatekeepers.

Dotcom mania is likely to become a forgotten chapter, not just by punters and vendors but also by new-media theorists, Internet artists and community activists. The dotcom stories are overshadowed by the much larger corporate scandals of ENRON, Andersen, Global Crossing and WorldCom. Both young geeks and senior technologists have already started to deny their involvement in dotcom startups, hiding behind their "neutral" role as technicians ("Don't shoot me, I was only a programmer"), forgetting their techno-libertarian passions of days gone by. For *Australian Financial Review* commentator Deirdre Macken, the legacy of the dotcom daze is symbolized by the Aeron designer chairs, still in their packaging, on offer at office furniture auctions. At the same time, the era has had a lasting influence on business culture. As Macken says: "From the casualization of work attire throughout the week, to the deconstruction of the office, the flattening of power structures and the creation of new layers of capital providers, the dotcom culture has much to its credit ... [yet] the Internet industry itself has failed to annex the future."[50]

Looking across the landscape of dotcom ruins, what remains is the unresolved issue of sustainable models for the Internet economy. The contradiction between developing free software and content and abstracting a decent income for work done, beyond hobbyism and worthy aims, is still there. The Indian summer of the Net has only postponed the real issues – for both business and the non-profit sector.

Deep Europe and the Kosovo Conflict

A History of the V2_East/Syndicate Network

Introduction

This is a case study of the rise and fall of the European cultural network and mailing-list community Syndicate.[1] In August 2001 the Syndicate list exploded and split in two. Founded in early 1996 as a "post-1989" East-West exchange network between new-media artists, Syndicate had grown into a network of 500 members Europe-wide and beyond. Syndicate organized its own meetings and publications, along with the "virtual" activities such as the list itself, the website and an electronic newsletter. I will not cover all aspects of its five-year existence. Instead, I will deal with three elements of its history. First of all, I will outline the formation of the network. Second, I will focus on the explosion of Syndicate postings during the 1999 Kosovo crisis. In the last part, I will analyze the demise of the list as Syndicate was unable to deal with the issue of moderation. Developed as an informal new-media arts network, Syndicate did not survive the polarizations of the debates which it plunged into. Its open architecture was vulnerable to the challenges of hackers, trolls and quasi-automatic bots, which eventually brought down the Syndicate as a social network.

The intensity of list traffic – and the circulating arguments and emotions – during the Kosovo war (March–July 1999) is the core subject of this chapter. The debates over the NATO bombing of Yugoslavia would turn out to be a turning point for the larger new-media arts community. No one had ever seen such fierce debates, such bitterness. The live reports and debates should be considered Syndicate's finest hour. While elsewhere on the Net dotcom greed raged, there was talk in the press of Kosovo as "the first Internet war." It was a time to go beyond normalcy and explore networked extremes. The Syndicate case could be read as an allegory of arts and politics in the outgoing "roaring nineties," both embodying and reflecting the technological intensities.

The inner life of a list reveals more than discursive threads and communication patterns. There are sophisticated forms of silence, repressed messages and unanswered remarks. Because of the intimacy of e-mail and the immediacy of open, unmoderated channels, lists foreshadow events to come. As "antennas of culture" they do more then merely discuss current affairs. Online communities do not just reflect events but have the potential to create their own autopoietic systems and provoke events. For mainstream media and its professional critics discussion lists are an almost invisible cultural phenomenon, yet they play a key part in the life of its participants. Lots of incidents happen on lists that become visible and emerge later in different form. The story of Syndicate is an instructive one because of the hatred that manifested itself in a medium which originally was meant to be collaborative and democratic. It can tell us something about the emergence of extreme cultures, the establishment of a culture of uncertainty and control, and operating way beyond the rational consensus paradigm.

The Formation of the Network

Syndicate was the brainchild of Andreas Broeckmann, a German new-media critic and curator who worked out of the Rotterdam-based new-media arts organization V2_. Broeckmann founded the initiative not long after the related Nettime and Rhizome mailing lists had started. Nettime, initially based on a vibrant USA-Europe exchange meant to establish a critical Net discourse with input from theorists, artists and other cultural workers, had quickly emerged as a broader community. Rhizome, although founded in Berlin by the American Mark Tribe and started on a server in Amsterdam (desk.nl), had soon after moved its operations to New York, where it would primarily focus on the US new-media arts scene.

In the autumn of 1995, Andreas Broeckmann had begun a new initiative called V2_East, aimed at creating a network of people and institutions involved with or interested in media art in Eastern Europe. "V2_East wants to create an infrastructure that will facilitate cooperation between partners in the East and the West, and it will initiate collaborative media-art projects," says one of the early statements. Syndicate was to be the vehicle for V2_East. The Internet mailing list started in January 1996 during the second Next Five Minutes "tactical media" conference held in Amsterdam and Rotterdam.[2] Ambivalent feelings towards a regional European identity were obvious: V2_East was to be "an important tool for fostering ties within the media-art community in Europe which makes it increasingly obsolete to think in term of 'East' and 'West', and which will eventually make the V2_East initiative itself redundant."[3] However, as this chapter will explain, it was not a peaceful synthesis that was going to make Syndicate superfluous but conflict and suspicion among its members.

In 1995 it was clear that within the context of new-media culture Europe would need its own exchange platform. However, "Europe" was not an easy category to deal with. Euro-skepticism aside, who would dare to define Europe? There was no place for a future-oriented "European culture" in all the EU plans. In the economic schemes culture was going to be the prime domain of the individual nation-states. In the Brussels terminology culture equaled heritage, a thing of the past which would compensate for the pressures of globalization. "European" new-media arts would be disdained as yet another hopeless initiative, backed by corrupt insiders with the sole goal of distributing resources among a limited group of arts bureaucrats. The "network4us" was a genuine danger. European networks of cultural organizations had an inherent tendency towards bureaucratic exclusion, favoring old mates with clearly recognizable nametags, employed by established institutions and brand-name corporations. Wherever one went in Europe in the 1990s, one was faced with resistance by established cultural institutions against "the new." In order to prevent any doubt about the intentions of its founders it was announced that V2_East/Syndicate was going to be "a no-budget network initiative rather than an institution."[4] As in other cases such as the Nettime, Xchange and Fibreculture networks, the zero money approach would result in speed, autonomy and the common pursuit of happiness.

East-West Relations

During the early to mid-1990s many of the exciting media/arts initiatives came not from the recession-plagued West but from the "wild" East, which had only recently opened up. To create a network of new-media artists and organizations throughout the 15 countries in the East would have been next to impossible before 1989. This was the time to do it. But how would an equal East-West network function, especially if it was run out of Western Europe? Conspiracy theories thrived, especially in an environment flooded with money from Wall Street speculator/philanthropist George Soros. Was there a hidden neo-colonialist agenda, which would start with new-media arts?[5] Easterners were a hard bunch to organize. For historical reasons there was a preference for informal gatherings over the official rhetoric of the next round of salvation, this time called "new media." There was an unspoken skepticism about exchanges planned from above – and good intentions in general. "Community" was a contaminated concept that came dangerously close to "communism."[6] On the other hand, this was not the right time to be dogmatic and reject opportunities. The longing for a "normalization" of East-West relations had been a sincere desire for decades. East-European Syndicalists were faced with the dilemma between going out on their own in the big world of the global networks and getting lost easily, and becoming a member of a "cool" network that would attract enough excitement to gain the critical speed to enter into another orbit, liberated from familiar geography (and inferior passports). The last thing they longed for was a cozy collective identity. The Syndicate agenda seemed pragmatic enough to be worth a try, even though there was a danger it would limit itself to networking arts bureaucrats.

The Syndicate network had to start off low-key and provide its participants with useful information, concrete assistance and collaboration on an equal basis. Building up such an informal network of trust was not going to be all that easy. Numerous informal exchanges took place in the background to lift Syndicate off the ground. By 1996 the Bosnian war had just ended and the Chechnya conflict was still going on. In most East European countries a tough neo-liberal "reform" climate had established itself, backed by a variety of political forces ranging from pragmatic post-communists to newborn conservatives and hard-line ethno-nationalists. 1989's euphoria and expectations of a generous Marshall plan for the East had all but faded away. Both the USA and individual European powers such as Great Britain, France and Germany continued with their well-known, contradictory Balkan *realpolitik*. With countless inspiring new works by artists from "the region" circulating, the overall climate in Eastern Europe was swinging between cautious optimism and the gray reality of growing poverty and mutual distrust (if not ethnic hatred). Former Eastern bloc countries had not yet entered NATO or the EU. These were the years of "transition," as the Euro-American officials had termed the process in such a clean and neutral manner. Expectations could not be too high.

As with Nettime, meetings were essential in order to build such a post East-West network. Syndicate needed a considerable trust among its participants if it wanted real outcomes. Trust was never going to be achieved just by e-mail. Not everyone had enough foreign-language skills to write online contributions in English. The first Syndicate meeting took place in Rotterdam in September 1996 during V2_'s DEAF festival, attended by 30 media artists and activists, journalists and curators from 12 Eastern and

Western European countries. More Syndicate meetings followed, most attended by a few dozen people. These workshops often took place on the edges of festivals and conferences – the DEAF festival in Rotterdam (September 1996), the Video Positive festival in Liverpool (April 1997), the Beauty and the East conference in Ljubljana (May 1997), Documenta X in Kassel (August 1997), Ars Electronica in Linz (September 1997), the Ostranenie festival in Dessau (November 1997), Shaking Hands, Make Conflicts in Stockholm (April 1998), a special Syndicate event in Tirana (May 1998), the Skopje Electronic Arts Fair (October 1998), and the Kosovo crisis gathering in Budapest (April 1999). In between, there were many smaller meetings and joint projects, presentations and workshops. Three readers, edited by Inke Arns, were published, collecting the most important texts from the mailing list.[7] Comparable to the Nettime mailing list in the 1995–98 period, Syndicate in 1996–99 was a traveling social network, moving from event to workshop to conference, from office to café to club, and further to the next airport, train station and bus terminal. Especially in the few years Syndicate existed as an accumulation of meetings, collaborations and "peer-to-peer" exchanges, with the list as a secondary tool for exchange.

Deep Europe

The term "Deep Europe," with which Syndicate became associated, goes back to Syndicate's participation in the 1997 Hybrid Workspace project, a temporary media lab that was part of the Documenta X art exhibition in Kassel, Germany. Syndicate was one of 12 groups that organized its own workshop, which was partially open to the public. A group of 20 artists, mainly from the former East, held debates, screenings and performances for ten days. The highlight was the "visa department" performance, in which all Syndicalists participated. Visitors had to stand in a long queue and be interrogated before being able to obtain a Deep Europe visa. The announcement stated: "The new lines that run through Europe are historical, political, cultural, artistic, technological, military. The role of the EU and its institutions, the notion of Mittel (central) Europe, old and new ideologies, messianic NGOs and late-capitalist profiteers contribute to a cultural environment in which we have to define new strategies and new tools, whether as artists, activists, writers or organizers."[8] The text warned against loading the Deep Europe concept with too much meaning – and that's exactly what happened.

The exact origin of the term "Deep Europe" remains unclear. It may have a multitude of sources. I can only provide the reader with my interpretation. "Deep Europe" was such a precise, timely and productive label exactly because of its ambiguity, being neither geographic (East-West) nor time-related (old-new). Deep Europe was proposed as the opposite of fixed identities. The overlapping realities were there to be explored.[9] Caught between regions, disciplines, media and institutions, the V2_East/Syndicate network was open to those interested in "Becoming Europe," working with "Becoming Media." Obviously, "Deep Europe" had an ironic undertone of essential values as opposed to superficial simulations. There was nothing "deep" about the 20th-century tragedy called Europe. Deep Europe would grow out of the tension between the crisis of ethnic nation-state and the promising poverty of globalism. I would reconstruct the term as a blend of Continental Europe (a notion used by English islanders) and the astronomical/science-fiction term "deep space." It is an unknown, yet-to-be discovered part of Europe, way beyond the bureaucratic borders drawn by the EU, the Schengen agreement, NATO and Russia. Europe in this context had to be understood as an open and inclusive, lively translocal network. It is not the Europe that claims universal ownership over civilization.

Deep Europe was a rust belt of history, a vast, green plain east of Berlin, Prague and Vienna, stretching out deep into Russia. It consisted of complex layers of provinces, languages and ethnicities, characterized by overlapping territories and dispersed minorities of different religions. For some, Deep Europe might be associated with Eastern Prussia, Thrace, Moldavia, Rumeli, Bessarabia, Hargita, and Gallicia. But these were historical names.[10] Beyond such nostalgic geo-historical associations filled with bittersweet memories of thriving communities, patriotic destiny and horrendous pogroms, Deep Europe was meant as an alternative, imaginative mental landscape, a post-1989 promise that life could be different. Europe could have a future, beyond its tourist destiny as a theme park. The danger of exotic orientalism could be countered with enlightened nihilism. It should be possible to wake up from the nightmare called history. There had to be another agenda, beyond the (necessary) containment strategy to stop Europeans from fighting wars, colonizing the world, and expelling and exterminating "others." Rejecting both superficial Western mediocrity and backward Eastern despotism, Deep Europe could be read as a desire to weave webs and tell stories about an unrealized, both real and virtual world. Deep Europe could be one of Italo Calvino's "invisible cities," a shared imaginative space where artists would be able to freely work with the technological tools of their liking, no longer confined by disciplines and traditions.

For moderator Inke Arns, Deep Europe expressed "a new understanding of Europe, an understanding which leads away from a horizontal/homogeneous/binary concept of territory (e.g. East/West) and – by means of a vertical cut through territorial entities – moves towards a new understanding of the different heterogeneous, deep-level, cultural layers and identities which exist next to each other in Europe."[11] UK new-media curator Lisa Haskel described what Deep Europe could be all about: "Not a political position, a utopia or a manifesto, but rather a digging, excavating, tunneling process toward greater understanding and connection, but which fully recognizes different starting points and possible directions: a collaborative process with a shared desire for making connection. There may be hold-ups and some frustrations, quite a bit of hard work is required, but some machinery can perhaps aid us. The result is a channel for exchange for use by both ourselves and others with common aims and interests."[12] Concepts such as tunnels, channels and rhizomes are used here to indicate how informal, decentralized networks with their "subterranean connections" (Deleuze and Guattari) cut through existing borders.

Syndicate as a Network

Unlike most Internet lists, Syndicate in its first years hardly generated debates or responses. Its one or two posts a day were mainly festival and project announcements. Inke Arns and Andreas Broeckmann: "Attempts to turn the Syndicate list into a discussion list and encouragements for people to send their personal reports, views, perceptions of what was happening, were met by only limited response."[13] As long as the offline community kept organizing meetings and collaborations, there was nothing wrong with a list focused on the exchange of practical information. But after a few years the novelty of sitting together in one room began to wear off. By 1998 Syndicate had reached 300 subscribers; it would further grow to 500 by 2000. Typical topics were access, connectivity, collaboration, and most of all the exchange of information about upcoming festivals, possible grants and new projects.

In the beginning people on the list knew each other and were lucky enough to meet each other every now and then. Syndicate facilitators Arns and Broeckmann, looking back: "The meetings and personal contacts off-list were an essential part of the Syndicate network: they grounded the Syndicate in a network of friendly and working relationships, with strong ties and allegiances that spanned across Europe and made many cooperation between artists, initiatives and institutions possible. The Syndicate thus opened multiple channels between artists and cultural producers in Europe and beyond, which is probably its greatest achievement. It connected people and made them aware of each other's practice, creating multiple options for international cooperation projects."[14]

By early 1999 Syndicate had found a better balance between new-media art and relevant politics, Eastern Europe and the rest of the world, and most importantly, general announcements and personal posts. Frequent meetings in real life had taken away some of the reluctance to post. The list had reached critical mass and by 1998 had become livelier. Gatherings had strengthened interpersonal trust in the initiative. Traffic had gone up. There were around 380 subscribers in March 1999. These were some of the subject lines in early 1999: "YOUR help needed!! – Russian artist under prosecution for his art"; "EU billions"; "ABBERATION: Interactive Visual Poem Generator"; "censorship in Poland"; "oppera teorettikka internettikka." The "no border" campaign, which focused on migration issues, had turned out to be an important topic, both on the list and at the third Next Five Minutes conference (March 1999), where a small Syndicate gathering had taken place. The topic had been "borderlessness." Jennifer De Felice remarked in her report of the meeting: "I find the 'no border' campaign a little in contradiction to the 'anti-multinational campaign.' I'm not brave enough to make overt statements about the repercussions of a rally for borderlessness but that utopian statement can be misinterpreted as freedom not merely for refugees and immigrants but for those same multinationals whose activity we are so adamant about protesting."[15]

NATO Bombings and List Explosions

On March 22, 1999, the Serbian nationalist Net artist Andrej Tisma, who had caused earlier controversies on Syndicate, posted: "Message from Serbia, in expectation of NATO bombing. Could be my last sending. But I don't worry. If I die, my website will remain."[16] It was the first reference to the deteriorating situation in Yugoslavia. Two weeks earlier, at the Amsterdam Next Five Minutes conference, the situation had not been an urgent topic, even though independent media producers from Belgrade, Pristina, Skopje and other towns in the Balkans had been present. Peace talks in Rambouillet between NATO, Yugoslav authorities and the Kosovo Albanians had failed to produce an agreement. With mass killings and armed resistance spiraling out of control, Kosovo was well on the way to becoming the next Bosnia. In the case of Bosnia it had taken Western powers three and a half years to intervene in a serious manner, after years of half-hearted diplomacy, broken ceasefires and limited UN mandates. The US bombardment of Bosnian Serb military positions finally brought the parties to the Dayton negotiation table. In the Kosovo case, with spring close and parties on both sides gearing up for the next big killing spree, NATO took action in a decisive manner, causing a spiral of effects. On March 24, 1999, "the most serious war in Europe since 1945" (Michael Ignatieff) began. The NATO bombing of Yugoslavia would last for 78 days, until the Yugoslav army withdrew from Kosovo in early June 1999.[17]

On the first day the independent radio station B92 had already been closed down and its director, Veran Matic, arrested by the Serbian police.[18] Local radio transmission no longer worked, but B92 continued its radio broadcasts via the Web. Not long after, the radio signal was retransmitted via satellite. News bulletins in both Serbian and English could be read on the B92 website. In one month the Syndicate group was to have its meeting in Belgrade. What was going to happen? Should the meeting take place, be postponed, be moved elsewhere? A first sign of life came from Branka in Novi Sad, Serbia, writing a telegram-style e-mail: "One night under pressure/stop/b92 shot down tonight/stop/internet as a tool of surviving horror?!/stop/without strength to completely control emotions (including fear)/stop/first degree alacrity/stop/every political opponent might be proclaimed deserter or enemy/stop/lots of love/stop."[19]

On that same day, March 24, 1999, Micz Flor, mailing from Vienna, announced that he had set up a message board where people could leave anonymous messages.[20]

Dejan Sretenovic (Soros Contemporary Arts Center, Belgrade) reported, not without sarcasm, that bombs had not yet been dropped, but the arrival of CNN's Christiane Amanpour in Belgrade was a bad sign. "Believe it or not, life goes normal in Belgrade. There's no panic, no fear, no rush for the goods or visible preparations of any kind for the attack. This paranormal state of normalcy indicates deep apathy and hopelessness of the Serbian people. Anesthesia. There's no general mobilization except for the antiaircraft fire reservists. The federal government has declared the 'state of immediate war danger' last night. But who cares? TV Kosava, which editor in chief is Milosevic's daughter, played an American movie last night. TV Pink, the pop-culture television station, played historical drama 'The Battle on the Kosovo,' full of pathetic national rhetoric and mythology."[21]

On that fateful day, March 24, Syndicate turned into a unique unfiltered citizens' channel, crossing geographic and political borders which had turned into enemy lines. It had taken three years to build up the community. Its direction had been unclear at times. This proved to be Syndicate's finest hour. Katarina of CybeRex from Belgrade, still on the 24th: "Already in the afternoon shops were out of bread and there were big lines in front of the bakeries. After the alarm sounds (around 8:30) people started getting out of the buildings with necessary things. Most of them are leaving town and a lot of them just standing on the open – commenting the situation, quarreling … public transportation hardly works, it's impossible to find a taxi. Kid with basketball, youngsters with audio players, and cans of beer – like any other evening in town is also part of the scenery. Telephone lines are overcrowded and out-of-Belgrade calls are impossible. We heard more than 20 targets all over Yugoslavia were bombed."[22]

Two weeks after the Next Five Minutes conference, the organizers spontaneously restructured their temporary office space in the attic of the Amsterdam cultural center De Balie into a base for the international support campaign Help B92. Help B92 provided technical support for B92's Internet broadcast and started a fundraising campaign. A few xs4all employees helped set up the global Web campaign in a matter of hours. Xs4all, a Dutch Internet provider, had been hosting B92 from the very beginning. The B92 site (www.b92.net) soon had 200,000 visitors a day. B92 increased its news bulletins in English.[23] As a result of the support campaign, the Austrian national radio station ORF began broadcasting B92 on medium-wave, reaching well into Yugoslav territory.

The Albanian art curator Edi Muka wrote from Tirana to his colleagues in Belgrade: "The situation looks really shitty and war tensions started to be felt in Albania too. Today several airlines canceled their flights to Tirana. Two jury members for the international photography exhibit that is going to open on Sunday couldn't make it. I just wanted to share the same support for our friends in Belgrade, since I know very well what it means when there's shooting out of your window, let alone repression without foreign support. But I just wanted to share the same, even more with the hundreds of thousands that are out in the snow, whose only purpose is to escape slaughtering."[24]

This is the first reference to the thousands of Kosovo Albanians, on the run from the retaliating Yugoslav army and paramilitary forces and NATO bombs. Over the next few months, messages from the "Albanian" side would be scarce. The Syndicate list would turn out to be primarily an exchange between Serbian artists and those in the Western world.[25]

One day into the event, political posts started to appear on the list. Nikos Vittis, writing from Greece, pointed to the possible oil in the Balkans as the reason for the US intervention.[26] Andreas Broeckmann, in Berlin, summed up the Western position: "The only person responsible for the attacks is Milosevic – this is not a war against the Yugoslav people – the military objective is to stop the killing and humanitarian catastrophe in Kosovo and to force the Serb leadership to sign the Rambouillet agreement – this agreement cannot be negotiated any further – the attacks will be stopped as soon as the Serb leadership commits itself to signing the Rambouillet agreement – it is not possible to fully exclude civilian and military casualties, but every precaution is taken that civilians and allied personal will not get harmed – the direct aim of the NATO initiative is to disable and ultimately destroy the Yugoslav military capabilities."[27]

Dejan Sretenovic responded from Belgrade: "It is hard to get reliable information on what's going on since all media give only short news about the air strikes. Local television, Studio B, is the only media giving prompt news about the air strikes. We heard that some military and police targets in the suburbs of Belgrade were hit, but there's no information on the damage or casualties. Most of the private TV stations in Belgrade transmit Radio Television of Serbia programs. And what's on the program? Old partisan movies from the 1950s and 1960s, patriotic military ads and news each hour. TV Politika played musical videos this morning. But, we are still blind for the things happening in this country. Those with satellite dishes are lucky. Thank God, Internet connections still function."[28]

Next day, March 25, Andreas Broeckmann suggested calling for international action to press EU governments to grant asylum to conscientious objectors and army defectors. Katarina heard sirens. "The days are sunny and warm. Streets in Belgrade are almost empty. Jewish community organized evacuation (of Jews) to Budapest."[29] From Skopje, Macedonia, Melentie Pandilovski reported anti-American demonstrations ("Let's hope things stay calm").[30] Nina Czegledy wrote about similar demonstrations in her city, Toronto. The overall picture in these first days was one of concern to stay informed and keep the communication channels open. There were no indications that Syndicalists themselves joined anti-NATO protests. The dominant angle on Syndicate was freedom of speech, tactically avoiding taking sides in the political conflict over the moral and strategic usefulness of the NATO bombardment. Independent media, both in Serbia and on the Net, symbolized the future, a way out, away from both NATO's brutal military solutions and the paranoid nationalism of the Milosevic regime. The presumption was that freedom of speech would benefit unheard, moderate voices. Both the NATO commanders and the Serb nationalists already had their war propaganda channels, and used them accordingly.

Stephen Kovats, in response to Andrej Tisma's "NATO democracy" concept: "NATO is not a democracy but a military alliance controlled by relatively democratic states in which praise, condemnation, pros and cons, critique and debate about its actions are freely debated, discussed and broadcast. I know that you all know that, but nationalist sarcasm is a part of the problem."[31] In a forwarded message from the Rhizome list an American artist called the Serbs not to rally behind a demagogue: "Nobody here hates YOU. This is not about invading your country; it is about protecting those under attack in another country that is being invaded by Milosevic's army. Frankly I think the NATO action is very cautious and gentle. Nobody should welcome bombing, I don't and I don't think many do, even those flying the missions. We have to choose between enabling an expansionist dictator and curtailing ethnic 'cleansing' in full swing in Kosovo right now. In fact now more than ever. Let's not repeat the Bosnian fiasco."[32]

Frederic Madre, reporting from Paris, sent in the following observation: "Yesterday I saw 30 guys on the Champs Elysees burn down an US flag. I stayed, I had some time to lose, if it was a French flag or whatever I would have done the same. They shouted 'USA out of Europe' and then 'Youth! Revolution!' they were fascists, I knew it from the start. Afterwards they distributed leaflets in which they were trying to be clever as being fascists. Like with big boots full of mud and blood."[33]

Net Activism in Wartime

Syndicate members had one thing in common. Their answer to the Kosovo crisis could be summarized like this: neither Milosevic nor NATO, but independent media, was the answer. This strategy of media liberty was offered as an alternative to the impossible choice between fear and anger on the Serbian side and solidarity with the Kosovo-Albanian population, now on the run. As a consequence of this strategy numerous Internet-based support initiatives sprang up in Budapest, Spain, the San Francisco Bay Area, Portugal, London, and even Tokyo and Taipei.[34] Groups were translating texts, putting up weblinks, producing radio programs, joining Help B92. Personal accounts arrived from Rome, Adelaide and Paris. The Open the Borders campaign was started, urging governments to give refugee status to Serbian deserters. The call for media freedom positioned itself as a "third-way" long-term contribution to resolving ethnic hatred. The position could be roughly described as such: We are not pro- or anti-NATO, pro- or anti-Serbian; we live in cyberspace. We come from the future and offer you hope for escaping the nightmare called history. Global communication is not just a tool for reconciliation – it is part of the solution. In this view new media do not just defuse tensions in order to impose a manufactured consensus. Digital devices will lead participants into a new world altogether – a view propagated by cyber-libertarians throughout the 1990s.

Meanwhile, Katarina was filming from the B92 roof. She captured the bombing of Batajnica airport and put the video file on the Net. Belgrade was in total darkness, Slobodan Markovic wrote in the early midnight hours: "There is no street light, no blinking neon banners, no light in houses and apartments. Darkness everywhere ... No clouds, no lights, only half-moon is shining over city. Totally amazing, scary and claustrophobic decoration."[35]

Within a matter of days the online diaries of Yugoslav citizens had become a literary genre.[36] The UK media-art curator Mike Stubbs associated the online exchange with a scene from *All Quiet on the Western Front* "where one soldier shares a fag or food or something another soldier throws a flower over at the front – the physical proximity and first 'closeness' of the respective 'enemies.'" He asked, "Will GSM phones work or will parts of commercial networks get closed down? How secure is this as a communications network?"[37]

The independent-media-as-part-of-the-solution argument was developed over the next three months in a variety of actions worldwide. However, those who rejected the need to choose sides between NATO and those who opposed its bombings were in danger of being ignored, crushed between the two sides. The Internet philosophy of globalism did not provide enough of a political program to be able to operate as a strong enough alternative. Global communication was not enough. The Western rational engineering discourse which presumed people could resolve their conflicts through talking (or even better, sending e-mail) was not equipped to tackle armed conflicts of this magnitude. When weapons speak, appeals to human rationalism are usually not heard. The usual superiority of rational discourse is bluntly overruled, forcing the engineers (and other techno believers) to either take sides and participate or remain silent. The technology agenda was no guide in a state of emergency. In 1999, the booming Internet sphere had not penetrated deeply enough in society to make a difference at the moment of truth. In retrospect, the Kosovo conflict turned out to be a bitter reality check for the Syndicate members and Net art at large, one year before the dotcom entrepreneurs would get theirs.[38]

Discussion was finally inflamed with a post from Sarajevo. Enes Zlater (Soros Contemporary Arts Center), responding to the posts from Serbia, said the Belgrade citizens were making too much noise: "They ARE NOT BOMBED! (military targets are). They are dealing now only with the aspects of fear and propaganda – but there are no bombs on Belgrade, on civilians, there are no snipers, there are no lacks of electricity, water, gas, food, etc. They can make telephone calls, they can send e-mails … That is not a state of war. I don't like anyone being attacked and bombed, especially bearing in mind the fact that I've gone through a real war for four years."[39]

Slobodan Markovic sent an emotional response from Belgrade. "The logic (personification) you are using is TOTALLY wrong: Serbs = Serbia = Yugoslavia = Slobodan Milosevic = criminal(s). This is the same logic NATO and USA are using. That is what I call propaganda. Go on and read some CNN news reports on www.cnn.com: They are talking about 'punishing Slobodan Milosevic', but his residence is not (even close) target of attack."[40]

Branka, writing from Novi Sad: "Every living creature has right to be frightened, never mind where she/he/it lives, attacked by snipers or just by bombardiers."[41] Doubts grew by the day about the effectiveness of the military air bombardment strategy. Annick Bureaud (Paris): "Today at the French radio they said NATO had bombed and destroyed important Serbian military facilities and headquarters. Fine, but what next? As in the case of Iraq, the military power of Serbia will be down and then, will it give the country democracy, will it give the people of Kosovo some peace?"[42]

Dejan Sretenovic, a Soros colleague of Enes Zlater's in Sarajevo, sent an elaborate response. "I can understand your feelings and anger towards Serbian regime, but I have to remind you that you have sent your message to a wrong address. All these reports from Yugoslavia are written by the people who are not supporters but opponents of the Serbian regime from the very beginning. People who were involved in various kinds of protests against the war in Bosnia. It is not necessary to remind us who is to blame for the Balkan catastrophe, but current situation in Yugoslavia is much more complicated than it was in Bosnia. We are talking about something that does not concern Yugoslavia only, but the whole international community. We are talking about the end of global politics and diplomacy, about UN transformation into a debate club with no influence on international relations, about double human rights standards. You in Sarajevo were, unfortunately, first to face disastrous results of the Western politics towards ex-Yugoslavia. Kosovo may be the last chapter of Balkan drama, but this time evil cannot be located in one spot only. We have a perverse coalition of two evil politics, local and global, which suits both sides at the moment. Both Serbs and Albanians are at the moment victims of such politics and if we try to look for the pure truth we'll discover that it does not exist at all. We have reached the blank spot of all international laws and standards, with no effective control mechanisms and the new rule of global totalitarian mind, which tries to arrange the world according to its own political standards. Does peace and democracy still have to come with bombs?"[43]

The question of why countries had to be bombed to turn them into democracies would circulate in private and public debates for months, if not years, to come. It would, for instance, be raised again two and a half years later, during the bombardment of Afghanistan in late 2001 by Western powers. Both Kosovo and Afghanistan were turned into Western protectorates with weak regimes that could not rule without a Western military presence and billions of dollars in support.

Andrea Szekeres and Adele Eisenstein proposed moving the upcoming meeting from Belgrade to Budapest, with the new-media center C3 as host. People from Serbia would be able to attend the meeting (the Hungarian-Serbian border would probably remain open). Western participants would not have to apply for Yugoslav visas, as if they wanted to be bombed.

The Syndicate list was exploding, with 50 or so messages a day. No one complained. Other lists and sites also became busy. While Syndicate was the channel for messages from "Deep Europe," Nettime focused on general news coverage and debates, while Rhizome had discussion among artists. But this division, which sounds good in theory, never really worked. As usual, there was a significant amount of cross-posting.

After a first wave of emotional solidarity, the question soon arose as to what could be done. New-media activists and artists should do what they are good at (making media), but humanitarian aid to the Kosovo-Albanian refugees flooding towards the Macedonian border seemed so much more urgent. The media and propaganda war had to make way for real, urgent needs. On the list, Enes in Sarajevo criticized the cuddly atmosphere: "Let's not just keep on sending senseless messages of solidarity and friendship. I also want to stay friends with you, but not in a way that I sit home eat popcorn, watch a film, take a look at news from time to time and say 'love you my friends in Serbia, it's awful what is happening to you,' or 'let's help them, poor things.'"[44]

More reports from nearby Sofia and Athens flooded in. Bombs had hit a chemical plant near Belgrade. The desperation reached ironic levels with an anonymous post called "info not bombs (make money not war)," sarcastically listing Western alternatives to bombing, indicating how futile and worn-out media strategies were in this situation: "Strong AM, FM, and UHF positioned at rest-Yugoslavian borders transmitters sending MTV, mixed with a new Alternative Independent Serbia Program, sponsored by Bennetton, Nike, Adidas, Siemens. B52 and stealth bombers dropping history books, McDonalds flyers and EU T-shirts."[45]

Moderator Andreas Broeckmann tried to prevent an atmosphere of flame wars: "We must have these arguments, but remember not to take the war here. I am fascinated to see to what a large degree some of us are still tied to the opinions generated by our physical environments" (thereby presuming that Internet users were indeed a different species).[46] From Ljubljana, Slovenia, Marko Peljhan posted a list of "what is to be done." Besides writing letters, he suggested, "Try to do everything you deem necessary so that the Serbian war machine in Kosovo is stopped and that NATO air operations stop as soon as possible. Link these two issues!" Marko's posts on media and military matters contrasted with reports from Luchezar Bojadjev in Sofia and Melentie Pandilovski in Skopje, only 50 miles from Kosovo, where refugees had started to arrive and the US embassy was fortified. Young male Serbs were mobilized into the Yugoslav army. Certain patterns begin to emerge on the level of discussion. The freshness of uncensored, direct e-mail communication began to wear off. A fight for "most favored true victim status" began to emerge.[47]

Reports from Kosovo about atrocities, deportations and robberies committed by the Yugoslav army and Serbian paramilitary forces appeared on Syndicate, but these stories remained distant echoes, forwarded messages from mainstream media and NGOs.[48] While Slobodan Markovic listened to U2's *War* all day, running back and forth to the shelter, Enes came up with the inevitable Hitler comparison – a sign in the land of lists that the electronic dialogue has reached its limits and is about to collapse.[49] One week into the bombing the full scale of the unfolding events was beginning to dawn on the Syndicalists. There were talk of NATO ground troops and further details about Kosovo Albanians systematically being expelled, while NATO planes bombed the main bridge over the Danube in Novi Sad.[50] B92 published two statements criticizing the NATO bombings. "Coverage from Kosovo is now completely impossible. Our principled position on the Kosovo tragedy has been known throughout the world for a long time and it has not changed one iota. We are sad to report that our prediction that NATO bombing could only cause a drastic exacerbation of the humanitarian catastrophe has proved true."[51]

Online Despair

The next day, April 2, B92 was permanently silenced. In the early hours police officers arrived to seal the station's offices and order all staff to cease work and leave the premises immediately. The radio studio, though without a local transmitter since March 24, had been in full operation, getting its message out on the Net. The Internet strategy to "rout around" the Milosevic regime had worked for a good nine days, with the B92 site getting 15 million visitors. The studio was taken over by the Milosevic student league. A Help B92 statement explained: "A court official had accompanied the police. He delivered a decision from the government-controlled Council of Youth to the station's manager of six years – Sasa Mirkovic – that he had been dismissed. The council of youth replaced Sasa Mirkovic with Aleksandar Nikacevic, a member of Milosevic's ruling Socialist Party of Serbia, thus bringing B92 under government control." Vuk Cosic immediately remembered a similar incident involving Nikacevic. "In March 1991 there were student demonstrations in Belgrade, and at one point, I think the third day, the students' coordination group was invited to negotiate with Milosevic. When our group came to the gates of the presidential palace, police told us that the student delegation was already having a meeting with the boss. We waited on the street to see who on earth had been inside. The chief of this bogus students' association was this same Nikacevic guy. Later that same day, much like in the case of the meetings with Rugova or the cardinals these days, there was a nice TV report on Milosevic's steps towards peaceful solution for the current difficulties. Milosevic has backup reusable puppet politicians for this type of task, and Nikacevic is of that profile."[52]

The final closure of B92 was a serious blow to the tactical-media strategy so many Syndicate members identified with. Independent media as an active solution, beyond narrow Balkan nationalisms and the NATO agenda of capitalist globalism, was about to collapse. There was no longer a "third position" available. Had it really become inevitable to take sides and join the intellectual crowd in its pro-/anti-NATO spectacle? Desperation slowly grew. Media could perhaps only be a long-term tool for conflict resolution. Doubts were growing that media could "evaporate" the fatal desires so prominent in "the region." The "civil society" forces were no party in this climate of ethnic conflicts, retaliation and abstract warfare from the skies.

Help B92, which had grown in a few weeks into a dynamic campaign with global appeal, had to reposition itself. NGO tendencies started to take over from the dynamic Net activism approach. Within B92 itself there had always been a productive tension between professional journalism, raving DJ culture and media activism. These different approaches were mirrored within the Help B92 strategies. After B92 was silenced, a strict low-key diplomacy became necessary. With paramilitary forces on the rampage, the lives of the well-known B92 staffers were in danger. Communication with the scattered B92 staff had become almost impossible. An odd mix of legitimate concerns over security and undirected paranoia superseded the near-ecstatic first phase of person-to-person communication after March 24. The group of volunteers shrank to a few staff members. Bit by bit, the B92 website itself, after being taken down, was reconstructed in Amsterdam with information dripping in from an unspecified location in Belgrade. April 1999 was B92's darkest hour. On May 4 the freeB92.net site was launched. In the war period B92's journalists could no longer work freely. They publicly announced that they could no longer guarantee independent newsgathering. The danger of being crushed by propaganda from whatever side had become too big. Atrocities could be committed by anyone: KLA, Serbian paramilitary forces, the Yugoslav army, NATO. In this war situation it was next to impossible to launch independent investigations. Since March 24 it had become very dangerous for journalists to travel to Kosovo. Independent reporting out of Kosovo, difficult enough before March 1999, had virtually ceased to exist. A free press in a country at war was an impossibility anyway. In the end, the whole media story was a political one. This fact was a hard one to swallow for the cyber generation, which had been dreaming of a "post-political" society in which old conflicts would be pushed aside by networked communication between global citizens.

The Help B92 campaign also ran into limitations of a different kind. Despite the fact that NGOs active in southeast Europe had been using e-mail extensively from early on, going back to 1991–92, there was surprisingly little up-to-date knowledge available about how the Web and streaming media could be used. E-mail had been used by NGOs as an internal communication tool. The gap between NGO officials and the "hacktivist" generation was substantial. The Internet at large was not understood as a medium for ordinary citizens. Tactical Net radio concepts, mobile-phone use, even ordinary websites were largely unfamiliar to media NGO decisionmakers, many of whom were of the baby-boom/1968 generation. To them, media was newspapers, magazines, radio and, if possible, television. NGO public-relations work consisted of sending out press releases, calling up journalists and organizing press conferences. In short, civil society was one of writers and theater directors doing roundtables, not ravers and geeks performing techno acts. Despite the enormous success of "tactical" Internet use, initiatives such as Help B92 in Amsterdam and elsewhere were confronted with a basic lack of understanding among established media-policy brokers and grant bodies about the potentials of new media. This cultural gap was not going to be closed overnight.[53]

Back to Slobodan Markovic, reporting on Syndicate. "Around 4:30 AM, cruise missiles hit Belgrade again. I've been responding e-mail when roaring detonation cut the night over Belgrade. I jumped to my window, when I heard another detonation and windows started lightly to shake. When I looked outside, I saw a great orange mushroom growing over the rooftops. That same orange light illuminated the whole night sky, not just one part. This time the target was a pure civilian object, a heating plant in New Belgrade, the western part of the city, with more than 100,000 citizens."[54] The 21-year-old computer science student slid smoothly into the 20th-century genre blending aesthetics, technology and war. "I'm sitting in front of my computer, listening to Radiohead's *OK Computer* (currently song number 10: 'No Surprises'), trying to write a piece of e-mail while outside I can hear very loud detonations and heavy anti-aircraft gun fire. I feel like I'm in the middle of *Terminator 2's* intro scene where Linda Hamilton is explaining the war between humans and machines. The sky is burning, the planes are flying over ..."[55]

Over the next few weeks of April, the mood on the Syndicate list changed. More and more protest letters from Belgrade were forwarded; they tried to make the point that anti-war did not equal pro-Milosevic. The Western logic seemed wrong: "You either accept my opinion or else I will attack you. Democracy cannot be learned by force, Mr. Clinton!"[56] On the Nettime list, US science-fiction writer Bruce Sterling answered the moral sentiments of the Serbian online diary writers. He wrote to Insomnia: "No matter how exciting it is to write your daily diary, you should be thinking ahead. Stop making melodramatic gestures that are obvious rehearsals of martyrdom and your own death. You should plan to join the Serbs who are going to survive this very dark period in Serbian history."[57] He further explained the US military logic. "American military leaders believe they can disarm and cripple nations like yours with modern strategic bombing. They can target and destroy anti-aircraft, aircraft, traffic systems, communications systems, electricity, telephones, radar, and fuel depots. And, yes, cigarette factories and pretty bridges. They are perfectly capable of bombing you for weeks on end. They could do it for months. Possibly years. This war from the skies should be interpreted as an experiment with the aim 'to see what happens to a living European nation as its infrastructure is methodically blown to pieces."[58]

The Slovenian psychoanalytic philosopher Slavoj Zizek gave his own reading of the event, in which he analyzed the blackmail position: "When the West fights Milosevic, it is NOT fighting its enemy, one of the last points of resistance against the liberal-democratic New World Order; it is rather fighting its own creature, a monster that grew as the result of the compromises and inconsistencies of the Western politics itself. My answer to the dilemma 'Bomb or not?' is: not yet ENOUGH bombs, and they are TOO LATE."[59]

According to Zizek, the lesson was that the choice between the New World Order and the neo-racist nationalists opposing it is a false one. They were two sides of the same coin. "The New World Order itself breeds monstrosities that it fights. Which is why the protests against bombing from the reformed Communist parties all around Europe, inclusive of (the German) PDS, are totally misdirected: these false protesters against the NATO bombardment of Serbia are like the caricaturized pseudo-Leftists who oppose the trial against a drug dealer, claiming that his crime is the result of social pathology of the capitalist system. The way to fight the capitalist New World Order is not by supporting local proto-Fascist resistances to it, but to focus on the only serious question today: how to build TRANSNATIONAL political movements and institutions strong enough to seriously constrain the unlimited rule of capital, and to render visible and politically relevant the fact that the local fundamentalist resistances against the New World Order, from Milosevic to le Pen and the extreme Right in Europe, are part of it?"[60]

The view of Zizek was certainly widely read and respected in Syndicate/Deep Europe circles. But the movement Zizek was talking about did not exist. There was no sympathy, neither with Milosevic nor with the Serbian people, who had so far failed to get rid of the corrupt nationalist regime. To portray the Serbs as victims was a bit too easy. However, the Zizekian refusal of the double blackmail (if you are against NATO strikes, you are in favor of Milosevic's proto-fascist regime of ethnic cleansing, and if you are against Milosevic, you support the global capitalist New World Order) had not translated into much action. More "tactical" media was not the answer either. The only option left, a weak and "neutral" humanitarianism, had only worsened the situation during the long year of the previous Bosnian war. Desperation grew over how to both support the Serb population living under NATO bombardment while at the same time assisting in the humanitarian aid crisis of hundreds of thousands of Kosovo Albanians on the run. Who was to blame for this mess? It was war in Europe again – and everyone was in shock.

Meetings and Actions

From April 23 to 25 the Syndicate meeting originally scheduled for Belgrade took place in Budapest, hosted by the C3 new-media center. The 35 or so participants from a dozen countries discussed proposals such as a traveling screening program, visa hurdles, a residency program, an emigrant library and a project nicknamed "The Future State of Balkania." Most importantly, the meeting served to diffuse virtual tensions. Kit Blake and Hedwig Turk reported to the list: "Stories exchange in the intro session, and a multi-focus picture emerges, from the distanced telephoto of media coverage, to the zoomed-in terror of eye contact laced with military hate. The meeting theme is default, and the favorite word becomes the 'situation.' What to do."[61]

Consensus over the capabilities of Syndicate's influence seemed to emerge quickly. What Syndicate members had in common was their involvement in contemporary media, arts and culture: "Attitudes are realistic, experienced. Most people operate in the media sphere, and the discussion singles out information exchange as the central issue."[62] Andreas Broeckmann, after returning to his home city of Berlin: "The whole situation is so heavy, that it is easy to get paralyzed by it. What the meeting in Budapest did for me and, I think, for other people as well, is that by seeing each other, confirming that we are no pure media-zombies but still the same real people, and by talking about our possible room for maneuver, it became clear that while there are lots of things now that we cannot change much about, there are very practical steps which we can take from our position as cultural practitioners."[63]

As no direct help to B92 could be given, the focus in Amsterdam changed to Kosovo itself. Press Now, a Dutch support campaign for independent media in former Yugoslavia, founded in 1993, together with what was left of the Help B92 crew, launched the "Open Channels for Kosovo" initiative. "We hope to give a voice to those journalists who are almost silenced, and give the visitor an alternative view on the crisis in the Balkans."[64] From early on, Press Now had been supporting the independent Kosovo Albanian weekly *Koha Ditore* and its charismatic editor-in-chief Veton Surroi. One of the first actions of Serb authorities on March 24 had been the closure of *Koha Ditore,* in an incident in which a guard of the newspaper had been killed. Open Channels installed a special telephone system to which journalists from the region could phone in and leave daily audio reports on media and politics. One of the outcomes of Open Channels was financial and technical support for Radio 21, which had managed to flee from Pristina to Skopje and resume its programs via the Internet.[65] Wam Kat, an early computer network activist and relief worker from the 1991–95 wars, began the Balkan Sunflower project to assist the tens of thousands of Kosovo refugees on the Albanian side of the border. All these projects started from scratch, and they were overwhelmed by the scale of the crisis.

Unlike many Serbian civilians, Kosovo-Albanian refugees, now scattered all over the world, were not hooked up to the Internet. Those in refugee camps, for instance, used global satellite phones to get in touch with relatives. But their faces on television remained anonymous. They were groups in the hands of governments and international relief organizations. The Budapest Syndicate meeting can only serve as a representative example: no Albanian from either Kosovo, Macedonia or Albania was present. They were not consciously excluded. Only a few were part of the Syndicate network (mainly from Edi Muka's circle in Tirana) and organizers had not been able to change this fact overnight. This situation only reflected the online absence of the Albanian side. KLA support sites, for instance, were maintained by Albanian immigrants in countries such as Switzerland and the USA. The "digital diaspora" had created the false image of a virtual presence on the Net, nonexistent in Kosovo itself.

Despite numerous messages forwarded from refugee organizations, the Syndicate exchange was unintentionally limited to a dialogue between online Serbs, most of them anti-nationalist Milosevic opponents, and those in "the region" and the West. The Syndicate microcosm reflected the situation on the Internet at large. In crisis situations it proved to be a near-impossible task to hear "other" voices from those who had been excluded for years. This asynchrony in the debate would become a repetitive pattern in world conflicts in the age of the Internet. McKenzie Wark, expanding his "vectoral theory," which he presented in his book *Virtual Geographies:* "The speed with which people can respond to each other is a significant factor, making lists a different media to print-based text exchanges. But then there's the strange spatial distribution that lists have. This was always going to be a strange intersection with the spatial aspect of state territoriality, and with the way that broadcast and print media usually are shaped by exigencies of state."[66]

Military and Civilian Targets

The only one posting consistently to the Syndicate list was Slobodan Markovic. The longer NATO bombings went on the angrier his reports became. April 30: "I was sleeping until around 02:20 am, when ROARING sound of airplane flying over woke me up! It was just like in the film: ssssshhhhhiiiiioooooossssshhhhh ... [small silence] BOOOOOOOOOM! That moment I jumped from my bed and felt that whole building was shaking (like it's at least 5 Richter scale earthquake). After that explosion I could see only a dense cloud of white smoke growing. One whole civilian block of houses on a crossing between Maksima Gorkog and Maruliceva Street was TOTALLY DEVASTATED. THERE ARE NO MILITARY OBJECTS IN A CIRCLE OF AT LEAST 4 km FROM THAT PLACE!" May 2: THERE IS NO SUCH THING AS AN ACCIDENTAL MURDER! Every civilian casualty is a terrible thing and should be treated as a topmost crime." May 3: "THERE CAN BE NO COLLECTIVE RESPONSIBILITY FOR ANY CRIMINAL ACT! EVER! This NATO's aggression on Yugoslavia is NOT a just war, it is not a humanitarian war, but a dirty war in which civilian targets are legitimate targets, not collateral damage! This is not 'a war against Milosevic' but organized terror over 10 MILLION citizens of Yugoslavia!"[67]

The time between a post and one replying to it began to slow down. If there was a good reply to a post within a short space of time, it greatly increased the likelihood of others taking up the debate. This was very much the case in the late March-early April period. By mid-May discussion had almost disappeared. What remained were forwards of open letters, essays and announcements of solidarity campaigns. The general news fatigue caused a shift from (fast) debates and flame wars to (long-term) action. To commemorate B92's tenth birthday a global 24-hour netcast was organized, starting in Vienna and ending in California. Its motto: "When reality fails us, we move to the virtual world. But pain is real and it stays with us."[68]

In May the NATO bombing strategy intensified. Besides bridges, factories and military installations, Serbian television and telecommunication infrastructure had been added to the target lists. On May 12 information circulated that the US government had ordered Loral Orion Company to shut down its satellite feeds for Internet customers in Yugoslavia. On May 25 it was announced that the Serbian television signal was to be taken off the Eutelsat satellite. After nearly two months of heavy diplomatic pressure from NATO, Eutelsat's member states had voted to pull the plug on Serbian television.[69] A May 26 press bulletin stated: "NATO military commanders won political approval today to attack some of Yugoslavia's most sensitive sites, including the country's civilian telephone and computer networks, in a bid to cut communications between Belgrade and armed forces in Kosovo, senior NATO sources said."[70]

This situation proved that it was impossible to distinguish between civilian and military targets. Highways, railway stations, airports, telephone switches, bridges, power stations and broadcasting towers: they were all military in essence. Destroying infrastructure from the air can topple a regime. In order to do this air superiority must first be established. This, in a nutshell, has been the post-Cold-War NATO doctrine. Within this paradigm Serbian indignation was understandable yet futile. Without infrastructure, sooner or later the Milosevic regime would comply with Western demands for the simple fact that power is not possible without modern infrastructure. According to this NATO doctrine, power should not be reduced to specific people in charge. Those in power were merely a special effect of society's infrastructure.[71] Drain the pond and you will have the fish. NATO's cold military structuralism outraged Serbs of all political colors. There were people amidst the attacked abstract power structures. Instead of turning against Milosevic, as they eventually would do 18 months later, many Serbs proudly wore "target" symbols, thereby, willingly or not, backing the sitting regime.[72]

The Moral Responsibility Debate

Once more, for the last time, in early June, the Syndicate discussed Serbia vs. NATO in a lengthy thread called "moral responsibility." However, the debate no longer had a new-media angle. The direct exchange had faded away. Instead, the big questions the Kosovo conflict had raised were once more put on the table. Was there such a thing as a Serb collective responsibility? McKenzie Wark: "A nation that can elect its leaders is morally accountable for the actions of those leaders – every Serb is accountable for what Milosevic does whether that Serb personally opposes or supports Milosevic."[73]

If there is no collective responsibility, there is no collective identity either, McKenzie Wark suggested. Slobodan Markovic countered: "You cannot take any responsibility for something YOU haven't done. There is no collective responsibility." He expressed the global feelings of the cyber generation: "I don't feel like a part of a nation which must be surrounded with state borders. I feel like an inhabitant of the Planet, but ... I don't think that all the Earthlings should speak one language, enjoy one drink, and have one flag and the same customs."[74]

Had any lesson been learned from the Bosnian war? Belgrade posts usually did not mention the Bosnian war. It hadn't been their war, any more than the backward Kosovo province had ever been on their radar. Why bother about misdeeds of primitive peasants in the Balkan outback? Once upon a time Belgrade had been part of the West. Cosmopolitans had traveled freely to Munich, Rome, Paris and London. Why were they suddenly haunted by the behavior of some criminal farmers in provincial outposts such as Vukovar, Srebrenica, and Pristina? War had always been elsewhere. The consensus beyond all political divides had been: We, the Serbs, are not responsible. Why would modern global citizens suddenly have a collective responsibility for the behavior of 19th-century bandits? Did Serbs have any more responsibility than Croats or Albanians? The Syndicate list wrapped up a discussion which had been going on ever since the breakup of Yugoslavia began in 1990. Andrej Tisma: "Kosovo was the first Serbia, where Serbian state exists since 13th century. Before the World War Two Serbs made 60% of the population in Kosovo and now make only 10%. So who is making the ethnical cleansing? Albanians of course, for last 50 years, supported by West."[75] Here we go again. This time no one took up the provocations of Tisma. McKenzie Wark, writing from Sydney, Australia: "When we say 'responsibility', this need not mean the same thing as guilt. I certainly am not guilty of killing any blackfellas. But I do think I am responsible for the fact that somebody did." Inke Arns responded from Berlin about her German background: "For my generation, accepting responsibility for what has happened in the past means that you accept responsibility for the future ... Personal, individual responsibility is about alertness ... about being aware that this should happen 'never again.'"[76]

At the end of these exhausting months these messages were sent from Sydney and Berlin. It would perhaps take years before "Belgrade" would express such thoughts.[77] McKenzie Wark again: "Just because I am not guilty does not resolve me of responsibility. If I want to belong to the human community, if I want to claim a right to it, then I must also face up to a responsibility. One that is quite minimal really – to hear the other. But also quite a burden, because the other tells me, again and again, about suffering. (...) One thing you get to see, in times like these, is who the people are who understand responsibility, not necessarily as a concept, more as a culture, as just something you do. It's there every day in my inbox, from syndicate and from Nettime and just from friends forwarding me things. The attempt to listen, to hear the other. To witness."[78] Syndicate had been one such timely "witness channel," to use Levinas' biblical term.

A Damaged Network

The month of June brought the end of the NATO bombings, the pullout of the Yugoslav army from Kosovo (June 12) and occupation by Russian and NATO forces. NATO had won the war and lost the peace. The general level of interest in East-European art had never been so high. In October 1999 the biggest survey show of contemporary Eastern European art was to open in Stockholm.[79] The presence of artists from the region, such as SubReal (Romania), at the Venice Biennale, which opened June 10, was prominent. Numerous openings, performances and presentations were announced on the list.[80] But the general feeling was one neither of victory nor of anger. Instead, the Kosovo episode had triggered the shameful memory of Europe with its dubious reputation of "making history," an inherently violent continent, locked up in identity traps, incapable of sorting out its own troubles. A small Syndicate meeting in Venice, taking place as part of the Oreste project, turned into a brief social gathering. The urgency felt in Budapest was not there.

Among its own antagonists the Kosovo conflict remained undigested. The Syndicate network was no exception. People moved on but the issues remained. The Kosovo conflict had drawn public discourse into a new, yet unknown era for good. Sooner or later the scar would rupture. In retrospect, remarkably little was published in book form that summarizes the heated debates. Besides Michael Ignatieff's *Virtual War,* Michel Feher's *Powerless By Design* should be mentioned here. Feher focuses on the debates within the Euro-US liberal and radical left, unraveling the countless paradoxes and contradictions of constantly shifting positions. "Western leaders who had been blamed in 1995 for doing what they finally ceased to do four years later were criticized in 1999 for not reverting back to their earlier policies."[81] According to Feher, the aim of the NATO bombings had been to undermine the authority of the UN, allowing the Pentagon to show that it could wage a war without US casualties. After so much complicity in Bosnia, violence was no longer linked to 500 or even 1,000 years of ethnic hatred "but to a decade-old regime whose representatives had relentlessly endeavored to rid what they saw as Serbian land of its non-Serbian population." The shifting positions, reflecting the pitfalls in the emerging Western doctrine, for instance expressed in The Nation, a US magazine Feher analyses, can also be found on the Syndicate list.

Like so many foreign-policy analyses, Feher's *Powerless By Design* lacks critical understanding of the media. It is as if government advisors and NGO experts and public intellectuals operate in a Platonic sphere solely devoted to the exchange of arguments. What we in fact witness is a spectacle of manufactured baby-boom celebrities, from Chomsky to Friedman, from Sontag to Zizek, that simulates a public debate, sanctioned by a small group of senior editors, gatekeeping the circulation of a limited pool of syndicated content inside the global corporate media. Within Internet list culture there is a visible tendency to fall back to the level of celebrity content, taken from the websites of established media, from *Die Zeit* and *The Guardian* to *The New York Times.* List subscribers are easily satisfied with significant contributions replicated from old channels. Such a regression in list culture happened on Syndicate after the turbulent exchanges slowed down in April–May 1999. New media give the opportunity to create dialogue forms of decentralized "public opinion." However, Feher, and with him countless other public intellectuals, does not reflect on such a shift in the media landscape.

The Future State of Balkania and Other Follow-Ups

A few projects emerged out of the tensions and clashes built out of information overload on cultural channels such as Syndicate. In August 1999 a special issue of the publication Bastard was produced in Zagreb by the Arkzin crew (Boris Buden, Dejan Krzic, Igor Markovic and others) together with Syndicalists such as Honor Harger.[82] The free newspaper, distributed Europe-wide in a circulation of 8,000, attempted to summarize critical discourses and projects related to the Kosovo crisis. In April 2000 the conference and exhibition "Kosovo: Carnival in the Eye of the Storm," curated by Trebor Scholz, was held in Portland, Oregon, bringing many of the controversies together retrospectively.[83] The conference included a film program featuring many Kosovo-related documentaries were screened. The project was a response to the significant non-activism in Europe and the US among cultural producers in response to the conflict. Trebor Scholz: "The complexity of histories in the Balkans paralyzed and split left and right and created a confusion that lent itself to 'productive silence', leaving the public discourse to politicians. In the exhibition a large number of Internet pieces were screened next to art of a wide range of media by artists of many generations. The question was, and still is, what can artists DO in response to war?"[84]

The proposal for a "Future State of Balkania," originally developed by Melentie Pandilovski (SCCA, Skopje) had been discussed at the Syndicate Budapest meeting.[85] Unlike the "Deep Europe" concept, which had drawn attention from mainly Western Syndicalists, Balkania originated in southeast Europe. The concept was further developed in October 1999, including demo design and both critical and speculative texts, at a Syndicate workshop in the Kiasma museum for contemporary arts in Helsinki. A dozen Syndicalists from all over the Balkans (and beyond) came together to design Balkania. From the announcement: "During a nightly meeting preceding the Dayton agreement, Holbrooke and Milosevic, consuming lots of alcohol, were playing around with an American army computer simulation of the Yugoslavian landscape. Was it the drinks or the technology that created that bird's-eye sensation in which suddenly an agreement seemed within reach? Parallel to the rise of the Internet, the situation of national states in Europe changed drastically. We witnessed both the ongoing European integration as well as the disintegration of the former Soviet Union and Yugoslavia. Among the many experiments with virtual communities that, particularly, the Internet gave rise to, virtual states are a regular phenomenon, ranging from exercises in political wishful thinking, to refugee republics, to game-like utopias. The virtual state offers possibilities to comment and criticize on real world situations, to fantasize and experiment."[86]

The Cyber-Yugoslavia project had been one of those "virtual states." Balkania was a less literal translation of the idea of building an alternative state inside cyberspace. It set out to spread ideas of regionalized artistic utopias. Melentie Pandilovski continued to work on Balkania at different levels, from 3-D VRML competitions to a series of Balkans conferences he organized in Ohrid and Skopje.[87]

By August 1999 the traffic on the Syndicate list was back to normal. Syndicate posts had jumped from 87 in February 1999 to 417 in March and 400 in April, down to 237 in May and 250 in June, and were back down to previous levels of 157 in July and 118 in August. The summer period was marked by a move away from Balkan news items. A small Syndicate gathering took place in Zittau on the German/Polish border where the second camp of the "No One Is Illegal" campaign was going on.[88] Freedom of movement had been a concern of many Syndicalists. A great amount of time was given to preparing conferences, workshops and festivals, writing travel grants and arranging visa applications. Other small meetings took place in early September during Ars Electronica in Linz (Austria) and during the opening of the After the Wall exhibition (curated by Karen Henry and Bojana Pejic) in Stockholm. From this period onwards, a paid staff member of V2_, Arthur Bueno, was hired to set up a proper Syndicate website mapping the ever-growing network of new-media initiatives in Europe.

ASCII Art and Serbian Revolution

In August 1999, the first indications of a change in the atmosphere on the list appeared. From an "anonymizer" server stationed in Trondheim, Norway, a short e-mail dialogue was forged, meant to create distrust and confusion among Syndicate subscribers.[89] A little later, in February/March 2000 the list got stuck in a loop several times, repeatedly sending out the same message dozens of times. Andreas Broeckmann and Inke Arns said about the slow changes taking place in this period: "Not only that there were no more meetings after 1999, one could also notice that since mid-1999 people felt less and less responsible for the list. Many Syndicalists of the first hour grew more silent (this was partly incited by the hefty discussions during the NATO bombings in Yugoslavia), perhaps more weary, perhaps less naive, many also changed their personal circumstances and got involved in other things (new jobs, new families, new countries ...). At the same time, the number of subscribers kept growing: more and more newbies kept flowing onto the Syndicate list."[90]

By April 2000 posts and Net art from individuals and groups such as HYPERLINK "mailto:propaganda@0100101110101101.org" propaganda@0100101110101101.org, net_CALLBOY, { brad brace }, Dr. RTMark, iatsu.pavu.com and data[h!]bleede began to increase. Noise levels, with or without meaning, were up. Approaching 500 subscribers and still open and unfiltered, Syndicate was an easy outlet for e-mail art, varying from low-tech ASCII art and Net poetry to hoaxes and anonymous personal attacks. While announcements had been an important aim early on, they now began to further increase the feeling of anonymity, which in turn encouraged Net artists to fill the gap left behind by the disappearing Kosovo exchange with more e-mail experiments. By May 2000 traffic had gone up to over 200 posts. A second Syndicate "Pyramedia" gathering in Tirana organized by Edi Muka got postponed until further notice at the last minute. And in August the list switched providers and was moved from Linz to Berlin because of technical troubles with the Ars Electronica server, which had hosted Syndicate since early 1996.

In the Kosovo aftermath the political situation in Serbia had grown more desperate, with both opposition activities and repression from the Milosevic regime increasing. The radio and TV station Studio B, which had started to relay the "real B92" signal on a vacant frequency, was forced to close on May 17, 2000. B92, which still had not returned to its studios and equipment, switched to satellite and the Internet to get its signal out. The rise of the radical Otpor student/youth movement in Serbia took place beyond the radar of Syndicalists. During the days of the "Serbian revolution" in early October 2000, when large demonstrations forced the fall of the Milosevic regime, Syndicate was revived as a peer-to-peer communication channel. For a brief moment Slobodan Markovic, Dejan Strenovic and Michael Benson reappeared on the list, but their thoughts were quickly overwhelmed by an ever-rising number of announcements from the global new-media arts sector. Posts no longer triggered responses. The last action of the Syndicate network was a spontaneous support campaign for the Albanian curator Edi Muka, who had been fired from his post as director of the Pyramid cultural center in Tirana.[91] While throughout 2001 Melentie Pandilovski regularly forwarded news updates from Skopje related to the crisis in Macedonia between Albanian (KLA) fighters and the army, the Syndicate list de facto fell silent over this topic. Owing to the aggressive NATO containment policy the Balkans had been neutralized. One of the effects was that news no longer sparked outrage. Once again ethnic conflicts were perceived as impersonal news items, echoes of some faraway region, a distant past.

In an overview of electronic mailing lists the Serbian filmmaker and diary writer Aleksander Gubas gives, in my opinion, an honest and precise description of the state of Syndicate in 2001: "Various hot activists, ASCII artists and other spammers fill your inbox every day. On the other side, Syndicate is a very useful source of the art information from Europe – especially from Eastern Europe, which is the region where I physically belong. Syndicate is an online source where the information can be freely available to the members, and at the same time is discreetly monopolized by the art managers who should spread it. Syndicate helped me in deciding to become the manager of my own. Unfortunately, it seems that in the last few months Syndicate somehow lost its informational function, being saturated by political quarrels on the Balkans items. I was also involved in such a quarrel on Syndicate, and I regret it. It was with an artist from Serbia whom I have never met – and I don't want to – although we live only 80 kilometers away from each other. When you're online, your compatriot can be more distant to you than somebody from Seattle or Mexico."[92]

To summarize Aleksander's observation: Syndicate was a window on the world that provided useful information about the region but could not be considered a close and homogeneous community.

Machine Talk

In January 2001 "Netochka Nezvanova" (NN), named after Dostojevsky's first full-length novel, began sending hundreds of messages to Syndicate, usually randomly responding to anything posted to the list. NN is a list spammer (or Net artist if you like), also operating under names such as integer and antiorp. The posts were a mixture of replies, cryptic political analyses, machine talk[93] and personal attacks.[94] NN had posted to Nettime and other lists before and was a well-known phenomenon. NN's aim was not just to dominate a channel but to eventually destroy the online community. Katherine Mieszkowski portrayed NN for the online magazine *Salon*, focusing on the unknown identity of the artist(s). "An appearance by Netochka frequently derails a mailing list, devolving it into a flame war about free speech vs. the rights of the community. Soon mailing-list members will be choosing sides: the defenders of freedom of expression at all costs! The fed-up denizens who just want her off the list! And the few who believe they see the brilliance in her indirection, the beauty in her sly, circumspect ways. All talk of anything else is soon abandoned." "As a community destroyer, she's fantastic," says Bernstein, the Brooklyn artist. "She's perhaps one of the Internet's first professional demolition experts. She's a real talent."[95]

In August 1998 the same person(s) had posted a few messages to Syndicate under the name antiorp but then disappeared after being unsubscribed by one of the moderators, without protest.[96] NN used a blend of software and Internet-specific styles of writing such as Europanto[97] and B1FF[98], combined with an agitated *Übermensch* attitude (perhaps inspired by the Extropians), showing off a machinic-futuristic "post-human" superiority over the all-too-human fellow subscribers and their petty and corrupt intentions.

In a brilliant textual analysis, *Mute*-magazine editor Josephine Berry unravels the NN/antiorp/integer grammar. Posting to lists such as 7-11, MAX, Nettime, music-dsp, Syndicate, Xchange and others, antiorp used a special language called Kroperom or KROP3ROM|A9FF. Berry: "This language, in part, relies on a logic of substitution to reformulate the Roman alphabet's phonetic system by including all the 256 different characters comprising the American Standard Code for Information Interchange (ASCII), the lingua franca of computing. For instance, in the case of a Kroperom word like "m9nd," the number "9" is incorporated into the word "mind" such that the "ine" in "nine" takes on a phonetic role. But Antiorp's system also extends beyond purely phonetic substitutions. In the example "m@zk!n3n kunzt m2cht . fr3!" not only do numerals and ASCII characters mix with alphabetic characters within the space of a word, but the unity of the phonetic system is broken by the logic of different character systems so that the reader is forced to employ a combination of strategies to decode the script. The substitution of letters for numerals, the script starts to mimic the functional potential of a program. In other words, textual self-reflexivity refers here especially to the computational environment."[99]

In a social context the phenomenon was known as a "troll." First used on the Usenet group alt.folklore.urban, a troll sends out messages designed to attract predictable responses or flames. The jargon file at tuxedo.org defines the troll as "an individual who chronically regularly posts specious arguments, flames or personal attacks to a newsgroup, discussion list, or in e-mail for no other purpose than to annoy someone or disrupt a discussion. Trolls are recognizable by the fact that they have no real interest in learning about the topic at hand – they simply want to utter flame bait. Like the ugly creatures they are named after, they exhibit no redeeming characteristics, and as such, they are recognized as a lower form of life on the Net."[100]

Trollers lure others into pointless and time-consuming discussions aimed at naïve and vulnerable users. Their aim, as described by one of the oldest sites on trolling, maintained by Andrew, is to sit back and laugh at all the idiots who will believe anything.[101] Trolling can often end in flame wars (online arguments) but isn't necessary the same thing. What trolls live for is attention. By disrupting ongoing conversations, trolls are testing the boundaries of the very foundations of the "attention economy."[102] Com2kid, writing on Slashdot, explains the success of trolls in this way: "If you piss people off, they will respond to you in droves. If you manage to gradually build up an argument and convince your readership that you are correct; well heck, what is left to be said? You win, case closed."[103]

One not infrequently sees the warning "Do not feed the troll" as part of a follow-up to troll posts. This was exactly what was about to happen on Syndicate. Unlike in 1998, in January 2001 antiorp/NN/integer was going stay. Unfamiliar with the troll phenomenon, Syndicalists jumped on a dialogue with NN, thereby unwittingly becoming complicit in the troll's strategy to become the center of the conversation. This time the strategy of hijacking the list and becoming the central online personality worked. Because the core community had eroded, the list got entangled in the constant stream of NN/integer postings. Some called for filtering of the NN/integer posts, whereas others tried to challenge the troll.[104] Others such as Diana McCarty took the liberal stand and defended the democracy of the delete button: "It takes 1–2 minutes of your time and you can file or delete and forget. Noise is sometimes music and sometimes incredibly intelligent."[105] For months virtually all attention went to the NN/integer troll. A dialogue between Eleni Laperi (Tirana), Edi Muka (Tirana) and Melentie Pandilovski (Skopje) about the Albanian-Macedonian tensions went under.[106] With a silent majority, a growing number of protest posts, a handful of fans and a growing number of "machine-talk" artists, Syndicate stalled. Because of the lack of internal electronic democracy (there were no voting systems in place on lists such as Syndicate) there was no way to find out what subscribers wanted to do. In June the debates intensified after Károly Tóth proposed to remove NN. It was another seven months before Syndicate exploded over the NN/integer case.[107]

One of the arguments used to defend NN's posts concerned the alien (female) "subhuman" robotic nature of integer as something which should rouse understanding and pity. Friddy Nietzsche, for instance, wrote: "Our beloved NN (we feel a certain sweet compatibility towards her, as one collective bio-tech organism towards another) is a being of another universe; her arrogance programmed in and conceptual, deprived of petty human motivations."[108]

Hijacking Lists

A similar debate had taken place on the Nettime mailing list from August to October 1998, when antiorp sent hundreds of messages. There was an essential difference, though: Nettime was a closed list and antiorp could not freely bother the subscribers. Nettime moderators only let a few messages through now and then. It was mainly the New York-based Nettime moderator Ted Byfield who took on the task of dealing with the flood of mail. In response to the filtering, Frederic Madre posted three rules: "1. hypermedia critics must do it the hypermedia way, or die. 2. forget 2.0: 0.0 is the right direction 3. moderation has to go."[109] Despite criticism by some, Nettime remained closed and could therefor not be hijacked. In early October 1998 antiorp was unsubscribed. Ted Byfield explained about the amount of work involved in maintaining a (closed) list: "Filtering out the spam, dealing with the misdirected subscriptions and unsubscriptions, passing mail to the announcer, cleaning up mail (quoted-printable cruft, ascii junk, bad formatting), and then stripping down multiple levels of headers that are generated by majordomo. It's not unusual for this to take a few hours a day."[110]

Antiorp sent around ten messages a day to Nettime. Ted Byfield: "If antiorp had been willing to listen or give me the benefit of the doubt when I asked it to slow down, or had recognized that getting its own mail bounced back might bear some theoretical relation to its own activities, then I wouldn't have unsubscribed it. But, instead, it went crying to the info.cops, playing fast and loose with the facts, and taking up my own and other moderators' time in order to radicalize the situation to "prove" that everyone except for poor little antiorp is an unenlightened fascist censor."[111]

An article by Austin Bunn in *Salon,* published in March 1999, describes the antiorp vs. Nettime case and mentions similar incidents such as the Jack Kerouac fan list beat-l ("exploding like a civil war"), Mediafilter's hijack of Nettime and Mark Stahlman's raving on the Technorealism list. "Take a close look at the wreckage and talk to survivors, and it's evident that mailing-list flare-ups are the handiwork of agent provocateurs determined to pump the bellows. They want to take your attention hostage and jam your mailbox with their agenda. At best, they're a kind of online performance artist trying to expose some elusive truth; but at their worst, they're rogues waging list-serv terrorism."[112]

What were these loose cannons after, Bunn asked? "And, perhaps more urgent, is there any defense against them?" Abandon ship and sign off? Install bozo filters? It's like trying to reason with someone holding a weapon. Bunn: "Often these provocateurs have something essential to contribute, but the sheer wattage of their energies endangers the connection they're trying to create."

Californian Net artist, programmer and former Syndicalist Amy Alexander suggested the trouble on Syndicate in 2001 had little to do with either subscribers or administrators. It was the very structure of lists that was outdated. "Any way you slice it, NN is a collective troll. Trolls are all over the net – and have been for years. Trolls as well as lamers, drifters and lurkers are all part of the assumed user-base. There are known ways to deal with them. A troll is not the Achilles heel that can knock down a list. It's 2001 and you just can't have a diverse Net community operate with a structure like it's 1985."[113]

Unlike in the early days, the motivation of participants could differ wildly. The Net had opened itself up in a radical way, allowing all sorts of people to express themselves. What was needed were new forms of collective security and filtering software. The majordomo mailing-list software from the early days was no longer capable of dealing with the new techno-social realities of the Net. In the midst of the fire, the recycle artist Steev Hise posted a cgi script intended to act like NN: a parody perl program that spits out a user's input in NN machine talk. This strategy was intended to fight fire with laughter. The software was meant to bring levity to the situation by pointing out and deconstructing the predictability of NN's texts in an amusing way. But the Syndicate was already beyond repair. Neither rationalism nor irony or humor could take away the bitterness that had grown.

Faced with the conflict between the desire to be noticed and the fear of being humiliated by taking sides in the conflict, most of the Syndicalists remained silent. The community lacked armor to defend itself and lost interest in the Syndicate project altogether. The fear of being labeled as a totalitarian advocate of censorship was omnipresent and lamed participants who might have acted at this crucial hour. Laissez-faire liberalism showed its brutal face. The choice was an impossible one. There was going to be violence in one way or the other: either a handful of posters would be excluded or the community would go under, self-destruct. After seven months of NN's presence and several thousand posts, not just by NN/integer but also by][mez][, Frederic Madre, Andrej Tisma, d u, pavu.com and others (and their opponents), Syndicate had passed the point when the issues could have been resolved through consensus. Suggested solutions such as mail filtering came too late. The whole idea of an online media-arts community which had to be "cleansed" of "unwanted elements" by voluntary filtering at the receiving end by individual subscribers seemed a veto of the original idea of egalitarian information exchange and collaboration. Only few Syndicalists filtered their mail; the majority remained fully exposed to the hundreds of NN postings.

While there had been some resistance on Syndicate against the ongoing flood of NN's postings in June and July, the protests began to gain momentum in early August. Julie Blankenship: "The life is being sucked out of the list by NN's constant posts and the responses they generate. I don't enjoy watching it die."[114] Igor Markovic from Zagreb, who had been challenging the integer troll for some time, wrote back that Syndicate was pretty much dead anyway, even if you filtered out NN and all the announcements.[115] Some insisted NN would have gone away if no attention were paid to the troll. Saul Ostrow: "I do believe (for it has been my experience elsewhere) that such vermin as these will migrate away if they come to be ignored – they live on negative attention and the desire of others to reason with them – I personally, readily use my delete key at the mere sight of this tag."[116] Others, such as Diana McCarty, described NN as "playful anarchy." "I thought of the NN posts as a bit like street theatre ... whereas antiorp was more like a mime, NN sort of used the list as a public space for interventions."[117]

The Death of a Community

On August 7, 2001, after hundreds of NN postings and an exhausting debate, Inke Arns unsubscribed NN, causing protest from a loud minority while receiving praise from others. The mood on the list was deeply divided. Inke Arns and Andreas Broeckmann seemed to have hoped that the Syndicate community, as a living entity, would defend itself against the ongoing humiliations of NN. Inke Arns: "If you don't take care of your list, and voice your opinion, the list will be taken care of by others. And you won't necessarily like it."[118] According to Arns, the suggestion that Syndicate was a utopian network with distributed responsibility was proven an illusion. "Regarding WORK the Syndicate mailing list is definitely NOT a non-hierarchic 'society' of equal members. How many times have I called for more support concerning the administration of the list? How few answers did I receive?" Andreas Broeckmann defended the removal: "I don't like filters. I like this list because it makes sense for me to listen to all the different voices. I don't want to censor what comes through. At the same time, I ask for some sort of respect for my position as somebody who is also on this list. This implies not being shouted at all the time. It more importantly implies not being spat on and insulted for writing this message. It implies not seeing messages that call me a criminal."[119] Annick Bureaud (Paris) also detested filtering and defended unsubscribing NN. "What I really disliked with NN postings was the flood. Once in a while, why not, but minimum 10 per day, as in the last week, come on! This is just a hijack of the list. S/he knew the rules, s/he didn't play by it. Too bad."[120]

Instead of a relief over the disappearance of NN, the mood on the list only got tenser, with Andrej Tisma crying censorship, complaining about a conspiracy of Soros swastika people, and Brad Brace equating NN to the martyr Mata Hari. At the "moment supreme," the Australian Net artist

][mez][started systematically forwarding NN's messages, stacked with personal attacks.[121] This was the signal for Andreas Broeckmann and Inke Arns to step down. They had enough of all the hate mail. The moderators made sure the handing over of the list was done "in a proper and friendly manner." While a small group, mainly Net artists, kept arguing, defending the anti-censorship case, in a matter of days Syndicate fell apart.[122] The rhizomes, tunnels and channels had insufficient defense mechanisms against those intending to hijack the "subterranean connections."

To conclude this story of the sad end of the V2_East/Syndicate network, I would like to quote Martha Rosler (a New York artist/activist) at length here, not only because of her thoughtful remarks but also because she was not directly associated with either side of the debate. "In my observation, Syndicate ceases to be interesting in pretty direct proportion to NN's posts, and it is somewhat arrogant to expect a participant to have to decode a private orthography in order to 'get it.' I wouldn't mind the posts if they didn't polarize and shrink the entire list to pros and cons about it. Indeed, I used to enjoy some of them, delete the rest. But when I get my e-mail while traveling, I resent the endless 'mutterings' that these posts seem to constitute. (The endless NN yenta, always commenting on everyone else, picking on their language, competes with a very nicely tuned NN anti-corporate, anti-bullshit set of remarks.) Freedom of speech is not the primary issue, and threats to call in the correctness police on the list are an ironic reversal of other authoritarian tropes, I humbly suggest; a list is neither society nor the public sphere in toto. I am not advocating asking NN to leave, for the decision is not mine, but ask yourself, when you play a game, what happens when the bully insists that it is always his/her turn at the bat; at a forum, what if she/he jumps up for the microphone after every remark someone else has made, simply to snipe, and not actually engage their points? Of course, this analogy is poor, because only one person can speak at a forum at once, but it is not wholly inappropriate. Pretty soon, the discussion is about rules and personality, not about substantive issues. I have been in many, many political gatherings where a bloc of extreme leftists (or a strongly vocal single representative) stood up to denounce the incorrect political 'line' each speaker was espousing, according to the commentator. This well-known tactic has a name: disruption."[123]

NN's strategy of disruption had proven successful. By mid-August 2001 the Syndicate list had effectively split in two. The group that had defended integer stayed on and moved the list (and the name) to a server in Norway.[124] Meanwhile, in early September, "Spectre," a successor to Syndicate, was announced. Spectre had been prepared on a cc: list during the turbulent weeks in August when it had become clear to Inke Arns, Andreas Broeckmann and a few others who had left the list in protest that Syndicate no longer could be saved. The Spectre announcement included the following "netiquette" rules: "No HTML, no attachments, messages < 40K; meaningful discussions require mutual respect; self-advertise with care!"[125] Soon Spectre had 250 subscribers. It continued with Syndicate's focus on announcements related to new-media culture. Spectre would no longer explicitly focus on East-West dynamics but still referred to the Deep Europe concept. "Deep Europe is not a particular territory, but is based on an attitude and experience of layered identities and histories – ubiquitous in Europe, yet in no way restricted by its topographical borders." As was the case with the original Syndicate, "many people on this list know each other personally." The aim of Spectre was going to be "to facilitate real-life meetings and favors real face-to-face (screen-to-screen) cooperation, test-bed experiences and environments to provoke querying of issues of cultural identity/identification and difference (translatable as well as untranslatable or irreducible)."[126] It was up to history if these initiatives would have the same vitality and timeliness as Syndicate once had. Spectre turned out to be an announcement list with hardly any debate, whereas the Norwegian initiative that carried on the Syndicate name mainly consisted of Net art/ascii-art devotees.

After Innocence

Syndicate was, relatively speaking, a late initiative. It blossomed as a pragmatist "second-wave" project, a belated response to the 1989 political turmoil in Europe and the cyberculture euphoria of the early and mid-1990s. Because it was situated in a different historical period, Syndicate missed both the euphoria of the aftermath of the fall of the communist regimes and the radical, speculative excitement of the early 1990s sparked by the rise of new media. Even one or two years can make a substantial difference in this context. Timing is crucial in building up social networks, performing actions and staging debates. Syndicate could no longer easily tap into 1989's energies. The V2_East Syndicate initiative had indeed expressed unease over the traditional networking practices of established NGOs and cultural organizations. It had the electronic means (mailing list and website) of building more open, decentralized and diffuse networks, and proved its potential during the Kosovo crisis. When the East-West network was in place, around 1997–98, it found itself in an environment of consolidation and growing suspicion. There was a hangover from the utopian techno promises of the free-marketers and the well-intentioned Western agendas of cultural officials wining and dining their Eastern counterparts. Syndicate itself had not expressed such tendencies but also proved unable to mobilize the simmering discontent.

Throughout its existence, Syndicate had had the feel of a somewhat non-binding and safe "Hegelian" project, struggling with the obsolete East-West dichotomy it had imposed upon itself in order to reach the synthesis of a united Europe, caught in an endless process of "reconstruction." Unconsciously, the project had been built on the Cold War strategy of culturally subverting power without naming the adversary. With old-school Communist officials having mutated and the EU and NATO not yet fully in charge, it was unclear which powers had to be questioned. Dutch sociologist Johan Sjerpstra, in a private e-mail exchange, looking back on Syndicate's role: "Lacking a critical apparatus to analyze the role of culture and the arts in the former East, Syndicate remained "positive" in its aims and attitude, demanding open borders and higher budgets. Being a potentially interesting international artist group, Syndicate lacked consistency to push its agenda (if there was any). Beyond the communication paradigm, which is not a particular Eastern approach anyway, there wasn't much else. No authority was explicitly questioned. The common denominator, working with networked computers in an arts environment, did not translate into a specific group aesthetics."[127]

Indeed, Syndicate did not end up as a movement or avant-garde group with its distinct style and agenda. The impoverished European new-media arts sector clustered around the Syndicate had too little in common to develop its own political aesthetics in terms of collaborative works such as manifestos. Identity-wise, Syndicate was neither "cool" nor did it create inspiring and controversial expressions of dissent. The exchange between the East and West never turned into a "hot" object of desire. The creation of a cultural Europe was perceived as a dull, pacifying project of arts bureaucrats attempting to repair 20th-century damage. Deeply rooted skepticism and distrust on both sides remained too big of an obstacle. The pragmatic drive towards consensus prevented interesting clashes from happening. When conflicts occurred, the mood turned nasty, causing the initiative to fall apart.

The question arises of whether anything is lost if a social network falls apart. Sentimental thoughts apart, was Syndicate sustainable in the first place? Virtual communities constantly dissolve and regroup and new initiatives pop up. People move on, and there is nothing to be said against that. However, in the case of Syndicate as a hybrid of real and virtual gatherings I would argue that in mid-2001 its time had not yet come. There are certain rules for the art of (dis)appearance and the Syndicate moderators were apparently not aware of them. They could have either dissolved Syndicate entirely or arranged a proper handover to the people they trusted. Without much effort Syndicate could have been transformed into a network of a different nature. Instead, the chaotic takeover in August 2001, when most list members were on holiday, prevented such a collective rite of passage into another project from taking place. Spectre, the successor to Syndicate, turned out to be nothing but a weak echo of a once-living entity.

The Syndicate case should be read as a Brechtian *Lehrstück,* a didactic play set in post-1989 Europe. The 1998–99 period around the Kosovo crisis was Syndicate's heyday. While elsewhere on the Net dotcom mania dominated the Internet agenda, the Syndicate network, symbolic of the new-media arts sector as a whole, tried – and failed – to claim moral superiority over war and ethnic tensions on the one hand and corporate greed on the other. Yet there was no cultural high ground to escape to. The quarrel of mid-2001 can only be read as a hostile attack on an already weakened body, covered up by lies and a massive abuse of democratic tolerance. The unspoken consensus of mediated communication based on tolerance, democracy and credibility fell apart, torn up by petty controversies. NN/antiorp/integer's (efficient) usage of anti-globalization rhetoric ("corporate fascists") with its roots in Stalinism and totalitarianism managed to overthrow an already minimal sense of belonging. It used populist anti-capitalist sentiments also found in the rhetoric of authoritarian rulers such as Malaysia's Mahatir during the 1997 Asian monetary crisis. The techno-organic rhetoric ("I am human plant"), masochistic sentiments against the English language and quasi-crypto-orthography pointed to a failed parody of content overruled by a manic backlash and driven by the desire for self-destruction (the troll being the Internet version of the suicide bomber). After August 2001 the remains of the Syndicate transformed into a nonsense communication community for a few insiders, a small circle of friends, mimicking a community, a mere parasite on the body of a dead project. Spectre proved irrelevant, caught in the pragmatics of a redundant, no-nonsense announcement list with virtually no discussion. Spectre's only reference to Syndicate was the Deep Europe term used in the footer, which by 2002 had turned into little more than an empty brand.

No genuine information appeared on Syndicate; most of the art info was forwarded from other sources. The main traffic became small talk: internal, nonsensical, repetitive, redundant textual content, very often with simple ("small is beautiful") messages, often no more than a URL. Johan Sjerpstra again: "The minimal e-mails can be a seen as a new movement in the quickly changing Net/Web art scene, like a counter-reaction to the earlier socially engaged and/or conceptual type of Net/Web art. We could call it a sort of Dadaist answer to the seriousness and tech orientation of the late 1990s. The significant difference with Dada is that instead of humor they use an aggressive and threatening (hacking) tone. Hate speak, targeted at those they dislike – a sign of an emerging new extremity."[128]

The Syndicate list takeover showed how the aggressive information warfare strategy of a small group could present tolerance as a form of weakness. The incident marked the end of the romantic concept of open, unmoderated exchange. This tendency of consciously extreme strategies is present, and even if it represents only a small percentage of users, within a growing Internet it is capable of penetrating existing structures with virtually no resistance, just as mediocre viruses are capable of bringing down millions of computers, and spam is becoming a major concern for businesses, so can Net artists dramatically increase their presence by using aggressive memes. There is no ethics of mediated usage yet. Such a networked ethics can only be situated within a living dialogue.

The fall of Syndicate marks the rise of information warfare. The "war zone" is no longer a distinct battlefield but stretches deep into society. It does not only affect the physical civil infrastructure but has also penetrated the civilian mindset. Strategies of tension, disinformation and uncertainty are now common practices among and between social groups. In the case of the Syndicate network, the good intentions of East-West exchange gave way to a dangerous, manipulative, unreliable network of abuse. This turning point, which may have happened earlier in some online communities, and later in others, both reflects and further accelerates the collapse of the dream of the Net as a utopian, parallel world. Like photography in the age of digital manipulation, the Internet has lost its credibility. For the Syndicate members this meant that free and open e-mail communication was no longer innocent.

Principles of Streaming Sovereignty

A History of the Xchange Network

Introduction

Xchange is a network of tactical non-profit organizations and individuals involved in "streaming media" since the birth of the technology in 1996–97.[1] This chapter focuses on streaming media,[2] usually described as audio and/or video, "streamed" from a dedicated Internet server, either live or on demand. Besides live webcasts, streaming projects build up online archives and databases. Unlike similar cultural networks and lists, the "cloud" of streaming initiatives I describe in this chapter has not evolved much since its genesis, and the reason for this is one of the main topics I will investigate here. Those who are not interested in network stagnation may as well skip this chapter. As a subculture of experimentation, Xchange remained in the shadow of events and by and large survived waves of commercialization, insisting on the original drive to seek new-media models that go beyond traditional broadcasting. The Xchange mailing list has had consistently moderate traffic and, with a few exceptions, refrained from intellectual theorization of the field. Like many radio initiatives, Xchange is weak on discourse and lacks even basic elements of reflection and (self-)criticism. Unlike the Nettime list, the Xchange community did not have controversies over the issue of list moderation. And unlike Syndicate, Xchange successfully managed to ignore trolls and ASCII artists begging for attention and trying to monopolize the channel. I have decided not to tell the Xchange history in a chronological manner. Instead I have chosen to highlight patterns in the activities and focus on practical limitations for streaming-media networks in terms of available and affordable Internet capacity.

I did not choose to cover Xchange because of its turbulent history. There has been none so far. I would propose to read Xchange's uncertain and somewhat flat state as a typical post-bubble allegory. Most of us would subscribe to the idea that "visual culture" has become dominant over the written word. But the Internet is an interesting exception. What happens if the technology is there (in this case streaming) but fails to be implemented? Why hasn't the Internet yet attained the immense importance of film, television and radio? What makes playing moving images and music on a computer network so uncool? Is it only the poor quality that keeps people away? Artificial life and virtual reality underwent a similar process after the hype ended. Mild stagnation also happens to certain advanced mobile phone applications. What could be missing here is the network sublime. Scrambled high resolution is by definition not cool low tech. In response, those looking for the instant satisfaction of utopian promises go away frustrated. In the case of streaming networks we are not just talking about "404 Not Founds" and broken streams. It is a larger, invisible infrastructure that simply does not deliver. Streaming is a field for pioneers with a long-term view. This chapter describes how cultural practitioners respond to such a state of sophisticated stagnation. Can creative and subversive concepts be freeze-dried and saved for another decade? What is the impact of working with advanced applications going nowhere? Technologies that have been sidetracked by history and placed in the waiting room for an indefinite period of time challenge dominant notions of speed and the boom-and-bust logic of information capitalism. It is not that the future is in ruins. Instead, streaming scapes, beyond excitement and disappointment, invite users to lie back, uphold their techno-expectations, stretch their time-space and enjoy the stumbling fuzziness on offer.

Over the first five years of Xchange's existence, issues such as bandwidth, standards and models for decentralized webcasting were remarkably stable. The immense popularity of MP3 file-swapping on Napster (around 2000) and other peer-to-peer networks such as Gnutella and KaZaa largely took place in a parallel universe, it seemed. Despite the worldwide growth in Internet users, who by now have installed media players on their PCs and increasingly also on PDAs and other wearable devices, this has not led to radical shifts in the independent arm of the streaming-media industry. Streaming has remained very much a desktop PC experience. Despite the steady rollout of broadband and cable modem connections since the late 1990s, independent non-profit streaming media did not witness a breakthrough comparable to the boom in e-mail, chatrooms, webcams and MP3-swapping. Partially in response to the worldwide stagnation of broadband, the central thesis of this chapter is to interpret "minor" collaborations as "sovereign media." But first I will present my version of the first five years of streaming media from the perspective of the Xchange network.

The Beginnings of Streaming

Before going into the life and work of Xchange, I will quickly go through the early history of "streaming media." All beginnings are arbitrary, but one starting point could be the release in April 1995 of the first version of the RealAudio player by a company called Progressive Networks (later Real Networks), founded by former Microsoft employee Robert Glaser in

Seattle. Early versions of the audio compression software provided only on-demand audio.[3] The first live broadcast was radio coverage of a basketball game: the Seattle Mariners vs. the New York Yankees on September 5, 1995. The RealAudio player (later RealPlayer) was freely distributed to users who, at that time, were typically connected to the Internet via low-bandwidth modems. The player supported connection rates as low as 14.4 Kbps, which delivered audio quality comparable to the sound of a decent AM radio. In October 1996, the first stable version of the Real-Audio server software went on sale, enabling users not just to receive live audio signals but also to stream out to the Internet. From then on, practically anyone could start his or her own radio station on the Net.

Another beginning important in this context could be B92's netcasts. The oppositional Belgrade radio station switched from air to Internet on December 3, 1996, after Slobodan Milosevic closed it down. For three days, B92 could only be heard via the Internet. The crucial lifeline was created by B92's in-house Internet provider, Opennet, set up by mathematician Drazen Pantic, who had heard of streaming media well before Progressive Networks launched its first player. Drazen, now based in New York at NYU and the LocationOne gallery, told me the story of early streaming software, from "multicast" to the very first versions of the RealPlayer. "Early experiments of Carl Malamud and the multicast group before 1996 were promising, but still out of the conceptual and infrastructural reach of many. I received all the announcements of the multicast group, including the announcement of their legendary live broadcast from the US Congress. Back then, one really had to be connected to what you could consider broadband in order to be able to receive a live stream. When Progressive Networks came out with their producer/server/player bundle it attracted a lot of attention. But early releases (up to version 3) were just not usable, even though compression software (called codecs) got better and basic stream could be delivered even to an ordinary 28.8 Kbps modem. However, the quality, delays and reliability remained bad for quite a while. A really interesting and progressive approach was that Real launched the version of their bundle for Linux as well as for Win and Mac. That fact kept many people focused on what Progressive Networks was doing."[4]

He went on to explain that early streaming-media networks were all about the "art of compression." The smaller the files were, the more people would be able to participate and the less the Internet at large would be congested. How many dropouts could one bear, having to re-open the connection to a streaming server somewhere on the other side of the world over and over again?

But let's go back to Belgrade. The closure of B92 came as a response to the massive student protests of late 1996. For weeks, hundreds of thousands of demonstrators protested the government's annulment of municipal elections won by Milosevic's opponents in Belgrade and 14 of Serbia's largest towns. Drazen Pantic: "When Milosevic banned Radio B92 in early December 1996, it was just one of those unimaginable synchronic situations that happen every once in a while. We immediately started distributing news clips in RealAudio format. We neither had the expertise, the bandwidth nor the software for live transmission on the Net. But XS4ALL and Progressive Networks jointly helped with bandwidth and server software. We got a server capable of 400 simultaneous connections, donated by Progressive Networks, installed at XS4ALL."[5] Within a day or two there was a live RealAudio stream from Belgrade carrying B92's programming. That same stream has stayed up and running, except for a few interruptions during the Kosovo conflict in 1999, to the present day.

Principles of Streaming

I will leave out the rich prehistory of streaming media here.[6] This chapter will instead focus on the post-1996 period, taking the Xchange network as an example of the stagnating independent and "tactical" Internet culture that emerged in the aftermath of the mid-1990s Internet hype (led by *Wired* magazine, and developing in 1998–2000, parallel to the dotcom hype). RealAudio technology made it possible to join a global network for the price of a local telephone call – and that made all the difference. The Xchange network was founded in late 1997 by three members of E-lab in Riga (Latvia), Rasa Smite, Raitis Smits and Janis Garancs who started an online audio project of the same name in July 1997. The three had participated in and helped organize the maelstrom of conferences, festivals and workshops during the European "short summer of the Internet" in 1996–97. This all led to the launch of Xchange.

Xchange is an example of the new-media cultural initiatives of Central and Eastern Europe that had started to flourish after the fall of the Berlin Wall.[7] As a mailing list and website, Xchange was meant for "alternative, non-commercial Internet broadcasters and individual audio content providers" and aimed at setting up a "Net audio network community."[8] The list was to provide its members with announcements of new radio links and timetables for collaborative live webcasts and texts. Since December 1997, E-lab's Ozone group has been doing live Web sessions every Tuesday, sending out Net radio experiments, live music and mix-jam sessions, sometimes together with other Net radio servers located elsewhere. Ozone invites local musicians, poets and writers to present their work to the global online Net radio community.[9] There is an IRC chatroom, an important tool for Net radiocasters to find out who's listening, who's picking up the stream for rebroadcasting, and who has content on offer to be downloaded. In the latter cases, the Ozone group in Riga might then go to the URL and rebroadcast the signal, integrating the incoming sound into the program.

In her 1997 welcome statement, Rasa Smite, member of E-lab in Riga and co-founder of Xchange, mapped out the terrain Xchange was to cover.[10] She described Net radio as a blend of different radio initiatives, some with a community/pirate background, others exclusively exploring webcasting. Net radio is not one, it is many. It is this blend that makes the culture, not Internet technology as such. Some streaming initiatives seek to serve both local (FM) and global (Internet) audiences. Others do live transmissions from festivals, parties and conferences. Others netcast from clubs. Some, like the Budapest-based Pararadio, webcast for a specific local audience; others aim at the global Internet population. In a posting to the Xchange list, Slovenian Net radio pioneer Borut Savski summed up the different elements of free webcasting:[11]

- (Live) real-time text;
- Audio and video transmission;
- Worldwide accessibility and international concepts;
- Synchronized broadcasting from multiple sources on the same platform (site);
- Atomized (international) production groups gathering as they wish;
- A differentiated (international) audience;
- Creation of no-copyright platforms of independent productions;
- Information banks (texts, interviews, music, archived live production);
- Individualized means of access to archived text, sound and vision files;
- No cost difference between local and international access; no repressive legislation (so far).

Over the coming years, the Xchange network would practice – and embody – these different elements. They define the Xchange network, keeping it separate from commercial currents. In the mid-1990s, non-profit Net radio pioneers enjoyed incredible freedom. The spirit was very much like that of pirate radio, an element the Amsterdam critic Josephine Bosma brought into the network through her writings, interviews and responses posted to the list.[12] Xchange could be described as a global network of audionauts festively exploring virtual frontiers. The authorities were oblivious, as were mainstream media and the corporate world. Intellectual property rights were a non-issue for the early non-profit streamers. Even though some Net radio stations occasionally played mainstream pop CDs, for the most part they webcast independently produced music and soundscapes. Out there on the Net they found the freedom to be left alone, to experiment with the new medium, connect it to local radio, pick up sounds in techno clubs and tiny studios, send soundscapes out into the cyber-plains. By 2002, Xchange had about 450 subscribers, almost all content providers – contributors who participated in building the community.

Webcasting, Not Broadcasting

Despite the open and pluralistic approach, there was one question on everyone's mind: what makes streaming media so different from broadcast media? Rasa Smite: "Everything! It is not just because audio is streamed via the Internet, thereby reaching a global audience. Streaming also gives you a certain freedom. The distributed and decentralized structure of network radio is very encouraging. It offers inexperienced artists possibilities to participate, to be involved and to 'network' – equally for everyone on the Net, and in particular for those in remote places, individuals, and micro-scale initiatives."[13] This is not just an idealistic statement. Small streaming-media initiatives active within Xchange have been operating in the way Rasa Smite describes. The practice, however, came at a cost, if you like: there was only a tiny audience for Net radio, despite the rapid growth of the Internet user base. But it was a reality most initiatives had no problem with. From very early on, the political economy of bandwidth defined the size of the Net radio projects. Non-profit projects simple could not afford the equipment and traffic costs to handle thousands of online listeners. Only a tiny fraction of Internet users had enough computing power, storage capacity and bandwidth to fully enjoy streaming technologies. On top of that, general interest in radio was limited anyway. Only those with stable and open connections and flat-rate prices would potentially be interested in tapping into streaming media. Berlin-based net critic, Nettime co-founder and streaming activist Pit Schultz: "The economies of streaming have to be put into consideration when the rather vague concepts are taken in. Narrowcasting is explainable when you look at the bandwidth costs. An average urban pirate station has more listeners than the biggest trance-streaming pipes on the Net, just for economic and technical reasons."[14]

Unlike academic IT researchers, the cultural sector does not have access to independent, non-commercial bandwidth. The only way to earn money with streaming media is to install banner and pop-up ads, ask for donations or require users to pay for content. Broadband is becoming available to a steadily growing (yet relatively stagnant) audience.[15] However, large backbone providers such as KPNQuest have gone bankrupt, partly because the content industry will not start streaming before "digital rights management" and tougher copyright laws are in place. Bandwidth prices might not fall until decentralized peer-to-peer networks have been tamed.[16] The overcapacity of bandwidth around 2000 was caused by a shortage of customers and content. Fights between telcos over last-mile access to households only made matters worse. Despite decent penetration of ADSL/broadband and cable, the streaming-media industry is still in its infancy. It might take years, even a decade, despite urgent calls from the technology sector for a new "killer app" that would create a new wave of global demand for IT products and drag everyone out of the 2001–03 economic malaise. Digital rights fees imposed in 2002 in the USA resulted in the closure of a number of online radio stations. While broadband users in the US doubled in 2001–02, the overall number of Internet users leveled off for the first time.[17] Online payment systems for (music) royalties might be another long-term solution. However, such a distributed system might not work unless it is a grassroots initiative. Standards pushed by the (US) media entertainment industry will most certainly face resistance from young consumers.

Online streaming, accessible via MediaPlayer, RealPlayer and other applications, is different from MP3 files that can be downloaded and then played offline. In response to the inherent limitations of the medium, streaming-media producers developed an ambivalent attitude towards high tech and the overly optimistic forecasts of telecoms. While the roll-out of fiber optics was welcomed, the daily online reality lagged behind the television advertisements promising frictionless speed. The enemy of the future was technofuturism. The future had become a glittering commodity, a merchandised myth unrelated to actual experiences. In response to ugly, baroque interfaces and obese 3-D files that took a lifetime to download, many independent Internet initiatives shifted to the low-tech ASCII art aesthetics of minimalist green on black. Streaming took an odd position in the bandwidth dilemma.[18] Streaming initiatives needed seamless capacity, but at the same time tried to prove that smarter encryption software would make more efficient use of scarce and expensive bandwidth.

This leaves us with the question as to what Net radio could be in a strategic sense, in the understandable absence of a mass audience. Responding to a post by the Amsterdam Net art critic Josephine Bosma on the Xchange list, Pit Schultz summed up a few "vectors of wishful possibilities":

- connecting old and new media (Net audio connected to real radio);
- random access: producing live and for archive (audio on demand);
- stretched time: geographically dispersed small groups producing from home studios;
- public content: experimental DJ performances making non-profit copyright-free productions;
- global sprawl: representing regional styles and mixing them with global ones;
- soundscapes: deconstruction of the song via remixing, sampling, overdubbing, cutting;
- free press: direct information without censorship, small news channels, talk shows, Net chat.[19]

Within this range of possibilities, archiving was an exciting new option for radio, which so far did not have the content-on-demand option. Once a program aired it was gone, unless taped – vanished into frequency nirvana. The only other possibility was that, in theory, civilizations in neighboring galaxies might pick up the program, and store, archive and properly metatag it. Or you could use a time machine to go back and push the record button. Many radio makers would agree: computer storage combined with streaming media has changed the very nature of radio. What now seems the normal option of looking up a radio program on the website if you missed it on BBC World Service, for example, is in fact a revolution in terms of what radio is all about. Rasa Smite: "Some net radios do serious archiving of live sessions. Some of us have experienced that sometimes there have been more listeners of a recorded 'last session' than during the 'real' live broadcast. But many others don't pay attention to archiving (too boring?). Doubts sometimes appear in between the necessity of archiving and the viewpoint that live shows are more exciting than recordings."[20]

For networks such as Xchange the issue of archiving is closely tied to audience development. By nature online archives are universally available. Sydney-based Net radio artist Zina Kaye explains: "If you missed a live stream you could go to the archive and listen to it for a whole week. The streaming-media database Orang in Berlin offered their services to Xchange members to archive radio shows and audio files, stored under categories chosen by the individual members." The Laudible server in Sydney wrote a piece of code that referenced the Orang database in order to give it a customized interface that displayed Australian and New Zealand content.[21]

Radio on demand had a great future. Now that information could be stored and spread all over the Net, the issue was how listeners could find content they liked. One did not easily find live netcasts through search engines or global portals. Announcements on lists and websites worked but reached a limited audience. The virtue of decentralization was also the problem. How could content be grouped in an archive, accessible through a Web portal, using a central interface, without any claim of ownership and control? The fact that files remained on their own servers, accessed via links, made databases unreliable in the long run, as URLs changed. As time passed, the Xchange list started to specialize in announcements of live webcasts, instead of theoretical debates about Net radio. The list developed slowly according to the users' needs. Many were looking for a place to announce their webcasts or get pointers to others' sessions. As an online "radio guide," the Xchange list was used by hundreds of streaming initiatives and events.

Meetings and Webcasts

Like other list-based networks, Xchange grew in a short amount of time through a series of meetings and collective netcasts where members met in real life. Net Radio Days in Berlin in June 1998 was an exciting early event of the newly formed network, directly followed by the Art Servers Unlimited gathering of independent Internet art initiatives in London in July 1998.[22] In the same month, there were live webcasts from the Polar Circuit workshop in Tornio, Finland. Perhaps the largest and longest Xchange project happened in September 1998, when around 20 members gathered in Linz, Austria, and performed *Open-X*, a live 56-hour webcast. The "webjam" included a long list of remote participants.[23] In November 1998, members gathered in Riga for the Xchange Unlimited Festival.[24] The next meeting took place in March 1999 during the third Next Five Minutes Festival in Amsterdam, with a special section devoted to streaming media.

The biggest festival/conference organized by and for the Xchange network was the Net.Congestion event in October 2000, sort of a micro-version of the Next Five Minutes tactical media festival, organized by (approximately) the same Amsterdam crew.[25] Panels included "The Network Is the Narrative," "Bandwidth Aesthetics," "The Hybrid Media Show," "Target.Audience=0," "Web Documentaries," "Tactical Streams," "Protocols and Alternatives," "The Art of Making Money" and "The Doom Scenario" (about congestion and the impact of streaming on Internet infrastructure). The festival statement struggled with the notion of the electronic avant-garde, the community having lost its grip on the medium it was affecting to direct. The contrast between the 80 million copies of RealPlayer in circulation by 2000 and the quasi-voluntary isolation of streaming artists was growing by the day. Why hadn't Xchange grown at a similar pace? Why had streaming remained such an unknown phenomenon, even among new-media artists? As a solution to this discontent, a "visionary scenario" was offered in which the artist would be a "toolmaker, directly effecting the production and distribution of streaming media."[26]

What was being cast? Only a minority of streaming initiatives labeled their content explicitly by genre: techno, rap, reggae, drum 'n' bass or industrial. More commonly Xchange streams 'map' ambient environments rather than transmitting messages. Unlike the star DJs familiar from clubs, regular radio stations and recording labels, most streaming DJs are low-profile or anonymous. The dominant presentation form is the live mix fusing music, spoken word and sound.[27] MP3 files or streams from the Net are often used. In Xchange's own streaming sessions every Tuesday, Raitis Smits explains, "Everyone can join with his or her RealAudio live stream.

The simplest way is to mix your sound source with another. Each of the participants is doing one part of the live session (for example, one is streaming voice, another background music)."[28] On an IRC chat channel running in parallel, participants exchange experiences and announce what's coming up.[29] A technical complication is the 5- to 10-second delay of each stream; this demands a sense of discipline and anticipation from participants.

Playing with Loops

Raitis Smits describes the "loop" as another technique that uses delay. You take a stream, re-encode it and send it to the next participant; the sound goes round and round, creating multiple layers. Eventually the stream turns into noise.[30] Another frequently used technique is sampling. Daniel Molnar: "Our generation grew up with information overflow; that's why we are into sampling. I'm just trying to sample the world, I ain't trying to synthesize any part of it, I'm just stealing the interesting pieces and putting them together."[31] These are the techniques used during the live sessions. The webjams' main difference from previous sampling practices and radio broadcasts is this collaborative, interactive aspect. The offline craft of sampling, often done in solitude at night, can now be done in a networked context. Software and critical discourse are also important elements, but the actual streaming between servers should be regarded as the essence of streaming art.

In 1998 the Ozone group in Riga started a series of "mobility" experiments to explore how streaming could escape the stasis of the PC-cum-radio station glued to the desk. The Riga group tested the minimum bandwidth and equipment needed for streaming. A mobile streaming studio was set up – RealServer 5 on a laptop. It was used at Net radio Days for encoding and running the server using a dual ISDN Internet connection. They did live streams from clubs, encoding via telephone line with a 28.8 Kbps modem.[32]

Later versions of the encoding software were unsuccessful at streaming through phone lines; they often produced noise. Obviously the software was made for higher bandwidth and could no longer compress audio for phone lines and 28.8 modems. Ozone also did a transmission from a train between Riga and Ventspils as a part of the Soros Contemporary Arts exhibition *Ventspils Tranzit Terminal*. Rasa: "We didn't try to encode signal via mobile phone (it had too narrow bandwidth, around 9 Kbps). Instead we used mobiles to transmit audio signals (sound, talk, music) from the train to the Ozone studio in E-lab in Riga, where it was received by another mobile phone. There it got encoded into RealAudio signal for further distribution on the Internet."[33]

Not all initiatives were minuscule by default. The choice of remaining invisible was open to every group and individual. Fashionable underground music genres such as techno, hip-hop, jungle and drum 'n' bass immediately drew online crowds, as did already established radio stations. By late 1997, the mailing list of the London streaming site Interface (started in January that year) had 1,400 members and reported 3 million hits on its site, a considerable number at the time, most coming from the club scene. When Josephine Bosma said only institutions had enough bandwidth to listen to Net radio, Interface member Eezee answered, "We at Interface have an average of 10,000 to 12,000 listeners on a daily basis now."[34] In contrast, mostly state-funded electronic "art" music usually attracted small, fairly specialized highbrow audiences. A third category, beyond the pop/avant-garde opposition, were the autonomous audio-nauts, webcasting in the great digital nirvana free of any consciousness of an online Other. All three models were to be found in the independent streaming scene: commercial pop culture, experimental sound art and autonomous "sovereign" webcasters.

Narrowcasts and Archives

The explicit aim of the Xchange participants was to set up temporary streaming exchanges, not to rebroadcast radio content. This contrasts with most broadcasting officials' belief that streaming was an ideal supplement to the conventional distribution channels of radio, recorded music, television and film. Remarkably absent on Xchange is the usual debate around commercialism, the clash between the not-so-secret aspirations of some to become big versus the determination of others to stay small, to avoid selling out. Japanese media theorist and experimental "mini FM" radio producer Tetsuo Kogawa wrote: "The point is not the stronger power of the transmitter. As long as it is alternative (later + native), it must be different from usual broadcasting. Forgetting 'broad'-casting, we insist on 'narrow'-casting. In my understanding, the more creative or positive function of the Web is not 'casting' but <weaving>. Unfortunately, the Internet is used as a new type of casting, though."[35]

The community aspect of Xchange remained small and pragmatic. In this context, Tetsuo Kogawa's one-watt transmitter could be seen as a good example of the Xchange approach. He wrote: "The coverage is proper for a community within walking distance and the technique is cheap and easy. In my workshop I built a set within an hour. In my workshop, I built a transmitter, showed something of radio art and invited an audience to the process: radio party. More aggressively than in Europe, the community culture in Japan has been destroyed. That's why we have few community radio stations in Japan. But this situation might be good for Web radio because the 'listeners' are separated and have no physical/geographical 'community' anymore. The Web may [reunite] them in cyberspace at least for the time that Web radio works."[36] The one-watt metaphor can easily be transported into new media. What makes the Net unique is not its ability to become one big metamarket but the potential for millions of exchange nodes to grow, an aspect that has yet to be fully understood.

Localization

Canada's Radio 90 is a good example of "localization" of net radio. It is a local station with an easy-to-use public streaming interface. UK Net artist and activist Heath Bunting founded the project. Zina Kaye explained, "Heath wrote a Web-based scheduler that steers the content of Radio 90. Xchange members would input the time of their shows and they would be heard via a one-watt transmitter, installed at the Banff Center for the Arts in Canada. The people of Banff no longer needed to have a computer in order to access streams that typically had no name or brand or advertising. No doubt the Radio 90 scheduler gave streaming-media initiatives more listeners."[37] Similarly, an FM transmitter installed at the Society for Old and New Media in Amsterdam rebroadcast Net radio streams, including B92's signal when the station was taken off the air in April–May 1999, to the Nieuwmarkt district on an irregular basis.

Another aspect of Xchange-style streaming culture is the link with "real" space, in most cases clubs. The Extended Life Radio project from Berlin emphasizes the link with locality. "Physical space is most important for us, and it doesn't need to be connected to the Net. The connection via Internet of two or more physical spaces gives the possibility to synchronize those spaces at least partly and for a certain time. It's an image, located in real time and real space, for and about information, experience, network, and communication. Translation. Inside and outside. Crossing and melting borders. For any activity in public space it's very important to create a certain atmosphere, an 'interface' which reflects what it is about. It's about this translation of (in this case) sound, which comes out of a machine without any body or human traces, into something you can experience which creates an atmosphere."[38]

Klubradio, also in Berlin, is based on the idea of users worldwide tapping into groovy underground clubs and listening to live DJs. With a good connection and a bit of luck users could, for instance, plug the stream into an ordinary amplifier and have their own Berlin techno party. This is all done at little or no cost, without complicated satellite connections or the interference of events agencies or telecoms or record companies.

Xchange is one of many "adagio" networks. Instead of picking up speed riding on techno storms, fired up by innovation and commerce, they place emphasis on slowly performed works that stretch time and space. The unknown and yet-to-be-defined "otherness" of streaming technology implies an outsider position. "Cyberspace is our land," as the slogan of Frankfurt-based webcasting artist group Station Rose goes. Analogous to "off-the-radar" free radio and club mixes that loop for hours and hours, streaming events reach out into the vast darkness of cyberspace. The streams promise to open up other dimensions of time and consciousness. Not interested in the size and mood of its audience, streaming media focuses on maximum interactivity among equals.

The different aspects of streaming listed here spring from technological circumstances: lack of bandwidth combined with a chaos of standards. Net casters have learned to redefine these limitations as virtues. Make no mistake; every streaming artist would love to operate in a situation of bandwidth abundance. Outside the corporate and academic IT worlds, scarcity rules. It is next to impossible to tell whether low tech is a passionate belief system or a necessity. Instead of a culture of complaint, there have been attempts to utilize streaming media's "micro" status in the best possible ways. Centralized experiments such as Web TV have so far failed. Berlin-based activist/artist Micz Flor has worked on Net radio projects in the UK, Central and Eastern Europe and Asia. He explains: "We are all still waiting for the new front end, the browser of the next generation, where all these media outlets come together at the screen and speakers and what else of the user, listener, or whatever you would want to call the next generation receiver. The ideal client 'solution' is not there yet. And that's a good thing. So far, not even multinational lobbies such as Microsoft or AOL managed to prune the Internet into the shape they would dream of. In fact, every attempt to shape the multitude of formats, players and codecs has only put strength to alternative solutions. Peer-to-peer distribution channels such as Gnutella are one example; alternative audio video formats such as Ogg or DivX are another."[39]

In the end it was all about playing with the limits of new technologies. Lack of bandwidth was countered with an abundance of imagination. Still, some of the borders were very real. In some instances streaming could become unpleasantly expensive. Matthew Smith, working for the Ars Electronica Center and the Austrian broadcaster ORF in 1998, discussed the cost of streaming and argued for the use of existing media. He wrote to the Xchange list: "If you want to find 'new' ways of providing content in a setting such as the Internet, it is not very efficient to clog up the net with high-bandwidth audio. The logistics of the net are not made for it, and who can really afford the necessary bandwidth to be able to serve 1,000 high-quality RealAudio streams, even after shelling out $5,000 for server software and about the same amount for a server. I don't believe that anything in that price class is for free, meaning distribution – to place your content on a setup like that will eventually cost the same as buying time on a 'classic' broadcast medium."[40]

Pit Schultz gave another example. "Our Klubradio server used about 1.5 terabytes over May 2002 and that is not even much compared to large streaming sites such as live365. A regular provider would ask about 4,000 Euro a month for this type of streaming traffic. Who is willing to pay that kind of money? Canalweb, our provider in Paris, closed down, like the other ones we previously used. After Canalweb disappeared we went down from 4,000 to 1,000 visitors a day. Our server capacity shrank from 2,000 concurrent users to 25."[41]

Xchange initiatives often used free demo versions of the RealAudio software that had a limited capacity (well under 1,000 streams) and an expiration date. Others got software donated by the Real Corporation itself. The potentially high bills of Internet access providers had an effect too. Without sponsorship and voluntary limits to capacity, streaming networks such as Xchange could not have flourished. Necessarily, experimentation would have made way for dotcom business models. As this did not happen because of self-imposed limits, Xchange partners still exist, whereas most dotcoms do not. In particular, those who were betting on a possible Web TV revolution have been badly burnt.

One of the problems Xchange successfully tackled was the question of how to find Net radio streams without a centralized portal.[42] The Xchange homepage offered links. Heath Bunting of the Radio 90 project in Banff, Canada, came up with a program schedule. Radioqualia (Adelaide, Australia) developed a similar idea, a global mini FM network, which it called Frequency Clock. The founders explained their project on the Xchange list: "A geographically dispersed independent network of Net radio stations, broadcasting on autonomously owned FM transmitters, could strengthen challenges to centralized institutions that are predominantly associated with FM radio, encouraging a rethinking of existing broadcast paradigms, and the incorporation of more open systems for determining content. In such models there is space to develop radically open-ended systems of content management, allowing for abatement of centralized program administration."[43] Do-it-yourself programming was seen as an effective answer to the "portalization" of the Web.

In November 2002 Radioqualia, which had moved from Adelaide to Amsterdam and London, released the 1.0 version of its Frequency Clock Free Media System. It is a shared resource for building streaming channels, open source software with a program database, a timetabling system and a customized streaming-media player. In the age of broadband and cable modems the "always on" mode is an important feature for streaming media. Users can schedule audio or video programs from the database in specific time slots, creating a continuous and ongoing channel, or alternatively, a channel that broadcasts only at special times. Producers can also instruct the timetabling system to play default audio or video when a time slot has nothing scheduled. This means audiences will always have something to see or hear.[44]

The Network Is Not the Organization

On November 10, 1999, at the height of dotcom mania, Adam Hyde and Zina Kaye posted a proposal to the list to upgrade the Xchange website to a dynamic portal. "Right now, we are at a stage where as a group we have the advantage, because we have been around for a long time and have a good relationship with each other. But the entertainment industry is catching up with us, and we will lose our lead and maybe our unique identity if we don't quickly distinguish ourselves from other mainstream streaming portal websites."[45] Three years after Xchange's founding, the Riga-based E-lab was still the only one really taking care of its activities. The website had not changed much and was nothing more than a list of links to the participating Net radio sites.

This proposal came at a time when projects such as the Frequency Clock, irational.org's World Service, Radio Internationale Stadt and TM Selector began to offer streaming radio guides, each in its own way. Riga, however, lacked the resources to bring the network to another level and turn the website into a lively hub. It proved hard, if not impossible, for a network with modest affinity among its participants to set up a decentralized working group to delegate technical and content-related tasks. The issue here was the true limits of non-profit and e-mail-based networks. Lacking formal organization, neither an NGO nor a dotcom, Xchange seemed to get stuck at the mailing list level. Nonetheless, a few months later, xchange.x-i.net was launched, but the portal initiative never really took off.[46] Xchange remained an announcement list with occasional short dialogues.[47]

Xchange chose not to formalize the network and turn it into an NGO or lobby group. Instead individual members moved their focus towards collective development of software, the material the Net is made of. According to Adam Hyde (Radioqualia), there were Jaromil (dyne.org), August Black (Kunstradio), Thomax Kaulmann (RIS, OVA, OMA), Pit Schultz (Bootlab), Micz Flor (LowLive), Drazen Pantic (Open Source Streaming Alliance), Alexander Baratsits (Radio Fro) and Heath Bunting (World Service); all were heavily interested in streaming software, as either developers, researchers, organizers or commentators.[48] The number of actual software developers within Xchange has so far remained relatively small. Streaming is not a traditional area for hackers and geeks – the proprietary nature of (mainly Real) software may be one reason. A cultural explanation could be the fact that music and video can only be dealt with on a higher application level. It boils down to the central question: why would you want to use the Net to rebroadcast old-media material? Streaming, therefore, was left to new-media artists plus some non-tech cultural types (read: those who remain on the easy-to-use desktop level and do not produce code). This could explain why there has been such a delay in the development of open source streaming-media software, compared to, for instance, the Linux operating system and the Apache server software.

Others involved in Xchange such as Rachel Baker, Lisa Haskel, Walter van der Cruijsen, Mr. Snow and Superchannel battle the technocracy by training others to use streaming software. Programmer and streaming art project organizer Adam Hyde explains, "These individual networkers within Xchange are very involved in issues surrounding software, these issues may not surface in discourse through the list (it's not a very "threaded' list) but certainly individuals within Xchange do their own work individually or collaboratively and then post the results."[49]

The politics of proprietary code as applied to streaming (e.g. proprietary codecs) is a well-known issue within Xchange but is not a focus for debate. Some members post news articles or links about the topic but it does not turn into a thread. Adam Hyde: "I think this is a very embryonic debate everywhere. The whole MP3 phenomenon as highlighted by Napster did not settle into debates on how the Frauenhofer Institute and Thompson (who own the MP3 standard) could close down anyone using an unlicensed MP3 algorithm; instead the hot ticket was how wonderful peer-to-peer technologies are. Proprietary media technologies (MP4/Ogg Vorbis/DivX) are just about to heat up and then it will be interesting to see if this groundswell will prompt Xchange into more political discourse."[50] After the introduction of Microsoft's MediaPlayer, Real gradually lost ground, though not as severe as the demise of Netscape in the face of the near-monopoly of Microsoft Explorer. Apple's QuickTime (mainly installed on Apple's own machines) is a viable third player.[51] The role of open source players is so far almost zero.[52]

Open-Source Streaming

In mid-2001 the Open Streaming Alliance (OSA) was announced. If Xchange had failed to set up a common portal/weblog or proper NGO, perhaps it could at least contribute to streaming software and test alternative network architectures. This shift in emphasis from collaborative webcasting towards software, driven by initiatives such as Radioqualia, had become visible during the Net.Congestion conference in Amsterdam in October 2000. In an e-mail Drazen Pantic mentioned scalability of capacity and platform independence as the two main aims of the alliance. From the beginning the proprietary nature of Real software had been a problem. There was little to say about the rise of Microsoft's MediaPlayer. The monopolistic marketing policies of Bill Gates were well known. But what about alleged alternatives such as Real and QuickTime? By 2000, open-source streaming software started to become available but wasn't widely used. Although Linux had gained a strong position in the server sector, desktop open-source software had not (yet) managed to reach the average consumer – not even avant-garde early-adopter Xchange artists. OSA planned to enable free and open-source tools for encoding and serving QuickTime, Real Media and Mbone streams, producing streaming content in one run, through just one encoding process, which obviously would save time, equipment and resources. Drazen Pantic: "Corporate software vendors try to monopolize streaming-media standards, using proprietary and closed code for encoders, players and servers. RealMedia, for example, started its operation with a noble idea to help independent broadcasters, but in the course of corporate battle – mostly with Microsoft – they sealed their code and became an opponent of creativity and innovation themselves. Closed code, and especially proprietary codecs, alienate content from the producers and enable control over distribution."[53]

Simultaneously, progress was made on the archiving front. With the motto "You don't have to know everything, you just have to know the reference," Berlin-based Orang Orang (Thomax Kaulmann and Frank Kunkel) launched its Open Meta Archive software. This open-source "context management system" was able to "categorize and publish rich media documents including text, photo, audio and video in RealMedia, QuickTime and MP3." Finally a variety of multimedia content could be stored on one database.[54] The future of community networks would be "hardwired" or, to be more precise, "softcoded" in software that would define decentralized (peer-to-peer) network architecture. The openness of software and the ability to use a variety of standards was going to be decisive.

Despite its low profile, the Xchange network could not escape the sea change in the general atmosphere. The Net was no longer a cozy family but a big and most of all anonymous place. In December 2001 the entire Orang Orang multimedia archive, used by many Xchange members to store their streaming files, was deleted by a hacker after several harmful intrusions. "There is nothing like 100% security. Sadly, this digital vandalism hits a site which always supported a community of free exchange and free access."[55] According to Pit Schultz, the result of such hacks is that "small providers or self-run co-locations, public access sites of universities and libraries move from a policy of the free digital commons to a strategy of paranoid enclosure, while the security experts and service industry prospers. In their midst, former hackers who still perform their sport like innocent boy scouts praised by the net culture, discourse as role models."[56] The attack was a rude wake-up call for a "minor" online community that for five years had successfully operated in the shadow of turbulent Internet events.

Xchange and Riga

Informal, decentralized networks such as Xchange may be indifferent to commercial interests, yet at the same time they are unable to represent the interests of their members in, for instance, negotiations about storage capacity, production of broadband content and financing of Internet traffic. Xchange suffered from the traditional stereotype of "organization" being "bad" because of the fear it results in bureaucracy and abuse of power. In this case, the lack of organization stalled the network. There was no moderation group to manage the direction of the list. Because of total reliance on contributions by individual members, the Xchange list eventually entered a state of regression (which pragmatists are perfectly happy with). The lack of organization resulted in the implicit expectation that "Riga" would take care of everything. But resources in Riga were scarce. Although Xchange had no official legal status, it was unofficially owned by E-lab. If Riga took no initiatives to improve the site or the lists, no one else did either. As a result, much like the Spectre list (the successor to Syndicate), Xchange ended up as a low-volume announcement list, with few personal messages, let alone debates.

The atmosphere on the list had not always been that friendly, and was slightly hostile at times. The "coziness" of assembling in cyberspace was missing here. Members had their common interests, but their moods were not always in sync. Postings were often written in a peculiar, impersonal style. By 1998 everyone knew all too well what the pitfalls of a list community were. The short summer of the Internet was over. This was the age of infowar and spam, of hacktivism and trolls. There was hardly any room left for naïveté. In October 1998 organizer Rasa posted a message to Xchange reflecting the growing unease. "There is confusion about what exactly we were/still are looking for. We are complaining and blaming and provoking each other or whatever (really funny, isn't it). We are dreaming about open spaces, but are we paying attention enough to the importance of personal relationships – understanding and respecting each other?"[57] As a response to growing tensions and the lack of real outcomes beyond limited collaborations, the Riga group began to lose interest in the list and focus on badly needed improvements to its own situation, both in terms of space and resources.

Over the years the E-lab group had been slowly shifting its Net radio focus towards the broader issues of "acoustic spaces." Looking back, Rasa Smite says she would no longer limit Net radio to just streaming media. According to her Net radio first of all means networked audio communications – and that is potentially an infinite field. Rasa: "Internet radio can, for instance, provide access to publicly inaccessible technologies such as secret military objects, or follow developments in the field of satellite networks. One could think about acoustic GPS space or combine wired and wireless, global and insular technologies."[58]

Riga shifted its attention to other projects that were close to Internet radio. I will mention two of them because they illustrate how networks try to escape impasses they have little control over. Acoustic Space Lab was a project initiated by E-lab aimed at obtaining new experiences beyond the usual Xchange webcasts, looking at what other shapes a streaming network could take.[59] It took place in August 2001 at the Irbene Radio Telescope in the Latvian forest, utilizing a former Soviet antenna with a diameter of 32 meters. It was a cooperation between scientists from VIRAC (Ventspils International Radio Astronomy Center) and an international team of 30 sound artists, net and community radio activists and radio amateurs, who experimented with the antenna, recording sounds and data from planetary observations, communication satellites and the surrounding environment.[60]

There was also the issue of work space. Since 1998 there had been talk of a center for digital culture in Riga. So far E-Lab had undertaken all its activities from a tiny attic room surrounded by artists' studios, in a gray government building housing a variety of cultural institutions. The view over the Daugava river was magnificent, but there was hardly adequate work space for the expanding group and the ever-growing number of PCs. Besides local initiatives, the Riga group had quickly focused on building links within the Baltic/Scandinavian region. In May 2000, the Riga Center for New Media Culture RIXC was founded.[61] The media space was to be located in the former sculpture studio, which needed serious renovation. In March 2002, an international architects' workshop met to develop conceptual guidelines for the design of RIXC.

Beyond Remediation

After presenting this version of the history of the Xchange network, I would like to bring together some elements of an independent streaming network philosophy. If the Internet was going be something truly new, as all the visionaries claimed, then streaming media would be a prime example of how to supersede the old, one-to-many model of broadcasting media. From their infancy, the Net radio initiatives featured here have tried to prove that decentralized networks are not just a weird idea but a viable practice. The hyped-up dotcom cycle, from startup to sellout and bankruptcy, was not inevitable. The "clouds" of webcasters and online audio archives took up the challenge of proving that Marshall McLuhan and contemporary "remediation" theorists such as Bolter and Grusin were not always right.[62] According to Bolter and Grusin, "remediation is a defining characteristic of the new digital media." (p.45) "Each act of mediation depends on other forms of mediation. Media are continually commenting on, reproducing and replacing each other, and this process is integral to media. Media need each other in order to function as media at all." (p.55)

Bolter and Grusin's remediation concept is common sense within media theory. Remediation may be the default option, but at least temporarily, in the shadow of corporate capitalism, it should be possible to unfold other practices – that is the claim critical Internet culture is making. McLuhan's law, which holds that the content of a new medium is by definition sourced from previous media, is not false and can easily become a self-fulfilling prophecy. But new media open up possibilities for other forms of narration and aesthetics. They are not just tools to tell the same old story over and over again. It is up to new-media practitioners to seize the opportunities and discover the language of new media, liberated from depressing laws of techno-determinism. If content and interfaces are merely special effects of hardware and software, then why bother in the first place?

Rebroadcasting existing audio, be it live or prerecorded, is not what (independent) streaming is primarily about. And, contrary to Bolter and Grusin's statement, streaming-media networks do not express "our desire for immediacy" (p. 35). They embody the desire to network, to link and stream. Long-term collaborations are much more characteristic than celebrations of the short-lived "live" effect. Communication does not need to be "real." In the post-hype period the aim of streaming networks such as Xchange is not necessarily higher image resolution or better sound quality. The bandwidth is not available to such civil networks anyway. But there is a general issue here, beyond the bull and bear market for telecom stocks. Networks in general do not attempt to gain higher levels of "reality" (in the sense of immediacy), as Bolter and Grusin claim. The genuine wish for faster machines and connections should not be confused with the desire for "more reality." The issue, rather, is: does the technology (in this case streaming software) give users access to information and each other? What fuels the imagination? Streaming media explore new network conditions and do not seek to rebuild the old audiovisual world into the virtual. Bolter and Grusin limit new media to the MP3 level of non-interactive customers interested solely in downloading their favorite "remediated" Metallica songs (soon available in Dolby quality), uninterested in contributing to the peer-to-peer networks they use.

Former B92 sysadmin Drazen Pantic reads the remediation issue as a misunderstanding. "Conceptually, streaming media is rarely understood as media per se, but instead as an extension or replacement of the corresponding classical media. So streaming video is taken as poor man's TV, while streaming audio for a while was considered as a replacement for radio. Neither of those either/or alternatives are actually realistic – both streaming video and audio are different media than their corresponding counterparts, with their own codes and structural rules. But this misconception has caused people to expect easy plug-and-play delivery and seamless broadcast quality delivery through ordinary telephone lines."[63]

In "Minima Memoranda," a short but rich collection of aphorisms, Tetsuo Kogawa investigates possible meanings of the streaming concept. Instead of using the obvious reference to water and nature (panta rhei), Kogawa investigates the line metaphor in a phenomenological manner. "Lines relate to binding, weaving and streaming. They can bind audiences into a tightly integrated "network," a marionette-like circuit. However, lines are not always tight but loose. Loose lines weave webs. In the weaving-weaved Web, the signal does not cast itself but streams by itself. Casting is a one-way process while streaming is interactive: streaming in and back."[64] Streaming resists remediation by its very definition. We can only speak of streaming media where there are open feedback channels.

Minor Media

Even though links have been made between Xchange as a "minor medium" and Deleuze and Guattari's concept of "minor literature,"[65] some would hate to see their network explicitly linked to the Parisian philosophers. Whereas some find useful concepts in the works of Deleuze and Guattari, others detest the academic fashion and theory hype that surround worn-out labels such as "rhizome." That's the danger when theory operates within the zone of popular (media) culture. Despite such reservations, I will look into the minor media notion as part of my search for independent streaming-media concepts. It was the German theorist and curator Andreas Broeckmann who placed this concept in the new-media context. Minor literature, he wrote, is a "literature of a minority that makes use of a major language, a literature which deterritorializes that language and interconnects meanings of the most disparate levels, inseparably mixing and implicating poetic, psychological, social and political issues with each other."[66] Strategies of "being minor" are intensification, refunctionalization, estrangement and transgression. In the context of media art, for Broeckmann "becoming media" is "a strategy of turning major technologies into minor machines."[67]

However, the usefulness of such statements within down-to-earth circles like Xchange remains more undiscussed than disputed. Whereas pragmatists hate to see such academism overruling actual practices, others see a limited role for theory as one of many alternative ways of storytelling. But what does it mean, in terms of social capital, to label your network project "rhizome"? Are "minor media" really proud to see themselves as such, despite the positive-productive meaning Deleuze and Guattari give to the term? Who wants to be minor? The strategy of independence may be a choice, but techno-cultural networks often do strive for more power and resources. The term "heterogeneous practices" sounds less pedantic. There is a wide consensus that networks such as Xchange are, in principle, based on mutual respect for difference, grown out of a process of "resingularization" to become ever more different.[68] Creating a nice, safe new-media ghetto can mean a one-way street; a situation in which growth and transformation are no longer options. If size doesn't matter, there should be no difference between becoming major and minor.

Nonetheless, in the case of Xchange, media freedom was created by the lucky circumstance that the mainstream ignored what was happening. If, for instance, there was a parallel between radio in the 1920s and stream-ing media in the 1990s, was the eventual outcome (state-sponsored cor-porate domination) likely to be the same? No, there was no such defeat. This is the point at which historical parallels and history as such could backfire on those who act. Networks were sparks of change. They either ignited processes or remained sparks in the dark. Though the streamers had little illusions about their actual power, the utopian promise was alive and well. Dancing nodes like Xchange seemed possible. Another pos-sible world was embodied in software and a lively decentralized network practice, which were supposed to spread like cultural viruses. If nothing worked out, at least the participants were having a good time, while turn-ing their backs on the system inside a self-created "temporary autonomous zone."[69] Such zones can be big, can fill up the universe – at least for a day.

The "minor" practices of Xchange questioned the eternal recurrence of the same (content). The cynical path from underground outlaw via fash-ion to sellout and mainstream market player could be avoided. While technology was a precondition for independent streaming networks, it did not dictate the form that "the social" would take. The technology was challenged not to determine the streaming politics and aesthetics. The content of new media is not by definition yesterday's papers. Both the content and form of new media can be radically different from those of previous media as long as network participants are aware of media laws and willing to negate and transcend them. This may not sound revolu-tionary but if a growing network of passionate media and art producers take the newness of digital media seriously, a lot can happen.

According to Erik Davis, DJ and author of *TechGnosis,* Internet radio is not part of the regulated and commodified spectrum. Comparable in this respect to early radio, it is a "space of openness, of indetermination, of the effects of the unknown."[70] Internet radio cannot be merely radio received via the Internet. Rather than emphasizing the convergence of media, for developers' communities it is more interesting to search for the radical and unconditional "autopoiesis" of new media. In this case: what is the unique quality of streaming and how can the self-referential dynamics be strengthened? How can the proclaimed autonomy of cyber-space be defended against the vested interests of film, radio, television and the recording industry?

For the Xchange network and numerous other streaming-media initiatives (including commercial ones) the proclaimed victory over old media comes at a price of voluntary marginalization. The media industry has been betting on a combination of technological convergence and syndication of content run by conglomerates. The response to this concentration of power in a few hands has been radical fragmentation. "Faced with the ubiquity of a zillion portals, channels, live-streams and file formats all screaming for attention, what's a net audio selector to do? Go niche. Go *überniche*."[71] Instead of fighting the mainstream or claiming territory within established channels using "pop" strategies, a multitude of parallel worlds were created.

The study under debate here touches the very essence of new media: its claim to be different from previous communication tools. Streaming media have the technical potential to question the iron necessity of the return of the "one-to-many" broadcasting model because everyone who is interested can install a streaming server and start webcasting. This ability to both stream out and receive streams has the potential to fragment the "mass" audience into dispersed user/producer groups. The technical peer-to-peer approach (as opposed to the centralized client-server model) may be obvious for some, but its consequences are far-reaching. In contrast to broadcasting, we may define streaming media as channels that make audio and visual material available on the Internet. That may sound pretty dry and straightforward.

With the porn industry as its avant-garde, state and commercial radio and television almost immediately started to dominate streaming media with their repackaged content. During dotcom mania, as some companies tried to define "Web-specific content," many jobs were lost and many internal Internet departments closed or lost staff after the dotcom bust. Remediation of existing material is a threat to independent streaming cultures, as it reduces the new medium to a secondary rebroadcaster. It is therefore of strategic importance to further investigate streaming models that go beyond repackaging others' content. This could also imply a critique of existing peer-to-peer networks, as their users hardly create and upload any of their own material and mainly download mainstream content.

Only a limited number of sites webcast live from clubs or events. The depressing reality is that nearly all mainstream content remains one-to-many rebroadcasted material. Xchange's collaborative netcasting techniques casting remain unknown, even to those in the field. The additional function of streaming technologies for mainstream media organizations, then, would be the ability to access material after its original broadcast (the on-demand feature). The value of streaming for existing media organizations is found in the storage and retrieval capacity of the Internet, and not so much in the "live" aspect. Independent streaming, on the other hand, stresses the importance of networked webcasting and, most notably, does not retransmit already existing signals. These initiatives provide the Net with new, as yet unknown content and forms of subjectivity. Becoming minor, in this context, can be described as the already mentioned strategy of "turning major technologies into minor machines."[72] Against the mass media, a heterogeneous network of networks could flourish. This is not mere theory. The listener-as-producer, submerged in immersive space, designing a unique, personal mix of up- and downstream data. Audiospace theorist Erik Davis: "Electro-acoustic spaces aren't simply a genre of music or a backdrop of good VR – they are interfaces with the machine."[73]

No More Audiences

In his text "Media without an Audience," Dutch media theorist Eric Kluitenberg, organizer of the Net.Congestion streaming-media festival, argues that the networked environment should be seen as a social space: "The active sender and the passive audience/receiver have been replaced by a multitude of unguided transmissions that lack a designated receiver."[74] Beyond broadcast hegemony, he traces the emergence of "intimate media," which have a high degree of feedback. Media without an audience were first described in a 1992 text about "sovereign media" written by the Adilkno group (of which I am a member).[75] Eric Kluitenberg further developed the idea, as did Joanne Richardson. Kluitenberg makes historical references to Bertolt Brecht's 1932 radio theory[76] and George Bataille's text "The Accursed Share," in which Bataille writes: "Life beyond utility is the domain of sovereignty."[77] According to Eric Kluitenberg sovereign media should be understood as media beyond use. "They should not be understood as 'useless' but rather as 'without use.' Sovereign media have emancipated themselves from the demands of functionality or usefulness to exist in their own right."[78] Erik Kluitenberg lists the Xchange network several times as an example of sovereign or intimate media.

The concept of sovereign media shows similarities with Andreas Broeckmann's reading of Deleuze and Guattari's idea of minor literature. Both emphasize the productive aspect of mediation. The difference, however, is that sovereign media no longer feel obligated to make references to the mainstream "majority." The act of declaring sovereignty over one's own mediacasting leaves behind dialectical polarities such as big/small, major/minor, broad/narrow, alternative/mainstream, and pop/elite. Sovereign media have long stated their declaration of independence and are not even indirectly focused on the "average user," "normal people" or "the Johnsons." The only function of mass media is to produce raw material, data garbage that sovereign media producers then freely use and reinterpret in their cut-ups. Remixing is not remediation. Mixes and cut-ups create entirely new art works and cannot be reduced to the nature of this or that source material. During the making of a mix there are no attempts to reach the higher plane of "immediacy." Instead of transplanting content from one platform to the next, sovereign media are getting serious about deconstruction. All meaning, all images and sounds, must be taken apart. Sovereign media no longer need the support or solidarity of the public (which the minority concept still appeals to). They have emancipated themselves from any potential imaginary audience. Live Internet radio often has few or no listeners. But this in no way bothers the streaming artists. That is true media freedom.

Tetsuo Kogawa speaks in this context of "polymorphous radio" or "polymedia." For him, communication is a "structural coupling." "The separation between transmitter and receiver is merely a political operation. Technologically, there is no separation between them."[79] In the same context, Lev Manovich theorizes about "micro-media," pointing at the growing importance of tiny wearable devices. The terms vary, but the overall direction is the same. If streaming networks are serious about their intention to overcome the broadcast paradigm, they will have to free themselves from the public as a database filled with subjects. Adilkno: "Sovereign media do not approach their audience as a moldable market segment but offer it the 'royal space' the other deserves."[80] Certainly there is a historical connection between the democratization (availability) of media and the miniaturization of technology (portability). It is now time to reflect on the unavoidable trend of becoming micro. Does the proliferation of media technologies imply a solution of the "media question"? Scarcity often leads to speculation. Absence fuels the imagination. Will the universal ubiquity of networked devices foster a diverse climate of digital creativity and discontent, or unleash a culture of indifference?

Towards a Theory of Humble Networks

Unlike the dotcoms with their promises of unlimited market growth, networks such as Xchange have high scalability awareness. "Think Big" was the dominant leitmotif of the cyber age. The liberating spirit of mega was usually associated with the "tiger" economies of southeast Asia (before their 1997 economic meltdown).[81] In *Wired* Bruce Sterling wrote a paean to the "overwhelming urge to be tall." "My beat is Jules Verne's idea of Big, the Prestigious Big – mega projects that exist because they exceed humanity's previous limits and break all the expected scales. Prestige mega projects are not big simply for functional reasons. They are not about the economic bottom line. Mega projects are about the top line – the transcendent, the beautiful, and the sublime. They are built for the purpose of inspiring sheer, heart-thumping awe – not unmixed with lip-gnawing envy from the competition. Mega is a very special conceptual world, a territory of fierce engineering ambition, of madly brash technical self-assertion. Mega is a realm that abolishes the squalid everyday limits of lesser beings."[82]

At the same time Dutch architect Rem Koolhaas made the rounds with slide shows and exhibitions featuring the growth-without-planning in Lagos, Nigeria, and the southern Chinese mega-cities designed overnight with the help of ordinary PCs. For Koolhaas, the "XL" strategy has been a liberating move away from petit-bourgeois politics and its bureaucratic regulatory regimes. The bold bigness of generic cities, their transurbanism, their mass-engineered towers, reflect the urgency of – and desire for – an anonymous mutated modernity.[83] In a swift move the metaphorical bulldozers destroyed the dusty microcosms of decades. The techno-imagination of the New Era was anything but viral. It took a while for the promoters of Big to realize that large-scale projects were solely driven by speculative financial setups. Bigness could easily collapse if financial resources were withdrawn and economic recession set in. In that sense

Koolhaas' XL approach is a product of the roaring nineties, the extraction of value from the post-1989 peace dividend. The gigantism of the Clinton era proved to be a special effect of short-term bubble policies, not a long-term trend. As *The Economist* formulated diplomatically, "the IT industry is becoming less of a growth story and more like a standard cyclical business. Traditionally, vendors have driven most big IT markets. But IT buyers are increasingly reluctant to play this one-sided game."[84] Paradoxically, less growth also leads to fewer players. In a stagnating market the Big becomes even bigger.

Minoritarian practitioners, working within the spirit of Deleuze and Guattari or not, do not seek open confrontations. The humble streamers, passionately tinkering and hard to distract, hide in the shadow of the Big gestures, ignoring the *Zeitgeist*, perhaps secretly hoping that the techno-cultural memes will one day burst out into society. They do not account for their tiny activities to the authorities and their "popular culture." Many never had revolutionary dreams in the first place. After the total disaster of existing socialism, leftist infighting snarled up long marches; it simply wasn't the time to Think Big. It was not a coincidence that the Xchange network was administered from a former Soviet republic. Let's conclude by saying that *petite* networks, cute or not, are here to stay. Time and again, pocket-sized nodes are proving immune to the fast-paced fluctuations of global capitalism.

Streaming Futures

Five years after its founding the Xchange network has found a modest, pragmatic way of operating. Despite the fact that a common Web portal-cum-Net radio scheduler has not yet emerged, collaborations do happen. The network regularly meets and puts out print publications. Pit Schultz (Klubradio, Berlin) stresses that, despite the loose ties, projects have emerged out of the Xchange network that do attract audiences. "I can only talk about the numbers I know. Sites such as Betalounge, Groovetech and Klubradio have thousands of visitors a day, not a gigantic number but certainly more than the average new-media institution with perhaps a 1,000-times-higher budget."[85] No matter how fragile independent streaming networks may be, the Xchange example shows that valuable collaborations are the result, perhaps not visible to the outside world, but so much more sustainable than the defunct dotcoms.

A critical streaming discourse is still in its infancy. Caught between the established 20th-century discourses on radio, (pop) music and sound art, streaming is still off the radar of most critics and curators. This is true even in the new-media arts system itself, with its recently opened centers and annual festivals. University departments and cultural institutions with their own dedicated streaming servers are still a rarity, even though streaming from live events is on an upward trend. System administrators do not like bandwidth-eating streaming servers. Yet the streams are silently streaming. Pit Schultz: "The role of 'sound' is really important, and what that means in a geographically diverse Internet context, is providing a platform for non-textual exchange. There is what one could call the 'Nordic element' in Xchange. Not talking much, but saying a lot. Much of this (invisible, silent) work is done on the local level, in developing nodes, interconnecting them in a loose way. Even during the most active times of Xchange, it would be difficult to describe where the fascination manifests itself – in the in-between, the actuality of the live element, the process of exchange, meetings and relationships."[85]

The broken dreams of Web TV still echo through the Net. Limited by underutilized broadband capacities ("dark fiber"), Xchange is setting out to explore what sound means beyond downloading MP3 files. Their message is a simple but challenging one: streaming is more than radio or television on your computer screen. Like peer-to-peer networks, independent streaming networks put on the table the question of what users have to contribute once they are confronted with the wide range of technical possibilities the Internet has to offer.

The Battle over New-Media Art Education

Experiences and Models

"We will be victorious if we have not forgotten how to learn."
Rosa Luxemburg

This text investigates methodologies of teaching "new media" in the arts and culture context.[1] Since the 1990s numerous schools have started new-media programs. The educators I will feature in this story are based in a variety of institutions, from art academies and design schools to cultural studies programs, literature faculties and media and communications departments. Despite the boom in new-media programs, little has been written about this field. The primary source for this chapter is a series of online interviews with practitioners who run such programs. I sent out early versions of the text to the interviewees so that they had an idea of what others and I had to say, which resulted in an open and collaborative sharing of ideas and experiences.

As "new media" is a system in flux, so are the concepts used to describe what newly established programs teach and investigate. The choice of a central concept, whether digital Bauhaus, new media or technoculture, is a delicate manner. The terms are related to the institutional framing of the program, and the choice will no doubt have repercussions further along the line. The dilemmas may sound futile for outsiders. Where does cultural studies end and digital media start? Why is contemporary arts so hostile to new-media arts? What's the use of an MA in "Internet studies"? Why are the "digital humanities" unaware of today's media theories? The term "new media" seems to be in competition with the rising "cybercultures" discipline. Who cares? some would ask. Why not call the entire field "intermedia"?

Pioneers who start new programs make a personal choice for a particular label. Each concept is a potential autopoietic system-in-the-making that will have to constitute and maintain its own organization. However, the creation of academic disciplines is no longer a secret. Those who know – and follow – the rules will be rewarded. Others will eventually miss out. Every initiative has to have its own mission statement, and market its leading concepts and pedagogy, which makes the field, at first glance, rather confusing. Instead of making a qualitative comparison and judgment, I will treat the labels in a more or less equal fashion, with a general preference for "new media." I find it too early to say that "digital media" is superior to, let's say, "interactive arts," "screen production" or "virtual architecture." One could take the liberal stance and let history judge, meanwhile letting a thousand flowers compete for eternal glory. But that's not the reality. In my experience, it is not so much the central concept that leads to "success," but factors such as an inspiring staff, generous support within the school and faculty, the right transdisciplinary chemistry, a balanced emphasis on both research and teaching and the way in which students open themselves up and get "electrified" by yet unexplored virtual worlds they create themselves. Schools need to be "cool," and that is by no means determined by a label. What relationship between theory and practice works best? Will students have the freedom to develop their own digital aesthetics? Is their work geared towards a larger audience from an early stage, or solely produced for the professor and a few classmates?

In the educational context it is easy to see how global technologies and design-related issues relate to specific local contexts. Whereas some places are traditionally strong in design or visual arts, elsewhere one can see new-media programs thriving within disciplines such as architecture, literature or social sciences. The ever-changing, hybrid nature of the new-media sector requires special educational conditions and tactical skills in order to build institutional alliances. New-media arts labs have to be open to other disciplines, while at the same time they have to fight for their own space and define, defend and expand the field. How do performing arts, music and cultural studies (all close to the field) respond to rise of new media as a separate entity? Literature, for instance, is already dealing with its own emerging subgenre of "electronic literature." Electronic music has been around for decades and has found its niche within music departments. So why suddenly buy into this overhyped generic "new media" term? Are there enough claims to be made for turning new-media studies into a separate department, just because it attracts scores of students at a certain moment in time? And how can artists talk to engineers, if indeed there is a wish for dialogue and a common language in the first place? And there are not only institutional concerns; the relationship of the new-media departments to "industry" and society at large seems as important.

Bauhaus: Reference and Model

A recent trend that I would like to begin with is the tension between "new media" and the visual arts. Animosities, or perhaps misunderstandings, are on the rise because art and technology are rapidly becoming inseparable. Today, hardly any contemporary art exhibition fails to include video or digital photography. What some see as a spiritual synergy might be better described as a culture clash. The more technology young artists use, the more uncertainty arises amongst the aging professors, curators, museums and galleries about how to judge all these "virtual works." Computers are invading all forms of art practice, even dance, sculpture and painting. It took at least 20 years for contemporary arts to incorporate video art. Many see the same drama being repeated in the case of digital/Web art. Instead of curiosity we can witness a backlash and rising tensions.[2] What are the consequences of this hesitance for art education? If you want your students to have a successful career start, the Internet is a no-go zone. What makes the art world so suspicious of the passion for technological experiments? Is it their secret disdain, à la Clement Greenberg, for kitsch – synthetic art that uncritically expresses the culture of the masses? During a debate at the Berlin Transmediale 2003 festival there was talk about the displacement of "media art" education away from the fine arts to the applied arts. Stephen Kovats reports: "There is a growing interrelationship between media arts and architecture faculties. Media art often becomes uncomfortable around sculptors, while architects move closer to 'fine' art through technology and find a new 'art/tech' way. This brings up the 'Bauhaus' issue and the idealizing role of the original Bauhaus idea, which may, in this new context, regain some lost meaning."[3] So let's look into today's fascination for the Bauhaus and what exactly it stands for.

Pelle Ehn, a founding faculty member of the school for media and communications in Malmö, Sweden, wrote the "Manifesto for a Digital Bauhaus" in 1998. It is a paradigmatic ten-page document containing a mix of moderate, rational, critical and visionary assertions. The manifesto, which combines postmodern notions with a flair of 1990s techno optimism, first of all deals with the chosen name, and what happened to the Bauhaus heritage. According to Ehn, the original social engagement of the Bauhaus transformed into an anti-democratic professional elitism. "Despite the high moral and aesthetic principles, there was no real feeling, insight or vivid realization of ordinary people's everyday life and conditions. Maybe the 'soft' ideas of participation and democracy never were a cornerstone of the Bauhaus."[4]

What is needed is "not a modernism caught in a solidified objectivity in the design of modern objects in steel, glass and concrete, but a comprehensive sensuality in the design of meaningful interactive and virtual stories and environments." Yet this criticism has not corrupted the use of the Bauhaus reference as such. Like its historical predecessor, the "Digital Bauhaus" is a project full of contradictions and runs the risk of degenerating into an adolescent doctrine of boundless individualism and technophilic hubris. Says Ehn, "We are left with a promising but overripe modern Bauhaus tradition in the background and an equally promising but immature postmodern third culture of nerds and digerati in the foreground."

Stephen Kovats, who worked inside the actual Bauhaus in Dessau during the 1990s, points out that "Bauhaus" originally referred to the role of the school in society. "Bauhaus" is associated with the problem of whether teaching serves a social, political and cultural role or an industrial and economic one. For a brief moment in time, the German Bauhaus, as a historical singularity, integrated a critical, autonomous practice with an industrial focus. But beyond the historical Bauhaus example, most current talk about "industry meeting the arts" is not going to go beyond good intentions. It is hard to develop a critical and innovative aesthetics within a commercial environment – and on top of that do multidisciplinary work. Collaborations often do not materialize beyond formalized exchanges for the simple reason that the self-interest of the partners involved is much too high. Despite a will to bring together eccentric artistic futurism with the hard-boiled skills required by commerce (embodied for instance in the "creative industries" approach[5]), it remains nearly impossible to "sell" new-media art, mainly due to a widespread wariness of experimentation among galleries, industry, NGOs and traditional media outlets. It seems as if society as a whole is conspiring against those who cross disciplinary boundaries. Then why should universities raise new generations of new-media artists whose future status will be so uncertain? Since the dotcom crash, information technology no longer guarantees a job, and the sector as a whole has lost its appeal for students. The education sector meanwhile has been a growth area, while at the same time being in state of permanent crisis due to ongoing budget cuts, privatization, bureaucracy and permanent restructuring. New-media art education is caught in the contradiction of a long-term demand for those with technical skills and an overall climate of diminishing resources and possibilities, delivering brilliant techno artists for whom there is no place.

No matter how much the modernist agenda has been taken apart, the Bauhaus is still considered a compelling point of reference, and I agree with that.[6] It is such a source of inspiration precisely because it promoted the artistic use of new technology yet did not produce kitsch. Its curriculum ignored the moralistic divide between visual and applied arts. Its ambition to create and participate in a transdisciplinary "dream team" producing both critical and innovative work exists to this day. One of the numerous websites dedicated to Bauhaus tells the story: "The intention with Bauhaus was to develop creative minds for architecture and industry and thus influence them so that they would be able to produce artistically, technically and practically balanced utensils. The institute included workshops for making models of type houses and all kinds of utensils, and departments of advertising art, stage planning, photography, and typography. By the mid-1920s Gropius had defined more exactly the starting points of modern design and its doctrines. Thus the Bauhaus curriculum combined theoretical education (a primary course and composition theory) and practical training in the educational workshops."[7]

The Bauhaus principles are echoed in electronic artists' wish to build prototypes of experimental interfaces and come up with a "digital aesthetics" that develops forms in which new communication devices and applications are used. The artist/designer is not a window-dresser. Instead of merely "freshening up" other people's content, new-media artists see themselves as inventors who operate on a meta level, beyond, or beneath, ordinary information exchanges. The will to interface with power is there. These days, artists do not merely derive inspiration from the media they work in (Greenberg);[8] they aspire to shape technology itself. It is not enough to deliver content for demo versions. The aim of a program should be to turn the student into a master of new-media language. As Nietzsche pointed out, education begins with habit, obedience and discipline.[9] But new-media students have already gone through that phase, having been subjected to the joystick, mouse, keyboard and mobile phone from early childhood. Atari, Gameboy and PlayStation have left their traces. It is the role of the student-turned-artist to simultaneously question and structure modes of communication – and that is where the Bauhaus legacy comes in. The shared passion for defining the medium is also the reason why so many new-media art works have no specific message or narrative. The medium is the object. It is more of a challenge to build a new browser than to design yet another website. Mainstream audiences and their guardians are known not to favor "vague" art pieces that "anyone could do." However, it is a matter of mass education to change this prejudice and create understanding of the importance of conceptual work on media interfaces.

Is there such a thing as an "artistic desire" that operates freely and chooses whatever medium it finds most appropriate? That might sound too good to be true. The computer might present itself as a universal device, but that does not imply the return of the universal artist. Not even a genius can play every instrument. The manuals are simply too thick. The specialization of knowledge makes it impossible for a single human being to keep up with developments to all tools. It is a lie that good artists can express themselves in any medium. The implication of this limitation is that technology-based departments remain necessary, even within a highly conceptual environment that thrives to be platform-independent. British media theorist Matthew Fuller, now teaching at Rotterdam's Willem de Kooning art academy, places the tension between conceptual and vocational teaching in a social context. The tensions new-media departments struggle with persist precisely as politically coded relations embedded in those of class, race and gender. Fuller: "We know what students are supposed to learn. We know that certain strata within educational systems are there to provide one kind of work force and others are there to service the production of another. Technologies are part of class composition, and so also are the educational devices built around, through and with them."[10]

Pelle Ehn sees less of a problem. For him, the aim of the Digital Bauhaus is "to create an arena, a meeting place, a school, and a research center for creative and socially useful meetings between 'art' and 'technology.'" Like many others in this field, the Malmö school has high expectations for a dialogue between art and science. Strangely enough, this often does not include hackers from the computer-science departments, as one would expect in this context. Often people are so familiar with computers that they leave information technology itself out of "science." For "science," the "soft-knowledge" sector usually thinks of "hard" yet exotic cutting-edge research within quantum physics, bio- and gene technology, cognitive science, chemistry, biology and astronomy. (The historic Bauhaus, by the way, did not have this fascination with natural science and worked within the constraints of a coalition between architects, designers, photographers and visual artists.)

Neoscene Pedagogy

The Digital Bauhaus concept may be a fata morgana amidst a never-ending institutional nightmare. The new-media subject appears at the end of a long global crisis in the education industry. Decades of constant restructuring, declining standards and budget cuts have led to an overall decline of the .edu sector. There are debates not only about fees, cutbacks in staff and privatization but also about the role of the teacher. For a long time the classic top-down knowledge delivery methods of the classroom situation have been under fire. In a response to the education crisis, the American-Scandinavian John Hopkins calls for a cultural shift towards alternative pedagogies. His pedagogy, close to that of Paolo Freire,[11] is based on a combination of face-to-face and networked communication, keeping up a "flow of energies from node to node." Hopkins, who calls himself an "autonomous teaching agent," has roamed between Northern European universities and new-media initiatives and currently teaches in Boulder, Colorado. His spiritual-scientific worldview might not match mine, but he is certainly my favorite when it comes to a radical education approach. Hopkins prefers the person-to-person as a "tactical" expression of networking, avoiding "centralized media and PR-related activities wherever possible." Hopkins' "neoscenes" networks are "a vehicle for learning, creating and sharing that does not seek stasis, spectacle and speed."

In a few instances, Hopkins' "distributed Socratic teaching strategy" has culminated in 24-hour techno parties with a big online component to make room for remote participation and exchange.[12] The challenge with the live remix streams was to find out collectively "how exactly to facilitate autonomy and spontaneity." For Hopkins teaching is a "life practice," an action that embodies "art as a way-of-doing." He calls his style "verbose and densely grown (not necessarily meaningful either ;-), but I do try to say what I am thinking and practicing ..."[13] Hopkins tries not to make a distinction between learning, teaching and being taught. "It is critical that I myself am transformed by the entire engaged experience."[14] As a visiting artist, and usually not a member of the "local academic politburo," Hopkins can build up personal connections within a local structure, free to "catalyze a flexible response that is immediately relevant," while maintaining a creative integrity that is based in praxis.

What makes teaching new media such a strategic and important topic? I do not believe that this preoccupation of many has grown out of a genuine concern with the well-being of the next generation. Often the young know more about technology then the 40- and 50-something .edu bureaucrats. Nor is the growing interest in academia a response to the long-term deterioration in education standards effected by the alarming budget declines. According to some, education is one of the few places where theorists, artists and activists can get jobs. The absence of sustainable models for building up a (money-based) new-media economy has driven many practitioners and critics into the arms of the education sector. Whereas a (declining) number of artists, for instance in Europe, can still live from grants, the dole and freelance jobs, this is not the case everywhere. Young professionals have to seek confrontation with the "digital economy," whatever that may be at any given moment. What started with video, photography and graphic design in the early 1990s moved on to multimedia and then straight into the gold mine of Web design. The idea to quickly (re-)educate scores of young people as professional Web editors stalled. After the dotcom golden age, the education sector has reached the stage of "transvergence," as UC Santa Barbara professor Marcos Novak calls it[15] – a new "epistemic cluster" that overcomes both the "convergence" crisis and its opposite, the tendency towards "divergence." Instead of delivering customized IT professionals, Novak's aim is to produce "aliens."

What remains after the heyday of Web design and the dotcom collapse is the promise of wireless applications, broadband content, computer games, digital cinema and DVD production (read: animation). Where to look next? Considerable differences between the communication paradigm of low-resolution networks and the high-resolution offline visuals remain to dominate both the market and the education sector. The early 1990s split between Silicon Graphics-style virtual reality and early text-only Internet applications such as e-mail, ftp and telnet is reproduced a decade later as SMS/text-messaging simplicity versus the aesthetic of Hollywood-style computer games coded by armies of cheap computer artists in Canada, Australia and Asia. Most programs now offer a bit of both, combining high-res image processing with low-res network explorations. Take Josephine Starrs, who teaches at Sydney's College of the Arts. She has students "give seminars on current trends in digital cultures incorporating virtual communities, tactical media, mailing lists, MOOs, computer games and Internet radio. We examine different conceptual approaches to making use of the 'network,' including issues to do with browsers, search engines, databases, shareware and social software."[16]

One could take a reassuring tone and emphasize the complementary character of high and low-res media. However, the reality of running a media course is messy enough and demands specialization. It is impossible for a small staff to cover the whole media spectrum. Choices have to be made. Many new-media departments are drawn to more complex offline visualizations. The manipulation of high-res images is perceived as being closer to commercial media practice. This has led to a whole generation of electronic artists who attempt to define the field of new-media education in the direction of virtual, immersive environments presented as products of the future. Funding bodies, university administrators and corporate representatives are easy to impress with 3-D environments. The promise of a killer app[17] in the field of artistic human-machine interfaces is a compelling one. If the Bay Area could generate Silicon Valley, and the whole country of Finland could become prosperous because of Nokia, local politicians are willing to try anything, as long as it looks fancy. Why not lure bureaucrats into the idea that their city could become the global capital of "interactive cinema" (whatever that may be)? Politicians in Dublin and Delhi have put millions of dollars on the table to host branches of the MIT Media Lab (though Delhi recently pulled out). In this global race for techno-supremacy, low-res applications are often ignored. Feeding off the desperation to keep up with the New Economy (RIP), offline high-res technologies are favored for their sexy and innovative appeal over the simplicity of low-tech social communication. The new-media education sector is playing a key role in the competition for research money. However, with the increasing split between research and teaching within tertiary educational environments, it is not clear how funds gained from attractive high-tech research proposals will translate or filter down to the teaching level. Hence real opportunities for most students to access the promise of high-end resources through their place of study are few. There is a paradox between the courseware offered and the lack of technical infrastructure and resources to deliver these courses – small amounts of time on low-end machines by industry standards. Consequently, students graduate with "below-standard" expertise.

Most new-media curricula include software classes in Macromedia Director, PhotoShop, Flash, and later perhaps C++, or 3D software such as 3D Studio Max or Maya. Besides offline multimedia packages, most programs offer Web-authoring classes, from basic HTML to Flash and the occasional Linux or Java course. More specialized programs deal with things like haptic interfaces, computer animation, interactive performance, browser design, robotics, wearable and wireless culture and computer games.[18] Having said that, for fundamental reasons, interesting and challenging new-media courses pay only minimal attention to vocational training on software packages. John Hopkins: "I start my workshops with a sketching of some absolute fundamentals of human presence and being in the phenomenal world. This beginning point immediately becomes a source of deep crisis for some students precisely because they are expecting the vocational top-down educational experience of learning a specific software platform and making traditional artifacts." John finds people who focus on software platforms "incredibly boring. It's like amateur photo-club members comparing the length of their telephoto lenses or having conversations about national sports. It's a code system for communication that is often mindless and banal. While at some level, my students are forced to confront the digital device, I encourage them to be aware of how they are interacting with the machine, what is comfortable and what is not."

This tension between vocational training and conceptual understanding has always existed – and probably always will. The main thing, however, is not to treat the computer merely as a tool. For design lecturer Brad Miller at the College of Fine Arts, Sydney, the computer is a universal machine. "It can emulate any process humans can articulate. Rather than the idea that we 'instill' knowledge to students about processes of conceptualization and they will pick up the software skills later in the workplace. As opposed to the vocational point of view the abstract conceptual approach should be synthesized as processes of creation within the realm of the computer screen and seen as an embodied process."[19]

The Freudian question, "What does a company want?" is the wrong one from the start. Problematic, off-track courses are much better for students. General skills last longer than the applications of the day. Schools that desperately try to comply with industry demands are often the least interesting ones. This also counts for schools that want to attract international students. Many warn that this is a volatile market. Changing currency exchange rates, rising fees for (international) students, wars, recessions and health crises such as SARS can suddenly change student interest in ambitiously marketed programs. The problem with the "market" approach is not so much commercialism, but the vulgar input-output model that fences off the curriculum against "alien" influences, thereby limiting students' opportunity to explore technology outside of the given frameworks. Matthew Fuller has a lot to say about this complex dynamic. "Rather than a fixed area with well-patrolled fences, we see our work as generating a context wherein students can aggregate and invent their own surplus of access to and understanding of new media. This means that they create value first for themselves and on their own terms. If we are to talk of 'industry demands,' then it is this surplus which makes students 'valuable,' but also that which allows them the possibility of self-determination against simple commercial expropriation in the way that market-driven instructional training shoehorns them into. Ironically, of course, it is this 'something beyond the market,' outside the reach of money, that drives capitalism. Perhaps in order to be of the highest level of potential service to commercial agendas one has to become funda-mentally anti-capitalist." This is another element vital to the Bauhaus story. It is unclear anyway what "industry" is and who is entitled to define its interests.

Universities still consider the computer/new-media industries as some-how emulating a film-industry model, with a stable set of skills each trained person goes out into the world with after graduation. According to Anna Munster, who teaches the College of Fine Arts, Sydney, "one of the hardest aspects of being involved in new-media education is to assist students to loosen up to a transient world of employment/work/play by disabusing them of the notion that there is an industry. This loosening up needs to occur through a thorough reinvention of the curriculum as well and, for example, assessment procedures and how these work in with course development and outcomes. Pedagogically we really need to think about what forms of assessment push this conceptual questioning in new media and go beyond simply testing a student's acquisition of software skills. We need to try to take the heat off assessment as 'final product' that gets the good marks, towards forms of assessment that include peer interaction and feedback and acknowledge the learning that occurs through process rather than product." Something Munster has found use-ful is to set up presentations of student work along the lines of a Socratic dialogue, where one student is asked to respond to another's work each week. "Students need to meet with each other beforehand and discuss the presenter's work and bring this discussion to the classroom situation. It's surprising how often students do not actually look at each other's work and engage with it."[20]

Teaching the Teachers

Despite all the opportunities to give shape to a still-undefined field, there is considerable pressure on staff to master an ever-widening range of technologies. Lisa Gye teaches in the Media and Communications program of Swinburne University in Melbourne. Gye has made the politics of new-media education one of her specialties. As a moderator for the Fibreculture community of Australian new-media researchers, she collects curricula of new-media programs to compare how different universities and professors structure their courses, information not usually publicly available owing to the obsession of today's corporatized universities with closing access to their intellectual property.[21] In an online interview, Lisa explained the "teaching the teachers" position. "It's really important to be able to cope with the possibilities that technological environments present to us. You have to be able to adapt to things like machine breakdown and develop fallback strategies. Many academics have been reluctant to accept that the new teaching environments we now inhabit demand that we develop more technical expertise – we'd be troubled if we went into, say, a library and found that the librarians had not mastered the cataloguing system and were unable to help us locate a resource. The same should apply to the teaching environment."[22]

Next, I consulted Minna Tarkka, a Finnish researcher, the organizer of ISEA 1994, and one of the driving forces behind the "m-cult" new-media organization.[23] From 1996 to 2001 she was professor of interactive and multimedia communication at the Media Lab at the University of Art and Design (UIAH) in Helsinki. As head of the new-media MA program, she initiated study and research projects on digital museums, interactive television and critical art and design practice. Minna: "An ideal pedagogical environment for me is one where technical practice coincides with cultural/critical practice, while 'theory' feeds this environment not as an abstraction, but more as a very concrete 'tool' for reflexivity – a source for grounding the practice socially and historically."[24] Tarkka finds herself often in opposition to the fashionable ideas of "problem-based learning" within a "community distributed expertise" that derides traditional academic forms of reading, lecturing and writing seminar papers. She says: "There is a friction between conceptualizing and questioning on the one hand and rushing to meet the brief and its deadlines on the other. But in the pedagogical environment this friction is only fruitful. In our discussions at UIAH we aimed at demystifying theory, defining it as a sensibility, or as just another kind of practice – a conceptual practice in dialogic relation to the productive practice."

Similar to John Hopkins, Lisa Gye stresses how important it is to understand and fully recognize the skills students bring in. "They very often have highly developed interpersonal communications skills which have grown out of their consistent use of networking technologies like the internet, e-mail, SMS, chat and game-playing. These kinds of skills provide us with the prerequisites for the development of effective collaborative strategies for learning." Often, teaching goes back to the old methods, running courses that end with the assessment of a written essay, a multimedia piece and a presentation. Measuring individual outcomes is still a requirement in many institutions. Lisa: "We need to draw on these skills more and rely less on the highly individualistic ranking systems, such as essay writing, that are currently used nearly everywhere. This is not to say, though, that we have to abandon the desire for the development of certain attributes that we've come to value in university graduates – the ability to think and write critically and independently, to synthesize ideas and so on – but we may need to develop more creative ways of getting students to that place."

I came across the education issue for the first time in Helsinki, at the August 1994 electronic arts conference ISEA. A panel called "Running to Stay in Place" dealt with faculty burnout in the electronic arts.[25] Cynthia Beth Rubin, Annette Weintraub and others discussed guidelines for faculty teaching in new media. They had drafted a document that was adopted by the US College Art Association in October 1995.[26] It discussed curriculum design, program management and the pressure on staff to keep current. "As a result of the rate of change in this arena, faculty staff must read a tremendous quantity of technical literature as well as keep up on aesthetics issues in the field."[27] The declaration, endorsed by 18 professors who supervised the incorporation of technology into visual arts programs, pointed out that "regular attendance at conferences and trade shows is a must. Aesthetic concerns shift as new applications emerge and changes necessitate intellectual exchange with like-minded colleagues." Another element that adds to the workload is the writing of grant applications. Specialized lab equipment is often expensive, and without resource-intensive support programs it becomes obsolete. Then there is the issue of who maintains and upgrades the equipment. Technical tutors have to be brought in to help students learn the programs, or the critical-conceptual element of the courses will suffer. Which genius can use Apple, PC and Linux platforms and simultaneously teach multimedia, Internet and 3-D software? Long working hours can easily cause burnout. The document warned: "Each year students enter into the field with more sophistication than the year before. If we do not keep pace then our programs become outdated and students suffer."

Australian-American robotics artist Simon Penny, one of the panelists in Helsinki, has dealt with new-media education policies for a long time. Simon Penny, who taught at Carnegie Mellon University and was recently appointed by the University of California at Irvine, was among those who endorsed the 1995 document. His ideal, he wrote me, "is that technical, artistic and historical-critical learning must be present in equal measure and with equal rigor, and must be negotiated together and interrelated, in order that the work be competent and insightful."[28] Penny is setting high standards. "I don't have much patience for dumb art. An artist in any medium should be intellectually activist, at the very least. Making smart, provocative art in or about such a complex cultural context seems to demand a supple, integrative, inquiring mind which can be equally at home with technical concepts, creative concepts, and theoretical concepts. And that mind has to have at its disposal theoretical tools in order to do that integrative work." At UC Irvine Penny drew up a graduate program in "arts, computation and engineering." He wrote: "Fifteen years ago, it was progressive to recognize that within the arts, there were skills which could enhance the production of computational projects and commodities. This is the premise of the MIT Media Lab. Given the transition from a technical agenda to a cultural agenda which is already in process, it is time to build a new model for the interrelation between the media arts and technical development."

Simon Penny argues for a transition from a technical to a cultural agenda. Traditionally, if creative and cultural sensibilities were recognized in the techno-economy, it was from the perspective that such sensibilities can be leveraged to generate better techno-commodities. "Increasingly, as we know, 'cultural' practices are the drivers of technical development: Napster, gaming, MUDs and MOOs, porn, eBay ... search engines!" According to Penny, it is time the contrary movement was explored: the leveraging of technical knowledge in the service of new and enhanced cultural practices. "In the traditional 'art in the service of techno-industry' context, artists have traditionally been brought in at the end, to window-dress, to make a 'cool-looking demo'. This idea of art as pretty artisan craft is so patronizing and romantic, it makes me puke. In the history I know, artists are integrative holistic thinkers who come up with novel techno-cultural formulations, and subject these formulations to critical assessment from diverse angles. This is the real value of art practice to industry, but to utilize that value, artists have to come in at the very beginning of the design phase, not at the end of research and development."

John Hopkins compares Scandinavia and the USA, places he knows well. "Because of a well-funded cultural industry sector in Scandinavia, artists who are potential teachers are not forced into teaching as happens in the US. This has kept the stagnation of the tenure-track system, something that dogs US higher education, out of the way. In the US, artists who have any desire to live by working in some way in their medium are more often than not forced into academia because there is no other social context for them. They may or may not be teachers in any sense. There tend to be more permeable and productive interchanges between the 'art world' and 'academia' in Scandinavia and northern Europe, realized by cycling a larger number of idiosyncratic individual teacher/artists into contact with students." Isolated campus life, slow and complicated bureaucracies, and the politically correct atmosphere at US universities are not ideal circumstances for a hybrid "trans-disciplinary" program to thrive. However, the campus setup does help to reduce distractions, once students know what they want and the resources are in place.

The Place of Theory

Theory in new media covers a wide field, from cultural studies to artificial intelligence and the history of cybernetics, including crossovers to the visual arts, film, television and sound. Most often we see a mix of postmodern theory and science on offer, combined with the new-media canon and its cyberculture readers. Minna Tarkka's students at the Helsinki design school have been hungry for theory and critical approaches. Tarkka explains, "This is probably due to the fact that I've taught a master's course in new media, with students who are already quite mature, have both previous degrees and a long experience from new-media design and production. They came back to education to learn to question the obvious and to expand the cultural and aesthetic aspects of new media." She stresses that there is no one ideal Theory, but rather a multitude of approaches whose "practicability" also varies.

For Simon Penny, theory helps practitioners negotiate the intellectual and social history of the "two cultures" and their current collision in digital culture. "This is a huge and demanding intellectual exercise. Without such grounding, a naïve combination of 'art' and 'tech' is digital 'Sunday painting,' or worse. Any historico-theoretico-critical perspective which helps a practitioner negotiate the relation between the technical-industrial and cultural practices is important. Science, technology and society, especially the qualitative side, is for me one of the most important theoretical developments of the last decade for digital cultural practice. The poststructuralist gangs are all relevant, as long as one avoids making a religion out of them. Postcolonial studies, feminism, situated anthropology, phenomenology, etc. are all important." In many programs, theory-as-such is seen as a source of inspiration, regardless of whether or not its authors deal with technology. In order to get students involved, it is important not to structure around "authors" and their famous books, but instead to organize theory around topics.

Marie-Louise Angerer is a German media theorist who worked in number of universities before becoming professor at the Cologne media-art academy KHM. For her, theory is not opposed to vocational training. "I understand theory as a different strategy of intervention. Theory shouldn't claim to be the better model for understanding media. Students should know the history and developments of the discipline they work in." She sees many different strands of media theory in Germany. "We still have the communication-versus-literature split and a materialistic versus an idealistic strand, even though the two can't be strictly divided. But I am advocating a broad and integrated understanding of media and the arts, which includes questions of perception, reception, production, time and space, body and gender." Matthew Fuller in Rotterdam agrees. "If you have a separate theory department you build such a division into the work of the school. We insist that 'theory' is drawn into 'technical' classes, that technologies are made to divulge their conceptuality and that theory is treated as material to work with, to make, not just to resent as an additional task." At the same time, text is different from everyday language, and it is different from code. Fuller: "These differences should be used to creates disturbances, reverberations. What is not needed are unified conceptual blocks or isomorphisms between theory and practice.

They can and should catch hold of each other, make something occur, act as attractors or models for particular currents or practices, but with an understanding of the materiality of each different media system."

Brad Miller's ideal theory would be a structure that can put logic into interaction and interface design. "I would, for instance, love to see a synthesis of Donald Norman's concepts on affordance and mapping with the developments in George Lakoff's work on metaphor and embodied realism." I asked Marie-Louise Angerer about her favorite places that integrate theory and practice. "In Linz, for instance, at the Kunstuniversität, they are appointing a professor for media theory, which should bring together artistic practice and theory and make use of the local Ars Electronica Center and its history. Amsterdam started a program that combines art, dance and theory, which should become the missing link between the art school and the universities. Then there are very qualified examples, such as Jan van Eyck Academy in Maastricht, with a very ambitious theory program I could only dream about. We at KHM are still working on establishing our own Ph.D. program, intending to combine art, media practice and theory on a high level."

As John Hopkins most often has taught non-native English speakers, he has drifted away from the tradition of assigning texts. He perceives this as liberating, "because it allows ideas to develop through 'live' thought and dialogue. It allows for something of a Socratic situation to arise that offers a fluidity that is often suppressed in 'discussions about a certain reading.' It allows for the spontaneous generation of theory that arises from individual experiential impressions." In recent decades, it was presumed that reading Lacan, Foucault, Deleuze and Guattari, Spivak, Baudrillard, Derrida, Jameson and other postmodern theorists was enough of a challenge to inspire students. Apart from the fact that contemporary theory should be general knowledge, which it obviously isn't, the questions the post-World War Two generation posed are slowly wearing out amid the daily avalanche of global real-time media events and technological advances.[29] Live videophone reporting from the battlefield no longer shocks, but is judged upon its aesthetic merits compared to other commercial products on the communications market. Poor image quality is seen as a reality effect, not a sign of technological imperfection. Real-time media form an ideal environment for students to practice their rip-mix-burn techniques, opening up a range of post-theoretical ways of reflection.

Since 1995, Richard Barbrook has heading the Hypermedia Research Center at the University of Westminster in London.[30] He teaches theory as cultural criticism, but would also like to raise the "economic competence" of future professionals. "Students need a mix of theory and practice. Ironically, being forced to read the old media of books is one of the things that is much appreciated. Of course, I avoid teaching po-mo theory where possible in favor of something more relevant, such as the political economy of 'really existing' capitalism. For instance, our course prerequisites include reading Adam Smith's *The Wealth of Nations*. One of our alumni told me that he has won various job contracts by lifting buzzwords from my lectures, e.g. Fordism, 'natural monopoly', gift economy, etc."[31]

Theory has not yet dealt enough with today's media-driven everyday life and the advanced forms of boredom, anxiety, saturation and violence reflected in its mediated experiences. Neither cultural pessimism nor a call for a return to "reality" seems an adequate response to the technological *a priori*. In short, theory is lagging behind, still struggling with the question of what technology is, whereas students have grown up with computers and often lack the passion for essentialist debates. As a result, a teacher needs a lot of inspiration to make a case for why all these complex pre-digital thinkers are interesting enough to read. Students cannot expect theory to reflect upon the latest software, gadgets and media-art practices. This leaves theory with two options: to maximize its speculative potential, speed up and project itself way into the 22nd century, or else make a case for abstract, quasi-timeless concepts. This again leads to the problem of why one should have to deconstruct yesterday's futurism. What is left is history. There is, indeed, growing interest in integrating "media archeology" (see Introduction) into the curriculum. Apart from this, texts five, 50 or 200 years old may as well deal with the issues of our time. Recent anthologies have tried to provide new media with its own intellectual history. However, the idea that the computer is a product of our culture, reflecting all its values, is still new for many. The opposition between technology and culture keeps haunting us.

John Hopkins' response to the crisis of theory is "deep praxis." "I see theory as a stimulus to start a discussion, a connection with an Other. But language, as arbiter of theory, is about re-presentation, and praxis is about be-ing and do-ing. A balance between the two is good, but lived experience should come before a textual representation of the same. Transcending theory is essential in this time, especially with the rapid erosion of many scales of personal freedom. A deep praxis must be brought into the learning situation. Deep praxis, a living moment-to-moment way-of-going, generates robust theory for those who need to play with re-presentations of active being."

Many question the linear model in which theory delivers concepts which are then "applied" by students. Lisa Gye refers to American scholar Gregory Ulmer, who, in his book *Heuretics: The Logic of Invention,* argues that theory is assimilated into the humanities in two principal ways – through critical interpretation and through artistic experiment. Ulmer points out that there is a symbiotic relationship between the former, hermeneutics, and the latter, heuretics. Gye: "Theorists are as much influenced by the making of arts and letters as they influence them. I don't think that acting in the world is that far removed from thinking about the world. One of the greatest teachers of all time, Socrates, provides us with a useful metaphor for thinking about the way in which theory should be integrated into everyday life. I like to think of theory as being able to 'talk the talk and walk the walk.' The beauty of his peripatetic approach to pedagogy is that you have to be out there engaged with the world in order to be able to perform it. This is vastly different to many approaches to theory that see it as something to be applied to the world as though theory is a thing apart from the world on which it comments."

None of the issues discussed here are new in ones for art and design education. Questions of how to integrate "theory" and "production" were being argued when Sydney media philosopher Anna Munster first began to teach communications courses during the mid-1980s. "During that time students were generally actively engaged with all kinds of theory and what's more, were making work at the same time. Consequently, the produced work felt speculative and the theoretical engagement felt picked-over and infused with pragmatism." Anna Munster doesn't think new media and theory issues introduce a radically new set of circumstances. "What is new are the attitudes towards theory that come from both the student and staff perspectives. What we see is exhaustion towards theory by people who should at least be bothering to inform themselves of recent intellectual developments. This disengagement results in feeling that theory has nothing to offer. Students develop their work within this atmosphere and within the broader cultural context of anti-intellectualism and fear of critical and speculative inquiry that is part of current Anglo-American (although not European) culture. Within this atmosphere, mixtures of highly speculative material and empirical or historical texts can work well, provided that whoever is teaching is engaged with new media as everyday practices as well and can draw out these connections."[32]

This brings the issue back to theorists, who must reposition themselves and start "walking" (like data dandies?) through the new-media environments. One obstacle doing this is the ongoing dominance of the book as a physical storage medium for knowledge. The dotcom promise of an Internet "attention economy" has not materialized, and the implications of this failure are far-reaching. The reputation system and the obtaining of income through grants are still closely tied to the output of books and articles. I am certainly no exception, nor is this book. A "Net critic" has to have other sources of income. Roaming around lists, blogs, virtual worlds and chatrooms doesn't pay off unless you rework your online ideas into traditional publishing formats. Serious academics would rather not mingle with the Internet at all, out of fear that their courses and texts will be stolen, and thus limit its potential as a digital public domain to private e-mail and Web searches. Posting on lists is widely seen as publishing (which it both is and is not). Indifference to the Internet is a strong current, a silent gesture backed by a multitude of roots and powerful forces. Many play it safe, preferring not to sacrifice their careers to what they see as a risky avant-garde passion headed nowhere. An exception to this rule might be publishing in peer-reviewed online journals – dead media anyway, in my view, as they most often exclude interactive possibilities[33]. In this conservative climate, even new-media theorists can only win fame through paper publications, preferably textbooks which are kept strictly offline by publishers for copyright reasons. The fact that these must be available in English speaks for itself. Language and translation are a separate issue which I won't go into here, but it is an immensely important factor in the worldwide formation of what is and is not going to be "theory." All these factors make it hard for theory and practice to blend in a virtual dialogue, though many nonetheless share and express the wish that they would do so. As a consequence, there is a growing discontent and disregard for theory, which feeds off a general increase in anti-intellectualism in many places.

Hypertext has long promised a synthesis between open, dialogic forms of theory and new-media practice. Lisa Gye thinks it provides students with an excellent platform for experimentation. "Essays as a mode of assessment are becoming increasingly outdated and problematic. For a start, essays, as they are generally written in universities, are pretty dull rhetorically. They teach students how to reproduce a particular mode of thinking and writing that is closed off to possibilities. And let's face it – most students hate to write them, hence the increasing incidence of plagiarism in Australian universities." Hypertext, and particularly online hypertext, is accessible, easy to write and not yet burdened with rigid, formulaic rhetorical strategies. Gye: "It allows students space to think about new ways of saying things – with words, pictures, sound – none of which are new, of course, but they are still fairly novel in terms of their application to academic writing. Part of this derives from my interest in Derrida's theories with regards to the technology of writing. So the hypertext course that I teach draws heavily on Derrida and Ulmer. But part of it also derives from my belief that practice and theory do not have to be cordoned off from each other."

The Eternal Return of the New

Over the past few years there has been a steep rise and fall in the Internet's coolness. What impact does this have on teaching? Should educators follow the latest trends in cell-phone/PDA culture, games, and so on? What is the use of raising armies of future HTML slaves for the labor market? Should students learn actual coding, or is it sufficient to stay with the graphic interface? How necessary, or strategic, is it to keep up with the latest? The pressure to produce a class of docile workers is enormous. Minna: "A key aspect of new media is the 'eternal return of the new,' so it is obvious that the 'latest trends' are always on the agenda. Design is a very political zone where many aspects of the 'new' can be contextualized and challenged. This is where the grounding provided by theory and history is important, since it shields against the worst hype and at least hypothetically allows the student to develop critical productive sensibilities." Marie-Louise Angerer in Cologne sees her students "going back." "They often use old media, such as 16mm film instead of video. Of course, then they do the postproduction on their computers, often using their machines at home. This trend indicates that old and new technologies are highly combined and used whenever, in whatever way needed."

The recent wave of artistic/social software is the outcome of a shift back to coding, away from just mouse clicks. Instead of pushing students into using the latest, we see growing interest in "unearthing" applications, peeling off bombastic usability layers and approaching problems using small, uncomplicated programs. However, the quest for low tech often borders on computer science. It remains unclear exactly how much emphasis should be giving to coding. In my experience, the best students all master programming, but only after developing a curiosity about theory and art history. Focusing first on IT skills and then doing some theory won't work. On the other hand, guest lecturers can only come in and realize interesting projects after students have worked with a range of different software packages. It is impossible to play around with software you are unfamiliar with. My solution to this never-ending dilemma would be to shift the problem to admissions criteria, and only admit students with a broad, critical interest in art, theory and society.

Lisa Gye in Melbourne says she can't see how to avoid the pressure to keep up with the latest. She is interested in all forms of media. "I live with a 12-year-old and a nine-year-old, so it's impossible to not know about the latest technological trends because they usually are desperate for them! I guess there's a certain level beyond which it's hard to go in terms of understanding technologies if you don't use them. Game culture is a case in point. There is so much misinformed critique of game culture from people who have never handled a Nintendo controller in their life. Teachers could learn a great deal about collaboration and cooperative group work from watching a bunch of nine-year-old boys play computer games – it's a very elaborate economy of information exchange."

Having been involved in photography, John Hopkins watched its retreat from special status as newcomer art form to being simply another way of putting a 2-D mark on paper. Hopkins: "Once, photography departments were the renegade areas in traditional fine art departments. The struggle of photography to be a 'fine art' expressed itself in a proliferation of medium-based museums, collections and academic departments, only to be superseded by 'electronic media' (video, and now 'new media')." Hopkins sees the same process, with variations, happening in new-media departments. Yet he does not think this process of integration fools serious students, who can still decide for themselves on a means of expression. But, Hopkins warns, "hipness, in terms of the cultural industry sector's focus on different materialist forms of expression, does have an effect on those people who are seduced by concentrations of cultural patrimony and spectacle."

As Lisa Gye suggests, in terms of Internet potential, we need to distinguish between networked culture and Internet culture. The Internet has been extremely influential in terms of encouraging the development of peer-to-peer networking, chat, e-mail, blogging and so on. Lisa: "I put all of this into the category of network culture, along with telephones, cellphone use and SMS. Applications seem to be pretty central for young people. I don't see that much evidence that Web browsing is as important as it used to be for them. It is really disappointing that not more of my students are interested in the publishing possibilities of the Internet. But then they don't seem to be that engaged with public radio or television either. Maybe it's the broadcast model that's lost its edge, rather than the Internet as such." Perhaps students prefer what the Japanese call "intimate media." There is a certain fear, mixed with uncertainty, of going "out there" and exposing yourself to the world. There is a growing reluctance to participate in the emerging real-time global public sphere, in part because it is often not a conscious choice. An e-mail sent to a temporary internal list is suddenly archived for eternity. On the other hand, there is good reason to cultivate students' excitement and organize a public presentation or contest at the end of the course, with publicity in magazines and on local radio, not just on the Net.

Simon Penny argues that engineering culture should not be idealized. "The engineering worldview and career path are predicated upon provability, reliability, optimization, efficiency. This demands a microscopic tunnel vision to identify a territory: say, the electrical behavior of a certain crystal in certain conditions, which can be claimed, isolated and proved. These criteria are generally absent from the judgments that determine value in artistic practice. Unfortunately, engineering education does seem to have the effect of eradicating expansive creative thinking. Art-critical practice brings diverse criteria to bear, it is inclusive, holistic, situated and 'macro.' The criteria for value in engineering and art are inherently orthogonal to each other, and would seem irreconcilable. Yet, paradoxically, a small community of inventor-artist types doggedly persist, and historically have originated prototype technologies and technosocial situations which do not occur in the academic-industrial research world for a decade or a generation ... it is a miserable fate to be too far ahead of your time."

Discipline or Transdisciplinarity?

Is the ultimate aim the abolition of new-media departments and integration into existing disciplines? Matthew Fuller sees little promise in the lure of absorption into disciplinary structures. "Roland Barthes suggests that an interdisciplinary object is one that cannot be owned by any one discipline, that requires an array of them to be discovered, renewed, invented. Dick Higgins proposed the Fluxus category of the Intermedia, that which exists outside of any existing media and its reception structures. Félix Guattari and others suggest the transdisciplinary. There are enough models for something that exists in between."

According to Minna Tarkka, the long-term goal should not be abolition and integration. "New-media departments are needed, but they need to constantly partner up with a multiplicity of other disciplines and departments. The 'latest trends,' such as mobility, may, for example involve that the right partners for questioning will not come from graphic/industrial design but from environmental architecture and urban studies. Besides cultural studies, the dialogue with engineering still needs further development, not to speak of the links with political economy." The Cologne school attempts to work towards an integration of media and the arts, resisting subordination to the interests of the media industry. Lisa Gye agrees with Tarkka. At Swinburne University, new media is taught from a variety of perspectives across a range of disciplines, from design to sociology, philosophy, political economy, engineering and applied science. Lisa: "When it was mooted, I strongly opposed the creation of a discipline of multimedia because I could see a situation where new media would be potentially ghettoized and existing programs would be gutted. This is what has happened to online education. Staff already engaged in developing the online potential of their curriculum have been undermined by the establishment of a non-teaching department of online education."

Inspiring Models

I asked Tarkka to name some inspiring schools. She said, "The best practices of European new-media schools are local – no universally good practice can be discerned. Some schools are excellent in highly conceptual, aesthetic work, some in very structured and productive design process, some in their effort to build a multidisciplinary dialogue and some in their ability to bravely venture into new areas." Matthew Fuller names a number of inspiring schools. "I really admire the crew in Buda-pest Intermedia, the fundamental commitment to art as a life process. One of the courses we collaborate with is the Zürich design school. There are some key overlaps in approaches there, in the prioritization of a mate-rialist approach to media. From InterMedium Institute in Osaka, we can learn a lot from the lightweight organization, the way it plugs into the city, using cheap office buildings and dedicated staff and thorough stu-dents. Perhaps there are opportunities for more distributed and cellular institutions that can learn from them, from 20th-century experiments in libertarian education and from networked organizational structures. The NetNetNet program that Natalie Bookchin ran in CalArts, and students there – again small, but setting some fundamental and inspiring chal-lenges. In Brussels, the link between Hogeschool St. Lukas and the ConstantVZW agency, too, makes a connection between education, the ongoing spaces and movements of the city, various currents in digital media, the curation of public events and a refusal to get locked into any one 'sector.'"[34] John Hopkins sums up what a good school should be all about: "The school has a trim and efficient interface with hierarchic state and organizational entities around it; not too much funding (that gener-ates too much internal fighting); a fresh flow of talent on both the stu-dent and teacher sides; no departmental territories; communally shared material production facilities; a permeable interface with the local com-munity; international connections; conditions that stimulate distributed experimentation and fun; fearless teachers who can still learn; and fear-less students who can give. The best practices are those that are rooted in a unitary life where open connection to the Other is the first path."

Most of the interesting new-media departments I encounter have an inherent interest in networking with other institutions and schools else-where in the world. Networked collaboration overcomes the traditional classroom situation and gives a sense of cultural difference. John Hopkins makes an ontological distinction between the use of computers as pro-ducers of "traditional" artifacts of text, image, audio and moving image and their use when networked. He likes to de-emphasize "materialist" categories in favor of flows and movements of energy. "The existence of the socially mediatory space of global networks represents a parallel field of social action that is not yet completely colonized by the hegemonic institutions of the cultural industry sector. When exposed to these ideas, students quickly see the significance of the interstitial regions that this approach outlines and are quick to take advantage of the possibility to develop creative practices that are deeply relevant to their lives. They are empowered to liquidate another rigid distinction that often surfaces when a creative individual is squeezed through a labeled degree program – the distinction between schoolwork and real (personal) life!"

Is the demand that students get "real outcomes" from courses a legitimate one? Why should anyone support the subjection of students to the "creative imperative"? The reason is simple: money. With the introduction of a fee structure comes the expectation of a job in "the industry," if only to pay off the accumulated debt. In a post to the Nettime list, Are Flagan argues against the idea that new-media arts should further boost the economy of "free": "The surplus of free labor in any field undermines the possibility of any sustainable employment down the food chain. Especially in the new-media art field, where new courses are popping up by the minute (arguably years too late), students pay big bucks to enter a field that is extremely limited, and that has virtually no economy to secure a return on their investment and fee."[35] Still, the "industry" focus often ignores the creative potential of students and is interested merely in a steady output of young, cheap pixel pushers and HTML slaves (when Web design was the cool thing to do). John Hopkins: "In Scandinavia, often the state-mandated education programs are driven closely by industry and state-media outlets, with little validation of student endeavors in their own media worlds, like the demo scene, the club scene, and the gaming communities, where innovative practices are developed."

For Simon Penny, what new media ultimately do is create their own environment, discourse and playing field. "I have maintained for over a decade that new digital-media cultural forms will generate their own venues and sociocultural practices, as did cinema and TV. This has already happened. There are anti-war protests in virtual worlds and art performance interventions in massively multi-user online games. Oil paint found no place in filmmaking, and film did not find its place in the art museum." Apart from the self-referential autopoietic qualities that every emerging discipline must have to survive in the savage institutional context of permanent budget cuts and commercialization of (public) education, there is the question of whether new media really offer a radically different worldview. John Hopkins: "A materialist model simply doesn't suffice to understand or model the social impact of new (or old!) media. Materialist-based programs are doomed to basically tread the same pathway as previous media. Only when radically new worldviews are explored can there arise a radical practice."

In the foreseeable future, new-media arts education will remain caught between the tendency to specialize and establish itself as a grown-up, self-referential discipline and an equally strong underlying drive to unfold its true transdisciplinarity so as to integrate into the general system, thereby anticipating its own disappearance after permeating every aspect of life. These forces seem to diverge, but in the long run their effects are the same. Following Nietzsche's 1872 observation, the maximum amplification and the maximum reduction of new media are two sides of the same coin, leading to the impoverishment of the field. The goals educators set are high, and are often complicated if not contradictory. In his Digital Bauhaus manifesto, Pelle Ehn sums them up: "What is needed are meetings between constructive knowledge and competence related to interactive and communicative possibilities and constraints when using the new mediating technologies: aesthetic knowledge and competence from fields like television, theatre, film, music, literature, architecture, art and design, and analytical-critical knowledge and competence from philosophy, social science and, not least, cultural and media studies." But what if the stakeholders are not interested in such meetings and collaborations? Competition between disciplines and their respective institutions is a really existing factor which educational new-media initiatives need to be aware of. Institutional politics will most likely lead to a segmentation of new-media programs. This almost inherent problem is countered by the growing certainty that students will most likely work within interdisciplinary teams. New-media work is not assembled by lonesome laptop geniuses. Teams usually consist of designers, programmers, editors, project managers and administrators. Then there might be a sound component, and collaboration with architects, interior designers or specialists in color, stage design, light or analogue animation. In this line, Pelle Ehn called for a design network that "embraces, penetrates and unites the arts, science and technology." That was in 1998. Five years later, it might be time to evaluate and reassess such calls and investigate the outcomes of actual networks and collaborations. What are the social dynamics within transdisciplinary teams?

New media can blossom in any environment. What counts is not so much financial resources and state-of-the-art machines, but an inspiring environment in which students and staff, often assisted by outsiders, can create work. Whereas some places have a strong, open experimental tradition in the performing arts, at others it is in architecture that the interesting projects happen. Such situations cannot easily be changed and should be recognized rather than ignored. Some schools will build up strong programs that drift off into the technical, whereas others will go for the overall integrative approach. Already computers are "invading" traditional art practices such as painting, textile-making and sculpture. This happens not so much by replacing "old" media with computer screens but rather by identifying existing practices as information-processing procedures. While the conservative agenda to play out "real" artworks against "virtual" artificiality may get popular support on the rhetorical level, it no longer reflects contemporary art practice. The introduction of "wired" school buildings, followed by the wave of wireless (WiFi) networks, combined with the trend towards better and smaller batteries to free up machines, illustrates that it is no longer useful to concentrate computers in separate lab spaces. The proliferation of digital technologies throughout academic institutions could soon be followed by the closure of young, still-fragile new-media programs, in particular those that compromised themselves during the dotcom boom with their techno superiority and digital Darwinism. The same could even be said of those who gambled on cultural studies and "identitarian" politics, which since 9/11 has rapidly been losing its hegemonic position. No doubt new media will also face a backlash over the next few years. The "new" label is obviously problematic. It will hit particularly hard those who have not made strategic alliances and stick to one type of machine and application (often Apple) and do not diversify and upgrade to, for instance, mobile devices, games and high-performance networks.

It seems unwise to label new-media design work as "art" in a desperate effort to plead with the established art world for a place in the sun. This is not going to happen. The contemporary art world with its curators, critics, magazines, galleries and museums has a vested interested in co-opting exotic and "alien" technological phenomena into established discourses and markets. To "reform" the art system in this respect is a daunting task and is not the task of educational institutions. We may have to wait a generation or two for things to change. Art Center College of Design professor Peter Lunenfeld suggests that the past decade has seen a rush to conjoin art and technology which may not have been in anyone's best interest. He questions the training, aspirations, and eventual

destinies of the students who flooded into emerging new-media arts programs with shaky pedagogical and aesthetic foundations. Lunenfeld notes
that most of these students never worked as artists, instead becoming
designers of some kind. He notes, "this disjunction between training and
career is not all that unusual, as only a tiny percentage of philosophy
majors ever become philosophers, but I do wonder about how the students in these digital arts programs could have benefited from a stronger
dialogue about the relationship between creativity and clients, and working within a brief, than they got. There is much lip service given in the
academy to collaboration, but little deep thinking about the power
dynamics of group work, much less the reality that most collaborations
have strict layers of management inherent in them."[36] The emphasis on
design research within Lunenfeld's graduate Media Design Program[37] tries
to keep questions like these at the forefront of students' work, in contrast
to the "beaux-arts digital pedagogy" which he first critiqued at the sem-
inal CRASH conference (the UC Berkeley Symposium on Critical and
Historical Issues in Net Art) during the very height of the bubble in early
spring 2000.[38]

Richard Barbrook (Hypermedia Research Center) suggests one solution to
the pressure to keep up is to build up alliances with local new-media
businesses. "The practical side of the course has to be taught by visiting
lecturers who work the rest of the time in the new-media industry. No
full-time academic can keep pace with the latest versions of the software
and the new, new thing of the moment. This is why our MA has always
had an association with a commercial new-media company: first ANTI-
rom and now Lateral. We can borrow their staff as visiting lecturers and
they get to cherry-pick people for their company from the course."[39]

Collaborative project-based education is a proven model for escaping
individual vocational training and the pressure to teach commercial software. Ned Rossiter teaches digital cultures courses at Monash University
in Melbourne, Australia. "There are all sorts of projects students can work
on, from building independent media sites – these could be a mix of lists,
weblogs, filtered news and commentary – to the mapping of urban spaces
and/or work places via strategically located webcams. Background
research into webcams would be a project in itself, investigating the logic
of surveillance, and the ways in which users are implicated in surveillance. The tracking of policy formation related to information societies,
identifying various players and stakeholders, their institutional loca-

tions/interests/motivations, and the impacts policy has on both producers and recipients of info policy would be another subject."[40] An example of such an integrated theory/practice approach could be to map the political and economic forces that drive the information society agenda. For instance, who are the representatives in international bodies such as the Internet Task Force, ICANN and the Internet Society? Which international telecoms companies are involved, and what has changed since the crash of their stocks? Students could also look into the "soft" approaches of the managerial class and their consultants. Who is driving the ideology of the knowledge society? What images of "knowledge workers" are circulating? Visual representations could be made of actual cables, connectivity and ownership of the telecommunication infrastructure. Ned Rossiter again: "I would like to bring students to issues associated with the politics of learning within technologically mediated terrains and neo-liberal cultures. Students can quite readily adopt very critical, reflexive understandings of their discipline, the university and society when the conditions of possibility are directly part of the curriculum as it unfolds. In this way, teaching new media is addressing its local situation, and the emergence of a politicized student culture and intelligence of 'new-media society' starts to come into being."

The tension between vocational training and conceptual learning can be overcome by making radical choices. It remains important to emphasize that the computer is not just a tool. Ideally, new-media programs should be modeled after laboratories, not schools. One short-term aim should be to build bridges between the arts and the geek community, and leave the world of "science" alone for a while. Interdisciplinary dialogues should start nearby, with the sysadmin who runs the department server next door. Forget the astrophysicists, biochemists and work first on, say, free software and open source inside your own institution. If the computer is to be an omnipresent work environment for all forms of artistic expression, it will be of strategic importance for us all to understand contemporary computer culture and those who program code. Computer science is not just "engineering" but an art form providing society with key concepts and metaphors. To understand the hacker's world and the history of computing at large is an obligation for us all. As Walter Gropius wrote in his 1919 "Bauhaus Manifesto": "Architects, painters, sculptors, we must all return to crafts! For there is no such thing as 'professional art.' There is no essential difference between the artist and the craftsman. The artist is an exalted craftsman. By the grace of Heaven and in rare moments of inspiration that transcend the will, art may unconsciously blossom from the labor of his hand, but a base in handicrafts is essential to every artist. It is there that the original source of creativity lies. Let us therefore create a new guild of craftsmen without the class distinctions that raise an arrogant barrier between craftsmen and artists!"[41]

Oekonux and the Free-Software Model

From Linux to the GPL Society

"Die guten Zeiten kommen nicht wie der Morgen nach einer durch-
schlafenen Nacht." Bertolt Brecht

Linux as a Model for a New Society

In the following account, I will use the German Oekonux mailing list to
discuss free-software-related issues.[1] Oekonux, whose name is a blend of
the words "economy" and "Linux," introduced the concept of the GPL
society. Literally, the term means a society based on the General Public
License, which was invented by Richard Stallman in 1984 and is the most
widely used legal foundation of "copyleft" software.[2] The GPL locks software into a form of communal ownership. Software authors who incorporate or modify GPL-licensed programs are obliged to publish the software under the GPL license if they intend to distribute it. This is why some
have called the GPL a "viral" license. The same could be said of a GPL society. This kind of society will not be established through revolution or by
Third Way reformist politics, but probably in a viral way. Cornerstones of
such a society may already exist, but cannot freely unfold to their full
extent within capitalism. For the time being, their growth will be invisible – but it is not impossible to identify the "network crystals"[3] that are
part of the future layout. A better understanding of the workings of such
transformations might help us to start building post-capitalist structures.

The GPL society transcends the level of opinion; it is not simply pro- or
anti- but goes "beyond" capitalism, thereby avoiding Leninist revolutionary rhetoric while bringing forward new practices, theories and debates.
Roughly speaking, three main figures define the free-software movement's ideology. There are Richard Stallman, already mentioned, and his
Free Software Foundation; Linus Torvalds, the key figure in the development of the Linux operating system; and Eric Raymond, free-software
developer, writer of *The Cathedral and the Bazaar* and promoter of the
"open-source" business model. In 1998, under the influence of dotcom
mania, a split took place between Stallman's "free-software" faction,
which stuck to the principles, and the business-minded open-source
community that gathered around "market anarchist" Eric Raymond. For a
brief moment in time, "sharing" and "shares" got mixed up. Torvalds tried
to stay out of the dispute but was de facto on the side of Raymond's open
source. The dispute between Torvalds and Stallman goes back to the early
1990s, when Torvalds surprised the developers of the GNU operating system grouped around Stallman by launching the missing kernel, which was

dubbed Linux. Ever since, there has been a rivalry between, on the one hand, those who talk about Linux and, on the other, the Stallman faction, which insists on the name GNU/Linux to emphasize the importance of the work done by the GNU developers. The free software-versus-open source debate has been played out at many conferences and on many lists and Web forums.[4]

GPL is by no means the only license. One of the earliest, the BSD license, dates back to 1979. The GPL was written in response to the limitations that the BSD license imposed on developers. What some see as an ever-increasing confusion of acronyms can also be read as a sign of a rich culture which has developed a sophisticated set of differences over the past two decades. There are now around 60 different free software and open-source licenses to choose from. Never mix up freeware with public domain software or shareware, geeks warn. Similarly, do not confuse Apple, SUN or IBM licenses with GPL. The essential point is GPL's "contaminating" character: changes in software cannot be privatized. Unlike open-source licenses, the GPL actively builds a commons. This is why the Oekonux initiators chose the GPL as their key concept.

In the post-dotcom era, free-software "memes" are replicating fast, yet have only been visible beneath the media surface. As many have already stressed, free software is about more than a clash between Microsoft and Linux. It is a utopian model for some and a business opportunity for others. This chapter is one of a thousand possible ways of telling the free software and society story. My point of view is that of a non-programmer, media theorist and tactical media producer with a particular interest in the Internet. Without wanting to deny the crucial importance of code and licenses, I read free software primarily as a metaphor. Software, in my view, is not just a tool but primarily a social and cultural artifact, a product and reflection of a specific historical formation that transcends the technical and legal functionality of "versions." It is no coincidence that I have chosen a German mailing list: 12.4% of free-software developers are German, meaning that nationality ranks second on the list.[5] Their motivation is often said to be related to concerns over the public domain. Many Oekonux members are involved in free-software development projects (which ones, exactly, are not discussed). To be clear, the Oekonux project does not propose an open-source model of its own. Like the majority of free-software developers, Oekonux members would be satisfied working with the GPL license. What Oekonux offers is a rich and deep, yet culturally specific, theorization of the field. Oekonux is one of the few online initiatives that reflect theoretically on free software, beyond technical issues, from a critical social-science perspective.

Many of the Oekonux debates are about the so-called *Keimform* (germ, embryo or seed) hypothesis, which claims that free software has the ability to "germinate" into larger political-economic structures. This model is neither one of a top-down Leninist "revolution" nor of social-democratic class compromises, but of a radical, "viral" transformation. The "germination" focus has the advantage that it does not get stuck in the dirty everyday reality of capitalism and end up as a reformist project, as has happened to many green parties and environmental initiatives. The idea of a GPL society draws lessons from the 20th century. How can a society be based on technology without ending up in a techno-determinist theocracy ruled by engineers? How can free-software projects transcend geek circles and "grow up" without making compromises or provoking fatal accidents?[6] How does technology, which itself clearly has social, political and cultural aspects, transform society beyond the instrumental level of code? And conversely, how are various free-software projects themselves becoming infected by society through their very own success? The Oekonux group, which addresses these issues, is small and primarily German-speaking, but there are similar lists in other languages, and it is certain that their debates will soon be carried out in other contexts and in wider circles.

We have entered a crucial period, with free software and open source on the brink of leaving behind the "geek culture" of IT and spreading in a multitude of directions, both as software and as a set of attractive, "infectious" ideas and concepts. Free software began the process of entering society at large in the late 1990s, but for many reasons – dot-com mania being one – its implementation remained an issue only for programmers and other IT experts. Part of the "socialization" of free software, in my view, will be to open up multidisciplinary channels of dialogue. This process involves more than instructing users how to install Debian, Open Office or KDE, although that in itself is also a fascinating and daunting task.

Users are no longer taking orders from an almighty engineering class that offers advanced "technical" solutions to human problems. Windows and Macintosh users are not "blinded" by corporate propaganda. Let's face it:

most computer users are not interested in their operating systems – not even when software is free of cost. What the free-software community needs is a critical understanding of economics, philosophy, global politics and contemporary cultural issues. One of the "hidden" impacts of free software/open source is the extensive transfer of economic values from rich countries to the developing world. It is in this respect as much geek culture as society that must open up and change. The argument between Richard Stallman and Eric Raymond over how to make free software more business-friendly is, luckily, wearing itself out. As a result, the free software/open source opposition is gradually losing its meaning – and many never bought into this polemic in the first place. I won't use the (politically) correct terms GNU/Linux or FLOSS.[7] Or maybe I will. In my view, linguistic jargon control such as that exercised by Richard Stallman is part of the problem, not the solution. Rigid vocabulary creates ghettos instead of interesting alliances. There is something to be said for conceptual clarity, but such an effort should not have the aim of policing others. I will not attempt to come up with new definitions or "debug" existing ones. It is much more interesting to report on debates and efforts around the world which are contextualizing free software. One such effort could be to make non-English material available to the global English-reading community (instead of the other way around, as is usual).

Wizard of OS Conferences

The Oekonux project is an outcome of the first Wizard of OS (Operating System) conference, which took place in Berlin in July 1999.[8] WOS's organization was in the hands of Berlin's Mikro e.V., a network of new-media artists and critics founded in 1998. Mikro was the result of growing discontent with failed new-media policies in the German capital.[9] Other than a series of successful monthly public presentations and debates, the Rohrpost mailing list for German Net culture, and the Bootlab media workspace, the WOS conference series has been Mikro's biggest and most visible activity. Mikro member Volker Grassmuck has been the driving force behind the WOS conferences. At the first WOS, the German programmer and Oekonux founder Stefan Merten called a group together after the "New Economy?" panel; the mailing list resulted from that informal gathering.

Wizards of OS should not be considered an ordinary Linux conference. Its agenda is a unique mix, and closely tied to Grassmuck's biography. At the theoretical level, there was input from theorists around the Berlin media professor Friedrich Kittler, who argued that computer operating systems were essentially the literature of our time. The subtitle of the event was "Operating Systems and Social Systems." Computer history was an important part of the program. The conference started off with a brilliant lecture by Wolfgang Hagen, an expert on computer history.[10] Hagen is a typical representative of the techno-determinist school, which states that hardware dictates software. In other words, software was, is and will always be, a byproduct of hardware and its logic. Speed and mode of calculation are merely a question of flip-flops – the frequency of electronic pulses. In the first generation of computers, software was literally inscribed in the architecture of the hardware; it had only gradually become a matter of language, Hagen claimed.

Arts-related topics remained marginal at the first WOS conference, with the exception of a presentation by the Russian Net artist Alexei Shulgin, but this element became more prominent at the second WOS in October 2001. In 1999, at the height of dotcom mania, debate centered around the economics of open source. Topics at the first WOS included open-source cryptography, biotech firms and the open-source code of life, and free software in education. Richard Stallman was the keynote speaker,[11] while Tim O'Reilly did the visionary dotcom talk about "infoware" replacing software. O'Reilly explained to the German audience that the open-source revolution would soon be over: commercialization and corporate takeovers were on the horizon. According to O'Reilly, "infoware" was turning both hard- and software into second-grade entities. The result would be a wave of free products and services. ISPs, operating systems, browsers, webspace and e-mail would all be free. Amazon.com, not Dell, HP or Microsoft, would be the killer app. Applications that could run on top of free software were the future, O'Reilly argued. In April 2001, a similar conference called Code was organized in Cambridge, England. It focused on collaboration and ownership in the digital age.[12] By then, the debate had shifted away from dotcom economics to the role of "open" science and culture in relation to "intellectual property" regimes.

WOS organizer Volker Grassmuck might, politically speaking, be close to Lawrence Lessig.[13] Lessig attacks monopolies like Microsoft and speaks of truly free markets, arguing for a climate of openness in which "open knowledge" can freely thrive. But Grassmuck is not a neo-liberal marketer. I would associate him neither with Nettime's aim of deconstructing the techno-libertarian hacker's agenda nor with the utopian Marxism of the Oekonux circle. His background as a Kittlerian techno-determinist makes him optimistic about the ability of technology to transform social relationships. As a European scholar he is convinced that the state has an important role to play in curbing monopolist power. Grassmuck favors a "marketplace of ideas" operating outside the money-based economy. According to Grassmuck, Lessig's pro-market stance must be understood as a strategic gesture. His Creative Commons initiative, for instance, is not at all targeted at the commercial realm. As a result of Grassmuck's efforts, WOS has given the German free-software community a cultural-academic arm, an element that was missing from the Chaos Computer Club (www.ccc.de), a hacker's group which resembles 2600 in the USA and Hack-tic/XS4ALL in the Netherlands. The idea of WOS and similar events is to insert "cultural intelligence" into the free-software community while at the same time opening up the academic world and the cultural sector to the free-software principles.[14] Grassmuck seeks to remind us that open-source ideas originate in the scientific community, which is now confronted with policies that commercialize publicly financed and owned knowledge production.

German Debating Culture

Soon after the Oekonux mailing list was started in July 1999, Stefan Merten opened the www.oekonux.de website, which contains links, common writing projects, announcements and the list archive. The site has a special English section. Oekonux has a unique feature, an internal project list which members can join if they want to help direct the initiative. In 2002 Oekonux opened a second, international list in English; in early 2003 it had a modest 90 subscribers. The German list has grown steadily and had reached 250 subscribers by early 2003. Traffic on the German list varies between 50–300 posts a month, usually about 6 to 8 a day. In mid-2003 its Web archive contained 6,700 postings. According to the intro page, the Oekonux website gets between 150,000 and 200,000 hits a month[15] and 500 to 700 visitors a day. The Oekonux list has so far organized two meetings, one from April 28 to 30, 2001, in Dortmund, and the second, which had significantly more international visitors, in November 2002 in Berlin.[16] A book project has been initiated; its progress can be followed on the Web.[17] There have also been calls on the English Oekonux lists for an anthology of (translated) Oekonux texts to be put together.

Over the years Oekonux has become a more international project, but the process is slow. For now, its core remains the German mailing list.

Stefan Merten emphasizes the pleasant atmosphere on the German list. Flamewars hardly ever happen, and only a few people have ever unsubscribed. Because of the sheer quantity, scope and depth of the discussions, I have to stress that this summary is strictly personal, and I by no means claim to give an overview of all the players and positions. The Oekonux discourse is dense. Threads can go on for months and stretch over hundreds of e-mails with different subject headers, which makes it hard to summarize debates. Insights that might be ignored and lost on another list are always responded to here. Replies to a post can be posted much later, often reviving a thread which might otherwise have died. The ultimate aim of Oekonux, as the intro file puts it, is "common learning" through discussion. The level of the debate can be pretty sophisticated. But, as the document says, only in a friendly environment can issues be raised that go beyond the common understanding. Oekonux is one of the most "rational" Internet mailing lists I know of. By that, I refer to a commonly shared passion for rationally digging as deeply as possible into each other's arguments and turning commonly used concepts inside out.

The Oekonux list gives a sense of what thorough German rhetoric is all about. It is proof that there are still online forums unaffected by trolls and spam – for those not allergic to traces of 1970s academic Marxist jargon. The Oekonux community is embedded in German intellectual culture, and there is little interest in what happens in the post- or late-Marxist world outside the German language zone. There is no proper English word for *auseinandersetzen*. The dictionary says it means to argue, tackle, confront or even clash with, but that only covers half its meaning. What is missing is the analytical, both hermeneutic and aesthetic aspect of, for example, the *Redebeitrag,* a contribution to a debate in which clauses, or principles and theorems, are taken apart. German polemics often are entertaining (as good rhetoric should be) even as they dive deep into the topic and the language itself. This widespread cultural practice should not be confused with the academic deconstruction school. I am referring here to a lively, in-depth, real-life debate, held during a lengthy plenary session (or *Plenum*). The Oekonux list echoes the orderly, precise, yet fascinating German debating culture.[18]

The two Stefans

Oekonux founder and list owner Stefan Merten is a computer science graduate in his late 30s who is based in the German town of Kaiserslautern. Merten describes himself as an "anarcho-libertarian" who keeps returning to Karl Marx. In one of his first e-mails to the list, he refers to one of his earlier projects, the "critical university." It was the work of Marxist theorist Robert Kurz and the Krisis group that had led Merten to the idea of the "socialization" potential of Linux.[19] Before starting Oekonux, he had tried to discuss free software within the context of the Krisis group, but it didn't really work. Still, the work of Robert Kurz and other Krisis members keeps popping up on Oekonux as a central reference area. The main thesis of the apocalyptic Marxists is the "crisis mode" of today's capitalism, which can no longer promise full employment and prosperity for all.[20] The welfare-state dream of full employment is over. There is no longer any way of producing surplus value, not even in automated factories. The global financial system only refers to itself and no longer needs labor in order to accumulate. The destruction of the environment combined with a shift away from the traditional exploitation of labor towards global financial markets leads to an inherently unstable, boom and crash form of "casino capitalism."[21] The problems are endemic. This is why the Krisis group often uses the term "catastrophic." Krisis has often been criticized for its fatalism in believing that capitalism will simply collapse under its own contradictions.[22] Having given up any hope of a possible role for the working class, this "Marxism without a subject" can only come up with radical negative thinking and has detached itself from any practical struggle. Theoretically speaking, many Oekonux members operate within the Krisis context yet emphasize the nucleus of another society in the free-software movement.

Another founding member of Oekonux is Stefan Meretz (not to be confused with the other Stefan), a Berlin-based IT expert who works for the large trade union ver.di. His background is in "critical informatics." At the moment he is one of the developers of a content-management system for trade unions that runs on free software (www.verdi.org). In early 1999, Meretz gave a talk about Linux as a social alternative. The original issues the list was meant to discuss included the economic model of Linux, to which part of society its principles could be transferred, whether these defied the concept of private property, and to what extent capitalism would be able to absorb free software.[23] Meretz runs the Open Theory project, which allows authors to post texts and others to comment on them.[24] The two Stefans do not share the same theoretical-political position. Whereas Merten tends towards a techno-determinist position, Meretz has no such illusions and often emphasizes the social dimension of things. Other Oekonux members bring in ideas from radical ecology movements, the New Age left, and socialist groups. With its alternative-left background, Oekonux could easily be positioned as opposing the open-source business.[25] But this is not the feeling one gets from the list. The free-software business is not perceived as a "renegade" that must be crushed in order to keep the movement pure. Rather, an unarticulated postmodern culture of tolerance and dialogue prevails. The fact that IBM is making billions of dollars with Linux is acknowledged, but not seen as a "betrayal" or analyzed in terms of (self-)exploitation of voluntary labor. So far, all these cultures coexist side by side. Sectarian fights do happen, but they are over metaphysical definitions, not markets or political influence.

Oekonux is an almost perfect Platonic debating environment of self-disciplined Germans such as many list owners can only dream of. Too good to be true, one would almost say. Indeed, the moderator's grip on the project is considerable. It's all deadly serious. Oekonux is yet another case of the "benevolent dictatorship" of the well-intentioned list moderator. In this case Merten's "power" is not just structural but also discursive: his voice on the list is omnipresent. Merten is the only list moderator I have so far come across who responds sincerely to literally every post. This leads to repeated sighs and complaints on his part, because obviously he cannot keep up. At times he responds to e-mails 30 or 40 days old. Merten finds it hard to shut up and let the list find its own way. This gives him the unintended image of a busybody. No one has yet explicitly accused him of being meddlesome. His grip on the project is almighty, and it almost seems like his sole hobbyhorse. He admits to have deleted several "non-relevant" posts from the list archive. On the other hand, the Oekonux project has become too big to be reduced to the private obsession of one person. Still, Merten's signature can be found everywhere, and the list revolts time and again against his dominant presence.[26] Subscriber Graham Seaman says, "I am often a 'mediator' – someone who brings people from different groups in touch with another, without having anything particular of my own to say. Stefan is rather a 'perpetuator', a person who will try to summarize everything other people have said, so that everyone feels they have been replied to, and there is a basis to continue an otherwise rather fragmented discussion."[27] Merten's consistent interference could be one reasons the Oekonux project has stagnated slightly over the nearly four years of its existence (as I write in mid-2003). Merten carefully marks out what is and is not acceptable within the aims of the Oekonux project and makes no secret of his personal tastes and opinions. His firm grip on debates has resulted in arguments starting to repeat themselves, with the effect that only a select group continues to post and exchange arguments with Merten, while others who do not fit into his ideological schematic disappear after a few posts.[28] In early 2002, the general atmosphere on the list deteriorated. Differences of opinion escalated, prompting Arnulf Pelzer to accuse Oekonuxers of being "more Christian than the Pope."[29]

Post-Capitalist Germs

The central question that occupies the Oekonux community is the extent to which free software could be described as a *Keimform* that can "germinate" while migrating to other parts of society, in a sort of socio-economic metamorphosis. Oekonux, one could say, is in search of new rituals beyond the obvious one of putting the Linux operating system onto the hard drive. What are the historical laws that promote the introduction of open-source principles in society? The Oekonux thesis says that free software is not just computer code but should be interpreted, analyzed and further developed as a part of a larger transformation called *Vergesellschaftung* (something between socialization and social dynamics: literally, becoming society). In early 2001 I did an e-mail interview for Nettime with Stefan Merten (in English). In it, he remarks that few Marxists have rethought the terms Marx developed. He says he rarely finds people who call themselves "Marxians" interesting. "My criticism of past leftist (Marxian) currents is their lack of a utopia. The 'utopia' they had was not more than an improved labor society, rather similar to the one they lived in."[30] Merten notes that there is a common sense within Oekonux of free software as "an early form of the new society embedded in the old society." As Linus Torvalds says, "With computers and programming you can build new worlds and sometimes the patterns are truly beautiful."[31]

The *Keimform* theory originates in the work of the West German Marxist psychologist Klaus Holzkamp; this theory is heavily promoted on Oekonux by Merten, Meretz and others. Holzkamp became well known in German academic circles in the 1970s as a representative of the "critical psychology" school. According to Holzkamp, changes in society can be described in five steps. In the first phase, the "germ" comes into being as a "collective invention" (Robert Allen).[32] In this early period, the new ideas are not all that visible. This changes in the second stage, when the dominant form encounters a crisis. During the third phase, the germ gains hegemony within the old, dominant structure. Next, it evolves into the dominating factor. It is only in the last, fifth stage that the entire system must subordinate the germ, which has become dominant itself. According to Merten, free software is currently in the third phase.[33] Glyn Moody, in *Rebel Code*, describes two distinct schools within the Linux networking community. One's philosophy is "Make it work first, then make it better"; the other's is "make it better first."[34] The Oekonux GPL society clearly works on the second principle. There is no rush. Society will be revolutionized from within, from the heart of the machine.

A important aspect of Oekonux is that we can set aside well-known topics of critical Internet culture for a while and see what happens in metal workshops,[35] car manufacturing and regular offices. There is a belief amongst Oekonuxers that the free-software principles they discuss are deeply rooted in economic structures – if not those of today's society, certainly those of the future. It can be interesting to compare algorithms with ordinary commodities you can buy in the supermarket, or discuss the use of new, lightweight materials, nanotechnology and computerized production processes. The question here is how to translate concepts applied to information into the material realm. Take, for instance, the Openeeg project, which tries to create a low-cost EEG device (for recording brainwaves using electrodes on the head).[36] Franz Nahrada points at an ideal *Keimform* example: the "rough-and-ready" chairs of Dutch-British interior designer Tord Boontje. Instead of selling objects, Boontje offers free drawings with building instructions.[37] The oft-made contradiction between "real" commodities and virtual information is no longer relevant. Cyberspace already envelops society.[38]

Today, most material goods production is based on information technologies. Like good old Marxists, Oekonux primarily focuses on society's work and production aspects, and not just the slippery simulacrum sphere of media, arts and culture. In the same way we can ask why no one thus far has analyzed supply-chain software from a sociocultural perspective. Millions work with SAP and with Baan products, and the entire planet depends on them, but they fall entirely outside the "social software" scope. It is to some extent a relief to see that there is no special interest in Oekonux within cultural studies or "the creative industries." For many Oekonux participants, the computer is capable of more than just communication. Merten: "The development of computers as universal information processors with ever-increasing capacity is shifting the focal point of production from the material side to the immaterial, information side. Today the development of the means of production in capitalism has entered a new historical phase."[39]

Stefan Merten admits that Oekonux doesn't have a full-blown concept of what a new society would look like, "and we better should not have such a drawing table model." Nonetheless, "NGOs share a number of interesting aspects with the development of free software and may be seen as a non-technical counterpart among the germ forms for the GPL society," he says. "In the midst of capitalism you can see how the production process starts to depend on information." According to Merten, the material side of production is becoming less important. "And information is something very different from the material world simply by the fact that you can copy it without losing the original." Since the invention of computers, and particularly of the Internet, the scarcity of digital information has become difficult to maintain, Merten says. Once digital information has been produced, it is reproducible at an extremely marginal cost. This is the reason corporations of all kinds are making such a fuss about so-called "intellectual property rights": IPRs could make digital information a scarce good to be profited from. Stefan Merten, with fellow Oekonuxers, is of the opinion that with the technical means of reproduction, now distributed among millions of households, "the bottle is opened, the ghost is out and nothing will be able to put it back in there." Free software is an example of non-rivalry goods.[40] However, there is an even more fundamental reason why Merten thinks the free production of information, and in the end of all material goods, will overcome exchange-based societies: they are supposed to be of better quality. There is a sense of superiority in the air here. Merten uses open-source science, fairy tales and recipes as examples that show how useful global cooperation and sharing of information can be in terms of realizing the GPL society.

According to Merten, free software is an anomaly, a contradiction to capitalism.[41] It is not a commodity, operates outside the realm of accumulation and thus, by its very nature, does not fit into the capitalist mode of production. To follow Merten's thinking, free software eliminates abstract, fetish-type exchange value and establishes an economy dominated by the practical (use) value of goods and services. Capitalism cannot develop a production method based on self-expression. Others have countered this claim by saying that capitalism is capable of appropriating virtually anything. Instead of presenting free software as an inherent contradiction, critics insist that its production is taken up as a creative provocation which, in the end, will be neutralized and integrated in the next wave of modernization.[42] Along these lines, Christian Fuchs accused Oekonux of being an elitist tech circle that does not recognize its "objective" role in the process of reforming capitalism.[43] Hackers clearly do not operate outside the capitalist economy. Their "leisure-time" work on free software is made possible by other entities. But this doesn't bring the debate much further. Cynical appropriation theories are valid, but boring because they are always right. They close rather than open strategy debates and rarely develop new practices. Merten responded to Fuchs that the "new" cannot develop itself in a vacuum and is impossible to separate from "old" structures. Coding is fertile, not futile. In my view, it is the task of the critical techno-intelligentsia to search within existing complex systems for "germs of the new" and stop complaining about the almighty power of the capitalist beast that eventually will absorb all dissent. There is an earnest search under way by the post-1989 generation to leave the 20th century behind and circumvent the "tired" choice between reform and revolution.

There are numerous "non-capitalist" tendencies within the history of hacking – they just need to be dug out. The growing importance of knowledge produces cracks in capitalist logic.[44] In his biography, GPL inventor Richard Stallman tells of a shift during the Reagan years towards selling software instead of treating it as a zero-cost commodity. "Selling software became more than a way to recoup costs, it became a political statement. More than a few programmers saw the hacker ethic as anti-competitive, and, by extension, un-American. At best it was a throwback to the anti-corporate attitudes of the late 1960s and early 1970s. Like a Wall Street banker discovering an old tie-dyed shirt hiding between French-cuffed shirts and double-breasted suits, many programmers treated the hacker ethic as an embarrassing reminder of an idealistic age."[45] The same could be said of Oekonux's discourse and rituals, which remind Germanophiles of the rigid "Stamokap" years in the 1970s,[46] dominated by "scientific Marxists," when thousands of "young socialists" (including Chancellor Gerhard Schröder) sat together in local study groups reading

Marx. One must overcome fears of such antagonism and ignore the *Zeitgeist* and the opinions of journalists and friends in order to extract from the Oekonux sandbox that which is useful for one's own context and needs.

Women and Other Topics

Topics discussed on the German Oekonux list vary from highly conceptual fare and the usual free-software news items to infobits from the everyday. Because of the sheer quantity and length of posts (often with quotes), I can't summarize them here, but subjects of debates included author payments, software patents, the debate about basic income (related to André Gorz, who appears to have an ideological position close to Oekonux's), or the question of "modes of dominance" *(Herrschaftsverhält-nisse)* and whether a world without rule, governance or power is possible.[47] Another issue that keeps coming up is the question of what the status of "knowledge" is in relation to (the crisis of) labor. To what extent can leftists buy into the rhetoric of the "knowledge society"? There was a discussion about Ulrich Sigor's concept of "media feudalism," in which political authority is centered in private organizations and based on the management of abstract forms of wealth.[48] The only time the list discussed a non-related topic was just after 9/11, when people all over Germany debated the anti-Semitic origins of the "War Against America." Oekonux's unquestioning relationship to cyberlibertarianism, North American ideas of liberty and the "founding fathers" is remarkable. The reason for this could be that the project's aim is not to deconstruct others' statements but to dig deep into the concepts themselves in order to come up with a comprehensive theory of the social future.

There are frequent references to the political science-fiction writer Christoph Spehr and his "theory of free cooperation."[49] Whereas some find useful elements in Spehr's work, others, such as Stefan Merten, reject Spehr's presumed "overidentification" with powerless and marginal groups, which he calls *maquis* (French for bush rebels, comparable to the concept of the multitudes).[50] Instead of contributing to a further conceptualization, Merten accuses Spehr of "leftist populism." One equipped with a literary imagination can easily fall out of grace in this dry scientific environment.[51] Stefan Meretz also made interesting remarks about Spehr, which he titled "The Wild Jungle of Cooperation."[52] Beyond good and evil, cooperation should not be presented in a moral fashion, Meretz argues. Cooperation is a complex issue, no matter the scale on which it takes place. It is making a false contradiction to play out the large-scale, complex society against small, simple groups. As Spehr says, the essence of free cooperation is the freedom to break up and move on.

The absence of women in free-software projects remains a challenge, and also is an issue for Oekonux. The few women, such as Annette Schlemm and Sabine Nuss, who frequently post have not changed the overall situation. It is not so much that the gender topic is ignored as that there is a general incapability to change gender relations within the free-software community, and Oekonux is no exception.[53] Whereas women play a key role as computer operators and have taken up the Internet quickly, their role in the IT sector remains marginal (around 10% of the workforce). The situation today is worse than in the 1980s and early 1990s, even in absolute numbers. The explanation that women are more interested in computers as tools, whereas men create their identity around the computer as a self-referential "bachelor machine," may sound plausible but does not point at any possible solution. The situation in free software is even more dramatic than in normal IT projects. If 98% of free-software developers are male,[54] while at the same time free software is being propagated as a model for a future society, isn't something fundamentally wrong? asks Benni Bärmann on the Oekonux list.[55]

Oekonux is not unique. Graham Seaman is one of the few people who can compare it with the Spanish-Portuguese list Hipatia, which discusses similar topics. Hipatia was originally Latin-American but now also covers Spanish- and Portuguese-speaking countries in Europe and has just started in Italy. Seaman says, "Some of the difference compared to Oekonux is just the geographic spread of the languages, but a lot of it is attitude. The Hipatia attitude is more outgoing, more assertive. Oekonux dissects issues in detail, whereas Hipatia skims over topics briefly. People always seem to want to be doing something. Discussions last about ten e-mails and then do not show up again. An example: most participants felt that the Hipatia manifesto should be improved, but the text had already been translated into languages including Farsi, Russian, Korean. There is very little clarity on shared goals; that they are shared is simply assumed." Seaman notices that Hipatia has a much larger proportion of women (who often dominate discussions) and goes out of its way to influence political groups. Oekonux, on the other hand, is wary of external politics. Other differences: Oekonux members inspect factories to try to understand the direction productive technology is going in; Hipatia visits factories to provide computing support for factory occupations. Oekonux rarely discusses software on the list; Hipatia often does. Seaman: "I'm just surprised how different two groups with a formally similar basis can be. Some of the difference, both positive and negative, is the Stefans. The people who were the original inspiration of Hipatia stay quiet, with only occasional magisterial interventions. A large part of the nature of Oekonux is simply nationality. There is an inheritance of endless theorizing (à la Young Hegelians), combined with a defensiveness and fear of imposing the world with well-meant German values, a lesson learned from recent history."[56]

"Self-Unfolding"

The "attention economy" meme, once so popular among New Economy academics, is criticized on Oekonux for its attempt to reintroduce capitalist money/exchange principles through the back door.[57] There is a free-software saying, "contribute nothing; expect nothing," which is a variation of the old "give what you can; take what you need" phrase (or even "produce what you like, consume what you can"). Merten: "I have used thousands of Web pages and millions of lines of code contained in free software without giving anything back. You simply take what you need and you provide what you like. It's not by chance that this reflects the old demand which says 'Everybody according to his/her needs.'"[58] Similarly, the anthropological models of gift and potlatch are rejected. There is no reciprocity, according to Merten, nor any expectation among free-software producers of getting anything back, excepting perhaps a reputation among their peers. It is arguable whether there is any accumulation of "cultural capital" (Bourdieu) within free-software production, but I would suspect that this is certainly the case.

In the interview, Stefan Merten explained to me that the future society will no longer be based on exchange and exchange value, and that this is why the whole term "labor" will no longer make sense. This new society will be based on principles such as individual self-expression *(Selbstentfaltung)* combined with self-organization and global cooperation. Here, Merten's ideas touch on dotcom fantasies about creativity, working conditions and the "free ideology" that were common among the wider Internet generation in the late 1990s.[59] "Goods in such a society are not sold but simply available and taken by those who need them. The GPL society transcends the industrial model of production into a new form, which allows human potential to really flourish." But Merten is quick to add: "Of course such a society is difficult to imagine for people who grew up with only money on their minds." The absence of exchange value (i.e. money), "self-unfolding," self-organization, and global cooperation are all key concepts of the Oekonux project that can be recognized in the principles of free-software development.

Self-development, or rather self-unfolding (to use the ugly, direct translation of the German term *Selbstentfaltung*), is another crucial (and deeply Protestant) notion. According to the Oekonux glossary, "individual and collective *Selbstentfaltung* is the main source of societal productivity, thereby potentially abolishing the current form of economy based on wage labor, money, and exchange." The Oekonux formula is: free software = self-unfolding + Internet. Disagreement remains about the correct English translation of the term. Personal unfolding is more than self-realization, a concept that focuses too much on the isolated individual and has nothing to do with altruism. "Self-unfolding understands humans as formed by their relations. Self-unfolding of the single person is a direct precondition for the development of all, and vice versa."[60] Some prefer the term "man's unfolding" or simply "unfolding." Stefan Merten explains why he prefers the "self-" prefix: "I don't do something explicitly 'for others' (altruistically), but I do it for me. However, this 'doing for me' does not go on costs of others. The self-unfolding concept starts from the 'self,' from me, not from anything outside – a higher knowledge, spirituality or stuff like that."[61]

The self-unfolding concept is discussed within Oekonux in an attempt to overcome the "work" imperative.[62] Self-unfolding is the opposite of alienated labor in a command economy. As with other German debates about "economy" and "money," here some Oekonuxers do not look for alternatives within the work category but reject the concept altogether. At least, some do; others question the use of such radical negations and seek more pragmatic solutions. On the English Oekonux list, Graham Seaman pointed to Ivan Illich's concept of "vernacular work": unpaid activities which provide and improve livelihood, but which are totally refractory to any analysis utilizing concepts developed in formal economics.[63] The "nature" of free-software production is important because it is done neither out of egoism nor out of altruism in the classic sense of charity work. *Selbstentfaltung* has two results: I create something that is useful for many, and I form myself. Both are in the interest of all. The importance of the first can differ: the degree of usefulness to others can approach zero. But the second element is always present.[64] Michel Foucault's more sophisticated concepts such as "techniques of the self," "sovereignty" and "governmentality" and Christopher Lasch's "reflexivity" are not discussed in this context but could nonetheless be of interest.

Oekonux is neither an avant-garde, despite its explicit interest in utopias, nor should it be seen as the technology department of some green or communist party. In my opinion it is a critical-hermeneutic laboratory (slightly Protestant, fair enough) centered on the development and assessment of ideas. Its untimely Marxism is something that can easily be criticized but may as well be accepted as the cultural condition of this particular online tribe. According to the Oekonux canon, the aim of the GPL society effort is not so much simply to overthrow capitalism but to get rid of its underlying principles. Money is usually seen as the tangible form of the appearance of value. Because capitalism is equated with the money economy itself, it is not possible to develop an effective "countereconomy" that develops free software based on the same money principle. This idea is widely accepted and has become a cornerstone of the Oekonux philosophy because its members work for free (and have paid day jobs). Unlike the "alternative economy" of co-ops that started in the 1970s and 1980s, including printing houses, organic farms, media and publishing ventures, health-food stores, café's, bookshops and more, all of which have a money component, the free-software movement is supposed to stay outside monetary circulation.[65] The moral stance that says money corrupts and itself prolongs capitalism goes beyond geek culture and can be traced throughout the Internet. Contrary to what one would expect from a Marxist circle discussing free software, the "free" ideology remains largely uncontested.[66] How free-software programmers make a living is a personal matter that is not widely discussed, let alone politicized.

An early topic on the Oekonux list related to this issue is the status of voluntary labor. Unpaid work is on the increase, and this could be read as both an expression of the crisis and as a sign of liberation. In some ways the debate reminds one of 1970s feminist theories on the political economy of domestic labor. However, in this case the "free" work is mainly done by highly skilled males who see their progressive contribution to free software as liberating from the (capitalist) monetary economy. Linux

is seen as a non-profit activity capable of both pushing for-profit products off the market and questioning traditional divisions between pleasure and work. Free cooperation is presented as superior to competition.[67]
According to certain Marxist formulas, writing free-software code is not
a private hobby nor can it be compared to reproductive (domestic) labor.
There is disagreement on the list about the normative distinctions between different types of work, with some activities strategically tied to
the productive forces and others not. Stefan Meretz insists that free-software production is not a hobby because a hobby has manual, 19th-centu-
ry characteristics. He argues that projects such as Linux should be positioned at the very edge of economic development, have general usage
and should not be disdainfully looked down upon.[68]

Projects Beyond Free Software

There are countless projects under way that apply the free-software principles to other fields in society. Many are mentioned or discussed on
Oekonux and together they might give an idea of where the GPL society
is heading. For instance, like Oekonux, www.ourproject.org provides tools
that "encourage the cooperative work effort of all types of people from
every part of the world, promoting the coming together of people and the
exchange of ideas and solutions to problems, with the condition that the
results of the projects will remain freely accessible to whoever may find
them useful."[69] The trick here is not to make the usual distinction between
technical and non-technical aspects of society. Technology has "invaded"
all dimensions of life. Computers and the employment of computer networks can be found in virtually all professions. This omnipresent technoculture makes it possible for general principles of free software to
"migrate" to other contexts. Within Oekonux itself, the Open Theory
Project assists in the writing of "open" texts. With the help of a Web
interface, readers can comment on the texts, which are installed and
managed by a maintainer.

Then there are free encyclopedias, such as Wikipedia,[70] and "free music" –
not that copied from commercial CDs but that offered for free from the
start and distributed in line with the GPL principle. There are visual artists
who experiment with "copyleft" and open content, using the Creative
Commons license and experimenting with the exchange of artworks on
sites such as www.opuscommons.net, operated by the Sarai new-media
center in Delhi. The question discussed on Oekonux is how open-source

theory can be applied to collaborative artistic practices. Members have extensively discussed so-called *Umsonstläden,* free shops where people can get goods at no cost. At the online front, a slow but steady "wikification" of knowledge production is happening that goes far beyond the Wikipedia project itself. One could also mention the free online scholarship (FOS) movement, which puts peer-reviewed scholarly literature on the Internet.[71] Open-source principles are also applied in the hard sciences – think of the fascinating open-source battle within the human genome project.[72] One could also mention OpenLaw, an experiment in crafting legal arguments in an open forum. With the input of users, OpenLaw develops arguments, drafts pleas and edits briefs online.[73] There are also projects like OpenMedicine, OpenBiology and OpenScience, all of which fight the scientific publishing houses and their rigid intellectual-property-rights regimes.

In an essay written in 2000, the Canadian academic Michael Century sums up elements of a cultural history of "open code" that goes beyond the well-known free-software canon as defined by Richard Stallman, Eric Raymond and Linus Torvalds. There is a certain dissatisfaction among humanities scholars with describing free-software production solely in ethnographic terms such as "gift economy" or "cooking-pot market." As possible alternatives, Century mentions the historic social construction of authorship (Woodmansee), the poetics of "open work" (Umberto Eco), and early hypertext ideas about linked documents such as Ted Nelson's Xanadu as the foundation of computer networks. Century also points at the collaborative traditions within the contemporary arts. "As personal computers became ubiquitous since the 1980s, several languages for programming interactive experiential art works became available; commonly, these were conceived initially to satisfy the requirements of a specific project, but then were adapted progressively to become quasi-standards. One such language, MAX, came out of the terrain of computer music research (IRCAM, Paris), to become a near lingua franca among the worldwide community of artists concerned with interactive performance."[74] One could also refer to film and sound cut-ups broadcast on radio and the Internet and at rave parties which mix news items and music samples. Century: "Generative music, in both avant-garde and popular ambient styles like Brian Eno, has been practiced since the 1960s. Eno's ideas about authorless music are being implemented in software today." However, it is not in the commercial art world, with its great need for identifiable celebrities and copyright regimes, that anonymous networked art thrives. This phenomenon can only be found on underground servers, on pirate/free-radio stations and in paper zines, where individual authorship can be overcome.

To sum up, the key elements of the GPL society are: "self-unfolding" as the main motivation for production; the irrelevance of exchange value and a shift in focus towards use value; and free cooperation between people and international teams.[75] "As well as capitalism with its industrial model was able to deliver better products compared to the former feudalistic models and therefore overcame feudalism, free production of goods will overcome the present model of capitalism."[76] Just as agriculture is no longer essential as a primary industry in the developed world, capitalism is relying less and less on industrial production. This historical "truth" is extrapolated into the future. Time and again, Benni Bärmann stands up and protests against Marxist techno-determinism. In his "Eight Theses on Liberation," Bärmann defines liberation as a never-ending process. He warns against the schematic idea that free-software principles inhabit a "historic truth" that will unfold over time and merely needs to be followed.[77] The fact that capitalism is in a crisis is meaningless in terms of the possibilities for liberation. A GPL society is by definition imperfect and not a totality. It needs to integrate its negation and cannot be top-down. Linus Torvalds denies that every innovation should be GPL'ed. "It should be up to the individual innovator to decide for herself or himself whether to GPL the project." In this context, Torvalds warns of religious fanaticism, which creates unnecessary political divisions.[78]

The comparison that some have made between the free software and civil-rights movements is of interest here. As the Oekonux debates illustrate, free software claims go way beyond "special interests" and address general concerns. Richard Stallman has rejected comparisons between him and Martin Luther King: "I am not in his league, but I do play the same game." According to Stallman, what does unite him and King is that each has a universal message. "It's a firm condemnation of certain practices that mistreat others. It's not a message of hatred for anyone. And it's not aimed at a narrow group of people. I invite anyone to value freedom and to have freedom."[79] Manuel DeLanda has commented on the universality of Stallman's mission. He writes: "Strategically, I have never thought it is a good idea to base one's philosophy on 'universal moral principles', particularly when they involve the generalization of one's morality into everyone's morality. The very fact that many hackers reject this moral stance should warn us against its universality. And if the relatively small hacker community does not identify with these moral values, one wonders where Stallman gets the idea that he is defending 'the prosperity and freedom of the public in general.'"[80] DeLanda remarks that in contrast to the high quality of free-software products, the philosophies in question are "shallow and brittle." Like myself, DeLanda does not wish to dismiss the real achievements of people like Stallman. This dilemma puts further theorization potentially on hold. DeLanda does contribute by connecting free software to the "transaction costs" concept developed by the New Institutionalist school. He interprets the GPL as an enforcement mechanism for community norms. Apart from his online essay, it is hard to find other "postmodern" criticism of free software.[81]

The central question for Oekonux is how society could be made compatible with free software – not the other way around. In an early mail to the list, Nettime co-founder Pit Schultz proposed moving the emphasis away from Marxist categories towards a more Deleuzian reading of free software production,[82] but this idea was never taken up. Concepts such as "immaterial labor" (Maurizio Lazzarato) do not really fit into the schemes of some Oekonuxers, who prefer to remain close to classic German Marxist terminology and its tradition of dialectical hermeneutics, in which terms such as use and exchange value get into those dazzling feedback loops German academic Marxism is famous for. What is missing here is a contemporary internationalism that could do away with the inward-looking German culture. One exception was a workshop at the second Oekonux conference on Michael Hardt and Antonio Negri's *Empire* facilitated by Stefan Meretz, Ulli Weiss and Benni Bärmann. In the runup to this session Bärmann wrote a text called "Free Software within Empire,"[83] which compares the pessimistic "value criticism" of the Krisis group, in which people are subjected to an abstract "cybernetic machine" that generates capital, with the optimistic viewpoint of the Italian postoperaists, for whom history is a product of social struggle between "empire" and the "multitudes." The new constitution of "immaterial labor" (as defined by Lazzarato) demands of working subjects that they are rich in knowledge and, as agile "active subjects," highly capable of initiating or even directing productive cooperation. Obviously free software perfectly fits into this category, as does "the right to reappropriation," one of Negri and Hardt's central demands, along with the rights to global citizenship and a social wage. Bärmann also points out the similarities between empire and Christoph Spehr's theory of free cooperation.

The search for the philosophical foundations of free software can be a daunting task. One could sum up the three positions as follows: Richard Stallman: I want a free society where everybody can use all software freely. Eric Raymond: I want free software because it's better software. Linus Torvalds: I want free beer. They say Eskimos have 20 different words for snow, and that's where we should be heading here with the term "freedom." Many have noted the deficiency of the English language in its inability to distinguish between free as in free of cost and free as in freedom. It is time for the free software community to catch up and start playing around with post-Kantian concepts of freedom which show that it can no longer be limited by rational absolutes and universal moral categories. Freedom's attachment to essentialist categories must at least be questioned. Given the Marxist background of Oekonux, it should come as no surprise that terms such as "free" and "freedom," as defined by diverse thinkers from John Stewart Mill and Max Stirner to Hannah Arendt, Friedrich Hayek and Isaiah Berlin, have not been widely investigated.[84] It is unrealistic and perhaps politically incorrect to demand for a *Kritik der Freiheit*, made in Germany. But history cannot be an excuse. Instead of deconstructing inflated terminologies, it might be better to invent new ones. The "free" reference has so far only caused confusion. In a similar way, it would be necessary to investigate the term "open," as in open source and open cultures.

It is equally remarkable that in most debates the legal nature of GPL remains undiscussed. The GPL society will potentially be run by professional "observers" who watch for the possible misuse of licenses and call in powerful lawyers to take GPL perpetrators to court. As Manuel DeLanda notes, the GPL has not been tested in court. "It is a piece of legal machinery which has demonstrated its power in practice but which may one day be challenged and show that it did not reduce enforceability costs after all. An important task for legal experts today is, I believe, to create imaginary scenarios where this challenge could be mounted and to invent new license designs which could avoid negative outcomes."[85] It is not sufficient to say that the utopian society no longer needs licenses because of the abolition of copyright. The legal blind spot in the debate thus far may not be the intention of the pioneers, but in my view it presents a considerable danger to the code-producing community. Lawyers could hijack the movement and make a lot of money in court. That's the risk a society based on licenses takes. Or does the GPL society perhaps presume that human nature will also change, and arbitration can take place outside the

courts? A careful study of the "libidinous economy" of the code producers would be invaluable, as "geek culture" remains the driving force
behind free software. Legal trouble could easily disturb or even fatally
damage the precious ecology of tribal techno-desires. This approach
could start with Pekka Himanen's call for a "passionate life" in *The Hacker
Ethic and the Spirit of the Information Age*. Himanen nicely sums up the
Oekonux philosophy when he writes: "From the point of view of a meaningful life, the entire work/leisure duality must be abandoned. As long as
we are living our work or our leisure, we are not even truly living.
Meaning cannot be found in work or leisure but has to arise out of the
nature of the activity itself. Out of passion. Social value. Creativity."[86]

Open Strategies

I would like to end with a few personal remarks as a half-insider/half-
outsider. After more than a decade of development I believe it is time to
leave behind the beta-culture and start some serious propaganda for free
software. Oekonux itself does not seem to be "viral." How could "weapons
of mass instruction"[87] be developed to win the hearts and minds of ordinary users?[88] How can "germs," once they have sprouted, transform and
become larger-scale? At what point do "memes" multiply exponentially
and cause a multiplicity of practices beyond the original group? Perhaps
biological metaphors should be abandoned altogether, so that more
explicit social agendas and marketing principles can come to the foreground. Remember, germs sprout, grow and blossom but also die. There
may be "smart mobs" (Rheingold), but how do they grow into masses? The
technodeterminist answer that copying in the digital age is free and
therefore free software will spread automatically does not take an
expected "revenge of society" into account. Technology alone does not
bring democracy, prosperity and freedom. Many confuse self-installing
CD-ROMs with thorough work on the educational front. One must also
take into account that technologies need to be "cool" and transmit a
seductive and semantically rich aesthetic. This is what free software has
so far failed to do. Clumsy interfaces, failing drivers and fonts, and software installation problems are (almost) a problem of the past but have
nonetheless cast a long shadow far into the future.[89] It might be time to
get rid of the geeky penguin logo and call for a radical cultural transformation.[90] From a certain point on, it is not functionality or "freedom" that
will convince people. Free software is not just a relationship, it can also

be a "thing" – so why not transform it into a desirable fetish? Perhaps this "popware" will not be a commodity, but it can certainly have symbolic and cultural value.

An interesting proposal has been made to classify free software as an intangible world cultural heritage object.[91] The fights against Microsoft in the late 1990s failed to get the majority of computer users on board. The "anti-" aspect might only appeal to a limited group of people. Back then, applications were not developed enough, but that is no longer the case. So what is the free software community waiting for? Is it the sectarian attitude of the believers that scares people off? How could cultural competence be injected into scenes that are doing such important work? Translation seems a key obstacle to realizing the free software society advocated by Oekonux. Are there still technical issues that make it difficult to transform works in progress and existing digital archives from one operating system to another? Or should we see the isolation of free software purely in cultural-political terms? Is the unresolved gender issue a crucial obstacle against the further spread of free software, alongside the obvious fact of corporate power blocking the way to utopia? Is the Microsoft lobby too powerful? Recent adaptations of free software by government agencies are encouraging signs, but they have not yet translated into a significant shift away from proprietary software.

Open-source and free software recently moved into the business-server area. One of the reasons could be that male geekiness is still an uncontested element within the corporate cultures of IBM, Oracle, Sun and other IT corporations that have taken up open-source software. Geek culture is actually a global phenomenon and is not confined to so-called Western countries. Shekhar Krishnan in Delhi remarks that Linux programmers are themselves becoming corporatist: they may scoff at the politics, but they vie for the contracts. "Most of the programmers on the one hand claim that Linux is the superior server and desktop solution for your business, while on the other hand claiming, somewhat tongue-in-cheek, that the reason they do Linux is because it is free and they believe in freedom first." This seems to be a contradiction. Krishnan: "Making money doesn't even enter into the debate, and the radicalism of free software is reduced to a rhetorical pose or a way to avoid the more complex issues of the market. Or worse, this position makes the politics of free software simply a question of the individual political choice of the user."[92]

Instead of utopian Marxism, Nettime moderator and www.openflows.org initiator Felix Stalder pleads for a precise critique of "intellectual property rights" (IPRs) and "knowledge monopolies." In his view, anti-capitalism and IPRs are very different issues, and the GPL has little to do with the former and everything with the latter. Stalder: "What the GPL does, and IBM understood this very well, is to provide a basis for turning everything it applies to from a commodity into a service. Software is a service. The raw materials to provide the service are freely available. The role model here is the lawyer (minus the certification). The raw material – the text of the law and legal precedents – is freely available, but still, most people feel comfortable paying people to 'customize it' for them. Is that anti-capitalistic? No. Does it need IPRs? No. In fact, it works better without it."[93]

What seems to be getting lost amidst the practical success of free software, Krishnan argues, is its politics, which Richard Stallman upholds, some would say obstinately. During the Delhi workshop at the Sarai New Media Center, a widespread disappointment was felt at how rigidly and dogmatically Stallman articulated the free software message to those to whom it could matter most. Free software's problem is not the usual profit-versus-non-profit controversy, but the absence of an overall communication strategy. Is free software really a disruptive technology, as some claim? Perhaps its meaning will not transcend the developers' community. In the end, the essence of free software remains the freedom to change the source code. But how many users are interested in this technical aspect? It would be better if the center of concern shifted from developers to users. All developers are users, but the inverse is not true, nor should it be presented as a desirable future. Oekonux's Austrian "global villages" advocate, Franz Nahrada, has often made this point. He has proposed "prosumerism" as a solution for getting rid of the user-developer dichotomy. In the context of free software, the prosumer can and may alter software, but doesn't have to. The act of using is part of a larger production process and is no longer seen as a passive activity at the end of the value chain.[94]

The lack of humor and subversive wit on Oekonux seems to be widespread in free-software groups. Linux instigator Linus Torvalds complains that people take him too seriously. In his autobiography, *Just for Fun,* he writes: "Some folks can't be content to just take things too seriously on their own. They're not happy unless they convince others to go along with their obsession."[95] This pretty much describes the atmosphere on Oekonux. The dark side of German debating culture is its obsession with discourse and its paradoxical attitude towards leadership – in this case, Stefan Merten. Like many German groups, Oekonux loves brilliant spokespeople who can lead the way, but bitterly fight over internal hierarchies. According to Bruce Sterling, open source is about hanging out with cool guys. "It's very tribal, and it's very fraternal. It's all about Eric, and Linus, and RMS, and Tim and Bruce and Tom and Larry. These are guru charisma guys. They're like artists, like guys running an art movement. Guys who dress up with halos and wear wizard hats."[96] Linus Torvalds, "a leader whose instinct it is not to lead," gets depressed by the expectations he faces as a self-styled antihero. "People will just follow anyone, including me. And it's scary that people will then want to impose their following-ness – if that's a word – on others, including me." We see the same social dynamics around Oekonux's anarcho-libertarian founder. In the predominantly male IT culture, personality cults seem to go hand in hand with decentralized, horizontal structures.[97] They are not contradictory, as one would expect. The guidance of leaders in the IT environment is anything but invisible. Merten follows Torvalds' leadership style in that he "let people do things because they want to do them, not because you want them to." According to Torvalds, "leaders enable others to make decisions for them."

As we have seen, there is a refusal to deal with wider money-related issues. For users in non-Western countries where hard currencies are scarce, free-of-cost software is indeed a necessity. However, according to the official free-software ideology, one must not publicly state that one is using free software for cost reasons. There is a constant fear that the "free cost" aspect threatens to drown out all others. But as Frederick Noronha from Goa, India, writes, "most of us (95%?) can't afford a legal copy of Windows. With free software I don't have to feel like a 16th-century thug roaming the high seas, butchering men on other ships and stealing their treasures. Otherwise, I would have been called a 'pirate.'"[98] What is FLOSS other than good software and bad philosophy? For perhaps the first time in the short history of computers and computer networks, people have a real option of building their own systems. This means a lot to the developing world in economic and political terms. Gaining independence from (neo-)colonial powers and corporate monopolies is no longer pure rhetoric. In most places on the globe, free software is part of a bigger "gray economy" which enables individuals and small businesses to use IT without having to pay Western license prices. In the West, how-ever, there is a diffuse fear that free products are of low quality and that high labor costs to service such software might overshadow the "free" aspect. It is time to publicly endorse the free-of-cost aspect of free soft-ware and insert free software and IPR critiques into the "digital divide" debates.[99] Jeebesh Bagchi of the Sarai New Media Center warns that the low-price argument is fraught with nationalistic discourses. "The Indian IT industry (is) working through a model of 'comparative advantage' and 'massive national wealth creation.' Here the euphoria is that 'we are now riding high on an advantage and let's make the best out of it.' Arguments of low price have very little to argue against the national wealth gener-ation model of IT growth. For this they will need massive IPL protective regimes, and free software will not find an easy argument base here."[100] Bagchi also fears that free software might get mixed up in the politics of "technological security" that is dovetailing with the emergence of the "national security state": "We may land up in a situation of the state using free software for its massive identification systems."

In his editorial to the open-source issue of the Finnish online magazine *Mediumi,* Tapio Mäkelä advises wariness toward the "ruse of metaphor" and calls for an end to the "cult of the individual" around Stallman, Raymond and Torvalds. Open-source software production so far has not been without hierarchies. Says Mäkelä: "Free-software 'lingo' is often heavily linked to neo-liberalist discourse, which praises the individual over a shared effort. These embedded political views are often not dis-cussed, because in some ways open source carries within it an assumed 'purifying ethic' that provides an excuse to talk about pure code as code, and consider the uses of software as secondary. Open-source-based soft-ware and servers do not guarantee a cultural and a social information society, unless they are designed for and by different cultural and social contexts – and connected to various open-content initiatives."[101] What the world needs now are gangs of intermediaries reaching out beyond introverted IT circles. Which memes should they install on today's net-works? It is time to decide. As Linus Torvalds writes: "You have to make the decision to be open. It's a difficult stance to take at first, but it actu-ally creates more stability in the end."[102] The Oekonux debate provides some clues. A relationship rather than a company, free software does not have the resources of a Microsoft to devote to self-promotion. The free-software story needs to be interspersed with feel-good user stories in order to appeal to non-developers. Obscurity is a far greater threat to authors and creative artists than piracy. This also counts for free software.

Defining Open Publishing

Of Lists and Weblogs

"The dilemma of information in the Internet era is not that there is insufficient content, but that there is too much of it. The situation has been called 'drinking from the fire hose.' The problem is to find a filter for relevance and quality. Personally, I am on the verge of unsubscribing – not because there is insufficient GREAT content but because there is too much GOOD content."[1]

Discontent in List Culture

Leaving general concerns over the state of the Net for what they are, the key purpose of this study has been to analyze the ways in which Internet culture deals with filtering and information overload. Fear and desire over the plethora of info are in permanent flux. In times of transition to the unknown, it makes sense to frequently change one's pink and black glasses. Plowing through online content, one experiences the fine line between meaning and noise. Yet it is liberal nonsense to say that this is all a matter of one's personal mood or taste. There is a growing discontent with the way e-mail lists operate. There seemed to be no way out of the dilemma between open and closed (moderated) lists. Open lists tend to become noisy and irrelevant to those who prefer less traffic and more content. Moderated lists, on the other hand, show a tendency to become quasi-edited magazines, thereby losing the "informality" of the e-mail exchange of ideas and material. Collaborative mail filtering, the motto of the Nettime list, is in danger of losing its lively, social aspect. The debate over open versus closed lists has exhausted itself and is showing signs of repetition.

Sydney Net scholar and Cybermind researcher Jon Marshall writes, "The Net has always seemed to be a place of suspicion filled with untraceable tension and despair. It is open to projections of hostility and love, to an awkward suspension of one's being before the uncertainty of the response of others. Flame wars and a sense that the end of the Net is nigh have always been common."[2] Besides moderation and filtering, the linear character of one post appearing after the other is another commonly mentioned constraint of e-mail lists, which can only deal with a certain number of topics at a time or users inevitably lose overview. Not more than three or four threads can take place simultaneously. Discontent about the limitations of lists goes back a while. As I remember, discussions inside the Nettime circle and on neighboring lists about the necessity of building Web-based multi-layered "workgroups" were going on in 1996–97. It took a few years for something to happen.

Despite all the technical changes in recent decades, electronic mailing lists have stayed pretty much the same.[3] The move in the 1990s from majordomo list software (Unix code) to mailman (an open-source application with a Web interface) did not make a real difference to the way in which list communities operated. In the second half of the 1990s, system administrators and programmers started their own Web platforms to discuss technical matters. Slashdot ("News for Nerds – Stuff that Matters") was launched in mid-1997. In 2000 Slashdot made available its "slash code" software, which a number of Web projects started using.[4] Around mid-1999, Catalyst, a Sydney-based activist group (with Matthew Arnison as a key member) developed Active, an open-source Web platform similar to Slashdot. Active would become the base for the global activist open-publishing site www.indymedia.org. Indymedia, the website of the Independent Media Centers (IMCs), was launched during the 1999 WTO protests in Seattle and rapidly spread with the growing movement against corporate globalization agendas.[5] Local initiatives, mainly in the USA and Europe, duplicated and modified the Active code and set up their own Indymedia sites.

Another community weblog is the New York-based Interactivist Info Exchange, run by the Autonomedia publishing collective and Interactivist.net, which developed its own Slashcode adaptation. On the Interactivist website anyone can post an article; still, "not every article posted to the InfoExchange appears on the front page, some will only show up in their section."[6] Slashdot and Indymedia are just two of many of community weblogs (another is Metafilter) that popped up between 1999 and 2001.

ABC of Blogs

Weblogs (or blogs) were originally frequently updated websites run by individuals and linked to other blogs. David Winer runs one the oldest, Scripting News. He defines a weblog as a continual tour with a human guide whom readers get to know. There are many guides to choose from, each develops an audience, and camaraderie and politics develop between them: they point to each other's sites in all kinds of structures, graphs, loops, etc.[7] It is important at this stage to differentiate between collective multi-user blogs and what are now commonly known as "weblogs." Journalists, including Andrei Orlowski of the Web magazine *The Register*, often equate weblogs to sites produced by individuals using out-of-the-box weblog software. Claims about who built up and therefore "owns" the blogosphere have become the dominant topic in 2003. The fight over the "essence" of personally run news sites goes back to the question of whether a medium should be defined through the content and culture of its first users. However, the debate over who can claim ideological supremacy in the blogosphere is not relevant here. In this chapter I will only briefly touch on the topic of individual weblogs and concentrate instead on collaborative blogs, as they are more similar to lists. What makes blogs interesting is their functionality and global potential, not the content of early adopters who voraciously link to each other in order to get higher on the Google search engine ladder.

First, I'd like to briefly look at the history and definitions of the weblog. Noah Shachtman once described blogs as a "constantly updated combination of diary and link collection."[8] According to David Winer, the first weblog was the first website, info.cern.ch/, built by Tim Berners-Lee at CERN. From this site, Berners-Lee pointed to every new site as it came online. NCSA's "What's New" page took over this role; later, Netscape's "What's New" page was, in a sense, a big blog from around 1993 to 1995, until the Web exploded. Other early weblogs included Robot Wisdom, Tomalak's Realm and CamWorld. In one of the first books on the topic, *We've Got Blog,* Rebecca Blood defines a weblog as a "frequently updated webpage with dated entries with new ones placed on top."[9] "Links with commentary, frequently updated" was the original formula. "Just as e-mail had made us all writers, weblogs have made all of us publishers," says Rebecca Blood.[10] This is an important remark in the context of this study. Lists do indeed get people to write – but they are not by definition publishing tools. Whereas lists are to some extent sensitive to copyright issues and leave authors the possibility of publishing their content elsewhere (and getting paid for it within an IP system), weblogs don't care about their relationship with print media. List owners often insist that posting to a list is not the same as "publishing" on a website (even though most lists have Web archives). Weblogs brought the emancipation of the Web as a mature medium a few steps closer.

Individual weblogs could be seen as a successor to the "home page." Their rise can be read as an indirect grassroots response to the corporate concentration of power by a few news portals and directories such as Yahoo! AOL, MSN and CNN. Many stress the empowering aspects of self-publishing. Users grew tired of the syndicated old-media content that flooded the Web during the dotcom days. They liked to link to global news sites but also had a lot to say about world events and the way in which they were reported – and weblogs enable them to say it (as "push-media" portals don't). Bloggers have seized the means of production, as Andrew Sullivan points out in *Wired* magazine.[11] In the past, "journalists needed an editor and a publisher. Even in the most benign scenario, this process subtly distorts journalism. You find yourself almost unconsciously writing to please a handful of people – the editors looking for a certain kind of story, the publishers seeking to push a particular venture, or the advertisers who influence the editors and owners. Blogging simply bypasses this ancient ritual." Blogging is also described as a sort of neo-geek sensibility. "Webloggers typically offer pithy, sarcastic commentary about the links."[12] Others emphasize the speed with which weblogs update news and links. *Salon:* "Weblogs, typically, are personal websites operated by individuals who compile chronological lists of links to stuff that interests them, interspersed with information, editorializing and personal asides. A good weblog is updated often, in a kind of real-time improvisation, with pointers to interesting events, pages, stories and happenings elsewhere on the Web. New stuff piles on top of the page; older stuff sinks to the bottom."[13] Evan Williams: "The blog concept is about three things: Frequency, Brevity, and Personality." It wouldn't be exceptional to say that weblogs are symptomatic of a cultural logic that celebrates excessive banality. Like mid-1990s homepages, many weblogs have an embarrassing tendency towards exhibitionism.

Some stress that blogs are essentially media platforms for individuals, just online diaries with a bit more structure. But for Ziod, Slashdot is more than just a blog: "I remember trying to tell my dad about Slashdot way back and told him it was like reading the newspaper and submitting your letter to the editor in a matter of seconds with other people commenting on your letter to the editor within a few minutes. He responded, 'so it's total chaos.' That's when I decided I had no idea how to explain Slashdot."[14] All seem to agree that blogs, whether run by user groups or individuals, need a lively, interactive audience. The users build up a collective personality and give the weblog its own unique characteristics. Over the years the blogosphere has become associated with the easy-to-install software developed for the genre. Software is the message, as is often the case on the Net, which initially brings together people with widely different interests and opinions. Greymatter, Blogspot, Movable Type, Pitas, Diarist, Groksoup and Blogger are examples of easy-to-install build-your-own weblog software.

By 2002, weblogs have been discovered by the mainstream media outlets. David Gallagher, writing for *The New York Times,* pointed to an emerging war between weblogs. Says Glenn Reynolds, a right-wing weblogger and law professor at the University of Tennessee, "The weblog world before 9/11 was mostly inward-looking – tech people talking about tech things. After 9/11 we got a whole generation of weblogs that were outward-looking and written for a general audience.[15] Gallagher describes a culture clash between the "war bloggers" who support George W. Bush's War on Terrorism and the "veteran weblogs" who are critical of the Bush administration's policy. Gallagher: "The war-blogging movement took off after 9/11 as people used blogs to vent their anger about the terrorist attacks. Though they are still commonly known as war blogs, these sites now address a wide range of news and political topics, usually from right of center."[16]

In 2002, it came as something of a shock for apolitical tech insiders when the "blog community" seemed suddenly to have divided over a political issue. The controversy over "war blogs" could be seen as an indication as the blogging phenomenon had moved from the underground to the mainstream. According to New York Internet analyst Clay Shirky, "The blogosphere is resolving itself into a power distribution, with many small blogs (small in terms of readership), some moderately sized blogs, and a handful of highly trafficked blogs. This in turn recreates all the difficulties the original Web users had in locating content, which created niches for search engines, directories, portals et al. Many of these solutions don't work well in the blogosphere, because weblog content is time-sensitive."[17] The discussion over the direction blogs will take is in full swing and can hardly be covered within the slow medium of the book. Individuals' blogs, supported by easy-to-install software, continue to spread. "Will readers flock towards trusted meta-blogs that filter and organize, or will other models of collaborative filtering arise?" Shirky asks.[18]

With the Internet still growing at a considerable pace, existing list channels are becoming slowly institutionalized. But how else can list owners manage the increased traffic? This is an issue that affects all users. There are growing suspicions of those who moderate and others who "chat" or even "spam." The net result is a standoff: a climate of tension from all sides, and even more troubling, silence – a gradual breakdown in communication, increased suspicion and the loss of an invaluable exchange of information and arguments. The spam avalanche has only made matters worse. However, many see no reason why the situation should be passively accepted. Weblog software, is one option that could bring critical new-media culture up to date, overcoming the current list problems. Existing new-media-culture websites and lists have not yet adopted open-publishing software. In late 2002, an initiative for a broad Web-based platform had yet to be developed.

List Culture in Australia

The Fibreculture list community, which I co-founded with David Teh in early 2001, proved once again that list culture wasn't quite dead. Teh and I met over coffee at Glebe Point Road in Sydney. We quickly agreed that we were both unhappy about the demise of the Australian new-media-arts list "Recode." Started in early 1998, Recode had become stuck in the complex funding politics which were plaguing the once-vibrant scene in Australia.[19] The list was locked up inside the Internet, and a climate of informal chat and rumor slowly exhausted the community. The incestuous relationship between artists and funding bodies contributed to a feeling of diminishing opportunities. With increased pressure to push arts, education and culture into the commercial arena, Recode failed to defend itself. In a right-wing political climate of decreased funding, artists treated their peers as competitors and a mutual sense of distrust emerged. Over the course of 2001, Recode slowly faded away and was closed in early 2002 after a conflict between moderator Julianne Pierce and Net artist][mez][.

Something had to be done to break the downward spiral. David Teh and I had the idea of focusing on the enormous potential of the new-media researchers and educators in Australia working at the crossroads of technology, design, the arts and activism. We could not solve the looming crisis of the shrinking new-media arts sector; others had to take initiatives at that level.[20] Within weeks the Fibreculture list was up and running. The interdisciplinary education, research, policy and theory angle seemed a productive one. Within half a year the list had 300 subscribers and six facilitators based in different parts of Australia. By early 2003 it had 700 subscribers. The list held its first meeting in December 2001 in Melbourne; there it presented its first publication, a collection of critical essays called *Politics of a Digital Present*.[21] A second and a third meeting took place in Sydney in November 2002 and in Brisbane in July 2003. The list remains open and largely unmoderated and runs a separate announcement list. As the example of Fibreculture shows, if they focus on topics and outcomes, lists can still be vital backbones for social networks.[22]

As an open and unmoderated list, Fibreculture soon had to deal with the handful of globally operating trolls that move from list to list posting messages some call spam and others call poetry. Classic cases of e-mail soloists are Brad Brace, Integer/N.N.,][mez][, Agricola de Cologne and Max Herman. Other well-known list provocateurs are Trevor Batten, Lachlan Brown and Paul Treanor. These schmoozers and self-hypers usually do not engage in debates. What unites these performers desperately seeking an audience is that they move from one list to the next, do their act, seek personal confrontations, are unsubscribed, and soon after appear on another online forum.

Open and unmoderated lists are ideal stages for trolls to perform on. Every time a troll showed up on Fibreculture, the facilitators and most of the subscribers would get confused, becoming divided in their response. Whereas most despised the egomania and ruthless self-promotion of the troll, many hesitated to remove him or her from the list. In the meantime, the troll had reached his or her goal by attracting a considerable amount of attention. As soon as a list becomes closed and moderated, the troll problem disappears, but in its first years the Fibreculture list wasn't big enough to do that, thereby exposing itself to exhausting debates over the continuing troll hijackings.[23]

Depending on the speed with which new technology spreads, critical Internet culture will have to move to the Web and "cellspace" and develop places where multiple threads, debates and news threads can take place in a way not possible within the linear electronic mailing list structure. As an example, the compilation technique that Nettime moderators use to filter related messages into single e-mails has partially helped, but the more moderation there is the less the participants have the exciting feel of an intimate, "live" exchange. Digests should be an option, not a default. And, importantly, moderated lists have proved very labor-intensive, which in itself contributes to power relations that are at times resented. Nettime is slowly losing its community feel. With over 3,000 subscribers (as of 2002), it is turning into a new-style publishing channel. The advantages of weblogs over lists are numerous. Whereas a list can only carry a limited number of parallel threads, weblogs can host an infinite number of conversations, including hundreds of responses on each individual post.

Allegories of Democratic Network Culture

Online forums can be compared to 19th-century salons. Like their historic ancestors, online salons form a keystone for democratic culture, but salons are not democratic, decision-making institutions themselves. Polling is now a common feature on weblogs and news portals – and so is vote rigging. The reliability of online polls is next to zero, since users can vote as many times as they like. Rival political groups call up their constituencies to go to certain sites and vote. Though reliable voting software is available, it's not widely used, mainly because of the anonymity of many Internet users. Its use within social networks is virtually unknown, mainly because of the strong belief in consensus. In the world of old media, it is taken for granted that neither publishers nor editors can be elected by the readership. Open-publishing channels, on the other hand, create an expectation of "freedom of speech" and online democracy by giving users a certain editorial control. Sooner or later, users will find out that there is no such thing as absolute freedom in the blogosphere either, and the fight over the degree of openness and moderation will start all over again.

Lists and blogs are not decision-making tools, and to suggest they are borders on ideology. What Internet forums do best is to create collective discourses. Much as in a Parisian salon, it is up to the list or blog owner who is included and excluded, despite all the thresholds. This very fact is often denied by those who run online forums, an attitude that only further fuels debate. It is to be expected that the tension between the traditional Internet ideology of consensus and access for all on the one hand and the actual power of the owners/operators on the other will escalate at some point. The contradictions described here could lead to an increase in fights and frustrations among users – or not, if people realize the limitations. On the other hand, yet-to-be-discovered limits of weblogs could lead to a new generation of software that would bring online dialogue onto a higher level of internal democracy without compromising expectations of quality on the content level – however high or low. As Buckminster Fuller said, "You never change things by fighting the existing reality. To change something, build a NEW model that makes the existing model obsolete."

It is important not to just complain about a corporate takeover of the Net, the rise of spam, the tragedy of the "digital commons," overly powerful moderators or the decline of virtual communities. One can actively reshape the Net by writing code, by developing new forms of lists, weblogs and interfaces. Yes, the Net is in danger, but there are also plenty of developments pointing to a renaissance of the medium. The dilemma between "noise" and "quality" should not paralyze us. The hotly debated issue of open channels versus edited ones, be it on e-mail or the Web, can be dismissed as a minor technicality only of interest to Internet nerds. But I don't think that is the case. The material presented in this study can be read as an allegory of the tensions peculiar to "electronic democracy."[24] Is the troll the online adversary in need of our sympathy? Or should dissent be classified as "noise" and filtered out? The fight over the architecture of Net-based conferencing systems goes to the heart of the question of what the new should look like. It is this uncarved, yet-to-be-defined element that makes the new different from the old. Otherwise we may as well position the evolution of the Internet into the eternal return of the same old "media laws." Media history has shown how revolutionary means of production were constantly retrofitted into profitable and controllable top-down channels. The cynical cycle from innovation and hype to mainstream adaptation and back to regression and discontent becomes a predictable pattern that can be undermined. One way to achieve this is to spread basic knowledge about group dynamics, point out actual power relationships and raise scalability awareness. By this, I mean the realization that a communication pattern in a group of 50 might not work when there are 850, and vice versa. Work groups of ten people have different goals than public discussion forums (potentially) followed by thousands.

Does Internet culture inevitably have to deteriorate? Are there ways to escape well-known patterns? What happens if users and developers suspend their belief in dotcoms and stop buying into the fateful-historical-cycle argument, from hype, start-up and IPO to bankruptcy? Appropriation and co-option are not inevitable. There are no natural laws of culture one must obey. After Gramsci, we understand that the scene of hegemony is one of contestation and negotiation. How can critical Internet culture get there and leave its self-created ghetto? Power, as Foucault demonstrated, is not static. Still, cyclical movements in both fashion and economics are all too real. Are there ways to sabotage the course of history from creative experiment to boom and bust? Weblogs and peer-to-peer networks are two encouraging phenomena pointing to a turn of the Internet away from corporate and state control. Are the innovative and creative forces Lessig speaks so highly of in *The Future of Ideas* condemned to start all over again each time a new round of technological innovation comes into view? As a lawyer holding liberal values, Lessig overlooks the capacity for dynamic Internet cultures to form "the new" in ways other than narrative of cyclical history would have it.

Democracy, in my view, is primarily an "agonistic culture," not a set of laws and legal procedures framed by models of rational consensus.[25] When democratic culture becomes technological, sooner or later democratic rules also have to be hardwired into the technical systems, for example in the form of software. Technology is not an alien force invading democratic societies. Instead of asking how representative democracy can be saved or renewed by using the Internet, the first question that needs to be asked is how democratic the Internet (and its culture) itself is. That is, one must inquire into the material dimensions of online communications.[26]

Democratic network culture starts and ends with the power of the user. Feedback channels for the user-as-producer have to be inscribed in software if the aim is to go beyond the polite, never-printed letter to the editor. If there is anything "new" about technical media, it should be the possibility of users becoming editors. In itself, it was not enough to have cheap means of production for digitally editing films or xeroxing zines if the distribution issue (how to reach a critical mass) was not dealt with. Hardware is a condition, but not a guarantee, for something interesting to happen. Dotcom portals addressed this issue through e-commerce marketing techniques (billboards, TV ads, T-shirts, etc.) but by and large failed to solve the mystery of how to build up a sustainable audience (and related revenue stream). How, in the future, will critical Internet culture address the topic of "wider" audiences and the inevitable conflicts associated with broader-based user communities? Some faction within critical Internet culture will one day want to go "out of beta" and release its debugged blueprints of the "network society." Who will radicalize Manuel Castells' third-way analysis of the Internet and transcend the quasi-neutral engineering culture that has dominated the Internet for so long?

Weblog architecture is one of many fields where network architecture is being contested. The key objective of community weblogs such as Slashdot and Indymedia has been to modify the grading system of incoming communications in order to keep the moderators in line. This is how Amy Alexander, a software artist teaching at UC San Diego, explains the Slashdot moderation procedure: "If someone turns out to be an unfair or wonderful moderator, everyone else gets to moderate that person's moderation. Someone who's considered a troll will tend to be consistently moderated down to 0 or -1, and then those users who want to set their threshold above that don't get annoyed with it, while those who prefer to see everything can either set their threshold lower or choose to view everything, thus ignoring the moderation altogether. You can easily choose to read N.N. and other trolls – or to not see them at all."[27]

The idea is to let the user customize – filter, don't filter, read threads, read in a specific order, and switch back and forth. Moderation according to the Slashdot definition involves ratings points given by participating users which give a post an overall rating somewhere between -1 and 5. Although some of the Slashdot readers are moderators at any given time, any reader can meta-moderate – which means keeping the moderators in check. Anyone who does bad moderation loses moderation privileges in the future. There are four goals of moderation mentioned on the Slashdot site: "1. Promote Quality, Discourage Crap; 2. Make Slashdot as readable as possible for as many people as possible; 3. Do not require a huge amount of time from any single moderator; 4. Do not allow a single moderator a 'reign of terror.'"[28]

The curious paradox of Slashdot is its exclusivity. To be "slashdotted" by an editor is arguably the highest honor on the Net – one's post is given headline status at the top of the home page. Which is harder: getting an article published by the online journal www.salon.com or getting featured on Slashdot? Slashdot moderators must go through hundreds of contributions a day. Its editorial filtering is some of the toughest on the Web. Ironically, Slashdot has turned into the opposite of "open publishing." The choices made by its moderators are anything but machinic. The editorial policy of the moderators can be described as apolitical and focused on mainstream games and gadgets: in short, 1990s techno-libertarian. But then … its (meta-)moderators are wizards in their own universe, ordinary geeks turned into gods. If someone wanted to attain that wizard level and change geek culture, they could probably work themselves up from user to moderator to meta-moderator.

Instead of featuring many editorial articles, the Slashdot model focuses on the democratization of the back end, the readers' comments, unlike online magazines that grant primary attention to contributors of top stories. The procedure for how main stories get selected (and then fiercely commented on) remains unclear. Core content remains tightly controlled. Slashdot is about the high art of administering commentary.

Slashdot gets a lot of comments: sometimes thousands a day, tens of thousands a month. At any given time, the database holds 40,000-plus comments. A single story might get a thousand replies – and let's be realistic, not all comments are great. In fact, some are downright terrible – but others are gems.[29] In the Slashdot model, users are first of all readers who comment on others' posts. The user as key author is not treated as a sovereign, singular content producer. S/he can submit a story, but that's not the essence. Slashdot commentator Platinum Dragon describes the Slashdot editorial process thusly: "It's not really anarchist. It's more of a dictatorship, quite frankly. The articles to be discussed are chosen by an unelected group of editors, and we just get to rant. 'News by consensus' would imply that the editors decide collectively which stories will be posted, all stories were unanimously agreed upon, and tossing in the word 'anarchist' implies that all participants have a say in which stories are posted, instead of the unchosen few."

Instead, Platinum Dragon suggests to look at the features of Indymedia: "Their center-column stories are developed by individuals or groups, and they're posted and edited on a collective, consensus basis. Anyone may submit a feature to any Indymedia site (generally, it's good to try to make a feature relevant to the local site you're submitting to, though this varies greatly), and anyone can get involved in the editing and decision process."[30]

The Indymedia model is much more transparent in its editorial policy concerning original posts. According to the site, Indymedia is a democratic news wire: "We want to see and hear the real stories, news, and opinions from around the world. While we struggle to maintain the news wire as a completely open forum we do monitor it and remove posts. You can see the decisions we have made by viewing the hidden articles page. In the overwhelming number of cases, stories have been removed for the following reasons: being comments, not news, duplicate posts, obviously false or libelous posts, or inappropriate content."[31] Indymedia says it is working on technology to make the editorial process more transparent, so that users can see when such decisions have been made, and why: "In future, we want our audience to be part of this process too."[32]

Weblog Conflicts: The Indymedia Case

In April 2002 Indymedia moved the open-publishing news wire from its front page. The idea was to decentralize power from the global site into the hands of local collectives. According to Indymedia insiders, the tension between being an open, anonymous, egalitarian weblog and being a credible news organization had become so obvious that something needed to be done. There were calls to build a system of credibility while remaining open and democratic. Reliability had become an issue because Indymedia had started covering hot and controversial issues such as the Middle East conflict. There were numerous cases of stories which could not be confirmed or which had been posted with the intent of spreading disinformation. The organization also faced increased police infiltration.

A solution was sought in an eBay-style reputation management system. Evan of Indymedia explains: "Unlike the traditional press that enforces consistent credibility through an authoritarian model of editorship we are trying to build up a networked credibility. In doing this we are developing effective strategies for fighting a Net war. Our information system covering the battle on the streets of Palestine has a very real effect upon the fighting. Indymedia operates as a fundamentally networked organization. There is no center or head office but we are very coordinated."[33]

Indymedia is testing the boundaries of the weblog as a (very successful) medium of substantial size. Whereas some within the organization would like to outdo *The New York Times* by claiming objectivity and replacing one worldview with another, others insist on "deep plurality," embedded in software. Evan: "We are not advocating the kind of world that fits neatly into one modernist perspective. Unlike the Marxist-Leninists, who had THE answer, today we have many answers and even more questions.

For credible media to be created in this new networked, postmodern if you like, world we need to fully reconstruct what we mean by credibility."[34]

In May 2002 it became known that US Indymedia groups were being stalked by an insider who used multiple identities. The case described here comes from an internal account of what happened written by Michel. Well-known activist James (the name has been changed) had become a member of one of the IMCs. There, he engaged in online disruption as well as attending meetings in person. He engaged in a number of activities to bolster his credibility. Michel: "He claimed to be a former reporter from a corporate television network. He did so in order to create the impression that the IMCs should value his participation because he had come over to the 'other side.' He then launched alternate personalities which were all set up with phone numbers attached to voice mail, addresses, job titles and manufactured histories." This was done in order to give depth and weight to his actions.

James's other critical tactic was to build upon existing sensitivities in the community. He would accuse people of taking power or control, of making decisions behind closed doors, of being racist, sexist, or authoritarian. To add strength to his denunciations of people or processes, he used the fact that he was black to cry racism. Many of his fake online personalities were minority or female. In his report, Michel describes James's tactic of creating dysfunction by raising issues people were most concerned about. This made it difficult to kick him out of the community or discount him; such e-mails resonated with people. Not knowing the history or that they were dealing with a disruptive person, many naïve people sent supportive e-mails demanding answers to the questions James raised. According to Michel, these issues actually were things that needed to be addressed – but James raised them not to resolve them but to bring the group into organizational paralysis.

To take it a step further, James provided reference for his activities. He did everything he could to make himself and his fake online personalities seem real. On one occasion he used forged e-mail and fake accounts to libel the real James. With the libel as "evidence" he then sued the other members of the group in small claims court. This legal maneuver increased tension in the group. The lawsuits were baseless, but the process of going through legal trouble is truly distracting for people with full-time jobs, kids and activism projects. At least once, Michel heard that James had gotten people to pay him off to drop the lawsuit and go away.

While James's actions were disruptive and caused Indymedia a lot of problems, Michel does not believe James was paid by anyone. Instead, he describes James as mentally ill and delusional. Michel: "He has written many publish-yourself books in which he attacks Indymedia and wraps up people he's met in long bad cyber-romance novels. Often he talks about traveling around the world and being a jet-setting media activist even though it is clear that all his e-mail is written from the same computer lab at his university." James and other disruptive people like him have been able to have such a large effect on Indymedia because of the open form of networked organizations. Michel: "We are creating a new kind of organization which is very strong in some ways yet also incredibly weak in others. For example, there are currently somewhere between three and six major legal battles involving Indymedia. But one place where Indymedia really runs into problems is when people intentionally manipulate the network communication by stoking tensions into flame wars. Instead of addressing problems in a constructive way it is easy to push people into misunderstanding and conflict. When a community member takes the step of 'becoming' two or more people they can stake out multiple sides of the issue and drive people into opposing camps. This polarization is used to stop constructive dialogue and refocus the work towards following and addressing the conflict. The flames turn people off from following the discussion and reduce interest in the group."

What are the lessons to be learned from this case? Michel: "We now start to know the people who have a history of being disruptive and when they post to a list we simply don't bite. If nobody responds usually the troll will get bored and search for other places to make trouble. Their actions only become a problem when we give them an echo chamber where other people can take up their 'cause'. To prevent the echo chamber from forming it is necessary to quietly inform people about the person's history of disruption. Whenever James posts to Indymedia lists now most people ignore him. If somebody does respond then they are sent a private e-mail explaining the situation off-list. This acts as a dampening force against disruption. By providing the context of the disrupter it takes away the constructed legitimacy of that person."

The answer to the challenges faced by community weblogs lies partly in software. Matthew Arnison, maker of the original Indymedia software, has written a proposal in which he tries to balance users' freedom with the need for collaborative editing, taking Indymedia to a new level. Arnison noticed that the Indymedia editing collective simply had more stories coming in than it could deal with. "Open publishing is about more than just open posting. It's also about open editing."[35] According to his proposal, an "automated open editing" procedure with ratings, as on Slashdot and Kuro5shin, would empower the users without creating an information overload on the front page. Arnison: "Users would be able to create highlights pages, updating them with the stories they are most interested in. They could choose a topic, or not, or have several different collections, and maybe share their highlights with a team of people. Indymedia would then survey all the highlighting every hour, and then build its front page based on whatever people are highlighting at the time."[36]

For Arnison, "open editing" would mean a return to the heart of open publishing. There is a lot at stake here. Proposals such as Arnison's may sound technical, and they are. But they are not techno-deterministic. The community is not a special effect of the software. The parameters of communication platforms used by millions of users, like Indymedia, are highly political. The drive to carefully renegotiate the roles of user and editorial team indicate that reaching a mass audience does not necessarily mean a rise in editorial control by a limited group. There should be ways to deal with growth without compromising the open character of networks – and software could assist in that transformation to larger, more diverse audiences.

Comparing Lists and Weblogs

So far, existing Net-art communities have not introduced open-conferencing weblog systems comparable to Slashdot or Indymedia.[37] Nettime, Spectre and Xchange have no plans to go beyond their list status. Electronic mail, for the time being, remains the lowest common denominator. Despite the rise of weblogs, it is not yet time to question the "supremacy" of e-mail communication over the Web. However, in some cases ASCII art and e-mail have become implicit excuses for stagnation. Instead of celebrating low tech as one strategy among many, list culture is in danger of becoming a habit, a dogma – in short, a symptom of regression. The steady rise in the use of broadband/cable and other forms of flat-rate Net access will no doubt bring weblogs further into the mainstream. There is also a generational aspect to weblogs. Users in their 20s seem to prefer the Web over e-mail and hardly subscribe to lists. Weblogs do not try to resolve the long, exhausting debate over the merits of e-mail and list culture; rather, they simply bypass the impasse of list culture altogether. Lists, no matter how open or democratic, are becoming outmoded vehicles.

Nothing is as subjective as the distinction between sense and nonsense. The challenge of every Internet project I have been involved in has consisted of aiming for the highest possible level of sophistication while keeping the channels open. The trick is to "seduce" users into posting quality content while preventing the project from becoming yet another publisher-to-customer business. An impossible task perhaps, but worth trying. In the age of networks, editing becomes anticipation of content. It is the task of those who run lists and weblogs to shape and facilitate the wishes of the users even before they are aware of them.[38] That's the true aim of moderation: to facilitate dialogue. Would it be possible to welcome the "alien" position without alienating the average participant who is wary of redundant information? Following Mouffe, at what point does the adversary become an enemy of the project? How does a controversy turn counterproductive? Weblog discourse doesn't set out to make the friend-enemy distinction; there is just arbitrary signal-to-noise ratios, set by each user in a different way.

The issue here is the tension between the unstoppable, all-too-human destructive forces and the belief that technology can protect humankind against itself. The Slashdot founders designed their software to be helpful. Amy Alexander: "There is something to be learned from geeks, and that is that they don't put any barriers between tech and life, meaning, if they see a people problem, they say: "How can we design the software to help us with the people problem?" It's very natural to them because software is just the result of their thought processes, whereas in non-geek circles that kind of thinking might be taboo, or at least kind of weird. Non-geeks see software as an inorganic 'thing,' not as a product of human thought the way writing is. But really software is just human writing – geeks write it, so they realize that."[39]

Computer geeks have almost unlimited confidence in self-regulation. "Ignoring technologies" such as e-mail filters and automated moderation are thought to take away the worries of users. I do not share their confidence. Ultimately, I would remove a user who endangered the overall project. This has little to do with the repression of differences of opinion. I would give the facilitators, those who put in so much work, the ability to block those who threaten the existence and growth of the online community. Survival and sustainability are more important than some absolute definition of freedom. Some opponents have fabulous rhetorical skills; others are just out to frustrate dialogue. A few could even try to bring down the site by sending hate mails, spreading rumors, and intimidating friends. It takes wisdom and experience to stay calm when you have invested a lot at a personal level. Most social networks have to deal with such cases. I personally can tolerate a fair bit, but not when the community as such is in danger of disintegration. It takes years to build up a social network – and only days to destroy it.

There is a difference between the high art of editing and censorship. I have never seen 100% "free" projects; there are always limitations, whether of knowledge, race and gender boundaries, or other cultural factors such as language. I remain suspicious of the libertarian "free-speech" argument and those who cry censorship, because they seldom create interesting clashes of difference. 1990s cyberculture never encountered serious cases of censorship like those that occurred in China, the Middle East or Africa. Instead, techno-libertarianism cried for the right to be left alone.

All interesting media projects are "staged" and have a performative aspect, even the most free and informal ones – and so do weblogs. Interesting parties are "seduced" into participating. In the case of Slashdot, for instance, writers are paid to contribute.[40] That's what it takes to have an interesting site. List culture has run up against the wall of volunteer labor. As the Net matures, it can no longer be presumed that everyone will work for free. A challenging Web project should at least raise the issue of money and think through alternative models to generate a (micro-)income for those without regular jobs. The dream of "free" is good enough for those who work on Internet projects in the evenings. But serious and reliable content for new media cannot be produced in a hobby situation. Can it?

We can see a growing awareness of the fact that the structure of software influences what is created and how people behave with it. Amy Alexander explains: "There's an old adage that goes 'If all you have is a hammer, everything looks like a nail.' Whatever tool you are used to using is going to influence how you perceive a situation and how you should respond to it. There are certain ways a community can work. If you're the list admin, you can decide who gets to post, who gets unsubscribed, whether you'll reject posts based on size, etc. It gives us a certain hammer that makes us approach every situation as more or less, a nail."[41] Larry Wall argued that Perl was a postmodern programming language because instead of giving you a hammer, it gave you a Swiss army knife.[42] Amy Alexander: "We should try hard to think 'outside the box' that the mailman/majordomo mailing list software has forced us into all these years, and see if we can build a more flexible structure. I don't expect new software to solve our human-relations problems, but we should recognize that old software has probably had a lot to do with creating or perpetuating our human-relations problems, and try to break out of the old ways of thinking."[43]

Unlike Slashdot-style weblog software, "scoop" weblog software allows a subscriber to post stories, not just comments. Some form of filtering is thus necessary. The idea of Scoop is that other users vote stories onto the front page and/or into other sections. Comments, on the other hand, always go directly on the site but can be rated up or down by other users. A certain number of negative ratings means a comment is hidden from other readers. Each reader can set his or her threshold to see as many or as few comments as he or she likes. This is how Slashdot works, and it's a nice feature that allows flexibility without the site being overrun by trolls. Scoop also allows moderators to set limitations on how many stories and comments a user may post in a certain amount of time. After that, the user is locked out from posting for a while. (Of course, a user could subscribe under multiple addresses to circumvent this if he or she really wanted to.) So the community moderation system becomes an important element in the software design, and eventually in the way collaborative weblog culture operates.

The Ownership Question

One thing current weblogs still lack is internal democracy. Founders and owners (also called "admins") of community weblogs cannot not be voted off, so the "enlightened dictatorship" regime of lists continues.[44] Like mailing lists, weblogs do not open up ownership. The implicit idea is that of an entrepreneurial individual who initiates a weblog and then "invites" others to participate, either as co-editors or moderators or commentators. The owner alone possesses the passwords to root access, domain name and server (space). It is the owner who, in the end, pays the bill for Internet traffic, server space, domain name renewal and other costs.

In many cases, such as that of the Dutch Digital City, it has been proven that those who own the domain name have power over a project in the end. Therefore, there is no real democracy for the "readers" unless they become owners themselves. Owners install and configure the software and have the ultimate say over its content and user base. This often unknown "last instance" is why there is always is an invisible meta-level on both lists and blogs that reduces the power of users to mere "partici-pation." Ultimately, the status of the user is downgraded to that of a guest. Like mailing lists, weblogs in theory could let the users elect the editors. In practice, however, this is not happening, at least not so far. Elections on lists and blogs are rare, though technically easy. Only with-in Usenet newsgroups has a voting culture been established: users are asked to vote for or against the opening of new Usenet groups. The "openness" of a weblog is confined to the content level. The explanation is a simple one. The admins/editors will not easily give up ownership of a project in which they have invested so much of their (free) time. Money is a secondary element here, as I am speaking about non-profit initiatives, but it can play a role as well. This all puts significant limitations on the idea of "free speech" within user-driven weblogs.

From Theory to Discordia

Invited by the Net artist Nathalie Bookchin, in February 2000 I worked at Calarts in LA for a week as a participant in the "net.net" lecture series.[45] There I met Amy Alexander, who was working at Calarts as a technical director of the computer animation labs. I had heard about her www.pla-giarist.org project. Alexander is a multitalented filmmaker, teacher, pro-grammer, network security expert and Net artist.[46] We discussed the ins and outs of Net art, theory and activism during hours of driving on the LA freeways and have stayed in contact ever since. During the last phase of the Syndicate list in mid-2001, Alexander publicly suggested looking for a weblog solution to the list's crisis.[47] One of the issues we agreed on was the way the current use of mailing list software was limiting Internet cultures. In late 2001, a few months after the collapse of Syndicate, we got in contact again. By then Alexander had moved to San Diego, where she had taken a job as assistant professor of visual arts in new media at UCSD. On a couple of occasions we had exchanged ideas about a possible weblog project; now it was time to get the project running.

We thought it was time for the new-media arts scene to move to the Web and build up a blog where multiple threads and debates could take place in a way that was not possible within the linear electronic mailing list structure. The Nettime moderators' filtering technique of compiling related messages into one only partly helped. The more moderation there was, the less participants had the excitement of a "live," intimate exchange. Nettime had slowly lost its community feel and was turning into a new-style publishing channel.

In the first months (December 2001–January 2002), Alexander and I defined the project, code-named "Discordia." Our aim was to adapt the Slashdot/Indymedia model and build a multi-channel Web-based discussion forum, a "weblog" for new-media culture that would bring together online artists, activists, theorists and techies. A letter was drafted to invite interested programmers. Soon after, designers and "content" workers would be asked to join the "Web-based social filtering" initiative.

First, our arguments had to take shape. As with every plan, the right wording was extremely important. As with dotcom business plans, the document describing the project had to contain all the right elements. It was all about finding a careful balance, not least between the two of us. Whereas Alexander stressed the open character of networks,[48] I emphasized the lessons that could be learned from list cultures. The first question we struggled with was to what extent the Slashdot moderation model could be altered. Would rating also work for non-nerds in the arts and culture context?

Discordia's intent was to encourage informality by filling the gap between a big list with thousands of subscribers and the intimacy of a chatroom. Alexander: "People shouldn't feel they have to be media theorists or scholars to post. It's easy to get that feeling on Nettime. In other words, I worry about mistaking form for content. There are a lot of talented writers on Nettime, but there are also those with interesting ideas without the talent or just the desire to do formal writing. Artists often fall into the latter category."[49]

What are the parameters for social Web filtering? What degrees of freedom would be given at the user, moderation and meta-moderation levels (to follow the Slashdot hierarchy)? Ideally, Discordia would be built by a group of programmers, designers and editors so that the technical and content-related issues would be thought through together. First a cheap, independent and sustainable prototype would be built. Later, international partners and non-profit foundations could be approached for funding once a beta version was up and running. At least, that was the idea. We were not in a hurry. The idea had been around for many years; there was no rush to release it overnight.

Getting the objectives right was most important. Discordia should not become a hugely complex coding job. Simple weblog software could even be installed within hours. The mythology of Web-based communication systems being complicated – read: expensive – had to be cracked. There was so much software to choose from. There was easy-to-use weblog software such as Blogger, Moveable Type and Blosxom, but also Phpnuke-based weblogs, Slashcode and Active. After looking around, the group opted for Scoop, which seemed the only one that allowed users to post stories directly onto the main part of the site. Amy Alexander installed a test version of the Scoop software on her server. The first impressions were positive. The software did not seem too difficult. RRS/RDF feeds, an application service that lets people insert news feeds from other sites, could be included. Which tools would work best? How could the current loop in the role game of the user-artist as adolescent rebelling against the moderating father be opened up?

In February 2002, Alexander and I met in Los Angeles to work out details. Our main focus was getting the chemistry of the team right. There did not seem to be enough cross-pollination between theorists, artists and programmers. Education still separates theory and practice. Alexander: "Programmers must also be concept people and concept people should get their hands dirty playing with the software. Programmers don't have to think 'Damn theorists, got their head in the clouds theorizing and not a clue how this thing really works,' and theorists don't have to think, 'Damn programmers, all they care about is the software, they don't understand or care about our concept.'"[50] Discordia would operate on the (idealistic) premise that the weblog's content would be shaped by every-one, not just theorists and critics. Multi-disciplinary teams may seem to be the rule rather then the exception within digital media, but the very idea remained controversial, problematic and, most of all, rare. Whereas Alexander emphasized the variety of skills each individual had, I stressed the reality of specialization. Whereas everyone could write, not everyone was a theorist. Whatever our differences, the overall aim was to overcome the inherent divisions of labor and rivalries between professional cultures, which sounds normal but is in fact utopian. Hackers, for instance, need respect, and lots of it, as do designers. Their time is precious. All IT projects must deal with this fact, even commercial ones. Discordia had to deal with the delicate problem of exploitation and find a balance. Amy Alexander: "Exploitation of programmers goes like this: 'Let's collaborate! I'll tell you my ideas, and you implement them!'"[51]

The first to join were Peter Traub, a Bay-area programmer and sound artist, and Saul Albert, a London-based Net artist and new-media lecturer. Alexander had collaborated with Traub on a number of projects. A little later, Trebor Scholz followed. A Brooklyn-based, East Berlin-born interdisciplinary artist, he had worked extensively on the role of media artists and activists during the 1999 Kosovo conflict. Alieen Derieg of Linz, Austria, also joined. She describes herself as a "translator and feminist theologian with a particular interest in computers and networked communication." Designer Pip Shea from Melbourne joined, as did Victor Sintron, a Perl programmer based in Troy, NY. With the text-messaging rage in mind, Saul Albert suggested expanding the project into other media besides the Web. He wrote to the internal list: "What I like about the idea of Discordia is the potential for multi-modality. Have it delivered to your Palm Pilot, to your text-to-speech synth, your mobile phone, your Braille reader, your washing machine's spin cycle."[52] In theory, content could finally free itself from its original carrier and be displayed and processed on any medium. Yet no one quite knew how to code such convergence. It was all a matter of time and commitment. How much was to be expected of an online volunteer group that had never met in real life? Alexander: "The current state of blogs is pretty limited and overly structured. We've got lots of good ideas for conceptual blog expansion, from visual design to communication flow design, but our hands are tied, as Traub has described ... In a perfect world, we'd write our own blog software, but we don't have time to do that, and apparently neither do the Scoop developers, since they didn't get around to cleaning up or documenting the code (a common problem of open-source projects written by unpaid volunteers – it's easy to burn out before you can make it user-friendly)."[53]

Coding of Discordia started in earnest in June 2002. The launch was initially planned for September 2002, but things proved more complicated than expected. People got busy with other projects, and the badly documented Scoop software complicated progress. The group of volunteers had to wait patiently for the coding and design process to be finished. Beta testing began in April–May 2003, when the first users were invited in. Discordia launched on June 20, 2003. There, the weblog discussion and Discordia prehistory breaks off and the actual collective weblog starts. The rest can be discussed on the site. See you at www.discordia.us.

Conclusion

The Boundaries of Critical Internet Culture

"Talk may be cheap, but dialogue is dangerous. It can lead to action."
James Kelman

In these concluding remarks I will point out a number of trends which are changing the nature of critical Internet culture. I will stress both technological and sociopolitical aspects. These developments will affect the character of virtual communities, raise the issue of the online "democratic deficit" and redefine the never-ending balancing act between openness and the "quest for meaning." The issues raised here should be read as examples of a wider debate about network architectures that involves lists and blogs but also the Internet as such. How can a digital public domain be designed that will flourish with as little state and corporate control as possible? What forms of "seductive criticism" and "cultural intelligence" (Konrad Becker) can be instigated against the culture of complaint? In new media there is no fight of the individual against circumstances. There are only blowbacks. Forget the battle against the gods. Everything is up for grabs. All the adventures are still there.[1]

After the Hype

With Internet growth peaking in Western countries, the cultural cutting edge is starting to lose its interest in the "new media" saga. Despite the global crisis in the telecom sector, some players are keen to move to the Next Big Thing, such as wireless networks (wi-fi) or mobile-phone applications (MMS, 3G). Others are turning their back on technology altogether and returning to school or university. Users are drastically reducing the amount of time they spend surfing the Web. They stop hanging out in chatrooms, unsubscribe from lists and quit ICQ (instant messaging). Today's cultural celebrities leave communication to their assistants.[2] New media is for the social trash that needs it. After a period of excitement about the speed and intimacy of e-mail, people have become used to "telephone letters" and have integrated new media into their already busy lives. The eagerness to be connected has vanished, despite the fact that one can now be "always on" thanks to broadband. Not only has there been a consolidation of mainstream news portals such as Yahoo!, CNN, MSNBC and AOL, a rise in conservative websites has also been noticed. The liberal hegemony of Clinton and his Third Way European counterparts has faced competition from neo-conservatives, and the overall turn of the political climate since 9/11 is reflected on the Web.

Diversification of Internet Access Devices

In 2002, 1 billion people worldwide possessed mobile phones – twice as many as have access to the Internet. Whereas most users still use their mobile phones only to make phone calls and perhaps do some SMS messaging, Internet usage via mobile devices will in the long run no doubt increase. The number of people accessing the Internet via cable television set-top boxes is also on the rise. Then there are personal digital assistants (PDAs) such as Palm Pilots. But we can also think of the rise of cyber cafés, telecenters and other public-access spaces. The advent of cheap PCs and tablets, such as the Indian Simputer prototype ($200), too, will change the user base. The many programs set up to overcome the "digital divide" worldwide are also contributing to an expansion of the user group. Wireless networks plus the steady rise of broadband also increase – and diversify – Internet usage. The cultural impact of PCs, wireless and wearable devices on critical Internet culture has not yet become fully visible. The culture as mapped in this study is by and large that of the desktop PC with a 56K modem, bound to the office/home environment. Despite enormous growth in its user base, the Internet is still mainly shaped by the engineering culture of programmers. Coders and producers of content (with their specific PC-desktop cultures) have so far remained relatively close to the user base. This might change at some point, once the Net becomes available in multiple ways and has a billion or more users.

Content: Triumph or Tragedy?

Now that the dotcom wave of "free" content and access has faded away with no system of micro-payments yet in place, the big question that remains is if (and how) users will pay for Internet content. Though the subscription model is on the rise, an overwhelming amount of content remains freely available. Content remains a spinoff of hard- and software precisely because these modes of informational exchange and production do not have a payment system in place. Critical Internet culture has by and large supported the classic hackers' position that "information wants to be free." In other words, regardless of commercial or political interests, information cannot be hidden behind passwords and should not be paid for. How content producers make a living is their problem. If information is "jailed" on secure servers, hackers will appear and "liberate" it. This has been the prime concern of the entertainment industry. The hackers' hegemony throughout the 1980s and 1990s prevented, with a few exceptions, serious attempts to create widely accepted pay-for-content systems. Building a sustainable network culture does not seem to be in the interest of hackers. The Internet currency "beenz," launched at the height of the dotcom age, failed, mainly because its business model required hypergrowth and immediate success. This leaves many with no other option than to ignore the "free" Internet and silently accept the intellectual-property conditions of publishing houses, state bureaucracies and the media industry. What would happen if all the academics, performers and other creative workers stood up and refused to sign away their rights? This would be a matter of digital civil disobedience, presented in the form of a clever media campaign.

After the 2000 NASDAQ crash many Internet professionals lost their jobs. Less and less money has been available for professional online-content production, and the situation has remained remarkably unchanged, suggesting that critical Internet culture will remain dominated by volunteer labor unless some sudden revolutionary discovery is made and a barter or micropayment system establishes itself. Some say this will never happen. Many would love to speed up the global implosion. Burn, Hollywood, burn, ransacked by smart pirates like you and me. The advantage of mobile phones in this respect is that there is indeed a payment system in place: the phone bill. Internet wi-fi enthusiasts, pretending to compete with third-generation mobile phone systems, are inclined to overlook this difference. To do would threaten the hegemony of the libertarian hackers' class. I am not saying "cellspace" is perfect. It's got its own tragedy of proprietary standards which only a few have started to address. Wi-fi wireless networks for PCs may extend access to the Internet and further speed up user mobility, but they avoid the issue of how such networks can be transformed into sustainable economies. Wi-fi networks are, once again, driven by the ideology of the "free," meaning that there is nothing in it for independent content producers. Critical Internet culture is a financial disaster for its own participants – and few seem to care. A decade into the culture, participants have accepted voluntocracy (governance by those who do the work). Those who do not agree with this mode of operation, or simply can't afford to participate, either have left or never showed up in the first place. From a content perspective, "community" is just another word for nothing left to lose.[3] Weblogs are not doing anything to change this situation. The popularity of free peer-to-peer networks such as Napster and its successors Gnutella and KaZaa not only harm the recording industry but also make it difficult for an independent pay-for-content culture to establish itself. This picture contradicts the dark views of experts such as Lawrence Lessig, who warns of a victory by the intellectual-property regime over the innovative and open character of the Internet. Tensions between free content and intellectual-property claims (from both artists and industry) are likely to rise, with no immediate resolution in sight.

From Internet to Global Capitalism

While, socio-technologically speaking, more and more people have access to the Internet, this by no means implies that the gender, race and class divides within the medium will simply fade away. This counts in particular for IT developers. After years in which there was a growing belief that technology might bring down global inequality, since 2000 the mood has been slowly shifting back to a general criticism of technology. Utopian promises have been slashed, and with them the hegemonic position of libertarian technological determinism. But what might on the one hand seem a healthy return to pragmatism could just as well become a skeptical backlash for many in the Net art, free-software/open-source projects and community networks that draw heavily on voluntary labor, driven by the collective belief that independent software, interfaces and infrastructure form the key battleground of the 21st century. Many post-2000 critical projects and individuals have shifted their concerns from technology to a broader analysis of global capitalism. The debates over Michael Hardt and Antonio Negri's theoretical epos *Empire* is one indication; *No Logo*, Naomi Klein's critique of corporate branding, is another.[4]

The series of global protests that started at the 1999 WTO meeting in Seattle has only grown. 9/11 has not led to a decline. Instead, we have witnessed the appearance of the largest (global) antiwar movement since Vietnam, in the protests against the US invasion of Iraq. Even though it is indisputable that these movements would not exist without the Internet, the so-called "anti-globalization movement" has so far not developed its own theory of technology and new media. Instead there is a withdrawal into a "Chomskyist" position – yet another form of determinism which states that all elements in society, including media and technology, are ultimately subordinated to imperial US foreign policy.

The "anti-globalization movement" has so far avoided specific new-media topics. It is the WTO, G8 and the World Economic Forum, not AOL or

Microsoft, where power is located. Politics is made undemocratically by a class of professional politicians who make deals with corporations behind closed doors. Even though the use of IT for social change has been discussed in detail,[5] the topic has by and large been absent from the agendas of the movements' own meetings, in Porto Alegre (early 2001 and 2002) and at regional "social forums" such as that in Florence (November 2002). Technology and new media have been remarkably absent in the movements' list of urgent social, economic and political issues.[6] The danger of a regression to previous activist arguments that "technology is evil" and "all media are propaganda" is lurking. E-mail, Web and mobile phones are widely used among activists but nonetheless seen as mere tools. Net activists and artists with an awareness of techno-politics are in the minority, and in danger of getting stuck in new-media-arts, open-source or streaming-media ghettoes. The David and Goliath struggle between Linux and Windows is followed with interest but by no means perceived as the mother of all battles. The rising criticism of techno-fetishism in new-media arts only further strengthens the general move away from technology.

Both progressive and conservative voices are calling for a "return to reality." In Chapter One, I discussed media ecologist Hubert L. Dreyfus. Regression might be on the rise, particularly in a time of corporate consolidation and increased censorship and surveillance, such as that after 9/11. Critical Internet culture could then seriously suffer, resulting in disengagement from key issues such as design of a digital public domain and related network architecture. The battle over the "network society" is far from over. Some would say it has not even started. However, it should not be taken for granted that significant numbers of artists, activists, academics and critics will identify themselves forever with the new media issue. The technology discourse (including its critics) must find its place in a broader theory of society, without being either talked down or overestimated.

Information Overload and Filtering

Time-wise, the Internet must compete not only with television, computer games, movies on VHS and DVD, radio and print media but also with "wearables" such as mobile phones, PDAs and MP3 players. The "attention economy" concept[7] once associated with the rise of Internet is turning against itself. There is no longer enough attention for the Internet, and not even the spectacular growth of the user base can hide this fact. For many websites, first impressions were also last ones. Users have moved on from initial curiosity about how to use the new medium to personal (crisis) management of ever-growing information and communication flows. A friend tells me how he copes: "I get about 80 e-mails a day. Remember the days when one's self-worth was proportional to the number of mails in one's inbox? I don't mind the large numbers of mails so much. I select the sources into separate mail folders. And then there is always is the delete button. Scanning is the problem for me: how do I know what will be of interest? So a brief summary at the top (or keywords) of the mail or a very clear subject heading is what helps me most."[8] Overload for individuals equals "scalability" for communities. How fast can they grow? What is their upper limit? Complex systems cannot grow forever and, almost by default, develop autonomous subsystems.

The use of e-mail is becoming more complex and unpredictable. As I pointed out earlier, a rapid "erosion of e-mail" is occurring.[9] The spreading of e-mail as a mass communication tool results in the paradox of longer reply times and increased disruptions. It is a communication tool that increasingly suffers from inflation and social fatigue while remaining the cornerstone of the Net. Getting an answer three weeks later, actually much slower than "snail mail" through the conventional postal system would take, is not uncommon anymore. Let's not even mention spam here – a topic that became the number one concern for system administrators in 2003. There are problems with overflowing mailboxes, crashed mail servers, bugs in Microsoft products, bouncing e-mails, broken transcontinental cables and bankrupt ISPs. Incidents such as these can no longer be blamed on the newness of the technology. Employees are warned that their e-mails are compressed and stored as possible evidence. With businesses generating 13 billion e-mails a day, it has never been more important for management to monitor and regulate the content of outgoing mail. It is urgent that users become aware that there is no such thing as privacy on the Net. Netiquette these days consists of a list of serious warnings, like: "Be professional, courteous, and careful, especially with sarcasm or humor. Cite all quotes, references and sources (when known), and respect author copyright. The responsibility over copyright is in your hands. Be circumspect when replying to others. Attempt to persuade with reason, facts and logic, rather than emotion. Don't write anything that you would not want your mother/father/boss or other assumed-hierarchically-superior person to read. Keep messages as brief as possible, succinct and to the point."[10]

Demise of Independent Infrastructure

Ownership of actual servers is not common within critical Internet culture, though one would think otherwise. Since the late 1990s there has even been a steady decline in the amount of small, independent Internet service providers. This has affected the cultural sector. Cheap and independent Internet access (e-mail, webspace, streaming servers, list software, chatrooms, etc.) available to activists, artists and NGOs is lost owing to a lack of sustainable models. The same thing happened to projects that used to run on university computer networks. Free access to servers hardly exists anymore. With this comes a loss of direct control. Cultural service providers such as The Thing (New York) have faced censorship by upstream providers because of "controversial" content. An increasing number of websites now run on anonymous commercial servers on the eastern and western coasts of the United States – so-called server farms where bandwidth and server space are still cheap. A further increase in intellectual property and copyright problems, however, could stop the decline of independent infrastructure. Since the dotcom crash, most 'free' Internet services have disappeared and fee-paying is on the rise. As described in the streaming-media chapters, the cost of bandwidth for streaming projects has risen. Instead of the predicted fall in the price of transferred gigabytes because of the rise in bandwidth capacity, the opposite is happening. Users may be forced into a pay-per-Mb-downloaded system, in particular for mobile devices and games. Now that the "funny money" (venture capital) has dried up, all the operators in the networks need to come up with real revenues. Unlike the dotcom logic of profit through an economy of hype, the pressure to make money within the information economy and its complex infrastructures will ultimately result in a user-pays system. Unless a comprehensive public domain economy is introduced, the rest is info junk, with the exception of some "creative commons" data.

From Consolidation to Isolation?

For critical Internet culture the telephone never rings. The cultural arm of the new-media sector has not had particularly prosperous years recently.

Ironically, its golden days could be located at the dawn of the World Wide Web, around 1990–95, when the air was laden with promises and mythologies.[11] Since the mid-1990s, business and technology have dominated Internet reporting, both online and in the old media. It is likely that IT industry insiders have never heard of the initiatives and topics discussed here. By 1998, when the dotcoms started to dominate the Internet, new-media culture's heyday was over. Artists and designers had failed to implement their avant-garde prototypes. Badly needed funding for Internet culture either wasn't there or disappeared into competing offline categories. Ever since, new-media culture's position within society has remained undefined. This may sound like a unique opportunity to shape the future while starting from scratch, but the reality looks different. In a time of shrinking budgets, the cultural establishment does not welcome yet another mouth to feed. Why would film, visual art or literature, let alone opera or theatre, support new media and voluntarily give up scarce resources?

As discussed in various chapters the emerging new-media culture has faced difficulties funding its own activities, depending instead on arrangements with other institutional support infrastructures. Despite modest growth in 1998–2002, we can hardly speak of an institutionalization of new-media culture. Volunteers do most of the work. While the funding structure differs widely from country to country, the overall trend is the same. Instead of the expected steady rise in funding by both governments and non-governmental foundations, spending on new-media culture has actually declined. As a result, critical Internet culture has not reached its potential – and perhaps never will, as its historical window of opportunity to intervene and invent is rapidly closing. The Internet, after all, has always been described in terms of a set of functions and a potential to transform society, be this in utopian or dystopian ways. It is therefore better to analyze the actual practices of new-media cultures instead of reading new media as embryonic forms of emerging landscapes. In analogy to the cyberpunk phrase "The future is now," we could say "The Internet is now."

The Democratization of the Internet

Sooner or later, critical Internet culture will have to confront the issue of its own democracy. I am talking not about digital rights of users but about power-sharing beyond the old boys' behind-closed-doors consensus culture. Contrary to Fareed Zakaria, one could say that the new media suffer from a lack of internal democracy, not from an abundance of liberty.[12] I am not referring to the big picture of the relationship between the Internet and representative democracy. What is at stake is an agonistic "electronic democracy," driven by "global governance from below," capable of addressing the plurality of difference that defines user communities ("Another network is possible"). This concerns the "cyber-rights" of both individuals and groups. Domain-name space needs an entire revamp, which will ultimately have to involve the transition of power from US authorities to a neutral global body. The emergence of such a polity will, in the first instance, bring forward the democratization of collective publishing platforms. The dream of an "Internet without adversary" has vanished.[13] It is important to note that users, communities, businesses and governments have different interests. This issue could be seen as the "cultural" version of the Internet governance battles (such as the one over domain names). Experiments with new forms of democracy and shared ownership of (global) Internet projects will also have to address legal issues of "open ownership."

Technical software for voting has been around for some time but has not yet been further developed or even used, at least not in the circles of artists, activists and critics that I have dealt with in this study. The same could be said of micro-payment systems that could enable content producers to develop independent revenue streams, beyond the goodwill gesture of giving it all away for free, which is the only option right now. Software for micro-payments has been around for a decade but has not reached a broader audience, beyond a few commercial attempts to establish private currencies. The telcos are currently in the best position to benefit from a centralized payment system. A peer-to-peer money economy (beyond one of attention) could do away with the hacker's dogma that one ought not earn income with the work one does online because everything should be "free." In this respect programmers are not the best advisers on how to shape the network society, as they get an income anyway. The same can be said of the telecommunication sector.

The democracy deficit can be explained in part by the libertarian *Zeitgeist* that emphasizes the right to be left alone: if you don't like our list or blog, then set up one yourself. Trust the engineers, they know what's good for all of us. If you don't like this or that digital city, then build one according to your own principles. There is infinite space in cyberspace, so the argument goes. The problem with this rhetoric is the fact that financial resources, necessary to install infrastructure, are not limitless. Nor do all users have the necessary technical skill to set up databases, servers or wireless networks or understand the ins and outs of free software. The argument that everyone is autonomous is used mainly by those who already have the technical skills and knowhow to run a list, blog or server. In short: users should be grateful for the service and shut up. The users, on the other hand, see themselves as the most valuable assets of a system – and rightly so. One can expect that the lingering conflict between operators and users will come to a head sooner rather then later.

Instead of recycling cyber-libertarian phrases, the Link Tank Report argues for the design of an Augmented Social Network (ASN) that could "revitalize democracy in the 21ˢᵗ century."[14] The report, written for the June 2003 Planetwork conference, calls for a new generation of online communications that will strengthen civil society by better connecting people who share affinities, so they can more effectively exchange information and self-organize. The paper couples political analysis with a description of a technical architecture that could be achieved with today's technology. In a remarkable move, the San Francisco-based writers of the report note the limitations of the engineers who once built the Internet. "They did not much consider what social interaction among millions of Internet users would actually entail. It was thought that the Net's technical architecture need not address the issues of 'personal identity' and 'trust,' since those matters tended to take care of themselves."

The four elements of the proposed ASN are persistent online identity, interoperability between communities, brokered relationships, and public-interest matching technologies. The ASN paper calls for a public-interest approach to online identity that would enable individuals to express their interests outside contexts determined by commerce. This approach would include a digital profile with an "affinity reference" that would facilitate connections to trusted third parties. The designers of the ASN architecture believe "identity" lies at the heart of today's Internet crisis. Trust between private users may be restored in such ways, but larger-scale solutions such as Internet governance remain untouched. Rather, the question should be: how can conflicts be publicly "staged," instead of played down or regulated on an individual level, without ending in global civil war? That said, the ASN approach is an interesting post-dotcom social alliance of technologists and activists in search of alternative network architectures.

In his conclusion to *The Internet Galaxy*, Manuel Castells calls for more institutions, political representation and participatory democracy. He admits that this is the weak link in the network society. In most societies, the practice of democratic principles is in a shambles. He writes: "Until we rebuild, both from the bottom up and from the top down, our institutions of governance and democracy, we will not be able to stand up to the fundamental challenges we are facing."[15] In an introduction to his website, Internet critic and blog expert Clay Shirky remarks: "More than once, new technologies have held out the promise of wider participation by citizens, only to be corralled by a new set of legal or economic realities, and the net, which threatens many vested interests all at once, will be no exception. Nevertheless, despite a 'two steps forward, one step back' progression, we are living through a potentially enormous shift in the amount of leverage the many have over the few."[16] The Internet may embody freedom, but as this study has shown, there is much to be learned from the Internet experience if we look at the ways it currently deals with its own decision-making procedures and the many conflicts that have arisen within social networks. Until recently the development of the Internet was run by a small consensus-driven group of (largely male) technologists. The medium has recently been taken over by business interests assisted by governments. In parallel, the increase in actively involved Internet users, in particular outside the United States, has been remarkable. Global civil society, if it is ever to exist, has to stand up and (re)claim the Internet. The case studies presented here do not answer Castells' call. Instead they point to increased levels of tension and conflict, accompanied by efforts to develop new communication architectures. The discomfort in critical Internet culture grows out of a wider unfamiliarity with new-media policy and economic power structures. One way out of this malaise could be the production, distribution and promotion of software that acknowledges the antagonisms in the society within which the Internet operates.

Notes

Introduction:
Currents in Critical Internet Culture

1. David Berlind, "IBM, Microsoft plot Net takeover," *Znet*, April 11, 2002. URL: techupdate.zdnet.com/techupdate/stories/main/0,14179,2861123,00.html.

2. "The Internet sells its soul," *The Economist*, April 16, 2002. URL: www.economist.com/agenda/display Story.cfm?story_id=1085967.

3. Jeff Chester, "How Industry Intends To Kill The Net As We Know It," October 24, 2002, URL: www.tom-paine.com/feature.cfm/ID/6600/view/print.
A Sydney-based friend wrote me the following response to Chester: "The USA has so far resisted use-based billing although non-use-based billing has all along disadvantaged customers who might not want to use streaming video etc. and just do a bit of email (after all still the really interesting part of net-life). Average users are actually subsidising the rich techno elite who do consume a lot of the bandwidth. My bandwidth is metered and it always has been."

4. Andrew Orlowski, "The Internet is Dying – Prof. Lessig," *The Register*, May 15, 2003, URL: www.theregister.co.uk/content/6/30733.html. Orlowski reports on Lawrence Lessig's gloomy prediction for the Internet's future, the relaxation of media controls which will leave most of the United States' professional media outlets in the hands of a tiny number of owners. Lessig: "When the content layer, the logical layer, and the physical layer are all effectively owned by a handful of companies, free of any requirements of neutrality or openness, what will you ask then?"

5. Lisa Guernsey, "As the Web Matures, Fun is Hard to Find," *The New York Times*, March 28, 2002. URL: www.nytimes.com/2002/03/28/technology/circuits/28WEBB.html.

6. See Rob Walker, "Work Daze," in *The New York Times Magazine*, June 23, 2002 (accessed via the Web).

7. Michael Geist, "US Extends Its Hegemony Over the Net," *Toronto Star*, June 9, 2003. URL: shorl.com/jegijotejivo.

8. Howard Rheingold, *Smart Mobs*, Cambridge, Mass.: Perseus Books, 2002, p. xii.

9. Linus Torvalds with David Diamond, *Just for Fun*, New York: HarperCollins, 2002, p. 244.

10. Alain Badiou, *Ethics*, London: Verso, 2001, p. 122 and pp. 67–68.

11. Karl Marx, "The Eighteenth Brumaire of Louis Bonaparte" (1852), URL: chnm.gmu.edu/revolution/d/580/. Source: Saul K. Padover (Ed.), *The Karl Marx Library, Vol. 1*, New York: McGraw Hill, 1972, pp. 245–246.

12. Erkki Huhtamo describes media archaeology as a way of "studying recurring cyclical phenomena which (re)appear and disappear and reappear over and over again in media history and somehow seem to transcend specific historical contexts. URL: www.uta.fi/~tlakja/GA/media01.html. See also Siegfried Zielinski, *Archäologie der Medien*, Hamburg: Rowohlt, 2002, pp. 46–47. For Zielinski, archaeology is "an-archaeology." See also Zielinski's "Media Archaeology," *CTheory*, www. theory.net/text_file. asp?pick=42.

13. This is what German media scholar Mike Sandbothe does in his *Pragmatische Medienphilosophie*, Weilerswist, Velbrück Wissenschaft, 2001. Sandbothe lays out the pragmatist foundations for a yet-to-be-founded academic discipline he calls "media philosophy." Frank Hartmann proposes something different in his study *Medienphilosophie*, Wien: WUV-Universitätsverlag, 2000. Unlike Sandbothe, Hartmann stays close to media-related issues and does not address the philosophy community directly in a plea for more understanding of media. Hartmann rejects technology-focused and archaeology-driven "media theory." Remaining close to Vilém Flusser's work, Hartmann emphasizes the "communological" capacity to demystify large-scale constructs (p. 14). Instead of distancing myself from media theory, I have chosen to politicize the field and give it another, perhaps more radical direction.

14. Elsewhere I have listed the different, competing names in this field such as digital studies, Netzwissenschaften, hypermedia studies (Lovink, *Dark Fiber*, p. 136). See also the debate on the mailing list aoir (www.aior.org) in early November 2002 over whether "Internet research" should become an academic discipline.

15. David Silver, "Looking Backwards, Looking Forwards: Cyberculture Studies, 1990-2000," in David Gauntlett (Ed.), *Web.Studies*, London: Arnold Publishers, 2000, p. 19.

16. I have no hesitation in presenting this volume as part two of *Dark Fiber: Tracking Critical Internet Culture* (Cambridge, Mass.: MIT Press, 2002), my collection of essays on critical Internet culture published by MIT Press in 2002. I closed the *Dark Fiber* manuscript in August 2001, one month before the 9/11 attacks on the World Trade Center and the Pentagon. I started work on *My First Recession* in late 2001, driven by the intention of doing more case studies on Internet-based social networks and continuing the research I started in the *Dark Fiber* chapters on the Digital City and the Nettime mailing list.

17. Thinking in the sense of Hannah Arendt's statement that "There are no dangerous thoughts; thinking

itself is dangerous. To think and to be fully alive are the same."

18. One example: Jean Baudrillard writes, "Video, interactive screens, multimedia, the Internet, virtual reality – we are threatened on all sides by interactivity." He then goes on to praise his typewriter (which he does not consider a machine). "The typewriter is an entirely external object. The page flutters in the open air and so do I. I have a physical relation to writing. I touch the blank or written pages with my eyes – something I cannot do with the screen. The computer is a true prosthesis." Jean Baudrillard, *Screened Out*, London: Verso, 2002, pp. 176–180.

19. GPL stands for General Public License, which is the legal backbone of free software production. See: www.gnu.org. "GPL society" is a term developed by the German-language Oekonux mailing list (www.oekonux.org).

20. Northrop Frye, *The Anatomy of Criticism,* London: Penguin Books, 1990 (1957), p. 3.

21. See McKenzie Wark, "A Hacker Manifesto," www.feelergauge.net/projects/hackermanifesto/version_2.0/

22. For my definition of the virtual intellectual, see "Portrait of the Virtual Intellectual," a lecture given at Documenta X, Kassel, Germany, July 13, 1997. Posted on Nettime, July 20, 1997. An updated version can be found in Lovink, *Dark Fiber,* pp. 30–39.

23. Ibid., p. 4.

24. Terry Eagleton, *The Function of Criticism,* London: Verso, 1984, p. 107 (Eagleton quotes Peter Hohendahl).

25. For instance, see www.textz.com (its slogans are "We are the & in copy & paste" and "Burn, Hollywood, Burn").

26. "We have no more beginnings" is the opening sentence of George Steiner's *Grammars of Creation,* London: Faber and Faber, 2001, p. 1. In analogy to Bruno Latour's *We Have Never Been Modern,* one could argue that "We have never been online."

27. Translation: "Net culture is all that is the case" (a reference to Wittgenstein's phrase *"Die Welt ist alles was der Fall ist").*

28. Together with Dutch designer Mieke Gerritzen, I have tried to map critical mobile phone discourse within the framework of two design competitions (the Berlin and Amsterdam Browsersdays, December 2001 and May 2002) and a publication of short texts and phrases, *Mobile Minded* (Amsterdam/New York: Bis Publishers/Ginko Press, 2002). See: www.browserday.com.

29. The artists' group Critical Art Ensemble first developed the term "electronic civil disobedience." See: CAE, *Electronic Civil Disobedience,* Brooklyn: Autonomedia, 1995. In his study *Future Active:*

Media Activism and the Internet (Sydney: Pluto Press, 2002), Graham Meikle dedicates a chapter to this topic (pp. 140-173).

30. Manuel Castells, *The Internet Galaxy: Reflections on the Internet, Business and Society,* Oxford: Oxford University Press, 2001, p. 158.

31. In Pekka Himanen's *The Hacker Ethic* (New York: Random House, 2001), hackers are portrayed as playful, passionate programmers, combining entertainment with doing something interesting, as Linus Torvalds puts it in his preface to the book. Crackers, on the other hand, are portrayed as computer criminals, "virus writers and intruders" and "destructive computer users" (p. viii). Himanen does not mention the historical fact that many hackers had to hack to gain access to the Net before it became publicly accessible in the early 1990s. Breaking a system's security is not by definition a criminal act, especially not if you put it into the context of another hacker ethic, "Information wants to be free" (which is more than just code).

32. Lovink, "An Insider's Guide to Tactical Media," in *Dark Fiber,* pp. 255–274.

33. Chantal Mouffe, *The Democratic Paradox,* London: Verso, 2000, p. 131.

34. Ibid., p. 103.

35. did., p. 104.

36. Quotations from Slavoj Zizek, *On Belief,* London: Routledge, 2001, p. 10.

37. The first two case studies, of the Digital City community network and the Nettime mailing list, can be found in *Dark Fiber.*

38. Peter Kollock and Marc A. Smith provide us with a useful definition of a mailing list: "Mail lists are typically owned by a single individual or small group. Since all messages sent to the list must pass through a single point, e-mail lists offer their owners significant control over who can contribute to their group. List owners can personally review all requests to be added to a list, can forbid anyone from contributing to the list if they are not on the list themselves, and even censor specific messages that they do not want broadcast to the list as a whole. Even open lists can be selectively closed or controlled by the owners when faced with disruption. Most e-mail lists operate as benign dictatorships sustained by the monopoly power that the list owner wields over the boundaries and content of their group. As a result, e-mail lists are often distinguished by their relatively more ordered and focused activity." Peter Kollock and Marc A. Smith, in the introduction to their reader *Communities in Cyberspace,* London: Routledge, 1999, p. 5.

39. Josephine Berry, "Introduction: Site-Specificity in the Non-Places of the Net," Ph.D. thesis, London,

2001, quoted from Berry's post to Nettime, August 22, 2001.

40. See www.w3.org/Talks/1999/0105-Regulation/all. htm.

41. A journalistic account would be David Bennahum's article on list culture in *Wired* 6.4 (April 1998). URL: www.wired.com/wired/archive/6.04/es_lists. html. One of the first studies into the population and behavior of a list was probably Stanley Brunn's "GEOGED as a Virtual Workshop," a paper presented at the National Council for Geographic Education's 83rd Annual Meeting, October 11–14, 1998, Indianapolis, Indiana, USA. See also the work of Radhika Gajjala (www.cyberdiva.org), who studies women-centered lists. Stefan Merten has written a German text on mailing lists which includes comments by other Oekonux members.

42. Jon Marshall's Ph.D. thesis is available online: www.geocities.com/jpmarshall.geo/T2/contents.html .Info on the list archives: www.geocities.com/ jpmarshall.geo/cybermind/archives.html.

43. From a private e-mail exchange, April 22, 2003.

44. Jon Marshall: "Community is not so much a 'thing,' but a term with political and social importance, carrying ideals of legitimacy. It is more interesting to look at how the term is used in a situation or among a group than it is to try and identify its characteristics." Private e-mail exchange, April 22, 2003.

45. Howard Rheingold, *Virtual Communities*, Cambridge, Mass.: MIT Press, 2000. In *Dark Fiber*, I analyze the new afterword (pp. 5–9).

46. David Bell, *Introduction to Cybercultures*, London: Routledge, 2001, pp. 92–113.

47. For me, the Internet is part of the "new media" landscape that extends from video art, computer graphics, CD-ROMs and virtual reality to digital cinema, mobile phones and DVDs. For a definition of new media, I would like to refer to Lev Manovich's *The Language of New Media*, Cambridge, Mass.: MIT Press, 2001. In the chapter "Principles of New Media" (pp. 27–48), Manovich sums up the characteristics of new media, such as numerical representation, modularity, automation and variability, all of which also apply to the Internet.

48. I have described my experience with an early dotcom project, Netural Objects, which was initiated by the Society for Old and New Media in Amsterdam and others. See: Geert Lovink, Nettime, April 21, 1998.

49. Dan Schiller, *Digital Capitalism: Networking the Global Market System*, Cambridge, Mass.: The MIT Press, 1999.

50. See Geert Lovink, "The Theory of Mixing," in Neil Straus (Ed.), *Radiotext(e)*, Brooklyn: Semiotext(e), 1993, pp. 114–122. URL: www.thing.desk.nl/bilwet/-adilkno/Radiotext/MIXING.TXT.

Post-Speculative Internet Theory: Three Positions: Dreyfus, Castells, Lessig

1. An earlier draft of the part on Dreyfus was published earlier in the German online magazine *Telepolis* on April 18, 2002. URL: www.heise.de/tp/english/ inhalt/buch/12345/1.html. The text was posted to the Nettime mailing list on April 22, 2002. Thanks to Felix Stalder for his comments on this chapter.

2. See Danny Hillis's and Stewart Brand's initiative to build a clock that keeps time for 10,000 years. URL: www.longnow.org/. Visionaries like Brand and Kevin Kelly seem to have shifted their emphasis from linear predictions of technological trends in an imaginary future towards thinking for the generations to come by defining long-term time standards, setting a conservation standard for digital archives (together with the Library of Congress), and mapping all the biological species. If you live in the future, you may as well work in the future, at least a couple of centuries from now.

3. The LA new-media theorist Peter Lunenfeld has a special interest in explaining why the US West Coast, and Southern California in particular, has lately become a major center for critical new-media research. For more on this topic, see my dialogues with Lunenfeld on Nettime, April 3 and July 31, 2000.

4. Hubert L. Dreyfus, *On the Internet*, London/New York: Routledge, 2001. URL of his bibliography: socrates.berkeley.edu/~hdreyfus/rtf/dreyfus_cv_5_0 0.rtf.

5. Ibid., p. 4.

6. Ibid., p. 102.

7. Ibid., p. 7.

8. See: Chris DiBona, Sam Ockman, Mark Stone, *Open Sources: Voices from the Open Source Revolution*, Sebastopol: O'Reilly Publishing, 1999.

9. See "The Revolt of the Media Ecologists" in Adilkno, *The Media Archive*, Brooklyn: Autonomedia, 1998, pp. 159–164 (URL: www.thing.desk. nl/bilwet/adilkno/TheMediaArchive/39.txt). An adaptation of this early-1990s essay, with examples of leading intellectuals' concerns about the nihilist nature of the Web: Geert Lovink and Pit Schultz, "Sinnflut Internet," in *Telepolis, Die Zeitschrift der Netzkultur*, No. 1, 1997, pp. 5–11 (URL: www.thing.desk.nl/bilwet/TXT/ angst.txt). See also Rüdiger Safranski's essay *How Much Globalisation Can One Bear? (Wieviel Globalisierung verträgt der Mensch?* München: Carl Hanser Verlag, 2003).

10. Dreyfus, *On the Internet*, p. 79.

11. Ibid., pp. 5–6. The following quotes are from the same pages.

12. Ibid., p. 79.

13. Ibid., p. 79.

14. David F. Noble, *Digital Diploma Mills: The Automation of Higher Education*, New York: Monthly Review Press, 2001.

15. The Dutch media theorist Arjen Mulder, like me a member of Adilkno, has dealt with the question of the "extramedial" extensively, for instance in his first book, *Het buitenmediale*, and also in *Het twintigste eeuwse lichaam* (neither has been translated into English). Building on Mulder's thesis is an essay in Adilkno's *The Media Archive* (Brooklyn: Autonomedia, 1998), "The Extramedial," which states: "Everything is medial. There exists no original, unmediated situation in which 'authentic' human existence can be experienced" (p. 192; URL: www.thing.desk.nl/bilwet/adilkno/TheMediaArchive/46.txt).

16. Dreyfus, *On the Internet*, p. 73 ff.

17. See Chapter Four, Chantal Mouffe, *The Democratic Paradox*, London/New York: Verso, 2000.

18. Manuel Castells, *The Internet Galaxy*, Oxford: Oxford University Press, 2001, p. 3.

19. See www.aoir.org. The archive of the list can be found at www.aoir.org/mailman/listinfo/air-l. Castells was a keynote speaker at the first AoIR conference in 2000. He refers, for instance, to studies by Steve Jones, Ben Anderson, Barry Wellman and Karina Tracey suggesting that the Internet seems to have a positive effect on social interaction. But there are conflicting studies on the effect of Internet usage on sociability. The Internet does support "networked individualism," while at the same fostering "specialized communities," thus "enhancing the capacity of individuals to rebuild structures of sociability from the bottom up" (p. 132).

20. Castells, *The Internet Galaxy*, p. 260.

21. Ibid., p. 272.

22. Ibid., p. 79.

23. Ibid., p. 36.

24. Ibid., p. 36.

25. Ibid., p. 61.

26. Ibid., p. 33.

27. Lawrence Lessig, *Code and Other Laws of Cyberspace*, New York: Perseus Books, 1999, p. 234.

28. Lawrence Lessig, *The Future of Ideas*, New York: Random House, 2001, p. vii.

29. Ibid., p. viii.

30. Taken from an interview with Lessig by Bill Thompson for *The Guardian*, March 13, 2003. URL: www.guardian.co.uk/online/story/0,3605,912616,00.html.

31. Lawrence Lessig, *The Future of Ideas*, p. 268.

32. Felix Stalder, "The Excess of Control," review of Lawrence Lessig's *The Future of Ideas*, first published in *Telepolis* (www.heise.de/tp/english/inhalt/buch/11504/1.html). Posted to Nettime, January 13, 2002.

33. "The Tragedy of the Commons" is the title of a famous paper by the biologist Garrett Hardin published in *Science* magazine in 1968 (No. 162, pp. 1243–1248). Garrett describes the decline of common pastures in villages owing to overuse. The tragedy of the commons is often used to warn against the dangers of overpopulation. Even though the ability to copy in the digital age is infinite, there are similarities. In this case the tragedy is man-made and not caused by natural scarcity of resources.

34. www.centerforthepublicdomain.org/commons.htm

35. Lawrence Lessig, "Reclaiming a Commons," speech at the Berkman Center, May 20, 1999; cyber.law.harvard.edu/events/lessigkeynote.pdf.

36. www.democraticmedia.org/issues/digitalcommons/

37. Jürgen Habermas, *Strukturwandel der Öffentlichkeit*, Frankfurt am Main: Suhrkamp, 1990 (1962) (in English: *The Structural Transformation of the Public Sphere*, Cambridge, Mass.: MIT Press, 1991).

38. Terry Eagleton, *The Function of Criticism*, London: Verso Books, 1984, p. 8.

39. Taken from the www.creativecommons.org website, launched in December 2002. Lawrence Lessig is the chairman of the Creative Commons board of directors.

40. Benjamin Barber, *A Place for Us: How to Make Society Civil and Democracy Strong*, New York: Hill and Wang, 1998.

41. Taken from www.syllabus.com/article.asp?id=7475. See also creativecommons.org/projects/founders-copyright.

42. Richard Sennett, *The Fall of Public Man*, New York: Knopf, 1977.

43. See Howard Rheingold, *Smart Mobs*, Cambridge, Mass.: Perseus Publishing, 2002. Weblog: www.smartmobs.com.

The Anatomy of Dotcom Mania: Overview of Recent Literature

1. Dotcom ethics, as described by Netscape employee Eric Hahn, in Glyn Moody, *Rebel Code*, London: Penguin Books, 2001, p. 195.

2. A part of this chapter was published in *Cultural Studies Review, Vol. 8, No. 1*, May 2002, pp. 130–154. Thanks to Chris Healy for editiorial assistance.

3. A selection: Lynne W. Jet, *Disconnected: Deceit and Betrayal at WorldCom*, New York: John Weley & Sons, 2003; Mimi Swartz and Sherron Watkins, *Power Failure: The Inside Story of the Collapse of Enron*, New York: Doubleday, 2003; Brian Cruver, *Anatomy of Greed: The Unshredded Truth from an Insider*, New York: Carroll & Grad, 2003; Barbara Ley

Toffler and Jennifer Reingold, *Final Accounting: Ambition, Greed and the Fall of Andersen,* New York: Broadway Books, 2003.

4. A third parallel universe worth mentioning here was the hacker/geek culture. The different communities of culture, commerce and programming were confronted with considerable communication problems. However, I will not look into the ways in which hackers responded to dotcom culture. They were certainly very much involved, as they did most of the work, but the vast majority of them stayed out of the business.

5. Early publications to come out in 2000 included *Cyberselfish* by Paulina Borsook, Robert J. Schiller's *Irrational Exuberance* and *One Market Under God* by Thomas Frank. A prime victim of speed could be *Wall Street* author Doug Henwood's *A New Economy?* announced by Verso Books in 2000. Its publication date was postponed a number of times owing to events. The book is now scheduled for 2003.

6. The June 2000 conference Tulipomania.dotcom (URL: www.balie.nl/tulipomania), held in Amsterdam and Frankfurt, organized by Geert Lovink, Eric Kluitenberg and others of the Nettime circle, could be seen as an exception. The symposium took place a few months after the dramatic fall of the NASDAQ index in April 2000. First indications of the dotcom downfall go back to late 1999 as clearly documented in Ernst Malmsten's *Boo Hoo* story.

7. An early overview of the dotcom bubble is *Dot.con* by John Cassidy, London: Penguin, 2002. www.fuckedcompany.com founder Philip J. Kaplan's *F'd Companies: Spectacular Dotcom Fallouts* (New York: Simon & Schuster, 2002) lists some 150 ill-fated companies.

8. Richard W. Stevenson, "Why a Business Scandal Became a National Spectacle," *The New York Times,* February 17, 2002.

9. Bill Keller, "Enron for Dummies," *The New York Times,* January 26, 2002 (online edition).

10. Timothy Noah, "Blaming Liberalism for Enron," www.slate.msn.com, January 21, 2002.

11. "Perhaps we, as a society, have become so accustomed to associating the act of running a business with the act of making money – or rather, the act of booking revenue in accordance with the arts of accountancy – that corporate analysts appear not to have had an institutional framework capable of distinguishing between an accounting trick and a business process, between a revenue stream and the production of value." (Jonathan Siegel, posted by Steve Brant on the Triumph of Content list, January 20, 2002.)

12. Karel Williams, "The Temptation of Houston," *Australian Financial Review,* March 15, 2002, p.3.

13. Kevin Kelly, "The Web Runs on Love, Not Greed," *Wall Street Journal,* January 4, 2002.

14. Ibid.

15. Rachel Konrad, "Trouble Ahead, Trouble Behind," interview with John Perry Barlow, *News.com,* February 22, 2002, news.com.com/2008-1082-84 3349.html.

16. Ibid.

17. Gary Rivkin, "The Madness of King George," *Wired,* Vol.10, No. 7, July 2002. URL: www.wired.com/wired /archive/10.07/gilder.html.

18. Manuel Castells, *The Internet Galaxy,* Oxford: Oxford University Press, 2001, p. 64.

19. Ibid., p. 67.

20. Ibid., p. 87.

21. Ibid., p. 111.

22. An analogy to Moholy-Nagy's warning of the 1920s that those who are ignorant in matters of photography will be the illiterates of tomorrow (see "Afterword," Hubertus von Amelunxen, in Vilém Flusser, *Towards a Philosophy of Photography,* London: Reaktion Books, 2000, p. 90).

23. Michael Wolff, *Burn Rate,* London: Orion Books, 1999, p. xii.

24. Michael Wolff, p. 63. In *Burn Rate* there is, in my view, an accurate description of Louis Rosetto's Amsterdam-based magazine *Electric Word* and the climate in the early 1990s which led to their move to San Francisco (not New York) in order to found *Wired* (described in the chapter "How It Got to Be a Wired World," pp. 26–51).

25. Michael Wolff, p. 8.

26. web.archive.org/web/20000619022736/http://ww w.valueamerica.com/ (the Value America website, as kept alive inside one of the world's biggest Web archives).

27. Value America's fall from $74.25 a share on April 8, 1999, to $2 a year later made it one of the first in a long series of dotcom crashes. John A. Byrne wrote a stunning reconstruction of Value America's doings in *Business Week Online,* May 1, 2000.

28. David Kuo, *Inside an Internet Goliath: From Lunatic Optimism to Panic and Crash,* London: Little, Brown and Company, 2001, p. 305.

29. Kuo, p. 306.

30. Kuo, p. 306.

31. *The Daily Telegraph,* May 19, 2000. Richard Barbook, in a private e-mail, remarks: "It was *4* Cs in the joke about Boo.com. Being an uptight Tory newspaper, *The Daily Telegraph* had to leave out the C which can make you feel very self-confident about everything: cocaine. Don't forget that the English consume more illegal chemicals per head than any other nation in the EU."

32. "Incompetence backed by less expert investors,"

review by a reader from Stockholm, Sweden, found on www.amazon.com.uk site, December 4, 2001.

33. Ernst Malmsten with Erik Portanger and Charles Drazin, *Boo Hoo: A Dotcom Story from Concept to Catastrophe,* London: Random House, 2001, p. 233.

34. Malmsten, p. 4.

35. Malmsten, p. 106.

36. Malmsten, p. 108.

37. Malmsten, p. 215.

38. Malmsten, p. 231.

39. Andrew Ross, *No-Collar: The Humane Workplace and Its Hidden Costs,* New York: Basic Books, 2003.

40. The complex dynamic between marketers and hip young rebels is well documented in the PBS television production *The Merchants of Cool.* URL: www. pbs.org/wgbh/pages/frontline/shows/cool/. The script of this insightful documentary can be downloaded at www.pbs.org/wgbh/pages/frontline/ shows/cool/etc/script.html.

41. A response to one of my "from the dotcom observatory" Nettime posts illustrates the gambling attitude: "It was pure dumb luck if a startup was successful or not. Many of the Netscapers went to other startups because they thought, 'Hey, we have the magic touch' (as everyone else thought as well … hiring magic lucky charms was very popular then) but nearly all of them failed. Most frequently massive misuse of money and no customers caused this (We have to hire 100 people in the next two months! … the ramp-up lie), but it is also being in the right time, right place, with the right connections. Dumb luck. Most people think it was their talent. Because the alternative is horrifyingly unfair. The ones who don't think it was their talent that made them successful, who made lots of money, have huge issues about deserving the money they made – I know one person who felt so guilty that he *gave* 2 million dollars to the girl he was dating … and she immediately broke up with him, of course. This is not to say that having a group of smart people in your startup wasn't important – it was, but I can count hundreds of startups that were just 'smart' experienced people that failed just the same" (Anya Sophe Behn, "re: nettime," From the Dotcom Observatory, December 26, 2001).

42. Michael Lewis, *The Future Just Happened,* London: Hodder and Stoughton, 2001, p. 135.

43. Lewis, p. 124.

44. Bill Joy, *Wired,* April 2000.

45. Steve Poole, *The Guardian,* July 21, 2001.

46. web.archive.org/web/20000815075140/http://www. purple-moon.com/.

47. Brenda Laurel, *Utopian Entrepreneur,* Cambridge, Mass.: MIT Press, 2001, p. 41.

48. Laurel, p. 84.

49. Laurel, p. 10.

50. Deirdre Macken, "Fitting end to dotcom daze," *Australian Financial Review,* March 8, 2002, p. 72.

Deep Europe and the Kosovo Conflict: A History of the V2_East/Syndicate Network

1. Research presented here has drawn heavily on the work of Andreas Broeckmann and Inke Arns, who not only put a lot of emphasis in building up the V2_East/Syndicate network but have also written about it on numerous occasions. In particular I would like to mention their *Syndicate history, Rise and Decline of the Syndicate: the End of an Imagined Community,* Nettime, November 14, 2001. The URL of the mail archive where the quoted postings can be accessed is: www.v2.nl/mail/ v2east/. Comments by Ted Byfield, Amy Alexander, Melentie Pandilovski and Trebor Scholz on previous versions of this text have been invaluable. Special thanks goes to Janos Sugar.

2. See www.n5m.org.

3. Andreas Broeckmann, *Syndicate Newsletter,* November 1996.

4. Ibid.

5. Concerns of a Western-led takeover of the East may have been fueled by historical precedents. The stalking-horse role played by abstract expressionism during the Cold War and revelations of CIA funding for US exhibitions were more then just wild rumors. Articles reconstructing such cases written by Max Kozloff and Eva Cockcroft appeared in *Artforum.* See also Serge Guilbaut, *How New York Stole the Idea of Modern Art,* Chicago: University of Chicago Press, 1983.

6. For instance, an "activist" during Communist times was a low-ranking Party member, spreading propaganda on the work floor, spying on others, always ready for betrayal if necessary. It was therefore not a surprise that Western "media activism" in the East was met with a certain disdain.

7. The three Syndicate publications: 1. *Reader of the V2_East/Syndicate Meeting on Documentation and Archiving Media Art in Eastern, Central and South-Eastern Europe,* colossus.v2.nl/syndicate/synr0. html. 2. *Deep Europe: The 1996–97 edition.* Selected texts from the V2_East/Syndicate mailing list, Berlin, October 1997, colossus.v2.nl/syndicate/ synr1.html. 3. *Junction Skopje,* selected texts from the V2_East/ Syndicate mailing list 1997–98, *Syndicate Publication Series 002,* Skopje, October 1998, published by SCCA Skopje, colossus.v2.nl/syndicate/synr2.html.

8. www.medialounge.net/lounge/workspace/deep_eur ope/. First announcement: Andreas Broeckmann, concept "Deep Europe," Syndicate, May 19, 1997; "Reports," Dimitri Pilikin, Syndicate, August 2, 1997; Kit Blake, "Deep Europe Visa Department," Syndicate, August 5, 1997; Andreas Broeckmann, "Discussion about a European Media Policy," Syndicate, August, 5, 1997; Inke Arns, "Report from Deep Europe," Syndicate, August 12, 1997; Lisa Haskel, "Tunneling to Deep Europe, a letter from my island home," Syndicate, August 15, 1997.

9. Andreas Broeckmann: "The war in Yugoslavia and Kosovo is the most current, pressing scenario with which cultural practitioners in Europe are faced. Other scenarios, like the slow-motion disintegration of the Russian empire, the re-emergence of the Baltic region, the hazy reality of Mitteleuropa, the precarious role of Albanian, Hungarian, German, Turkish, Basque, Roma, and other minorities in different parts of the continent, are equally precarious, both potentially productive and destructive. The site of these scenarios is Deep Europe, a continent which has its own mental topography and which is neither East nor West, North nor South, but which is made up of the multi-layeredness of identities: the more overlapping identities, the deeper the region." "Changing Faces, or Proto-Balkanian Dis-Identifications," Syndicate, July 7, 1999, beta version, written for Stephen Kovats (ed.), *Media Revolution,* Frankfurt/New York: Campus Verlag, 1999.

10. One of the German contemporary essayists who writes about "unknown" parts of Eastern Europe is Karl Schloegel; see, for instance, his book *Promenade in Jalta,* Munich: Hanser Verlag, 2001.

11. Inke Arns, "Beyond the Surfaces: Media Culture versus Media Art or How we learned to love tunnel metaphors," Syndicate, August 23, 1999, written for Stephen Kovats (ed.), *Media Revolution,* Frankfurt am Main/New York: Campus Verlag, 1999.

12. Lisa Haskel, "Tunnelling to Deep Europe. A letter from my Island home," Syndicate, August 15, 1997, quoted in Inke Arns, "Beyond the Surfaces," Syndicate, August 23, 1999.

13. Inke Arns and Andreas Broeckmann, *Rise and Decline of the Syndicate: the End of an Imagined Community,* Nettime, November 14, 2001.

14. Ibid.

15. Jennifer De Felice, "lurking in the minds of individuals," Syndicate, March 16, 1999.

16. Andrej Tisma, "U.S.A. Questionaire," Syndicate, March 22, 1999.

17. For an overview of the Kosovo conflict, see Ivo Daalder and Michael O'Hanlon, *Winning Ugly,* Washington DC: Brookings Institution Press, 2000; Wesley Clark, *Waging Modern War: Bosnia, Kosovo, and the Future of Combat,* New York: Public Affairs, 2000; Independent International Commission on Kosovo, *The Kosovo Report: Conflict, International Response, Lessons Learned,* Oxford: Oxford University Press, 2000.

18. Drazen Pantic, "Radio B92 closed, Veran Matic arrested," Nettime, March 24, 1999. See also Katarina's e-mail, posted on the same day, for more details about the police raid on the B92 offices.

19. Pticica (Branka), "Re: news," Syndicate, March 24, 1999.

20. Micz Flor, "anonymous postings," Syndicate, March 24, 1999. He also set up a mailing list to be able to post anonymous e-mails. Pit Schultz sent a critique of the use of anonymous e-mail to Syndicate on April 20, 1999. An excerpt: "who needs such an anonymous service in Kosovo these days? Who even has Internet access there? People lost their passports, their homes; contact to their relatives, now they should symbolically give up their names? (...) How would *you* deal with dubious mail personalities not willing to tell their 'true' name if asked?"

21. Dejan Sretenovic, "Belgrade report," Syndicate, March 24, 1999.

22. Katarina, "B92-home-B92," Syndicate, March 24, 1999.

23. The Help B92 press release lists the following founding organizations: B92, De Balie, The Digital City, Next 5 Minutes, Press Now (Dutch support campaign for independent media in former Yugoslavia), the Net radio initiative Radioqualia (Australia), De Waag (Society for Old and New Media), Public Netbase (Vienna) and XS4ALL. See: helpb92.xs4all.nl/supportgroup_eng.htm and Eric Kluitenberg, "Help B92 campaign started tonight," Syndicate, March 24, 1999. See also "HelpB92 press release," Syndicate, March 27, 1999.

24. Edi Muka, "message from edi," Syndicate, March 25, 1999.

25. I made this argument first in an essay published in the Arkzin *Bastard* newspaper (June 1999), posted on Nettime in August 1999 and reprinted as "Kosov@: War In The Age of Internet" in Geert Lovink, *Dark Fiber,* MIT Press, 2002. The essay published here can be read as a continuation and extension of the arguments made in *Dark Fiber.* Because of security concerns for those posting from Yugoslavia, the Syndicate list archive for the March–July 1999 period was closed. Its reopening in January 2002 enabled me to do this more extensive research. After the Serbian revolution of October 2000, with Milosevic on trial in The Hague and a "tense peace" in Kosovo, the relative distance in time and space enabled me to come up with a fresh rereading of the

Syndicate material.

26. Nikos Vittes, "re: Bombings, Syndicate," March 25, 1999. See also his posting on March 26 in which he states that the whole region is under US control. Nikos denies that his analysis is ethnically biased. "I don't say that you have to agree but I don't accept the ironic message about disliking the neighbors. I personally come from the Greek Macedonia. I grew up playing in the summer [with] kids from Serbia and Macedonia."

27. Andreas Broeckmann, "Berlin news," Syndicate, March 25, 1999.

28. Dejan Sretenovic, "Belgrade news," Syndicate, March 25, 1999.

29. Katarina, "Belgrade," Syndicate, March 25, 1999.

30. Melentie Pandilovski, "Developments in Macedonia, part 1 and 2," Syndicate, March 25, 1999.

31. Stephen Kovats, Syndicate, March 25, 1999.

32. Ivan Zassoursky, "Re: RHIZOME_RAW: Bomb Thread," Syndicate, March 26, 1999.

33. Frederic Madre, "re: morning report," Syndicate, March 26, 1999.

34. See Lisa Haskel's "Radio Deep Europe report," Syndicate, March 28, 1999.

35. Slobodan Markovic, "Amazing night in Belgrade," Syndicate, March 26, 1999.

36. On the Syndicate list there were regular diary-type messages from Branka and Andrej Tisma (Novi Sad), Larisa Blasic, Dejan Sretenovic and Slobodan Markovic (Belgrade), Melentie Pandilovki (Skopje), Marko Peljhan, Vuk Cosic and Michael Benson (Ljubljana), Zvonimir Bakotin (Split), Adele Eisenstein (Budapest) and Enes Zlater (Sarajevo). Regular posts from outside "the region" came from Andreas Broeckmann, Inke Arns, Ivan Zassoursky, Honor Harger, Sally Jae Norman, Frederic Madre, Florian Schneider, Micz Flor and others.

37. Mike Stubbs, "re: what is new(s)," Syndicate, March 26, 1999.

38. The Dow Jones index hit its historic 10,000 mark on March 30, 1999, one week into the NATO bombing campaign. It was back at that same level during the bombardment of Afghanistan in November–December 2001.

39. Enes Zlater, "a message from Sarajevo," Syndicate, March 26, 1999.

40. Slobodan Markovic, Syndicate, March 26, 1999.

41. Pticica, Syndicate, March 26, 1999.

42. Annick Bureaud, "serbs against peace," Syndicate, March 27, 1999.

43. Dejan Sretenovic, "re: a message from Sarajevo," Syndicate, March 26, 1999.

44. Enes Zlater, "another message from Sarajevo," Syndicate, March 26, 1999.

45. "We at Nettime, info, not bombs (make money not war)," Syndicate, March 27, 1999.

46. Andreas Broeckmann, "some general list-related stuff," Syndicate, March 27, 1999.

47. See, for instance, the dialogue between Paul Treanor and Michael Benson, Syndicate, March 29, 1999.

48. Frequently posted information came from websites such as IWPR'S Balkan Crisis Report, International Crisis Group, Phil Agre's Red Rock Eater News Service, the Kosova Crisis Center and B92.

49. "It might be useless to try and convince our friends from Serbia that they suffer from the same syndrome as the Germans 50 years ago. As Hitler succeeded in convincing Germans that a real Aryan is tall, beautiful, blond, with blue eyes – while he himself was short, ugly, black-haired, with brown eyes, why shouldn't Milosevic succeed in explaining Serbs that NATO are criminals and that they (Serbs) are fighting for a just cause." Enes Zlater, "a thought from Sarajevo," Syndicate, March 30, 1999. See also Paul Treanor on "Hitler near Milosovic," Syndicate, March 31, 1999.

50. Branka: "Those of you have visited Novi Sad and who fucking can remember the old bridge, near the fucking oldest bridge which is in Danube, as remembrance of fucking WWII and thousands of Jews, Serbs and others fucking thrown alive in January cold water under the fucking ICE by fucking nazi destroyers? If you can, than fucking keep that fucking memory, THERE IS NO OLD FUCKING BRIDGE ANYMORE, there is no fucking symbol of Novi Sad, there is just tower left and fucking awaiting next bombing to be destroyed. Fucking time for going over the bridge to the office, factory, clinic … fucking 1st of April." "Baza, fucking 1st of april day of fucking joke," Syndicate, April 1, 1999. See also the personal account of Andrej Tisma, who also lives in Novi Sad.

51. "Keeping the Faith, B92 Statement," Syndicate, April 1, 1999.

52. Vuk Cosic, "re: Radio B92 Closed Down and Sealed Off," Syndicate, April 3, 1999. For more information on the "patriotic left" takeover and the launch of "real B92," see the press release "Will the real Radio B92 please stand up!" fwd. to Syndicate, April 15, 1999.

53. "The call for discussion What to Do?" posted by B92's Gordan Paunovic on Syndicate (September 4, 1999) only indirectly raises some of the issues mentioned here. The text is limited to a general political analysis of the strategy of the Milosevic opposition after the Kosovo crisis. The thread that followed did discuss the dependency of B92 and other independent media on funds provided by US philanthropist George Soros and his network of Open Society NGOs. See also Mihajlo Acimovic's "B92 criticism," Syn-

dicate, September 30, 1999.

54. Slobodan Markovic, "Belgrade is burning again," Syndicate, April 4, 1999.

55. Ibid.

56. "Open letter from Nade Proeva (Skopje)," Syndicate, April 6, 1999.

57. Bruce Sterling, "Open Letter to Insomnia," Nettime, fwd. to Syndicate, April 6, 1999. Related is his "Open Letter to Slobodan Markovic," Syndicate, April 7, 1999.

58. Ibid.

59. Slavoj Zizek, "Against the Double Blackmail," Syndicate, April 7, 1999 (translation from German, originally published in *Die Zeit,* March 31, 1999).

60. Ibid.

61. Kit Blake/Hedwig Turk, "Budapest report," Syndicate, May 2, 1999.

62. Ibid.

63. Andreas Broeckmann, "... but keep the faith!," Syndicate, April 26, 1999.

64. "Open Channels for Kosovo press release," Syndicate, April 18, 1999.

65. See Jo van der Spek, "Visit to Radio 21 in Skopje," Syndicate, May 14 (and 21), 1999.

66. McKenzie Wark, private e-mail correspondence, February 4, 2002.

67. Slobodan Markovic, Syndicate, April 30, May 2 and May 3, 1999. Not all messages from Belgrade were like this. For instance, an in-depth analysis by Dejan Sretenovic, "The European pariah," Syndicate, May 21, 1999, discussed the thesis of the lack of guilt among the Serbs.

68. "Net Aid announcements," Syndicate, May 14 and 15, 1999.

69. Steven Pearlstein, *Washington Post* Foreign Service, "Serb TV Gets Notice It's Cancelled, Satellite Firm Bows To NATO Pressure," May 23, 1999, fwd to Syndicate, May 25, 1999. Quoted in Slobodan Markovic, "Civilian communications again in danger!," Syndicate, May 28, 1999.

71. NATO spokesperson Jamie Shea: "What we are doing is we are attacking the military facilities of Belgrade. That electricity, those facilities, drive the military machine of Milosevic, that is why they are a target." Brussels, May 25, 1999; quoted in Slobodan Markovic, "My Goodness ...," Syndicate, May 26, 1999.

72. In his war diary Aleksander Gubas made the following critique of the target logo: "I don't feel like being target. I don't like to be treated as target, and I think none of us was supposed to be in the situation of being bombed. This has had to be avoided. And not only NATO is to be blamed for this situation – which many people forget, even the greatest enemies of the regime. The other reason is that this mark is

invented and promoted by the regime itself, and it's some kind of trademark for demonstrations against NATO, which actually support the regime and ARE organized by the regime. And I don't want to take part in anything like this, and I'm not willing to give this regime my amnesty for its former evil deeds. And last but not least – this target mark has become the new symbol for unification of people's minds. Instead of former communist red star, now we have the target mark. Wearing this mark is the certification that you are patriot, good Serb, loving your country and following The Right Line. I doubt the proclaimed Right Line. I resist any kind of mind unification." Quoted from his Syndicate post, September 14, 1999.

73. McKenzie Wark, "re: moral responsibility," Syndicate, 18 June 1999. See also his posts of June 18 and June 30, 1999.

74. Slobodan Markovic, "re: moral responsibility," Syndicate, June 18, 1999.

75. Syndicate moderators tolerated Tisma's postings. "Many perceived his tirades against the West and against NATO as pure Serbian propaganda which became unbearable at some point. Later, Tisma came back to the list and continued his criticisms by posting links to anti-NATO webpages he had created. For us, he was always an interesting signpost of Serb nationalist ideology, which it was good to be aware of. And it was good that he showed that people can be artists 'like you and me', and be Serb nationalists at the same time. The Syndicate could handle his presence after he agreed to tune down his rants." Andreas Broeckmann/Inke Arns, *Rise and Decline of the Syndicate: the End of an Imagined Community,* Nettime, November 14, 2001.

76. Inke Arns, "re: moral responsibility," Syndicate, June 18, 1999.

77. The "moral responsibility" thread took place on Syndicate in the June 18–30 period with postings from Jennifer de Felice, Michael Benson, Slobodan Markovic, Bruce Sterling, Frederic Madre, McKenzie Wark, Inke Arns, James Stauffer, Sally Jay Norman, Zvonimir Bakotin and others. There is an interesting posting from the Albanian curator Edi Muka, writing from Tirana a few days after the debate (June 22), in which he calls for Serbian intellectuals and artists to take a public stand about the atrocities committed against the Kosovo-Albanian population. "It is important because I want to normally talk to my Serbian colleagues, invite Serbian artists to Tirana, I want Serbian artists to have shows in Pristina and I don't want to fear for their security. It is important because we must find a common language, because Serbs must not flee Kosova." See also Geert Lovink, "Interview with Edi Muka," Syndicate, June 1, 1999.

78. McKenzie Wark, "Collective Responsibility," Syndicate, June 30, 1999.

79. Bojana Pejic, "After the Wall, Venice press conference," Syndicate, June 5, 1999.

80. See Irina Cios, "Romanian presentation in Venice," Syndicate, June 7, 1999; Nebosja Vilic, "unofficial presence of Republic of Macedonia at 48th Venice Biennial," Syndicate, June 6, 1999; Melentie Pandilovski, "Venice Biennial," Syndicate, June 3, 1999; Miran Mohar, "Transnacionala book in Venice," Syndicate, June 3, 1999.

81. Michel Feher, *Powerless By Design: The Age of the International Community,* Durham and London: Duke University Press, 2000, p. 7.

82. Honor Harger, "special edition of *Bastard:* the war in Yugoslavia," Syndicate, August 24, 1999.

83. URL: www.molodiez.org/overviewkosovo.html.

84. From private e-mail correspondence, January 27, 2001. Subsequent projects by Trebor Scholz related to the same issue were the "Aestheticization of War" symposium in 2001 at PS1 in New York (together with Nomads and Residents) and events at the Santa Fe Art Institute and the Weimar Bauhaus University. These events all dealt with the issue of collective and individual responsibility in response to war. Another of his projects in that line was an exhibition/open forum on activist responses to 9/11 at the Bauhaus (www.molodiez.org /acc/).

85. Melentie Pandilovski, "The Balkans to the Balkanians," Syndicate, April 3, 1999.

86. Geert Lovink, "Temporary Media Lab, Kiasma/ Helsinki, Oct 8–Nov 14," Syndicate, September 7, 1999.

87. See announcement of "Understanding the Balkans Conference," Syndicate, July 18, 2000. The first conference took place in Ohrid (Macedonia), October 13–16, 2000. The second conference, "The Balkans and Globalization," was held in Skopje, December 1–2, 2001. URL: www.scca.org.mk/utb/index.htm.

88. Lisa Haskel, "syndicate/border camp," Syndicate, July 24, 1999.

89. Atle Barcley, "re: enough (message from the provider)," Syndicate, August 11, 1999: "According to the source code the (supposed) forged mails (in the name of Geert Lovink and tbyfield) have been sent from White-mail (www.kit.ntnu.no/stud/barcley/white-mail/). Anyone can access, and I have no idea who is using White-mail."

90. Andreas Broeckmann and Inke Arns, *Syndicate history, Rise and Decline of the Syndicate: the End of an Imagined Community,* Nettime, November 14, 2001.

91. The campaign started with the message from Edi Muka in which he announced that he had been sacked (Syndicate, November 29, 2000). A petition was written and signed by Syndicate members.

92. Aleksander Gubas, "The Flock of Netgulls, a Personal View to the Mailing Lists," Syndicate, May 22, 2001.

93. An example: "ue = g!vn d!sz g!ft dont u knou. dze ab!!!t! 2 knou. + through uz mattr kan knou !tzelv. out ov dze uomb ov t!me + dze vaztnesz ov zpasz dzat u!ch = uz – h!drogen. karbon. n!trogen. ox!gen. 16-21 elmntz dze uatr. dze zunl!ght – all hav!ng bkom uz kan bg!n 2 undrztnd uat dze! r + hou dze! kame 2 b." integer@www.god-emil.dk, Syndicate, January 18, 2001. More on the ideas behind NN can be found in the Syndicate posts of January 28, January 29, February 2 and February 11, 2001.

94. A closer look at posts shows that NN's vocabulary was rather limited. Someone would either be a "inkompetent male fascist" or a "korporate male fascist." Whereas some contributions contain traces of brilliant poetry, the personal attacks often show signs of repetition.

95. Katharine Mieszlowski, "The Most Feared Woman on the Internet," www.salon.com/tech/feature/2002/ 03/01/netochka/index.html.

96. a9ff@hell.com, f1f0@m9ndfukc.com and meter@ flicker.dk were some of the other e-mail addresses used by antiorp/NN/integer. An example of an antiorp post: "== addtl lo.tekk pozer mattr c ub!ku!touz komput!ng + xerox park + !nvert m9ndkonta!nr \\ humanzukc ++ .edu == .krapmattr, humanz = _ komputat!onall+e def!c!ent \+\ sub. opt!mal – ztat!ond at 1 local m!n!ma." Syndicate, August 19, 1998.

97. See Diego Mariani, "Europanto," fwd. by Ted Byfield, Nettime, April 25, 1997.

98. "B1FF /bif/ [Usenet] (alt. 'BIFF') /n./ The most famous pseudo, and the prototypical newbie. Articles from B1FF feature all uppercase letters sprinkled liberally with bangs, typos, cute' misspellings (EVRY BUDY LUVS GOOD OLD BIFF CUZ HE'S A KOOL DOOD AN HE RITES REEL AWESUM THINGZ IN CAPITULL LETTRS LIKE THIS!!!), use (and often misuse) of fragments of talk mode abbreviations, a long sig block (sometimes even a doubled sig), and unbounded naïveté. B1FF posts articles using his elder brother's VIC-20. B1FF's location is a mystery, as his articles appear to come from a variety of sites. However, BITNET seems to be the most frequent origin. B1FF was originally created by Joe Talmadge <jat@cup.hp.com>, also the author of the infamous and much-plagiarized 'Flamer's Bible.'" jargon.net/jargonfile/b/B1FF.html.

99. Josephine Berry, "M @ z k ! n 3 n . k u n z t . m2cht . fr3!: Antiorp and the Meaning of Noise," Nettime, August 23, 2001.

100. www.tuxedo.org/~esr/jargon/html/entry/troll.html.

101. Andrew, www.altairiv.demon.co.uk/afaq/posts/troll-faq.html (1996). See also Judith Donath, "Identity and deception in the virtual community," in M.A.

Smith and P. Kollock (eds.), *Communities in Cyberspace*, London: Routledge, 1999, pp. 29–59. I found this material in Susan Herring's case study "Searching for Safety Online: 'Trolling' in a Feminist Forum," yet to be published, sent to me by the author.

102. In Michael H. Goldgraber's essay "The Attention Economy and the Net," there is no explicit mention of the possibility to "hijack" an online community (www.firstmonday.dk/issues/issue2_4/goldhaber/). As in the case of publicity, it might be impossible to distinguish between "good" and "bad" attention. Unwillingly paid attention seems not to fit in the consensual models of electronic democracy in which reasonable actors appear to exchange rational arguments, puzzled by the irrational Other.

103. Com2Kid on www.slashdot.org, "re: Blogs are lame," June 6, 2002.

104. An example would be Darko Fritz: "oh, I love women media activists in uniforms ... please please spam me. spank me. oh yes. more. Even more. spam me. (...) what a pity that there is no moderator here so you can masturbate only with no resistance to a father figure, as in good old years. what unforgettable incest scenes ... and everyone can watch ..." Syndicate, February 1, 2001.

105. Diana McCarty, "re: another small syndicalist," Syndicate, February 3, 2001.

106. Eleni Laperi, "about Macedonian crisis," Syndicate, March 28, 2001; Edi Muka, "hi from edi," Syndicate, March 31, 2001; Melentie Pandilovski, "re: hi from edi," Syndicate, April 2, 2001.

107. Károly Tóth, spams by integer, June 12, 2001, writing to the list owner: "I have at least 284 messages (monologs) (ca 4 MB) in my mailbox written by the mysterious 'integer'. Please: be the tide to go against. It would be: a small step for a man (male, corporate) and a big leap for mankind (social, org)."

108. Friddy Nietzche, "regarding integer," Syndicate, June 15, 2001.

109. See two digests, Nettime, August 12 and 18, 1998. These digests largely contain of representative antiorp postings.

110. Ted Byfield, "re: gated communities," Nettime, October 10, 1998, in response to the protest of Net art critic Josephine Bosma against the removal of antiorp from Nettime (and Syndicate), demanding an open list. An answer by xchange list administrator Jaanis Garancs, Xchange, October 9, 1998: "It might be good for both us and antiorp to live in peace. Why throw away such a talent and keep so much overestimated academic bullshit?" ("gated communities," Nettime and Xchange, October 9, 1998). The Xchange list had its own antiorp debate in the same period.

111. Ibid.

112. Austin Bunn, "Molotovs and Mailing Lists," *Salon*, March 3, 1999. URL: www.salon.com/21st/ feature/1999/03/03feature2.html. Whereas some suggest that NN is a New Zealand female audio artist, others insist that it is a collective, probably based in Europe.

113. Amy Alexander in a private e-mail, December 26, 2001. Amy wrote to the Syndicate list: "the people who had been successfully (for their own purposes) filtering were reading a different list than everyone else, and tended to be surprised that other people were so upset about the volume of NN mail. Some people suggested, 'filter – don't censor!' and other people responded with 'how do you filter?' or 'I can filter but only on the client side so it ties up my bandwidth'. it seemed there were have and have-nots of filtering, and though that might sound like some sort of geek minutiae, really it comes down to access to control of reception – which I'd argue on a listserv is at least as important as access to control of broadcast. If the information coming in is too tangled or cumbersome, then it can't be read effectively." (Syndicate, August 22, 2001). More info on trolls: www.cs.ruu.nl/wais/html/na-dir/net-abuse-faq/ troll-faq.html (posted by Derek Holzer, Nettime, March 3, 2002).

114. Julie Blankenship, "re: [ot] [!nt] \n2+0\," Syndicate, August 7, 2001.

115. Igor Markovic, "re: [ot] [!nt] \n2+0\," Syndicate, August 7, 2001.

116. Saul Ostrow, "re: concerning the Mosquitoe Integer," Syndicate, August 8, 2001.

117. Diana McCarty, "Re: Syndicate's love-hate relationship with NN," Syndicate, August 10, 2001.

118. Inke Arns, "re: what happened," Syndicate, August 14, 2001.

119. Andreas Broeckmann, "re: Jaka Zeleznikar: NN – what happened?," Syndicate, August 13, 2001. The essence of the Syndicate project is well summarized in a posting by Eric Kluitenberg, "A short comment on the identity of the Syndicate list," Syndicate, August 13, 2001 ("In the last year or so I saw the essence of the list get lost in a cloud of confused autistic ascii experiments that had really nothing to do with the initial character of the list."). See also Patrick Lichty, "Bans & Free Speech," Syndicate, August 14, 2001.

120. Annick Bureaud, "re: what happened," Syndicate, August 14, 2001.

121.][mez][, explaining her decision to forward integer messages: "y* I'm sending NN's replies to the list ... as NN has been uns*bbed without a list consensus, I'll continue 2 4ward her replies as I assume a rite-of-reply should be allowed under the paradigm the

Syndicate list has adopted."][mez][, "4warding of NN's mails," Syndicate, August 16, 2001. In the same period a similar conflict between][mez][and the Australian mailing list moderator Julianne Pierce took place. Even though the recode list was already in decline, it was the Net art versus spam controversy that eventually led to the closure of recode on January 30, 2002 (see Nettime, January 31, 2002). Mez documented a variety of e-mails concerning this case at the following website: www.hotkey.net.au/~netwurker/recodebacle.htm.

122. In retrospect, Honor Harger (London) reflects on the cynical NN/integer/antiorp strategies and the "nato" software used during the list raids. "I find it deeply ironic that an entrepreneur so well known for revoking licenses to use her software (nato) when she encounters even the smallest criticisms of her programming – effectively censoring nato users – would react with such petulance when she herself is asked to minimize the 'noise' of her postings. Considering the NN_construct is so intolerant of others views on her work and ideas, I find it rather galling that so many have tried to defend her in the name of 'free speech.' This is something laughably alien to the NN_construct's philosophy of doing business, and it is unfortunate that Syndicate has collapsed based on this issue. Not that this would be of any interest to the NN_construct, who has little concern for this discussion space, absolutely no awareness of the network which has formed around this list for the past 5 years, and no care if her incessant flood of posts destroys the character of this list. This is simply one of the many spaces for the NN_construct to advertise her commercial products, and to raise her profile as a practitioner. I find it very sad that her promotional tactics have been so effective in redirecting the course of the list." "Re: future," Syndicate, August 18, 2001.

123. Martha Rosler, "banning," Syndicate, August 14, 2001.

124. Those who took the name "Syndicate" with them to restart the list elsewhere included yaNN@x-arn.org, Claudia Westermann, Clemens Thomas, Atle Barkley, Frederic Madre and Jaka Zeleznikar. The administration team changed, and from August 27, 2001, the Syndicate mailing list and webspace were hosted by Atelier Nord in Norway. The homepage of the renewed Syndicate provided information about mail filters and how to use them. "Sometimes it might seem to be necessary to set mail filters, in order to avoid getting your inbox stuffed with mails that are not of interest to you" (anart.no/~syndicate/subpages/filter.html).

125. Andreas Broeckmann, "new mailing list: SPECTRE: info," Spectre, September 14, 2001. He also stated:

"Requests for subscription have to be approved by hosts. Subscriptions may be terminated or suspended in the case of persistent violation of netiquette. Should this happen, the list will be informed. The list archives are publicly available, so SPECTRE can also be consulted and followed by people who are not subscribed." URL of the Spectre list archive: coredump.buug.de/pipermail/spectre/.

126. Andreas Broeckmann, "new mailing list: SPECTRE: info," Spectre, September 14, 2001.

127. Johan Sjerpstra, in a private e-mail to the author, February 25, 2002.

128. Johan Sjerpstra, in a private e-mail to the author, March 3, 2002.

Principles of Streaming Sovereignty: A History of the Xchange Network

1. This chapter was based on research into the few thousand or so postings to the Xchange list from December 1997 to July 2002, Xchange members' related websites, and relevant publications. I would like to thank Joanne Richardson, Rasa Smite, Pit Schultz and Adam Hyde for their valuable comments.

2. A random "googled" definition of streaming media states: "Streaming media is a way to enhance World Wide Web sites by integrating video and audio with a site's text-based content. Unlike downloading a video or audio file separately and then playing it back later, streaming media plays when a Web page (with the embedded streaming video or audio) downloads on a user's browser. To include streaming video or audio, the server hosting the Web site must support the application. To play streaming media embedded in a Web page, the user must have a helper application such as a viewer or plug-in. Viewers are typically offered free to users" (members.tripod.com/Lori_Sylvia/stream.htm).

3. A technical explanation: "Uncompressed CD-quality WAV and AIFF files are too large to stream over the Internet for playback in real time. Instead, lighterweight compressed formats such as MP3 and RealAudio are employed for streaming network audio. These formats use what are called 'lossy' compression schemes, reducing file sizes by eliminating certain inaudible data from the original files without too significantly degrading playback sound quality. MP3 and RealAudio are excellent streaming formats, achieving performance factors great enough to allow real-time encoding/decoding over current network bandwidth conditions while delivering satisfying audio quality." From: linux.oreillynet.com/pub/a/linux/2001/03/23/streaming_media.html?page=2.

4. E-mail interview, January 17, 2002.

5. Ibid.

6. There had been early networked sound-arts experiments in the early-mid 1990s, before the Internet, using BBS systems and direct telephone connections. Heidi Grundmann of Kunstradio (ORF) in Vienna was one of the pioneers. See the interview with Heidi Grundmann by Josephine Bosma, Nettime, July 15, 1997. URL: www.kunstradio.at/. We could also mention Gerfried Stocker, whose Horizontal Radio project in June 1995 connected 36 radio stations for a 24-hour program in which listeners were able to control the audio mix via a Web interface. URL: gewi.kfunigraz.ac.at/~gerfried/horrad/.

7. We could mention here the first and second Art+Communication festivals organized by E-lab in Riga in November 1996 and 1997; a workshop during the second Interstanding conference in Tallinn, Estonia, in November 1997; the radio workshop at the Hybrid Workspace during Documenta X (organized by Kunstradio, Vienna) and the weekly radio shows from Kassel; and the network (hosting) activities of Radio Internationale Stadt (Berlin) and Xs4all (Amsterdam).

8. "Introduction," Xchange, December 2, 1997. URL of the list archive: www.xchange.re-lab.net\m\index.html.

9. During the first live session, on December 2, 1997 Peteris Kimelis was interviewed about his work 3 Frequencies. "He has made a sound just from 3 frequencies – > 3000Hz, 5000Hz, 8000Hz. These are natural frequencies of the human ear but what you actually hear is beeeep and it's hard to listen to this sound for a long time." Raitis, Xchange, December 3, 1997. The Xchange live Web sessions are archived at ozone.re-lab.net/sessions.html.

10. For more on Pararadio see the interview by Josephine Bosma, Xchange, December 11, 1997.

11. List adapted from Borut Savski's posting to Xchange, December 15, 1997.

12. See, for instance, Josephine Bosma, "Interview with Pararadio," Xchange, December 11, 1997; "net, 'radio' & physical space: E-lab/RE-lab/Xchange/OZOne," Nettime, January 7, 1998; "From Net art to Net radio and back again," written for the 1998 Ars Electronica catalogue, posted on Xchange, July 11, 1998.

13. E-mail exchange with Rasa Smite, January 13, 2002.

14. Pit Schultz, in an e-mail, June 13, 2002.

15. See www.ecommercetimes.com/perl/story/21537.html. On May 18, 2003, the Pew Internet Project published the research paper "Broadband Adaptation at Home": "In the survey Pew found that 57 percent of dial-up users had no interest in upgrading to faster access, even in areas where such service was already available."

16. On June 25, 2002, US Representative Howard L. Berman proposed a bill aimed at the "unbridled" piracy taking place on decentralized peer-to-peer file-sharing networks by introducing legislation that lets copyright holders employ tools to prevent illegal trading. Berman said copyright holders were at a disadvantage against P-to-P pirates under existing legislation. "While P-to-P technology is free to innovate new and more efficient methods of distribution that further exacerbate the piracy problem, copyright owners are not equally free to craft technological responses." Berman's bill came on the heels of a slew of legislative efforts to curb piracy in the digital realm. Another bill, proposed by Senator Ernest Hollings, sought to incorporate digital rights management technologies in all consumer electronic devices. Source: PC World, June 26, 2002.

17. Source: Arbitron/Edison Media Research: Internet 9, "The Media and Entertainment World of Online Consumers," July 2002. URL: www.edisonresearch.com/I9_FinalSummary.pdf. By mid-2002, seven in 10 US Americans had access to the Internet. In early 2001, 13% of those with Internet access had had a broadband connection; as of July 2002, this number had grown to 28%. The inquiry only asked if users had had streaming-media experiences. Users are defined here as consumers of media products, not as potential producers of content and social networks.

18. The dilemma for individual artists between high and low bandwidth was based on the growing paradox between promises and technical capacities on the one hand and the actual availability of affordable high-speed connections on the other. George Gilder in August 2000: "Since the commercial advent of wave division multiplexing in 1996, bandwidth has been increasing at least four times as fast as Moore's Law, if not faster, and promises to continue to do so for at least the next several years." (www.forbes.com/asap/00/0821/097.htm). The reality, however, was one of rising costs and a stagnation in Internet usage due to telcos withholding "dark fiber" (unused capacity) from clients for profit reasons. See: Geert Lovink, "The Bandwidth Dilemma," posted on Nettime, March 26, 2001 (originally published in German and English in Telepolis online magazine (www.heise.de/tp).

19. Pit Schultz, "re: A Stimulus to Make the Most Productive Use of Radio," Xchange, May 19, 1998.

20. Rasa Smite, Xchange, December 9, 1997

21. Interview with Zina Kaye, Sydney, May 31, 2002.

22. Report of the Art Servers Unlimited meeting can be found in Acoustic Space 2, Riga: E-lab, 1999, pp. 14–24.

23. xchange.re-lab.net/56k and www.openx.aec.at/xchange/. See also report in *Acoustic Space 2*, Riga: E-lab, 1999, pp. 34–40, and Zina Kaye's post on Xchange, September 7, 1998, which includes the names of the participants and a program.

24. For the program of the webjam see Rasa Smite's posting on Xchange, November 29, 1998.

25. First international Net.Congestion streaming-media festival, Amsterdam, October 6–8, 2000, net.congestion.org. The website contains an archive of all the panels. The initial concept was developed by Adam Hyde. The first announcement was posted on May 3, 2000, by Honor Harger.

26. Conceptual Background, *Net.Congestion Reader*, Amsterdam: De Balie, 2000, p. 4.

27. More on the philosophy of mixing: Geert Lovink, "An Inventory of Amsterdam Free Radio Techniques," in Neil Straus (Ed.), *Radiotext(e)*, Brooklyn: Semiotext(e), 1992.

28. Raitis Smits, "Xchange Open Channel: Co-broadcast Experiments in the Net," in Nettime (Ed.), *Readme!* Brooklyn: Autonomedia, 1999, p. 349–350.

29. An IRC chat at the #xchange channel, dated March 31, 1998, was printed in the Nettime reader *Readme!* Brooklyn: Autonomedia, 1999, pp. 343–350. An example of the city-to-city cast: "Listen to RA radio aura today 8PM(GST): active. llaky.fi/aura/aura.ram, music/sounds/and/ambience by >scott scott >radio Banff >pk >martins ratniks >sera furneaux >matti adolfsen.. sydney((o)) tornio((o))stockholm((o))banff((o))scotland((o))riga." Xchange, August 27, 1998.

30. As described in Raitis Smits, "Xchange Open Channel: Co-broadcast Experiments in the Net," in: Nettime (Ed.), *Readme!* Brooklyn: Autonomedia, 1999, pp. 349–350.

31. Daniel Molnar, Xchange, January 4, 1998.

32. E-mail exchange with Rasa Smite, January 13, 2002.

33. URLs for the Pulkvedis club event in May 1998, with participation of D:U:M:B, hardcore techno DJs and VJs from Rotterdam: ozone.re-lab.net/archive/dumb.ram and ozone.re-lab.net/archive/dumb2.ram. URL of the train transmission: ozone.re-lab.net/archive/vtt/train.ram. Information provided by Rasa Smite via e-mail, June 4, 2002.

34. Josephine Bosma and Eezee E, Xchange, August 17, 1998.

35. Tetsuo Kogawa, "The Other Aspects of Radio," *Acoustic Space 3*, Riga: E-lab, 2000, pp. 26-28. Also: "Minima Memoranda," *Next Five Minutes 3 Workbook*, Amsterdam: De Balie, 1999, pp. 103–104.

36. Xchange, February 25, 1998.

37. Interview with Zina Kaye, Sydney, May 31, 2002.

38. "Extended Life Radio," Xchange, February 12, 1998.

39. For the entire interview with Micz Flor by Geert Lovink, see Nettime, "Tactics of Streaming," April 26, 2002.

40. Matthew Smith, "re: G2," Xchange, June 2, 1998.

41. Ibid.

42. "Portal" is a late-1990s term for a website that brings together Web resources for ordinary users on a central page. A portal usually imitates the layout of a newspaper front page. At the left and right are small menu bars for links. In the centre are the headlines of the main stories. A definition of a portal, found with the Google search engine, reads: "A portal is an entry point or starting site for the World Wide Web, combining a mixture of content and services and attempting to provide a personalized 'home base' for its audience with features like customizable start pages to guide users easily through the Web, filterable e-mail, a wide variety of chatrooms and message boards, personalized news and sports headlines options, gaming channels, shopping capabilities, advanced search engines and personal homepage construction kits." URL: www.auburn.edu/helpdesk/glossary/portal.html.

43. Radioqualia, Xchange, October 13, 1998. URL: www.radioqualia.va.com.au.

44. See: "Radioqualia, streaming-media software for arts released," Nettime, November 7, 2002.

45. "An Open Letter from Adam and Zina," Xchange, November 10, 1999. See also Adam Hyde's report of the Streaming Media Europe Conference, November 22, 1999, which contains interesting comparisons between Xchange and commercial streaming portals. "During the conference it quickly became apparent to me that the Xchange community is very advanced in its use and thinking about streaming media. In fact many of the ideas I heard coming from businesspeople working with streaming media did not (generally) reflect that same quality of ideas and breadth of understanding about the medium that I know to exist in Xchange. I found this very surprising and exhilarating as I personally was beginning to think that we (Xchange) were being left behind by industry."

46. Rasa Smite, "Next steps for the Xchange Website," Xchange, February 20, 2000.

47. An exception which should be mentioned here is Xchange's involvement in streaming projects related to the Kosovo conflict in 1999, sparked by the closure of the Belgrade independent radio station and streaming pioneer B92 (see Chapter Three on the history of the Syndicate list).

48. This part of the essay draws heavily on an e-mail exchange with Adam Hyde in May 2002. The quotes are from the same exchange.

49. E-mail interview with Adam Hyde, May 20, 2002.

50. E-mail interview with Adam Hyde, May 20, 2002.

51. Here are some statistics compiled by Nielsen/NetRatings: in April 2002, RealMedia reached 17 million at-home viewers, compared with Windows Media at 15.1 million and QuickTime at 7.3 million. At work, Windows Media drew about 12.2 million unique viewers, compared with RealMedia at 11.6 million and QuickTime at 5 million. Nielsen/NetRatings' last multimedia report, for December 2001, showed that RealNetworks reached some 32 million users at home and 16.3 million at work; Windows Media hit 14.6 million at home and 9.9 million at work; and QuickTime reached about 7.4 million people at home and 5.5 million people at work. Source: news.com.com/2100-1023-938423.html?tag=rn.

52. "Linux Media Player" (linmp), a solo project so far, has been in development since late 2001. See: sourceforge.net/projects/linmp/.

53. E-mail interview with Drazen Pantic, January 17, 2002.

54. Pit Schultz, "OMA alpha release party," Xchange, June 21 2001.

55. Pit Schultz, "orang.orang.org is getting reconstructed," Xchange, December 31, 2001.

56. Pit Schultz, "digital hooliganism," Nettime, March 16, 2002.

57. Rasa Smite, Xchange, October 17, 1998.

58. E-mail exchange with Rasa Smite, January 13, 2002.

59. Derek Holzer, "Call for Inputs: Acoustic Space Labs!!," Xchange, June 28, July 2, and August 3, 2001, and e-mails from other Xchange members in the same period. For a report see Mukul, The Wire, September 2001, posted on Xchange, September 3, 2001.

60. Rasa Smite, e-mail interview, January 13, 2002.

61. RIXC is a joint effort by a number of independent local cultural groups based in Riga, Liepaja and other cities in Latvia working in the fields of new media, art, film, music, youth culture and the social field. The founders of RIXC are E-lab, the film and TV production studio Locomotive, and the Baltic Centre, an NGO for alternative education and social projects. URL: rixc.lv.

62. Jay David Bolter and Richard Grusin, Remediation: Understanding New Media, Cambridge, Mass.: MIT Press, 1999. "Remediation is a defining characteristic of the new digital media" (p. 45). "Each act of mediation depends on other forms of mediation. Media are continually commenting on, reproducing and replacing each other, and this process is integral to media. Media need each other in order to function as media at all" (p. 55).

63. E-mail interview with Drazen Pantic, January 17, 2002.

64. Tetsuo Kogawa, "Minima Memoranda," in Next Five Minutes 3 Workbook, Amsterdam, 1999, p. 104.

65. Gilles Deleuze and Félix Guattari, Kafka: Towards a Minor Literature, Minneapolis: University of Minneapolis Press, 1986.

66. Andreas Broeckmann, "Minor Media – Heterogenic Machines," in Acoustic Space 2, Riga: E-Lab, 1999, p. 78. URL: english.uq.edu.au/mc/9909/minor.html.

67. Ibid.

68. Félix Guattari, quoted in Andreas Broeckmann, "Minor Media – Heterogenic Machines," in Acoustic Space 2, Riga: E-Lab, 1999, p. 82.

69. Reference to Hakim Bey, Temporary Autonomous Zone, Brooklyn: Autonomedia, 1991. In the early 1990s the anarchist TAZ concept became part of the cyber-libertarian Wired generation vocabulary. Some claimed the entire Internet to be an autonomous zone. This could more accurately be said of certain virtual communities such as Xchange.

70. Erik Davis, "Acoustic Cyberspace," Xchange, December 29, 1997. Also in: Acoustic Space 1, E-Lab, Riga, 1998, p. 23.

71. TMs in TM.SELECTOR#2, a connoisseur's guide to net listening published by the www.irational.org group (October 2001).

72. Andreas Broeckmann, "Minor Media – Heterogenic Machines," in Acoustic Space 2, Riga: E-Lab, 1999, p. 78. Staying close to Félix Guattari's terminology, Broeckmann features the Xchange network as an example of "heterogenesis" and "molecular revolution." "Xchange is a distributed group, a connective, that builds creative cooperation in live-audio streaming on the communication channels that connect them. They explore the Net as a soundscape with particular qualities regarding data transmission, delay, feedback, and open, distributed collaborations. Moreover, they connect the network with a variety of other fields. Instead of defining an 'authentic' place of their artistic work, they play in the transversal post-medial zone of media labs in different countries, mailing lists, netcasting and FM broadcasting, clubs, magazines, stickers, etc., in which 'real' spaces and media continuously overlap and fuse." See also Andreas Broeckmann, "Konnektive entwerfen! Minoritaere Medien und vernetzte Kunstpraxis," in Stefan Muenker and Alexander Roesler (Eds.), Praxis Internet, Frankfurt am Main: Suhrkamp, 2002 (posted on the Rohrpost list, May 15, 2002).

73. Erik Davis, "Acoustic Cyberspace," Xchange, December 29, 1997. Also in: Acoustic Space 1, E-Lab, Riga, 1998, p. 24.

74. Eric Kluitenberg, "Media without an Audience," in Acoustic Space 3, Riga, 2000, p. 7.

75. Bilwet, Media archief, Amsterdam: Ravijn, 1992. English translation: Adilkno, The Media Archive, Brooklyn: Autonomedia, 1998, pp. 12–15. This essay

has been updated and commented on in 2001 by Geert Lovink and Joanne Richardson, "Notes on Sovereign Media," Nettime, November 14, 2001, and published on the Web in *Subsol* magazine: subsol.c3.hu.

76. Bertolt Brecht, "Der Rundfunk als Kommunikationsapparat. Rede über die Funktion des Rundfunks" (1932), in *Bertolt Brecht Werke, Schriften I (1914–1933),* Band 21, Frankfurt am Main: Suhrkamp Verlag, 1992, pp. 552–557.

77. Quoted in Eric Kluitenberg, "Media without an Audience," *Acoustic Space 3,* Riga, 2000, p. 7, posted on the Xchange list, October 19, 2000. George Bataille, *The Accursed Share,* Cambridge, Mass.: The MIT Press, 1991.

78. Kluitenberg, p. 7.

79. Tetsuo Kogawa, "Other Aspects of Radio, From Mini FM to Polymorphous Radio," in *Acoustic Space 3,* Riga, 2000, p. 27. See also: Tetsuo Kogawa, "Minima Memoranda," *Next Five Minutes 3 Workbook,* Amsterdam, 1999, pp. 103–104.

80. Adilkno, *The Media Archive,* Brooklyn: Autonomedia, 1998, p. 14.

81. See Jee Greenwald, Thinking Big, *Wired* 5.08, August 1997, on Malaysia's Multimedia Super Corridor. After the 1997 monetary crisis and the 2000 NASDAQ crash, "big equals good," ideas became less prominent.

82. Bruce Sterling, "The Spirit of Mega," *Wired* 6.7, July 1998. URL: www.wired.com/wired/6.07/mega_pr.html.

83. See: Rem Koolhaas and Bruce Mau, *OMA: S M L XL,* Rotterdam: 010 Publishers, 1995, and Lars Spuybroek meets Rem Koolhaas, "Africa Comes First," in: Joke Brouwer et al. (Eds.), *Transurbanism,* Rotterdam: V2_Publishers, 2002, pp. 160–193.

84. Reprinted in *The Australian,* August 27, 2002, p. 31.

85. Pit Schultz in a personal e-mail to the author, June 13, 2002.

86. Ibid., June 14, 2002.

The Battle over New-Media Art Education: Experiences and Models

1. In part, material for this research was gathered in preparation for the European Media Academy Day (February 27, 2003) which I coproduced with Stephen Kovats for V2_'s Dutch Electronic Arts Festival (DEAF). Thanks to Anna Munster (COFA, Sydney) for her comments on an earlier draft.

2. This tendency can be exemplified by the Walker Art Center's layoff in May 2003 of Steve Dietz, one of the world's few Web art curators. The Walker's termination of its new-media curatorial program sent shockwaves through the community. See the protest letter written by Sarah Cook with 690 signatures: www.mteww.com/walker_letter/index.shtml.

3. Thanks to Stephen Kovats of V2_ for his Berlin report (private e-mail, February 11, 2003).

4. Pelle Ehn, "Manifesto for a Digital Bauhaus," in: *Digital Creativity,* vol. 9, no. 4, 1999. Ehn refers to Tom Wolfe's ironic critique of the "white gods" (Gropius, Moholy-Nagy, Mies van der Rohe, et al.) and their "success" in the US in *From Bauhaus to Our House,* London: Jonathan Cape, 1982. Another recent Bauhaus manifesto is Jürgen Claus, *Das elektronische Bauhaus, Gestaltung mit Umwelt* (Zürich, 1987). In 1999, the exhibition "Digital Bauhaus: A Vision of Education and Creation for the New Century" took place in Tokyo at the NTT InterCommunicationCenter (1999). See also Heinrich Klotz, *Eine neue Hochschule (für neue Künste),* Stuttgart 1995. For a critical overview see Stefan Roemer, *Digitales Bauhaus, Die Konstruktion der Neuen Kunst- und Medien-Hochschulen neu durchgesehen,* 2003.

5. An example is the recently established Creative Industries faculty at the Queensland University of Technology (www.qut.edu.au). For a critique of the CI model and the "Queensland Ideology," see Danny Butt and Ned Rossiter, "Blowing Bubbles: Post-Crash Creative Industries and the Withering of Political Critique in Cultural Studies," posted to *Fibreculture,* December 9, 2002.

6. On several occasions Lev Manovich has pointed to a structural analogy and historical continuity between the 1920s contructivist style and the language of new media. In this context Bauhaus is used as a source of inspiration because of its teaching methods. See: Lev Manovich, "The Engineering of Vision from Constructivism to Computers," www.manovich.net/EV/ev.pdf.

7. www.uiah.fi/presentation/history/ebauha.htm. Quoted in www.uiah.fi/presentation/history/ebauha.htm.

8. Reference to Clement Greenberg, *Art and Culture,* New York: Beacon Press, 1965, p. 7.

9. Reference to Nietzsche's 1872 lecture "The Future of Our Educational Institutions." See: www.vusst.hr/ENCYCLOPAEDIA/nietzscheenglish.htm and Rosa Maria Dias, *Nietzsche Educator,* Sao Paolo: Scipione, 1993.

10. Private e-mail exchange, April 11, 2003. More on Matthew Fuller's program within the Piet Zwart Institute, the postgraduate and research institute of the Willem de Kooning Academy: pzwart.wdka.hro.nl/.

11. As a source of inspiration John Hopkins also mentioned the work of J.L. Lemke at CUNY Brooklyn

(www.kovacs.com/EJVC/lemke.htm, infosoc.uni-koeln.de/etext/text/lemke.93b.txt and academic.brooklyn.cuny.edu/education/jlemke/papers/cfppaper.htm).

12. For more information about the multi-locality events Hopkins is involved in, visit the www.neoscenes.net website. Three relevant articles of Hopkins link the neoscenes events with education issues: "1 + 1 = 3" (neoscenes.net/texts/xchange3.html), "learning and networks" (neoscenes.net/texts/xchange2.html) and "neoscenes occupation" (neoscenes.net/texts/xchange1.html).

13. Private e-mail exchange, January 30, 2003.

14. John Hopkins, e-mail interview, February 4, 2003. All other Hopkins quotes in this chapter have the same source.

15. "Convergence, divergence, transvergence: at the beginning of a new century already marked by accelerating advances in science and technology, we are presented with a unique opportunity: the bringing together of several once-distinct disciplines into previously unattainable formations. Art, architecture, electronic music, computer science, engineering, nanotechnology, each with frontiers of its own, are here brought together to face the challenge of their encounter. What new forms of practice and theory might these spawn? How can we set aside disciplinary boundaries and explore the edges of what is conceivable now that new floodgates of possibility have been opened? What are the futures we imagine, and how do we begin constructing them?" URL: www.centrifuge.org/marcos/.

16. In: Mike Leggett, "Managing Multiple Media," RealTime 50, "Education Feature: Training the New Media Artist," August/September 2002, p. 25. URL: www.realtimearts.net/rt50/legget.html.

17. Howard Rheingold defines the killer app as "the software application that turns an underused technology into an industry" (Smart Mobs, Cambridge, Mass.: Perseus Publishing, 2002, p. 71). This, of course, presupposes the presence of underused technologies and how to develop "underusement cultures."

18. The website of the CaiiA-STAR network, a networked research community and Ph.D. program in interactive arts, mentions more fields of research: "telematics, immersive VR, Mixed Reality, Alife, architecture, hypermedia, telepresence and agent technology, transgenics, data imaging, intelligent environments, generative music, technoetics" (caiiastar.net/mission/index.html).

19. Private e-mail exchange, April 17, 2003.

20. Private e-mail exchange, May 1, 2003.

21. www.fibreculture.org/newmediaed/index.html

22. Lisa Gyle, e-mail interview, February 5, 2003. More on Gyle's work can be found at halflives.adc.rmit.edu.au/

and www.swin.edu.au/sbs/media/staff/gye/.

23. History of the m-cult organization: www.m-cult.org/archive_en.htm. General info page: www.m-cult.org/index_en.html.

24. Minna Tarkka, e-mail interview, January 16, 2003.

25. See: Minna Tarkka (Ed.), ISEA '94 Catalogue, UIAH, Helsinki, 1994, pp. 196–197.

26. The College Art Association, founded in 1911, "includes among its members those who by vocation or avocation are concerned about and/or committed to the practice of art, teaching, and research of and about the visual arts and humanities. Over 13,000 artists, art historians, scholars, curators, collectors, educators, art publishers, and other visual arts professionals are individual members. Another 2,000 university art and art history departments, museums, libraries, and professional and commercial organizations hold institutional memberships." Quoted from: www.collegeart.org/caa/aboutcaa/index.html.

27. www.collegart.org/caa/ethics/teaching.html.

28. Simon Penny, e-mail interview, January 19, 2003.

29. US media theorist Willard Uncapher sent me the following about a class he gave. "I was trying to explain about the link of the Whole Earth Catalog to initial Web ethos and culture – with a mind to the California Ideology – and then asked if they had ever heard of the Whole Earth Catalog. Nope. Brenda Laurel, Ted Nelson, Donna Haraway for my students in the media arts class. Nope. The key problem for a teacher is discovering what students know, but one can't move forward too quickly. I wanted to explore the issue of Deleuze and Guattari's 1,000 Plateaus and I first wanted to see if they understood the context – so I inquire if they had heard of Derrida and Deconstruction. Nope. OK, what about structuralism, or poststructuralism? Nope. Um, hmm. What about James Joyce, particularly Finnegan's Wake (nope), or Gödel and the question of incompleteness or undecideability? Nope. Foucault? It makes me wonder – the chances are better that they will know something about theorists from 150 years ago who have made it into a canon of sorts (Hegel), rather than someone like Derrida from the last 40 years. This whole system has to be redesigned. Obviously one can contrast the students from one school with another, one discipline with another, but I worry about equality and opportunity when so much of what you learn in school depends not on a sophisticated, useful, and engaged curriculum, but on outside knowledge" (private e-mail, February 5, 2003).

30. URL: www.hrc.wmin.ac.uk/.

31. Private e-mail exchange, February 27, 2003.

32. Private e-mail exchange, May 1, 2004.

33. The decision not to open up Web journals is an editorial one, unrelated to technical limitations. The

"blogification" of science is going to be a palace revolution, which still lies ahead and may require as much civil courage as did the democratization of the university in the 1970s. As in more and more instances, this will require a "cultural revolution" that builds on today's possibilities. Technologically speaking, we have already reached the "omega point" of the information society.

34. Private e-mail exchange, April 11, 2003. URLs of the schools Matthew Fuller mentions: Budapest Intermedia department: www.intermedia.c3.hu/im/main.html; Osaka InterMediumInstitute (IMI): www.iminet.ac.jp/; Zurich design school: www.snm-hgkz.ch/SNMHome/info.htm; Nathalie Bookchin's NetNetNet course: www.calarts.edu/~ntntnt/ (1999–2000); Brussel St. Lukas School: www.sintlukas.be/.

35. Are Flagan, "re: One Day Left," Nettime, January 16, 2003.

36. Private e-mail exchange, April 22, 2003.

37. Information on the program: artcenter.edu/mdp.

38. His rancorous back-and-forth about these issues can be found at www.conceptualart.org/features/crush/crusha.htm.

39. Private e-mail exchange, February 27, 2003.

40. Private e-mail exchange, March 25, 2003.

41. Walter Gropius, "Bauhaus Manifesto," 1919: www.bauhaus.de/english/bauhaus1919/manifest1919.htm.

Oekonux and the Free-Software Model: From Linux to the GPL Society

1. Thanks to Volker Grassmuck, Jeebesh Bagchi, Benni Bärmann, Felix Stalder, McKenzie Wark, Seppo Koskela, Benja Fallenstein, Graham Seaman and Ned Rossiter for their comments on earlier versions of this chapter.

2. It is not my intention to explain again in detail what free software is and exactly how the GPL works or reconstruct the 1998 ideological split. For more on the ideas and history of free software, see for instance Richard Stallman's autobiography, *Free as in Freedom*, and his collection of essays *Free Software, Free Society;* Linus Torvalds' *Just for Fun;* Eric Raymond's *The Cathedral and the Bazaar;* and Glyn Moody's *Rebel Code* (see Bibliography for details).

3. I am using the term "network crystals" here in much the same way as Elias Canetti used "crowd crystals" in *Crowds and Power:* "Crowd crystals are the small, rigid groups of men, strictly delimited and of great constancy, which serve to precipitate crowds" (p. 86). Canetti stresses their historical permanance. "Even in the midst of the greatest excitement the

crystal stands out against it."

4. See Chris DiBona, Sam Ockman and Mark Stone, *Open Sources: Voices from the Open Source Revolution,* Sebastopol: O'Reilly Publishing, 1999. For online debates, see for instance the FSB (Free Software Business) list, www.crynwr.com/fsb/.

5. See www.infonomics.nl/FLOSS/report/FLOSSFinal_2b.pdf.

6. The relationship between growth, transformation and technical media is described in the work of the independent German media theorist Klaus Theweleit, who combines psychoanalysis, literary criticism and popular media culture in a search for egalitarian, non-violent forms of power. For more on this see Adilkno, *Media Archive,* Brooklyn: Autonomedia, 1998.

7. FLOSS stands for Free/Libre Open Source Software. See www.infonomics.nl/FLOSS/, a survey of users and developers of open source/free software (OS/FS), conducted by Rishab Gosh in 2001-2002.

8. See report (in English) by Bettina Berendt. "Protocol of Meeting at OS," Oekonux, August 3, 1999. The URL of the conference proceedings: www.mikro.org/Events/OS/frameset_e.html?Submit1=english. www.wizards-of-os.org.

9. For more information on Mikro's activities: www.mikro.org/Doku98-99/allg-e.html (report in English).

10. Text of the German lecture by Wolfgang Hagen is available online at www.mikro.org/Events/OS/reftexte/hagen/index.html.

11. See my interview with Richard Stallman, taped at the WOS 1 event, Nettime, July 21, 1999. I posted a report of the WOS conference on Nettime, July 19, 1999.

12. URL: www.cl.cam.ac.uk/CODE/.

13. See Volker Grassmuck's introduction (in German): *Freie Software,* Bonn: Bundeszentrale für politische Bildung, 2002. URL: freie-software.bpb.de/. His homepage: waste.informatik.hu-berlin.de/Grassmuck/.

14. See for instance the Open Cultures conference, organized by Public Netbase in Vienna, June 5-6, 2003. URL: opencultures.t0.or.at.

15. See www.oekonux.de/projekt/statistik/. There is a general text on Oekonux which summarizes the history, data and themes of the project at www.opentheory.org/wasistox/text.phtml.

16. For conference announcements and proceedings, see: www.oekonux-konferenz.de.

17. See www.opentheory.org/buchprojekt. It is unclear whether this project is succeeding or has died.

18. During his presentation at the first Oekonux conference, Kim Veltman made another connection between Germany and open source. "When printing began in Germany, it was largely out of a conviction

that this was for the public good. Interestingly enough Germany is also the most active contributor to Open Source." URL: erste.oekonux-konferenz. de/dokumentation/texte/veltman.html.

19. Stefan Merten, "Vorstellungsrunde," Oekonux, July 22 1999.

20. More on Robert Kurz, the Krisis group and their magazine can be found at www.krisis.org. Increasingly their texts are being translated into other languages. In early 1993, together with other Adilkno members, I visited Robert Kurz in Nürnberg and made a radio program in German about his work for Amsterdam's Radio Patapoe. The interview has not been transcribed or published. I did, however, write a review (in English) of Robert Kurz's *Die Welt als Wille und Design, Postmoderne, Lifestyle-Linke und die Aesthetisierung der Krise* (Berlin: Edition Tiamat, 1999), part of the essay "Relaxed Stagnation: Diederichsen, Bolz, Kurz and the German Cultural Condition," posted to Nettime, September 1, 1999.

21. There are a number of Robert Kurz translations available online that can be used as an introduction to his work, for instance, www.giga.or.at/others/krisis/r-kurz_marx2000_englisch.html. For more see www.krisis.org.

22. According to New York critic Doug Henwood, crises are nothing but "normal competition – part of the 'beauty of capitalism', as Paul O'Neill said of Enron. Winners, losers; fortunes, liquidations; expansions, recessions. It's misleading to call these crises, because the word implies some dramatic break. If they happen every day, they're by definition routine. Most Marxists who use the word are either consciously or unconsciously echoing a 'death agony' rhetoric <www.marxists.org/archive/trotsky/works/1938-tp/>. This is finally really the Big One that's going to reveal all the hidden contradictions, and the System will come smashing down. Even if users of the concept don't mean to, they're evoking that discursive register." *Lbo-talk digest*, Vol. 1 No. 735, July 5, 2003.

23. Stefan Merten, "Info-Text," Oekonux, July 25, 1999.

24. See www.opentheory.org.

25. *The Boston Globe* reports on a group of researchers that looks into the success of Linux. One of them, Mark Blaxill, says: "What's interesting about open source is not free love and openness but its performance. This thing is competitive. It takes on Microsoft and wins. Therefore there must be important economics and strategy principles that underlie it." The researchers look into the way open source takes advantages of the Internet, the influence of the lowered transaction costs that come with these electronic networks, the leadership style of Linus Torvalds and the motivational factors that inspire thousands of programmers to work on projects for free.leadership style of Linus Torvalds (published March 16, 2003, www.boston.com/globe).

26. See for instance the "Prinzipielles/Teil II" thread, instigated by Sabine Nuss (April 2001).

27. Personal e-mail exchange, July 6, 2003.

28. Frequent posters include Benja Fallenstein, Benni Bärmann, Christoph Reuss, Enrico Weigelt, Franz Nahrada, Hans-Gert Gräbe, Holger Weiss, Horst Ribbeck, Stefan Seefeld, Kurt-Werner Pörtner, Hartmut Pilch, Casimir Purzelbaum and Thomas Uwe Gruettmueller.

29. Arnulf Pelzer, Oekonux, April 1, 2002 and the "Warum seid ihr so verbiestert?" thread.

30. Interview with Stefan Merten, Nettime, April 24, 2001.

31. Linus Torvalds (with David Diamond), *Just for Fun*, New York: HarperCollins, 2002, p. 75.

32. See Alessandro Nuvolari, "Open Source Software Development: Some Historical Perspectives" (opensource.mit.edu/papers/nuvolari.pdf).

33. Another origin is a 1997 essay by Robert Kurz, "Anti Economy, Anti Politics" *(Krisis 19)*, in which he discusses the status of "germs" in the present capitalist society after the fall of communism. URL: www.giga.or.at/others/krisis/r-kurz_antioekonomie-und-antipolitik_krisis19_1997.html.

34. Glyn Moody, *Rebel Code: Linux and the Open Source Revolution*, London: Penguin Books, p. 77.

35. See for instance Stefan Merten's report of his visit to a metal construction firm, Oekonux, November 19, 2001.

36. See openeeg.sourceforge.net/doc/index.html. The OpenEEG project is concerned with making available free plans and software for do-it-yourself EEG devices. Another example is OpenCola, which the *New Scientist* claims is the world's first open source product. Unlike Coca-Cola, it openly advertises its recipe (www.newscientist.com/hottopics/copyleft/copyleftart.jsp).

37. Tord Boontje: "It is about offering an awareness of choice. Providing information instead of stuff. Home-made instead of factory produced. To date about 30,000 drawings have been distributed for free." From: www.tordboontje.com/rough-an.htm.

38. See the statement written for the third Fibreculture meeting, Brisbane, July 11–13, 2003. "The myth of a separate, containable 'cyberspace' persists despite all evidence to the contrary. Rather than perpetuating new age visions of leaving the body behind to virtually 'inhabit' cyberspace, it is important to begin to realize that cyberspace, or fiberspace, already envelops society; is society. How can disciplines integrate Internet content, literacies, and technologies as part of their core activities rather than as an

adjunct afterthought?" Posted to Fibreculture by Axel Bruns, June 18, 2003.

39. Joanne Richardson, "Interview with Stefan Merten," Nettime, December 5, 2001.

40. Graham Seaman explains: "In addition to the general meaning rivalry is an economic term, used especially in 'Welfare Economics', defined negatively: if something is 'non-rivalrous' the consumption/use of it by one person has no effect on the consumption/use by other people. In many cases that means I can give you something non-rivalrous and still have it myself. Examples are ideas, software, broadcast TV programs, etc." Oekonux-en, February 2, 2003.

41. See Sabine Nuss and Michael Heinrich, "Warum Freie Software dem Kapitalismus nicht viel anhaben kann," posted on Oekonux, July 3, 2001.

42. See debate on Oekonux, July–October 2001.

43. Christian Fuchs, "Die Anwendbarkeit der Wertkritik in der Informationsgesellschaft," Oekonux, November 30, 2000. See also his December 10, 2000, post: "Du bist der Depp des Kapitals, Stefan Merten." Someone else responds: "I hate you all! Help, where is my chain saw?" Since then, Fuchs has come up with his own theory (in English) of software engineering and the production of surplus value, in which he states that "informational capital has a material base and the surplus value objectified in information commodities is in need of a physical-material carrier/medium." URL: eserver.org/clogic/2002/fuchs.html.

44. A recent publication in which these ideas are investigated is André Gorz, L' immatériel. Connaissance, valeur et capital, Paris: Galilée, 2003.

45. Richard Stallman, quoted in Sam Williams' biography, Free as in Freedom, Sebastopol: O'Reilly, 2002, p. 101.

46. "Stamokap" stands for state-monopoly capitalism. According to Lenin, state monopoly capitalism does not evolve into socialism. It does, however, in Lenin's view, create the material prerequisites for socialism by concentrating and centralizing production and finances, and promoting specialization, cooperation, and improved methods of economic organization, accounting and control. In the 1980s neo-liberalism took over and stamokap vanished from the theory horizon. (Ref.: venus.spaceports.com/~theory/economy_1.htm).

47. A special conference was organized on this topic. URL: www.projektwerkstatt.de/herrschaft.

48. See Oekonux, late August 2001. In this debate Robert Gehring makes a reference to Abbe Mowshowitz's "Virtual Feudalism" (in Peter J. Denning and Robert M. Metcalfe (Eds.), Beyond Calculation: The Next Fifty Years of Computing, New York: Springer Verlag, 1997).

49. PDF version of the (German) essay "Gleicher als Andere" ("More the Same as Others"), Foundation of Free Cooperation: www.rosaluxemburgstiftung.de/Einzel/Preis/rlspreis.pdf.

50. Christoph Spehr, in an interview I did with him: "My work inspired some very interesting controversies in Oekonux between the GPL model that everything should just be free and the free-cooperation model that everything should be a balance between powerful groups or individuals. I'd like to take that discussion further. But to build bridges between activists and nerds, the nerds should be more open to produce things the activists and their groups need. There should be more bargaining and cooperation between these two groups." Posted on Oekonux-en, June 7, 2003.

51. See lengthy debate on Oekonux, October 2001.

52. Stefan Meretz, "Der wilde Schungel der Kooperation," Oekonux, October 4, 2001. URL: www.opentheory.org/dschungel.

53. See "Patriachat und Netzaktivismus debate," Oekonux, November–December 2001. Oliver Frommel writes: "There is a certain conservative tendency in most of the free software movement that also extends to the obtainment of power. More than often I found FS people talking about market share as a value of its own with no other higher aim. It is also very interesting to observe an attitude that goes hand in hand with this and is also a confirmation of patriarchal structures: the sometimes crypto-fascist tendency in system administration (very often the gainful occupation of FS developers) and in general a mysogynist and homophobic tendency." Oekonux, December 4, 2001.

54. See the Hackers Survey by the Boston Consulting Group (Lakhani, Wolf and Bates). URL: www.osdn.com/bcg/BCGHACKERSURVEY.pdf.

55. Benni Bärmann, Oekonux, November 27, 2001. More on this topic in Francis Hunger's "Open Source – Open Gender?" (in German; English translation available soon), a chapter of the thesis Computer als Männnermaschine, www.hgb-leipzig.de/~francis/txt/comamama/index.htm. Seppo Koskela (Helsinki) reports two exceptions. In the Finnish Linux User Group (FLUG) there is a subgroup of women that calls itself, sarcastically, Linux Blondes. The other one is in Brazil and has a name derived from local folklore.

56. From a private e-mail exchange, July 6, 2003. More on Hipatia at www.hipatia.info.

57. Many critique the attention economy concept, but Linus Torvalds certainly supports the idea. In his autobiography he writes: "Open source hackers aren't the high-tech counterparts of Mother Teresa. They do get their names associated with their con-

tributions in the form of the 'credit list' or 'history file' that is attached to each project. The most prolific contributors attract the attention of employers who troll the code, hoping to spot, and hire, top programmers" (p. 122).

58. Joanne Richardson, "Interview with Stefan Merten," Nettime, December 5, 2001.

59. For a rich empirical description of the dotcom work ethic, see Andrew Ross, *No Collar,* New York: Basic Books, 2003.

60. www.oekonux.org/introduction/blotter/default_7. html.

61. Stefan Merten, Oekonux-en, January 13, 2002.

62. See "Manifesto Against Work" by the Krisis Group. Their slogan: "We can win a world beyond labor. Workers of all countries, call it a day!" (www.giga. or.at/others/krisis/manifesto-against-labour.html). Also Norbert Trenkle, "Terror of labor" (www.giga. or.at/others/krisis/n-trenkle_terror-der-arbeit-englisch.html).

63. Graham Seaman, Oekonux-en, November 23, 2001. Web reference to Illich's work: www.oikos.org/ecology/illichvernacular.htm. Seaman also found that Paolo Freire used the term "personal unfolding."

64. See improved translation by Benja Fallenstein of Stefan Meretz's posting from the German Oekonux list on Oekonux-en, December 17, 2001. Meretz: "The point is not to get good products in the short term, but to get people in the long term who, in their own interest, take care of a good life for everybody."

65. As a random example of this argument, a quote from Stefan Merten: "How I create a context for musicians who'd like to unfold themselves in an undisturbed fashion that benefits their performance as well as their listeners? The fact that payment disturbs this process may be undisputed, in particular if you look at the practices towards computer-generated products by the music industry. The consciousness of payment for achievement has to be broken down" (my translation). Oekonux, October 21, 2001.

66. I have tried to bring together a few elements of the "free" ideology in the online Free for What? Project (www.waag.org/free), produced during the Kiasma temporary media lab, Helsinki, November 1999.

67. Stefan Merten, "Ehrenamt und Tauschwert," Oekonux, July 29, 1999.

68. Free interpretation of Meretz's position in an early e-mail to Oekonux, August 1999.

69. Posting of Vincente Ruiz to the English Oekonux list, April 23, 2003. URL: ourproject.org.

70. See www.wikipedia.org. "Wikipedia is an international, open content, collaboratively developed encyclopedia. As of May 2003, it covers a vast spectrum of subjects and has over 120,000 articles in English as well as over 75,000 articles in other languages. The project started in English on January 15, 2001, and projects to build Wikipedia in other languages are very active." Wikification could be a synonym for collaborative work environments on the Web where users add entries and comment on each other's entries. In order to make this work, contributors have to share Wikipedia's presumption that there is no objective knowledge. "Because there are a huge variety of participants of all ideologies, and from around the world, Wikipedia is committed to making its articles as unbiased as possible. The aim is not to write articles from a single objective point of view – this is a common misunderstanding of the policy – but rather, to fairly and sympathetically present all views on an issue" (accessed May 3, 2003). See also: www.wikipedia.org/wiki/History_of_Wikipedia.

71. See Peter Suber's blog of the WOS movement: www.earlham.edu/~peters/fos/fosblog.html.

72. URL: www.ornl.gov/TechResources/Human_Genome/home.html. The question here was who would own the "source code" of the human genetic sequence. The sequence and analysis of the human genome working draft were published in February 2001 in *Nature* and *Science.* See also open-bio.org/, bio.perl.org/ and other sites for developers interested in open-source tools for bioinformatics.

73. URL: eon.law.harvard.edu/openlaw/. Another initiative, the Free Archictecture list, "discusses the application and implications of the ideas and methods of the free software movement to architecture and the design of the built environment." www.e-maillists.org/mailman/listinfo/freearchitecture. The examples given here can only be random.

74. Michael Century, "Open Code and Creativity in the Digital Age," May 8, 2000, on www.mikro.org/wos.

75. Taken from Joanne Richardson, "Interview with Stefan Merten," Nettime, December 5, 2001.

76. All quotes in this paragraph come from my interview with Stefan Merten, Nettime, April 24, 2001.

77. Benni Bärmann, "8 Thesen zur Befreiung," Oekonux, December 27, 2001.

78. Linus Torvalds (with David Diamond), *Just for Fun,* New York: HarperCollins, 2002, p. 195.

79. In Sam Williams, *Free as in Freedom,* Sebastopol: O'Reilly, 2002, p. 77.

80. Manuel Delanda, "Open Source, a Movement in Search of a Philosophy," 2001. URL: www.btinternet.com/~cyberchimp/delanda/pages/opensource.htm. He quotes Richard Stallman, "Why Software Should Be Free," www.gnu.org/philosophy/shouldbefree.html, p. 6.

81. As always, there are inspiring exceptions, such as Tiziana Terranova's "Free labor: producing culture for the digital economy," posted to Nettime, March 31,

2000, and published in *Social Text 63*, Vol. 18, No. 2, summer 2000, pp. 33–48; and Richard Barbrook's "High-Tech Gift Economy," (www.firstmonday.dk/issues/issue3_12/barbrook/).

82. Pit Schultz, "begriffe," Oekonux, July 26, 1999, and also Thorsten Schilling, "re: Ehrenamt und Tausch-wert," July 29, 1999, in which Schilling raises a whole range of issues at the edge of Marxism and late-20th-century postmodern discourse. Early debates in this direction did not continue.

83. See: www.opentheory.org/fs_empire/text.phtml, posted on Oekonux, June 28, 2002.

84. Exception is the thread "Ein paar Gedanken zum Freiheitsverständis," Oekonux, August 2001.

85. URL: www.btinternet.com/~cyberchimp/delanda/pages/opensource.htm.

86. See summary and comments of Stefan Merten on Himanen (in English), Oekonux, May 19, 2002.

87. Subtitle of the Books Not Bombs petition signed by librarians against the war in Iraq, September 2002. URL: www.libr.org/peace/Iraq.Sept.2002.html.

88. An encouraging initiative that emerged out of the Oekonux context was the Linux Bildungsbande (education gang). URL: www.oekonux-konferenz.org/documentation/texts/Rehzi.html. See also work by two Amsterdam-based initiatives, the activist-run Internet workspace ascii (squat.net/ascii) and www.tacticaltech.org, which focuses on NGOs.

89. In a typical response, Chris Zielinski writes to the Community Informatics list: "Open Source is made for those who are highly adept technologically (a vanishingly small minority of the population). If, like me, you have never had the desire to decompile your operating system or rewrite your printer drivers, the thrill of being able to do so thanks to an open architecture is not so potent" (posted July 17, 2003).

90. Despite all the talk of a free-software takeoff, Linux still accounts for just 1% of operating systems used to access the Google search engine (www.google.com/press/zeitgeist.html).

91. See www.fsfeurope.org/projects/mankind/.

92. "Report from the South Asian Tactical Media Lab, organized by Sarai, Delhi, November 14–16, 2002." Posted to TML-list, December 10, 2002.

93. Private e-mail exchange, July 9, 2003.

94. Franz Nahrada, "Globale Dörfer und Freie Software." URL: www.opentheory.org/globale_doerfer/text.phtml. Posted on Oekonux, July 18, 2001.

95. Linus Torvalds (with David Diamond), *Just for Fun,* quotes from p. 121 and p. 192.

96. Bruce Sterling, "A Contrarian View on Open Source," O'Reilly Open Source Convention," San Diego, July 26, 2002, posted on Nettime, August 5, 2002.

97. As David Diamond writes in the introduction to Linus Torvalds' autobiography, *Just for Fun,* "Most folks one meets in Silicon Valley have a cult-like zeal about them. They focus so intensely on their business that nothing else seems to exist. Nothing interrupts the continuous loop of self-congratulation that passes for conversation" (p. 23).

98. Frederick Noronha, in response to Alfred Bork, who wrote: "Do not believe there is any case for open source as a way of avoiding the digital divide, or for providing education for all. It is a 'red herring.'" Posted to bytesforall_readers, January 30, 2003. See also the responses by Ajit Maru and Vivek Gupta.

99. For a general report by Niranjan Rajani et al. (closed in May 2003) on the uptake of FLOSS in developing countries, see: www.maailma.kaapeli.fi/FLOSS_for_dev.html.

100. Private e-mail exchange, June 28, 2003.

101. Tapio Mäkelä, "Open Source and Content: the Cultural Move," www.m-cult.net/mediumi/, Issue 2.1.

102. Linus Torvalds (with David Diamond), *Just for Fun,* p. 229.

Defining Open Publishing: Of Lists and Weblogs

1. Millard Johnson, posting to the Triumph of Content mailing list, January 1, 2002.

2. Jon Marshall, private e-mail exchange, April 22, 2003.

3. An exception that should be mentioned here is BumpList (www.bumplist.net/). BumpList is a mailing list concept that re-examines the culture and rules of online e-mail lists. The site explains: "BumpList only allows for a minimum amount of subscribers so that when a new person subscribes, the first person to subscribe is 'bumped,' or unsubscribed from the list. Once subscribed, you can only be unsubscribed if someone else subscribes and 'bumps' you off. BumpList actively encourages people to participate in the list process by requiring them to subscribe repeatedly if they are bumped off. The focus of the project is to determine if by attaching simple rules to communication mediums, the method and manner of correspondences that occur as well as behaviors of connection will change over time."

4. Slashcode.com/sites.pl lists the projects that use its source code.

5. The history of the independent media centers (IMCs), the Indymedia weblog and the Active software is well described in the chapter "Open Publishing, Open Technologies," in Graham Meikle, *Future Active,* Sydney: Pluto Press Australia, 2002, pp. 88–101.

6. See: slash.autonomedia.org. Other examples of weblogs are www.peek-a-booty.org/pbhtml/index.php, www.blogskins.com and www.kuro5hin.

org/. For a list of various blogs that use Scoop, see scoop.kuro5hin.org/?op=special;page=sites.

7. Dave Winer, "The History of Weblogs," URL: new-home.weblogs.com/historyOfWeblogs.

8. Noah Shachtman, "Blogging Goes Legit, Sort Of," *Wired News*, June 6, 2002. URL: www.wired.com/news/print/0,1294,52992,00.html. The article reports on the use of weblogs by professional journalists and university departments.

9. Rebecca Blood's introduction to John Rodzvilla et al., *We've got Blog: How Weblogs are Changing our Culture*, Cambridge, Mass.: Perseus Publishing, 2002, p. ix.

10. Ibid., p. x.

11. Andrew Sullivan, "The Blogging Revolution," *Wired* 10.5, May 2002. URL: www.wired.com/wired/archive/10.05/mustread.html?pg=2.

12. *The Chicago Tribune*, July 9, 1999 (quoted from David Winer's site).

13. *Salon*, May 28, 1999 (quoted from David Winer's site).

14. Ziod.com on www.slashdot.org, "re: Slashdot a blog?," June 6, 2002.

15. David Gallagher, "A Rift Among Bloggers," *The New York Times*, June 10, 2002. URL: www.nytimes.com/2002/06/10/technology/10BLOG.html.

16. Ibid.

17. Clay Shirky in *Europe Online* newsletter, May 2002, www.europeonline.com.

18. Ibid.

19. There is no online archive of the Recode mailing list yet. See also: www.netculture.gr/eng/showdocwars.asp?view=76.

20. In January 2002, the Australian Net artist Melinda Rackham initiated the Empyre list. "Although - Empyre- is an international list it first evolved to address the gap in the Australian regional online terrain after the decline of the recode list, presenting a companion list to Fibreculture." URL: www.subtle.net/empyrean/empyre.

21. Hugh Brown et al. (Eds.), *Politics of a Digital Present*, Melbourne: Fibreculture Publications, 2001.

22. For more information, see www.fibreculture.org. During 2001, the facilitators' group consisted of Hugh Brown, Geert Lovink, Helen Merrick, Ned Rossiter, David Teh and Michele Wilson. In 2002, Chris Chesher, Danny Butt, Molly Hankwitz and Lisa Gye joined the group.

23. In order to solve the troll problem on Fibreculture, on February 14, 2002, posting guidelines appeared on the list, formulated by the eight facilitators. "The following kinds of posts are not suited for Fibreculture: announcements (send to fibreculture-announce); flames, unannotated URLs/forwarded articles, fiction, long (>5000 wd) academic papers/thesis chap-

ters, text-art-one-liners (unless *really* funny or insightful), promotional material."

24. I define electronic democracy as a practice within Internet culture, in contrast to experts such as Steven Clift who talk about electronic democracy in terms of transparency through bringing (local) government documents online, promoting electronic voting and raising citizen participation through online forums. Electronic democratic culture, in the context of this thesis, is not confined to the relationship between citizens and government. See also Clift's homepage: www.publicus.net.

25. See the introduction of this thesis for an explanation of the term "agonistic democracy" and Chantal Mouffe's interpretation of the concept in her book *The Democratic Paradox*. London: Verso, 2000.

26. In this study I have not looked at the ICANN domain name controversy to try to answer that question. This is the battle over who owns and administers top-level domains such as .com, .org and .net. Since 1998, the Internet Corporation for Assigned Names and Numbers (ICANN) has been responsible for this task. Ever since its founding, the legal structure of ICANN and its accountability have been highly controversial. To many, ICANN is the exact opposite of what Internet democracy could be. See www.icannwatch.org. Castells points out the conflicts and shortcomings but still praises ICANN: "Without prejudging the effectiveness of these new institutions, the truly surprising accomplishment is that the Internet reached this relative stability in its governance without succumbing either to the bureaucracy of the US government or to the chaos of decentralized structure" (p. 33). Lawrence Lessig does not mention the ICANN drama of Internet self-governance either in *Code and Other Laws of Cyberspace* or in *The Future of Ideas*. One of the first critical ICANN studies is *Ruling the Root: Internet Governance and the Taming of Cyberspace* by Milton Mueller (The MIT Press, 2002).

27. Amy Alexander, in a private e-mail, December 18, 2001.

28. slashdot.org/moderation.shtml

29. Ibid.

30. Platinum Dragon on Slashdot, June 7, 2002.slashdot.org/comments.pl?sid=33810&cid=3658121.

31. Indymedia.org/publish.php3.

32. Ibid.

33. Evan, Indymedia, "Credibility, & Covering Palestine," April 5, 2002 (from a closed internal list).

34. Ibid.

35. Matthew Arison, Fibreculture, November 10, 2002 (posted by Graham Meikle). URL: www.cat.org.au/maffew/cat/openpub.html. Related text about open editing by Dru Oja Jay: www.dru.ca/imc/open_pub.html.

36. Ibid.
37. More on Scoop: scoop.kuro5hin.org/special/whatisit.
38. Reference to Robert Altman's film *Gosford Park*.
39. Amy Alexander to Geert Lovink, December 31, 2001.
40. Many Phpnuke-based weblogs have the following restriction: "People who have admin access get to upload/download files, add articles, and review submissions if they want."
41. Amy Alexander to Geert Lovink, January 6, 2002.
42. See www.wall.com/larry/.
43. Amy Alexander to Geert Lovink, January 6, 2002.
44. Eric Raymond, in a similar context of open-source software development, speaks of "benevolent dictators." Eric Raymond, "Homesteading the Noosphere," URL: www.tuxedo.org/~esr/writings/cathedral-bazaar/homesteading/x349.html. Quoted from Felix Stalder and Jesse Hirsch, "Open Source Intelligence," *First Monday,* issue 7/6. Stalder and Hirsch: "They are not benevolent because the people are somehow better, but because their leadership is based almost exclusively on their ability to convince others to follow. Thus the means of coercion are very limited. Hence, a dictator who is no longer benevolent, i.e. who alienates his or her followers, loses the ability to dictate."
45. Documentation of the Calarts net.net series (November 1999-May 2000), organized by Nathalie Bookchin: www.calarts.edu/~ntntnt/.
46. Amy Alexander's old home pages: emsh.calarts.edu/~amy/index2.html and shoko.calarts.edu/~alex/. There is a great variety of projects to be found on www.plagiarist.org, such as thebot (a spiking Web spider), netsong (a singing Web search engine), Interview Yourself! (a collection of self-interviews by artists) and b0timati0n (live Net art performance for the geek age).
47. Amy Alexander, Syndicate, August 15, 2001.
48. She would say things like: "The big thing is to remember what we've set out to do, and let the structure help us do it, rather than start out by assuming we're still in the old structure and we have to have this top-down censorship to solve every problem – i.e. 'the old way'" (private e-mail exchange, January 6, 2002).
49. Ibid, December 28, 2001.
50. Amy Alexander to Geert Lovink, January 12, 2002.
51. Amy Alexander to Geert Lovink, March 16, 2002.
52. Saul Albert to Discordia members, February 24, 2002.
53. Amy Alexander to Discordia members, June 10, 2002.

Conclusion: The Boundaries of Critical Internet Culture

1. Phrase used by Kodwo Eshun in my interview with him posted on Nettime, July 25, 2000, and printed in my collection of interviews *Uncanny Networks* (MIT Press, 2002).
2. Take the editor of the Freud translation, Adam Phillips. He doesn't do e-mail. "It's not clear whether this is a Luddite impulse, a shrewd maneuver designed to enhance his glamorously elusive aura or simply a pragmatic decision not to squander hours at the beck and call of everyone with a keyboard and a screen name. 'I don't want to be in touch,' he explains. 'I want less communication'" (Daphne Merkin, *The New York Times,* July 13, 2003).
3. Reference to Ditherati, June 21, 2002: "I never got into this in order to lure all of you here and sell you to advertisers." Rusty Foster, on discovering that community's just another word for nothing left to lose, *Kuro5hin,* June 17, 2002 (www.kuro5hin.org/story/2002/6/17/23933/5831). The reference can be found in the Ditherati archive: www.ditherati.com/archive/.
4. Michael Hardt and Antonio Negri, *Empire,* Cambridge, Mass.: Harvard University Press, 2000; Naomi Klein, *No Logo,* London: Flamingo, 2000.
5. See, for instance, Graham Meikle, *Future Active: Media Activism and the Internet,* Pluto Press Australia, 2002.
6. A change might take place during the World Summit of the Information Society which will take place in Geneva (December 2004) and Tunis (November 2005). During the Geneva event, a counter-summit on communication rights and other activities to raise critical perspectives on the "digital divide" and global governance have been announced. For more see www.crisinfo.org.
7. See Michael H. Goldhaber, "The Attention Economy and the Net: The Natural Economy of the Net." URL: www.firstmonday.dk/issues/issue2_4/goldhaber/. The attention economy is a classic late-1990s attempt to explain how founders of a free website could turn into millionaires overnight. How "eyeballs" were miraculously transformed into overvalued stock options is explained on this website: www.newmediastudies.com/economic.htm.
8. Personal e-mail from the new-media artist, activist and curator Trebor Scholz, June 26, 2002.
9. See "Sweet Erosions of E-mail," posted to Nettime, June 13, 2000. Published in Geert Lovink, *Dark Fiber,* Cambridge, Mass.: MIT Press, 2002, pp. 176–180.
10. Quoted from www.alia.org.au/e-lists/netiquette.html. See also Karen Dearne, "E-mail minefield," *The*

Australian IT, March 11, 2003, p.1.

11. I discussed the mid-1990s switch from speculative theory to a more critical approach in a lecture at InterCommunicationCentre, Tokyo, December 19, 1996, called "From Speculative Media Theory to Net Criticism." The essay was published in *Mute,* Issue 7, Spring 1997, pp. 1–2, and *InterCommunication Magazine,* Tokyo, No. 20, 1997. The text was first posted on Nettime, January 13, 1997, and rewritten for *Dark Fiber* (MIT Press, 2002).

12. Fareed Zakaria, *The Future of Freedom: Illiberal Democracy at Home and Abroad.* New York: W. W. Norton & Company, 2003. The "wave" of democracy that swept the world in the 1980s and 1990s has not yet reached (or missed) the Internet. This can be argued for the entire mediasphere, which is still, by and large, pre-democratic. It is a truism that democracy alone doesn't guarantee freedom. Political Internet liberty has yet to be outlined. Zakaria's solution of impartial experts insulated from the democratic fray is exactly the Internet's problem.

13. Reference to Chantal Mouffe's last chapter, "A Politics with Adversary?" in *The Democratic Paradox,* London: Verso, 2000.

14. The full version of the ASN paper can be downloaded at: collaboratory.planetwork.net/linktank_whitepaper/ASN2003-05-15.pdf/file_view
The URL of the conference: www.planetwork.net/2003conf/frames/index.html.

15. Manuel Castells, *The Internet Galaxy,* Oxford: Oxford University Press, 2001, p. 282.

16. URL: www.shirky.com (accessed April 4, 2003).

Bibliography

Consulted mailing lists and newsletters

Nettime-l, an international mailing list for Net criticism, www.nettime.org.
Nettime-nl, a Dutch list for Internet culture and criticism, www.nettime.org.
Syndicate, a European list for new-media arts and culture, www.v2.nl/syndicate.
Rohrpost, a German-language list for digital media and networks,
    www.nettime.org/rohrpost.
Rhizome Digest, a New York-based Net-art portal and newsletter, www.rhizome.org.
Fibreculture, an Australian list for critical Internet research and culture,
    www.fibreculture.org.
Triumph of Content, a list that collaboratively filters (mainly US) mainstream news
    channels, triumph-of-content-l@usc.edu (no website).
Oekonux, a German discussion list (and a parallel English one) about free software and
    society, www.oekonux.org.
LINK, an Australian discussion list about IT policy, sunsite.anu.edu.au/link/.
JUST-WATCH-L, an international list for human rights and media,
    listserv.acsu.buffalo.edu/archives/justwatch-l.html.
LBO-talk, the Left Business Observer discussion list, www.panix.com/~dhenwood/lbo-
    talk.html.
Politech, Declan McCullagh's newsletter on technology and politics,
    www.politechbot.com.
Fast Company's Fast Talk, a business management newsletter,
    www.fastcompany.com/homepage/.
Philosophy, a discussion list moderated by Alexander Bard, bard@bullgod.se (no web-
    site).
Air-l, the list of the Association of Internet researchers, www.aior.org.
Reader-list, the discussion list of the New Delhi-based Sarai new-media center,
    www.sarai.net.
Bytes for All, and the related Bytes for All Reader-l, www.bytesforall.org.
Edupage, an EDUCAUSE newsletter about higher education and information technolo-
    gy, www.educause.edu/pub/edupage/edupage.html.
NowEurope, Europe's Online Business Forum, moderated by Steven Carlson,
    nowEurope.com.
gir-l, a German-language Internet research list, www.online-forschung.de/.
Free Software Business list, www.crynwr.com/fsb/.
Tornado-Insider: Connecting Innovation, Capital and People, a European venture-capi-
    tal newsletter, www.tornado-insider.com/info/
Europemedia.net Newsletter, a European new-media research newsletter produced by
    Van Dusseldorp & Partners, www.europemedia.net/.
DITHERATI, a daily critical quote from a leading IT industry member, edited by Thomas
    Owen, www.ditherati.net/archive/.
The Industry Standard's Daily News and Media Grok, a daily newsletter published by
    the dotcom magazine The Industry Standard (January 1998-September 2001),
    www.thestandard.com/.
Corp-focus, a weekly corporate watchdog newsletter published by Russell Mokhiber
    and Robert Weissman, www.corporatepredators.org.
Pandora, a newsletter on the PR industry, compiled by Eveline Lubbers.
Generation-Online, a discussion list about Negri and Hardt's book *Empire*,
    coyote.kein.org/mailman/listinfo/generation_online.

Red Rock Eater News Service, Phil Agre's link list and newsletter about information technology and society, dlis.gseis.ucla.edu/people/pagre/rre.html.
Solaris, a mailing list on critical issues in IT and development, mail.sarai.net/mailman/listinfo/solaris/

Frequently used websites

www.google.com, the search engine.
www.heise.de/tp, a German online magazine.
www.indymedia.org, an independent news blog.
www.wired.com, the online technology magazine.
www.firstmonday.dk, a peer-reviewed journal on the Internet.
www.salon.com, the US online opinion magazine.
www.amazon.com, the online bookstore, with reviews.
www.perlentaucher.de, German literary reviews.

Books

Adilkno, *The Media Archive*, Brooklyn: Autonomedia, 1998.
Badiou, Alain, *Ethics: An Essay on the Understanding of Evil*, London: Verso, 1991.
Baudrillard, Jean, *Screened Out*, London: Verso, 2002.
Becker, Konrad, *Tactical Reality Dictionary*, Vienna: Edition Selene, 2002.
Bell, David, *An Introduction to Cybercultures*, New York: Routledge, 2001.
Berlin, Isaiah, *The Sense of Reality: Studies in Ideas and Their History*, New York: Farrer, Straus and Giroux, 1997.
—, *The Proper Study of Mankind, An Anthology of Essays*, New York: Farrar, Straus and Giroux, 1998.
Berners-Lee, Tim and Fishetti, Mark, *Weaving the Web*, New York: HarperBusiness, 2000.
Bey, Hakim, *Temporary Autonomous Zones*, Brooklyn: Autonomedia, 1992.
—, *Immediatism*, Edinburgh: AK Press, 1994.
Blood, Rebecca, *We've Got Blog: How Weblogs Are Changing Our Culture*, Cambridge, Mass. Perseus Pub., 2002.
Bolter, Jay David and Grusin, Richard, *Remediation*, Cambridge, Mass.: MIT Press, 1999.
Borsook, Paulina, *Cyberselfish: A Critical Romp Through the Terribly Libertarian World of High-Tech*, London: Little, Brown and Company, 2000.
Canetti, Elias, *Masse und Macht*, Frankfurt am Main: Fischer Verlag, 1980 (1960).
Castells, Manuel, *The Information Age: Economy, Society and Culture, Vol.1: The Rise of the Network Society*, Oxford: Blackwell, 1996.
—, *The Internet Galaxy*, Oxford: Oxford University Press, 2001.
Cassidy, John, *Dot.con: The Real Story of Why the Internet Bubble Burst*, New York: HarperCollins, 2002.
Davis, Erik, *TechGnosis: Myth, Magic and Mysticism in the Age of Information*, New York: Harmony Books, 1998.
DiBona, Chris, et al., *Open Sources: Voices from the Open Source Revolution*, Sebastopol: O'Reilly Publishing, 1999.
Dreyfus, Hubert L., *What Computers Can't Do*, New York: Harper and Row, 1979.

–, *On the Internet,* New York/London: Routledge, 2001.

Eagleton, Terry, *The Function of Criticism: From the Spectator to Post-Structuralism,* New York: Verso, 1984

Feher, Michel, *Powerless by Design: The Age of the International Community (Public Planet Ser.),* Durham: Duke University Press, 2000.

Frank, Thomas, *One Market under God: Extreme Capitalism, Market Populism and the End of Economic Democracy,* New York: Doubleday, 2000.

Gleick, James, *Faster: The Acceleration of Just About Everything,* New York: Random House, 1999.

Grassmuck, Volker, *Freie Software,* Bonn: Bundeszentrale für politische Bildung, 2002.

Groys, Boris, *Unter Verdacht,* München: Hanser Verlag, 2000.

Hardt, Michael and Negri, Antoni, *Empire,* Cambridge, Mass.: Harvard University Press, 2000.

Hartmann, Frank, *Cyber-Philosophy, Medientheoretische Auslotungen,* Wien: Passagen Verlag, 1996.

–, *Medienphilosophie,* Wien: WUV, 2000.

Hayles, Katherine N., *How We Became Posthuman: Virtual Bodies in Cybernetics, Literature and Informatics,* Chicago: University of Chicago Press, 1999.

Himanen, Pekka, *The Hacker Ethic and the Spirit of the Information Age,* New York: Random House, 2001.

Horkheimer, Max, and Adorno, Theodor W., *Dialectic of Enlightenment,* New York: Continuum, 2000.

Ignatieff, Michael, *Virtual War: Kosovo and Beyond,* New York: Henry Holt & Company, 2000.

Jole, Francisco van, *Valse Horizon,* Amsterdam: Meulenhof, 2001.

Fibreculture (Ed.), *Politics of a Digital Present,* Melbourne: Fibreculture Publications, 2001.

Frank, Thomas, *One Market Under God: Extreme Capitalism, Market Populism and the End of Economic Democracy,* New York: Doubleday, 2000.

Frye, Northrop, *The Anatomy of Criticism,* London: Penguin, 1990 (1957).

Kelly, Kevin, *New Rules for the New Economy: Ten Ways the Network Economy is Changing Everything,* London: Fourth Estate Limited, 1998.

Kittler, Friedrich, *Eine Kulturgeschichte der Kulturwissenschaft,* München: Wilhelm Fink Verlag, 2000.

Klein, Naomi, *No Logo,* London: Flamingo, 2000.

Kuo, David J, *Dot.Bomb,* London: Little, Brown and Company, 2001.

Laurel, Brenda, *Utopian Entrepreneur,* Cambridge, Mass.: MIT Press, 2001.

Lessig, Lawrence, *Code and other Laws of Cyberspace,* New York: Basic Books, 1999.

–, *The Future of Ideas,* New York: Random House, 2001.

Lewis, Michael, *The New New Thing: A Silicon Valley Story,* London: Hodder and Stoughton, 1999.

Lewis, Michael, *The Future Just Happened,* London: Hodder and Stoughton, 2001.

Lovink, Geert, *Dark Fiber,* Cambridge, Mass.: MIT Press, 2002.

–, *Uncanny Networks,* Cambridge, Mass.: MIT Press, 2002.

Lunenfeld, Peter, *Snap to Grid: A User's Guide to Digital Arts,* Media and Cultures, Cambridge, Mass.: MIT Press, 2000.

Malmsten, Ernst (with Portanger, Erik and Drazin, Charles), *Boo Hoo,* London: Random House, 2001.

Manovich, Lev, *The Language of New Media,* Cambridge, Mass.: MIT Press, 2001.

Maresch, Rudolf and Rötzer Florian (Eds.), *Cyberhypes, Möglichkeiten und Grenzen des Internet,* Frankfurt am Main: Suhrkamp, 2001.

Meikle, Graham, *Future Active,* Sydney: Pluto Press Australia, 2002.

Mitchell, William J., *City of Bits: Space, Place, & the Infobahn,* Cambridge, Mass.: MIT Press, 1995.

Moody, Glyn, *Rebel Code: Linux and the Open Source Revolution,* London: Penguin Books, 2001.

Mouffe, Chantal, *The Democratic Paradox,* London: Verso Books, 2000.

Mulder, Arjen, *Het fotografisch genoegen,* Amsterdam: Van Gennep, 2000.

—, *Levende systemen,* Amsterdam: Van Gennep, 2002.

Negri, Antonio, *Time for Revolution,* London/New York: Continuum, 2003.

Nettime (Ed.), *Readme! Ascii Culture and the Revenge of Knowledge,* Brooklyn: Autonomedia, 1999.

Nielsen, Jakob, *Designing Web Usability,* Indianapolis: New Riders Publishing, 2000.

NL-Design (Ed.), *Everyone Is a Designer! Manifesto for the Design Economy,* Amsterdam: BIS Publishers, 2000, reprinted as *Emigre No. 58,* spring 2001.

—, *Catalogue of Strategies,* Amsterdam: BIS Publishers, 2001.

—, *Mobile Minded,* Amsterdam: BIS Publishers, 2002.

Noble, David F., *Digital Diploma Mills,* New York: Monthly Review Press, 2001.

Oosterling, Henk, *Radikale middelmatigheid,* Amsterdam: Boom, 2000.

Oy, Gottfried, *Gemeinschaft der Lüge, Medien- und Öffentlichkeitskritik sozialer Bewegungen in der Bundesrepublik,* Verlag Westfälisches Dampfboot, Münster, 2001.

Paternot, Stephan, *A Very Public Offering,* New York: John Wiley & Sons, 2001.

Plant, Sadie, *Zeros + Ones: Digital Women and the New Technoculture,* London: Fourth Estate Limited, 1997.

Poster, Mark, *What's the Matter with the Internet?,* Minneapolis/London: University of Minnesota Press, 2001.

Raymond, Eric S., *The Cathedral and the Bazaar,* Sebastopol: O'Reilly & Associates, revised edition, 2001.

Rheingold, Howard, *The Virtual Community: Homesteading on the Electronic Frontier,* revised edition, Cambridge, Mass.: MIT Press, 2000.

Rheingold, Howard, *Smart Mobs,* Cambridge, Mass.: Perseus Publishing, 2002.

Rifkin, Jeremy, *The Age of Access,* London: Penguin, 2000.

Rogers, Richard (Ed.), *Preferred Placement: Knowledge Politics on the Web,* Maastricht/Amsterdam, Jan van Eyck Akademie Editions/Uitgeverij De Balie, 2000.

Ross, Andrew, *No Collar: The Human Workplace and Its Hidden Costs,* New York: Basic Books, 2003.

Sandbothe, Mike, *Pragmatische Medienphilosophie,* Weilerswist: Velbrueck Wissenschaft, 2001.

Sarai (Ed.), *The Public Domain, Sarai Reader 01,* Dehli: Sarai/CSDS, 2001.

—, *The Cities of Everyday Life, Sarai Reader 02,* Dehli: Sarai/CSDS, 2002.

—, *Shaping Technologies, Sarai Reader 03,* Dehli: Sarai/CSDS, 2003.

Schiller, Dan, *Digital Capitalism: Networking the Global Market System,* Cambridge, Mass.: MIT Press, 1999.

Schiller, Robert J., *Irrational Exuberance,* Melbourne: Scribe Publications, 2000.

Schwartz, Peter et al., *The Long Boom: A Vision for the Coming Age of Prosperity*, Reading: Perseus Books, 1999.

Shapiro, Carl and Varian, Hal, *Information Rules: A Strategic Guide to the Network Economy*, Boston: Harvard Business School Press, 1998.

Shapiro, Andrew L., *The Control Revolution*, New York: Century Foundation Book, 1999.

Sloterdijk, Peter, *Globen, Spähren Band II*, Frankfurt am Main: Suhrkamp, 1999.

—, *Die Verachtung der Massen, Versuch über Kulturkämpfe in der modernen Gesellschaft*, Frankfurt am Main: Suhrkamp, 2000.

Smith, Marc; Kollock, Peter, *Communities in Cyberspace*, London: Routledge, 2001.

Spehr, Christoph, *Die Aliens sind unter uns!* München: Goldmann Verlag, 1999.

—, *Gleicher als andere, Eine Grundlegung der freien Kooperation*, Berlin: Karl Dietz Verlag, 2003.

Steiner, George, *The Grammar of Creation*, London: Faber & Faber, 2001.

Torvalds, Linus and Diamond, David, *Just for Fun: The Story of an Accidental Revolutionary*, New York: HarperCollins, 2001.

Ulmer, Gregory L., *Heuretics: The Logic of Invention*, Baltimore: Johns Hopkins University Press, 1994.

Williams, Sam, *Free as in Freedom: Richard Stallman's Crusade for Free Software*, Sebastopol: O'Reilly, 2002.

Waag Society for Old and New Media (Ed.), *Next Five Minutes 3 Workbook*, Amsterdam: De Waag, 1999.

—, *Metatag: 26 Hits on Technology and Culture*, Amsterdam: De Waag, 2001.

Wark, McKenzie, *Virtual Geography: Living with Global Media Events*, Bloomington: Indiana University, 1994.

Wolff, Michael, *Burn Rate: How I Survived the Gold Rush Years on the Internet*, London: Weidenfeld & Nicolson, 1998.

Zakaria, Fareed, *The Future of Freedom*, New York/London: W.W. Norton & Company, 2003.

Zielinski, Siegfried, *Archäologie der Medien, Zur Tiefenzeit des technischen Hörens und Sehens*, Reinbek: Rowohlt, 2002.

Zizek, Slavoj, *Did Someone Say Totalitarianism? Five Interventions in the (Mis)use of a Notion*, London: Verso, 2001.

—, *On Belief*, New York/London: Routledge, 2001

Acknowledgment

A good two-thirds of this writing was submitted to the University of Melbourne as a Ph.D. dissertation. It was Scott Mcquire of the Media and Communications program in the English Department who believed in my work and guided me through the jungle of applications and regulations to make it all happen. During 2002, an international student scholarship from the University of Melbourne enabled me to concentrate on research and writing. Both Scott Mcquire and Nikos Papastergiades have been fantastic supervisors, and they substantially shaped my thesis. After I submitted the thesis I made slight changes for the version that appears in this book.

Generous support from the Rockefeller Foundation enabled me to take time off and finish the manuscript; may Joan Shigekawa and the Trustees rest assured of my gratitude.

Another part of the research is the result of my work as a post-doctoral fellow at the Center for Critical and Cultural Studies, University of Queensland, Brisbane (Australia), where I started in January 2003. I wish to thank its director, Graeme Turner, and administrator, Andrea Mitchell.

A Digital Cultures fellowship in April 2003 provided by the English Department at the University of California, Santa Barbara, facilitated by Professor William Warner, made it possible for me to write, visit libraries, enjoy bandwidth abundance and exchange ideas with fellow theorists.

Strong intellectual and editorial support came from Ned Rossiter. Readers of individual texts are mentioned in each chapter. Thanks also to Mr. Snow and Felipe Rodriguez for crucial computer tech support and the Waag Society in Amsterdam for administrative assistance.

I am especially indebted to Joke Brouwer of the V2_Organization for taking on *My First Recession* with such trust and speed. It's an honor for me to open this V2_ series and to have Joke Brouwer do the design. My longstanding friend and co-member of Adilkno, Arjen Mulder, took up the role as series editor. I am grateful for his editorial comments and support. Another old acquaintance, Laura Martz, did the final copy editing. Thanks to those at V2_ and NAi Publishers for the production, marketing and distribution of this book.

Looking back, this period of study has, most of all, been marked by the joyful birth of our son Kazimir. I would like to dedicate this book to the one who went through so much to get there: my wife and the love of my life, Linda Wallace. In particular, I thank her for her unconditional support. It's amazing how far we've gotten – with so much more to come.

Brisbane, July 2003

Geert Lovink's text archive: www.laudanum.net/geert.
Contact: geert@xs4all.nl.

Editorial team: Joke Brouwer, Arjen Mulder, Laura Martz
Production and design: Joke Brouwer

This book was made possible by the financial support of the Prins Bernhard
Cultuurfonds (The Prince Bernhard Cultural Foundation), the Netherlands.

Available in North, South and Central America through
D.A.P./Distributed Art Publishers Inc, 155 Sixth Avenue 2nd Floor,
New York, NY 10013-1507, Tel 212 6271999, Fax 212 6279484.

Available in the United Kingdom and Ireland through Art Data,
12 Bell Industrial Estate, 50 Cunnington Street, London W4 5HB,
Tel 208 7471061, Fax 208 7422319.

Printed and bound in the Netherlands

ISBN 90-5662-353-2

Other books published by V2_: http://publishing.v2.nl